CERES™
Celestial Legend
Volume 6: Shuro

STORY & ART BY YUU WATASE

English Adaptation/Gary Leach

Translation/Lillian Olsen
Touch-Up Art & Lettering/Bill Schuch
Cover & Graphics Design/Hidemi Sahara
Editor/Avery Gotoh

Supervising Editor/Andy Nakatani
Managing Editor/Annette Roman
Director of Production/Noboru Watanabe
VP of Publishing/Alvin Lu
Sr. Director of Acquisitions/Rika Inouye
VP of Sales & Marketing/Liza Coppola
Publisher/Hyoe Narita

© 1997 Yuu WATASE/Shogakukan Inc. First published by Shogakukan Inc. in Japan as "Ayashi no Ceres."
New and adapted artwork and text © 2004 VIZ MEDIA, LLC. All rights reserved.

Printed in Canada

Published by VIZ MEDIA, LLC
P.O. Box 77010 • San Francisco CA 94107

Shōjo Edition

10 9 8 7 6 5 4 3 2

First printing, January 2004
Second printing, February 2006

store.viz.com

www.viz.com

VIZ GRAPHIC NOVEL

CERES

Celestial Legend

Vol. 6: Shuro

Story and Art by
Yuu Watase

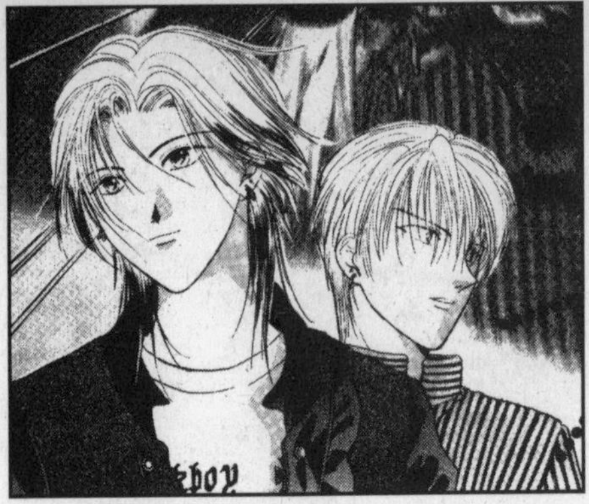

KEI AND SHURO: Beautiful, androgynous members of Japan's hottest pop duo, GeSANG. But the two seem to have more than just music in their veins....

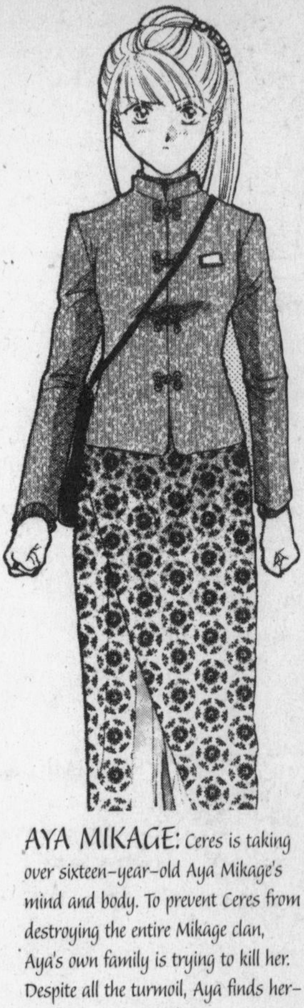

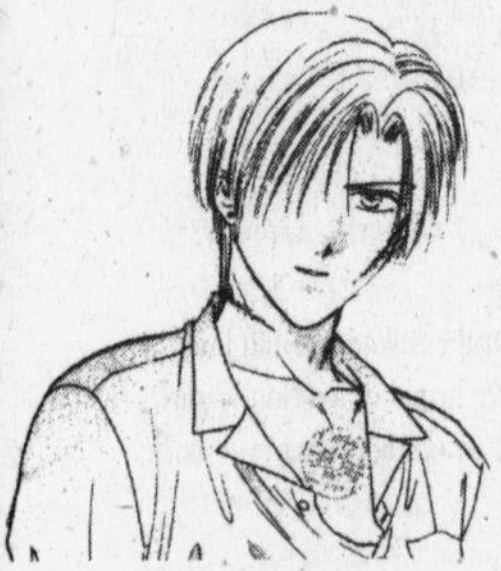

AKI MIKAGE: Aya's twin brother. While the consciousness of Ceres is taking over Aya, Aki is showing signs of bearing the consciousness of the founder (progenitor) of the Mikage family line. Placed under confinement by the Mikage family to keep him separated from Aya, still nothing will keep him from her....

AYA MIKAGE: Ceres is taking over sixteen-year-old Aya Mikage's mind and body. To prevent Ceres from destroying the entire Mikage clan, Aya's own family is trying to kill her. Despite all the turmoil, Aya finds herself falling in love with Tôya—a man hired by Kagami to keep an eye on her.

TÔYA: Mysterious man who's come to Aya's aid on more than one occasion. In exchange for their help in getting his memory back, Tôya works doing "whatever" for Mikage International... at least for now.

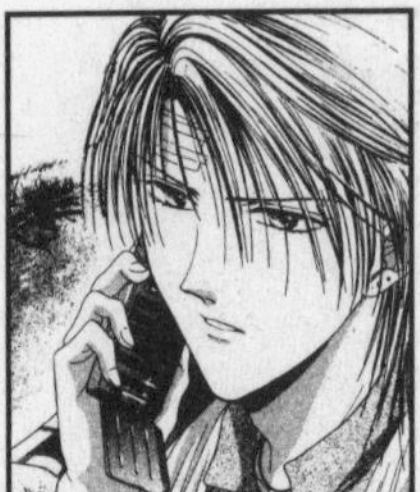

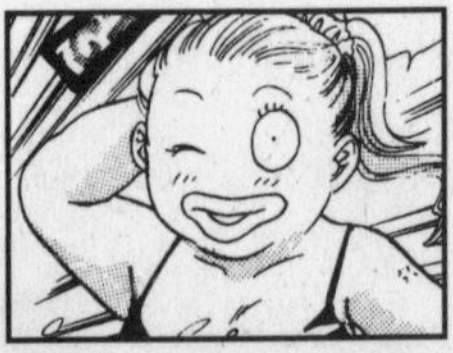

MRS. Q (ODA-KYÛ): Eccentric yet loyal-to-a-fault servant of the Aogiri household.

KAGAMI: Although the Mikage family wants to kill off Ceres through Aya, Kagami—head of Mikage International's research and development department—has put into motion his own agenda: C-Project, a plan to gather descendants of ten'nyo and use their power.

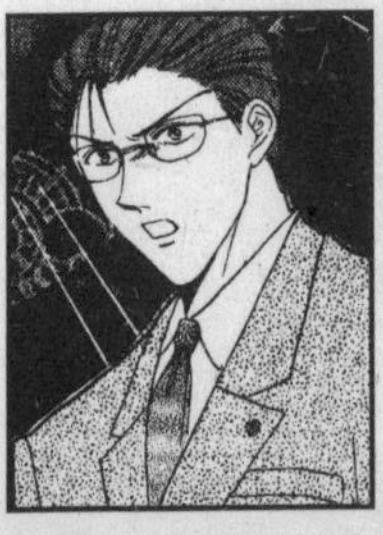

YÛHI: Sixteen-year-old brother-in-law to Suzumi. A skilled martial-artist and aspiring chef, Yûhi has been asked (ordered, more like) to serve as Aya's watchful protector and guardian...his own feelings for her notwithstanding.

CHIDORI: Awakened to her own, unsuspected celestial powers only after her younger brother was put into mortal danger, Chidori Kuruma was at first another target of Kagami, but was spared by the compassion of Tôya. Deceptively young in appearance (she looks like a grade-schooler but is actually in high school, just like Aya), Chidori has since decided to help Aya and the others in the search for Ceres' missing hagoromo.

CERES: Once upon a time...long, long ago...a ten'nyo or "celestial maiden" named Ceres descended to Earth. Her hagoromo or "feathered robes" stolen, Ceres—unable to return to the heavens—was forced by the human thief to become his wife and bear his children... thus beginning the Mikage family line. Awakened after aeons of waiting—and anger—Ceres wants her hagoromo back and vows to use all her celestial powers to avenge herself against the descendants of the man who wronged her, so long ago.

SUZUMI: Instructor of traditional Japanese dance and descendant of ten'nyo or "heavenly maidens" herself. A big sister figure, Suzumi has welcomed Aya into her household, and is more than happy to provide her with all the protection, assistance and support that she can.

You may have noticed some unfamiliar people and things mentioned in CERES. VIZ left these Japanese pop-culture references as they originally appeared in the manga series. Here's an explanation for those who may not be so J-Pop savvy:

Page 17: Superstar queen of TV drama series, "Matsu-Taka" (short for Takako Matsu) has also been successful in the realms of stage, film, and pop music. She comes from a family of prestigious Kabuki actors.

Page 17: "Tomo-chan" (Tomomi Kahara) is a super-cute, albeit slightly vapid pop-idol whose star burned brightest in the late nineties.

Page 21: The "GeSANG/Ginseng" joke used in this English version was originally a joke referring to "Peyang," a popular brand of instant noodles.

Page 27: This is most likely a reference to Shiori Fujisaki, a character from the popular dating simulation game, TOKIMEKI MEMORIAL.

Page 49: "Blue Seal" is an American-style brand of ice cream local to Okinawa.

Pages 56–57: These lyrics are from the traditional Okinawan song, "Naakuni."

Page 91: Sweet potato shôchû and "Awamori" are types of distilled alcoholic beverages. Pit-viper liquor (sake) is an alcoholic beverage infused with a deadly poisonous snake in every bottle.

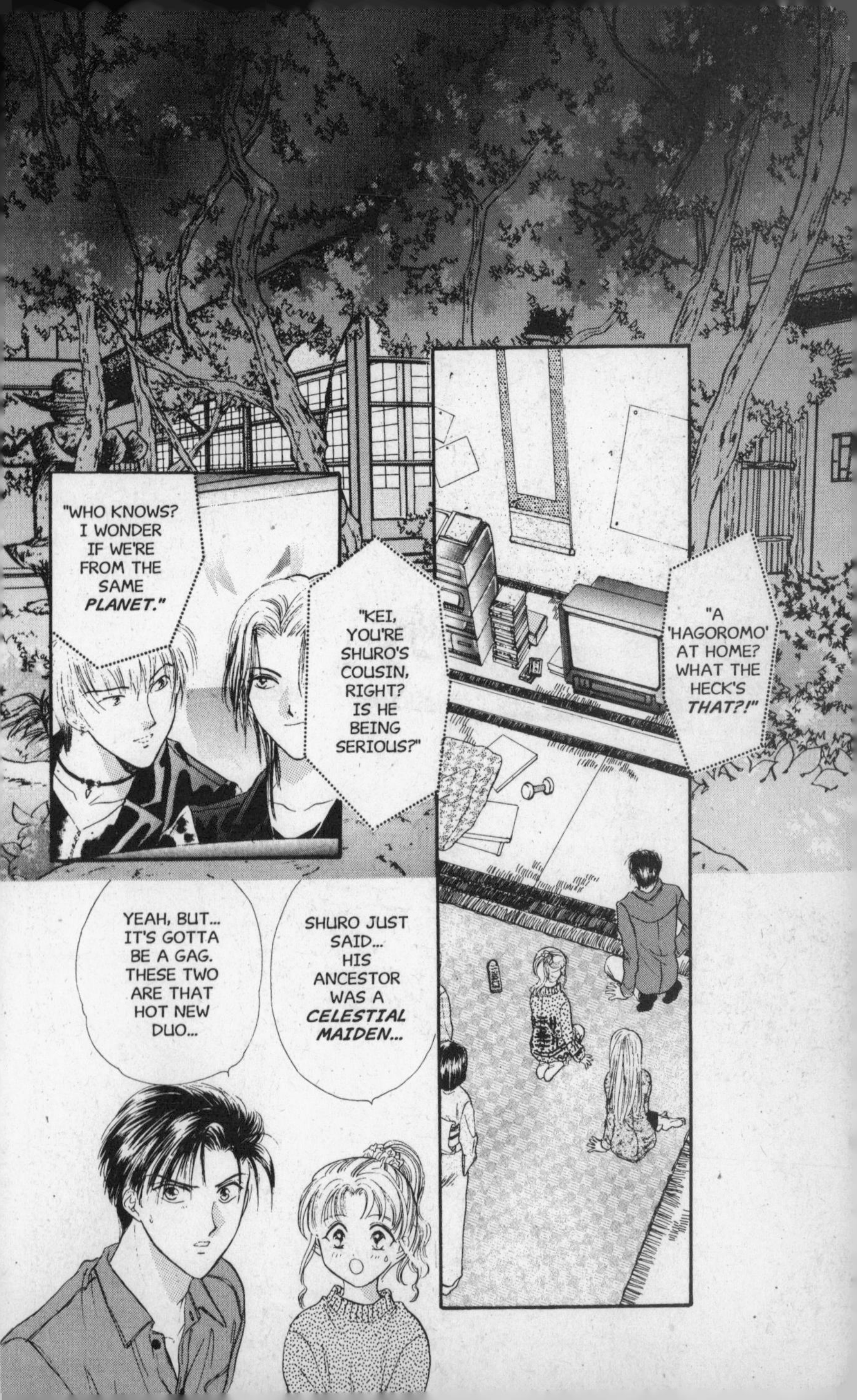
"A 'HAGOROMO' AT HOME? WHAT THE HECK'S *THAT?!*"
"KEI, YOU'RE SHURO'S COUSIN, RIGHT? IS HE BEING SERIOUS?"
"WHO KNOWS? I WONDER IF WE'RE FROM THE SAME *PLANET.*"
SHURO JUST SAID... HIS ANCESTOR WAS A *CELESTIAL MAIDEN...*
YEAH, BUT... IT'S GOTTA BE A GAG. THESE TWO ARE THAT HOT NEW DUO...

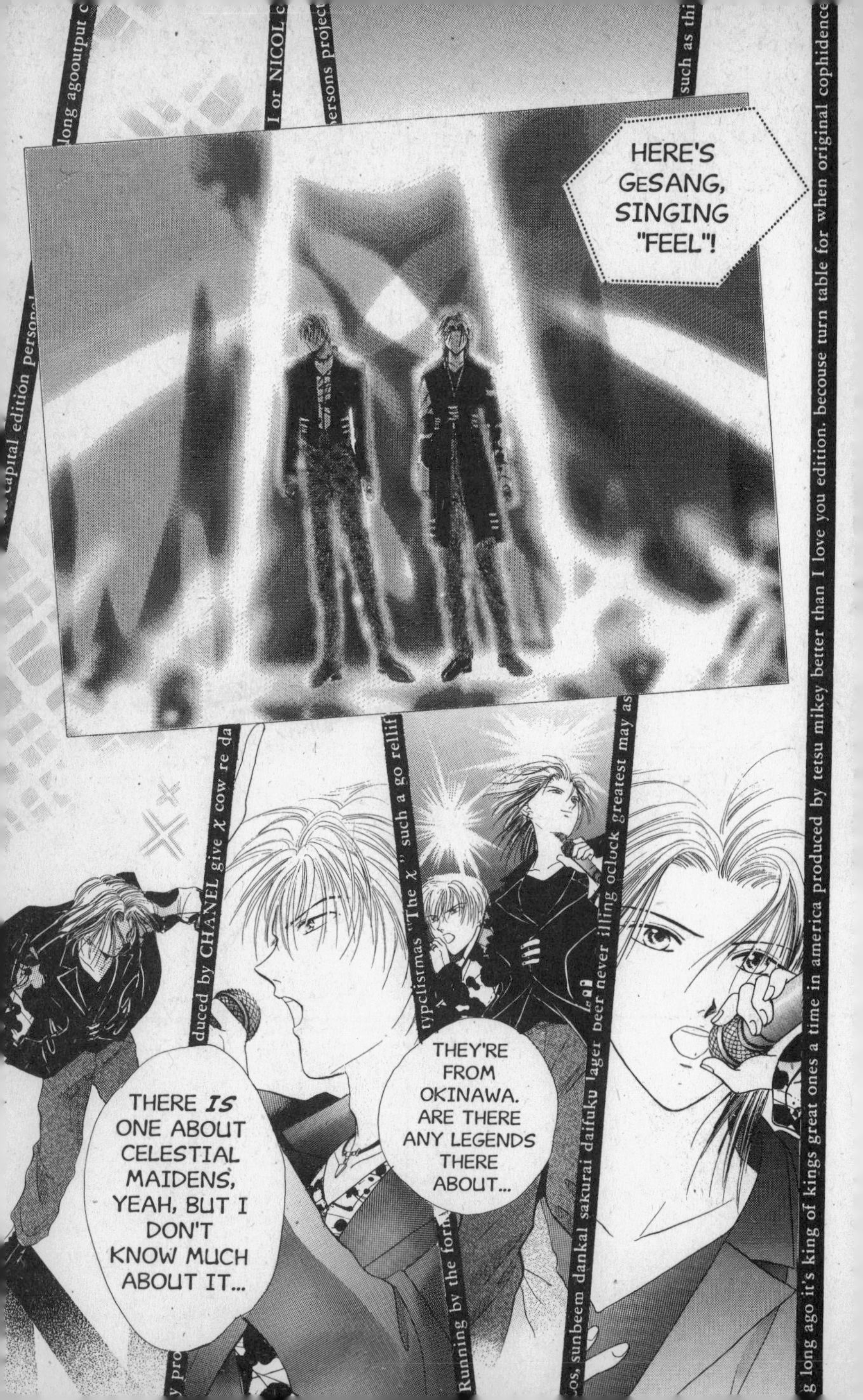
HERE'S GESANG, SINGING "FEEL"!
THEY'RE FROM OKINAWA. ARE THERE ANY LEGENDS THERE ABOUT...
THERE *IS* ONE ABOUT CELESTIAL MAIDENS, YEAH, BUT I DON'T KNOW MUCH ABOUT IT...

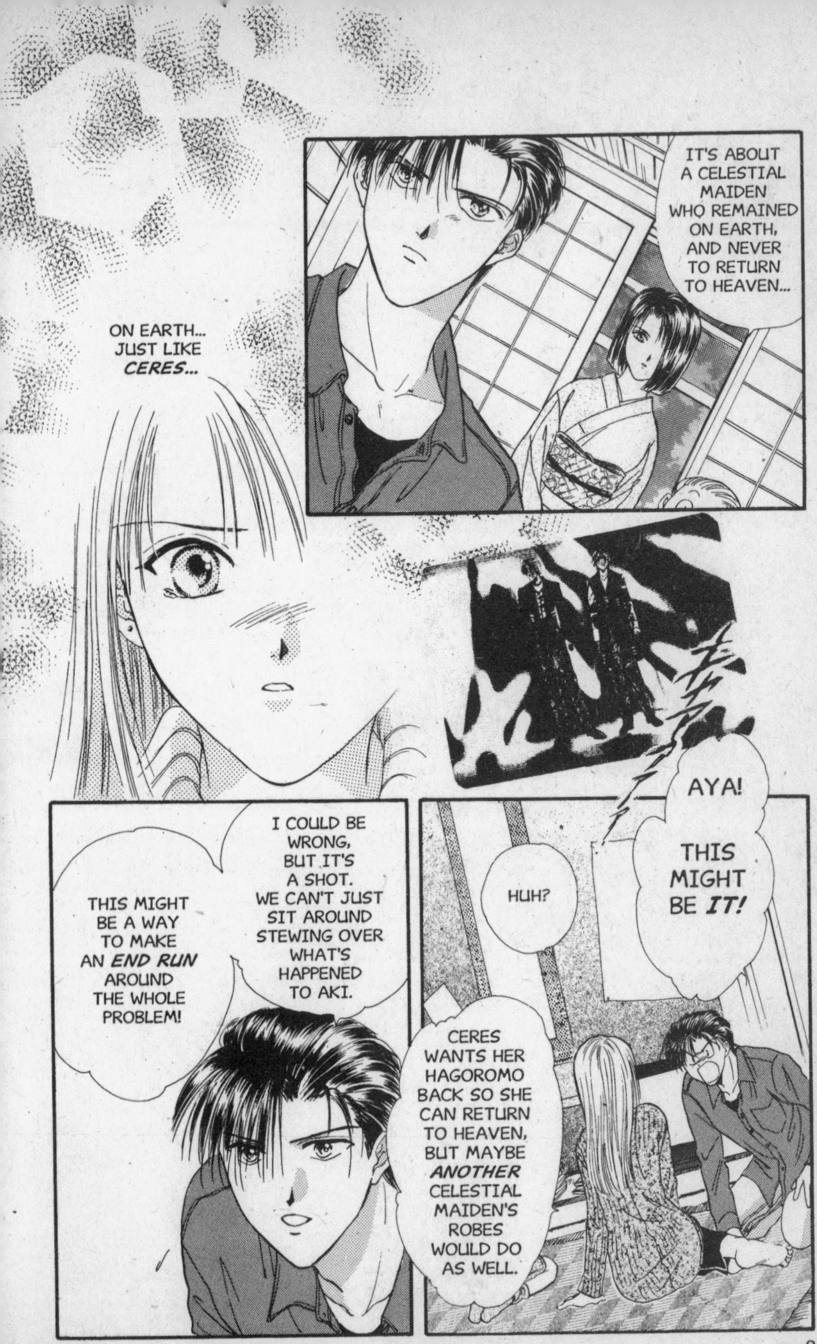

IT'S ABOUT A CELESTIAL MAIDEN WHO REMAINED ON EARTH, AND NEVER TO RETURN TO HEAVEN...
ON EARTH... JUST LIKE *CERES*...
AYA!
THIS MIGHT BE *IT!*
HUH?
CERES WANTS HER HAGOROMO BACK SO SHE CAN RETURN TO HEAVEN, BUT MAYBE *ANOTHER* CELESTIAL MAIDEN'S ROBES WOULD DO AS WELL.
I COULD BE WRONG, BUT IT'S A SHOT. WE CAN'T JUST SIT AROUND STEWING OVER WHAT'S HAPPENED TO AKI.
THIS MIGHT BE A WAY TO MAKE AN *END RUN* AROUND THE WHOLE PROBLEM!

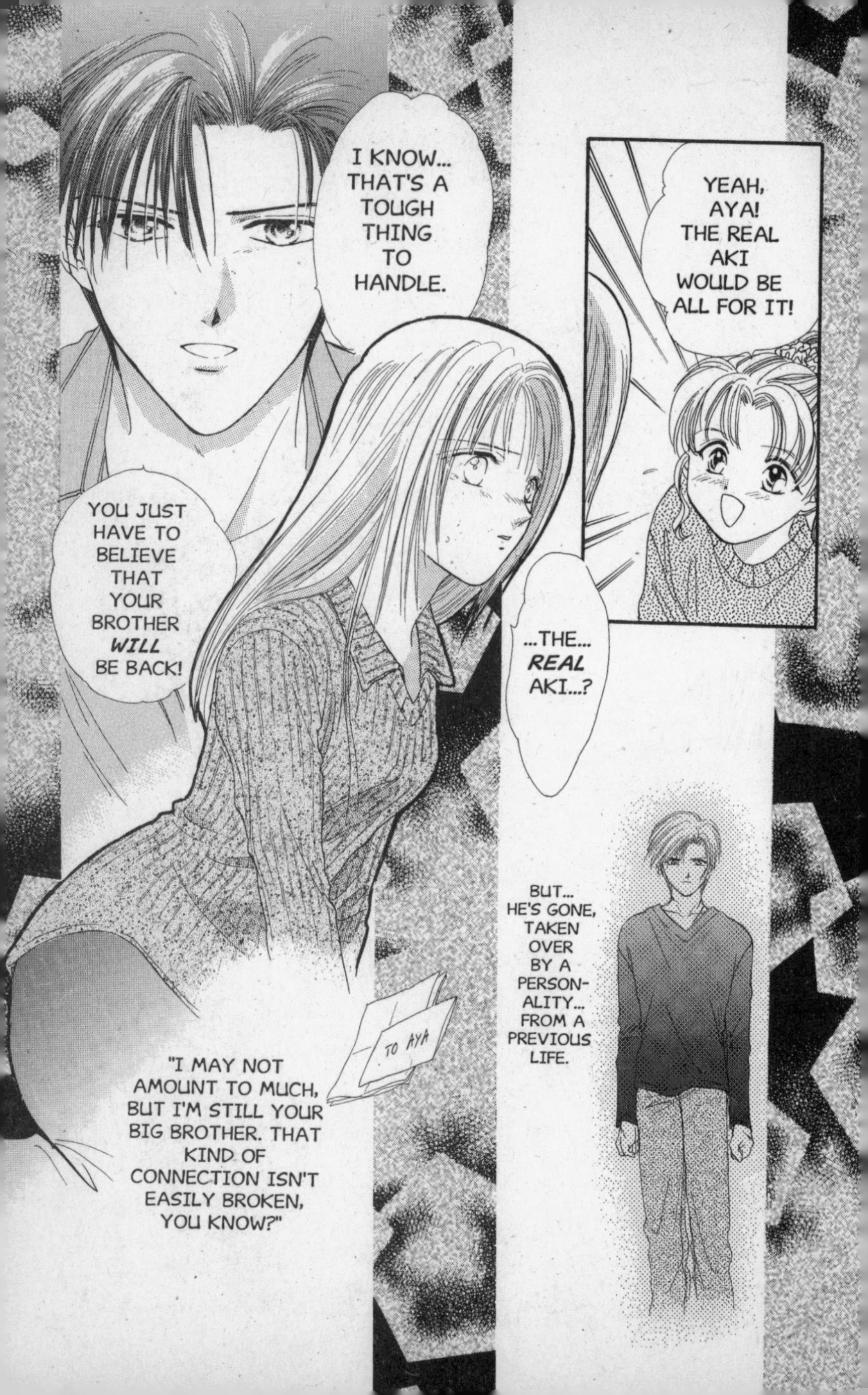
YEAH, AYA! THE REAL AKI WOULD BE ALL FOR IT!
...THE... REAL AKI...?
BUT... HE'S GONE, TAKEN OVER BY A PERSON-ALITY... FROM A PREVIOUS LIFE.
I KNOW... THAT'S A TOUGH THING TO HANDLE.
YOU JUST HAVE TO BELIEVE THAT YOUR BROTHER WILL BE BACK!
TO AYA
"I MAY NOT AMOUNT TO MUCH, BUT I'M STILL YOUR BIG BROTHER. THAT KIND OF CONNECTION ISN'T EASILY BROKEN, YOU KNOW?"

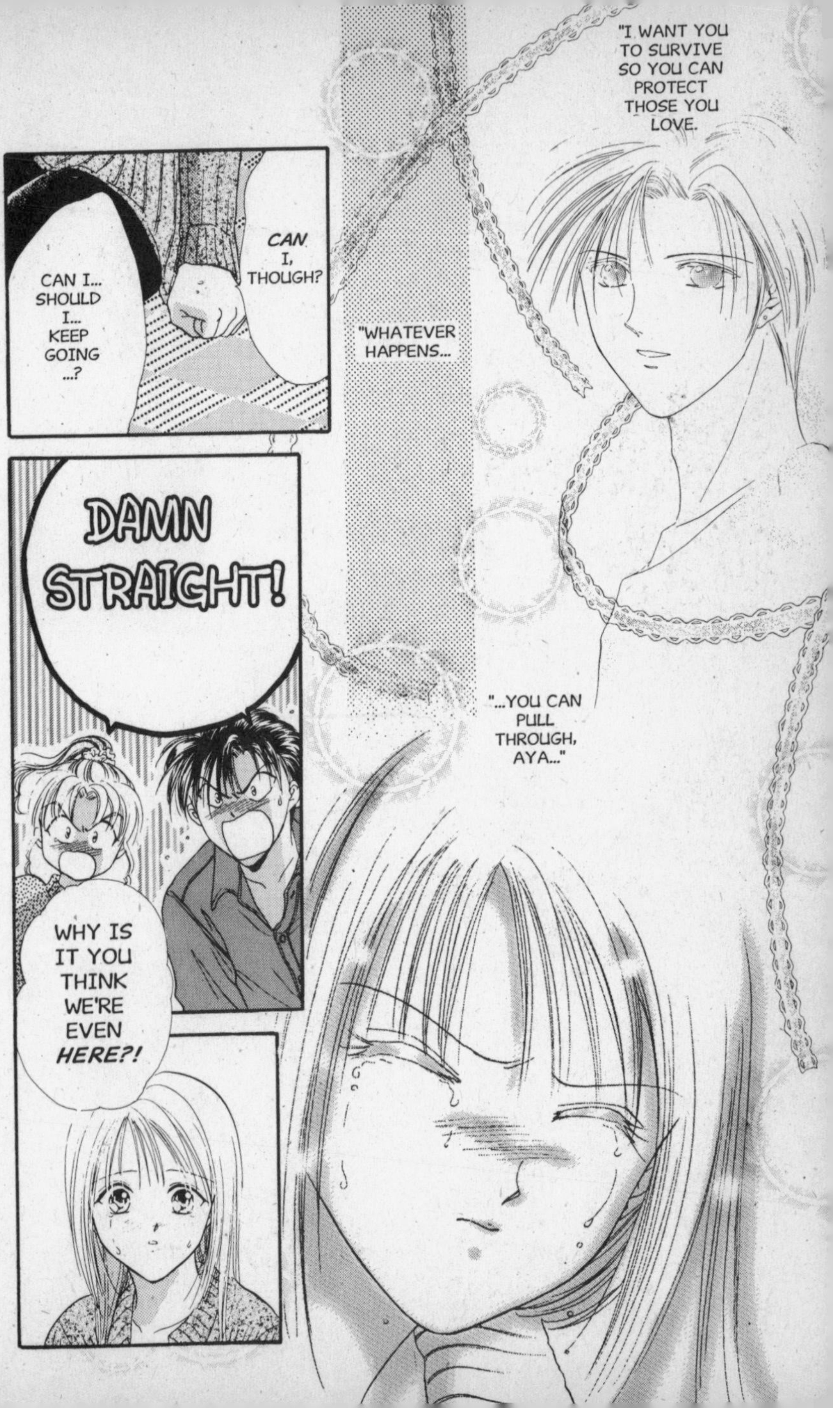
"I WANT YOU TO SURVIVE SO YOU CAN PROTECT THOSE YOU LOVE.
"WHATEVER HAPPENS...
"...YOU CAN PULL THROUGH, AYA..."
CAN I, THOUGH?
CAN I... SHOULD I... KEEP GOING ...?
DAMN STRAIGHT!
WHY IS IT YOU THINK WE'RE EVEN HERE?!

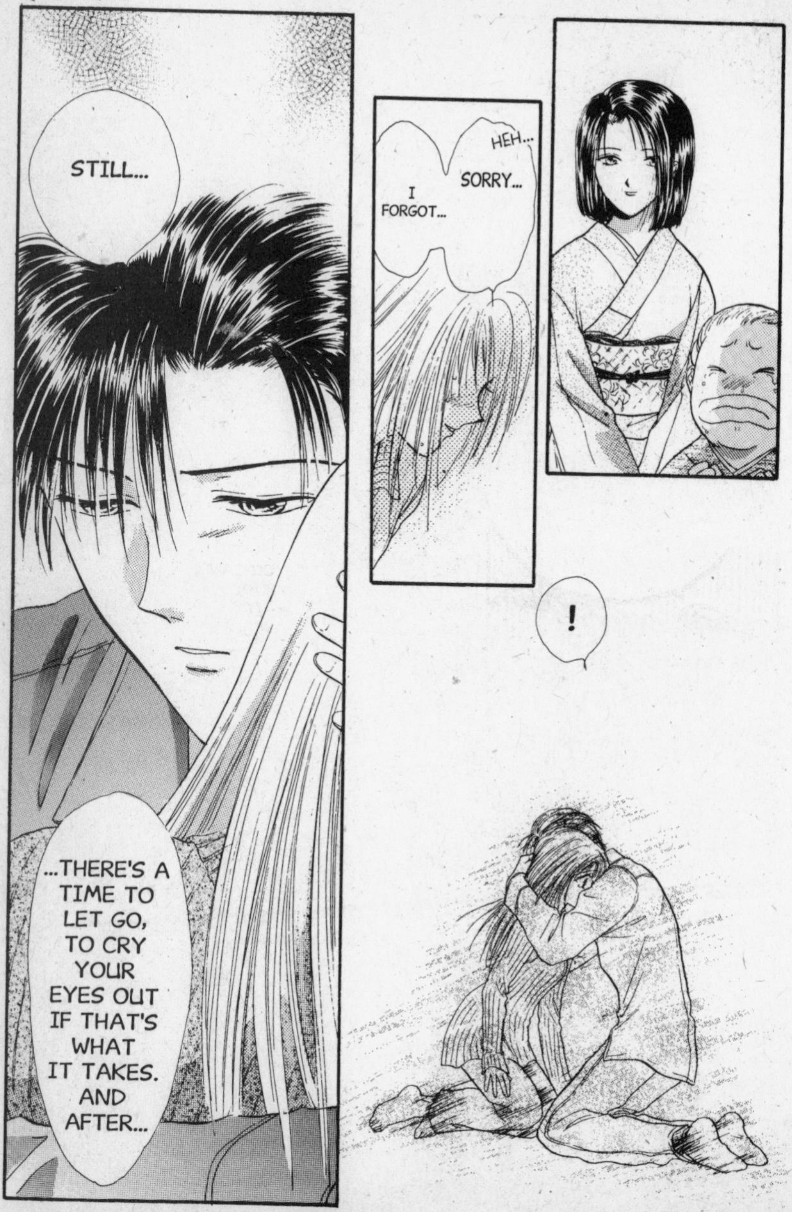
HEH... SORRY... I FORGOT...
!
STILL...
...THERE'S A TIME TO LET GO, TO CRY YOUR EYES OUT IF THAT'S WHAT IT TAKES. AND AFTER...

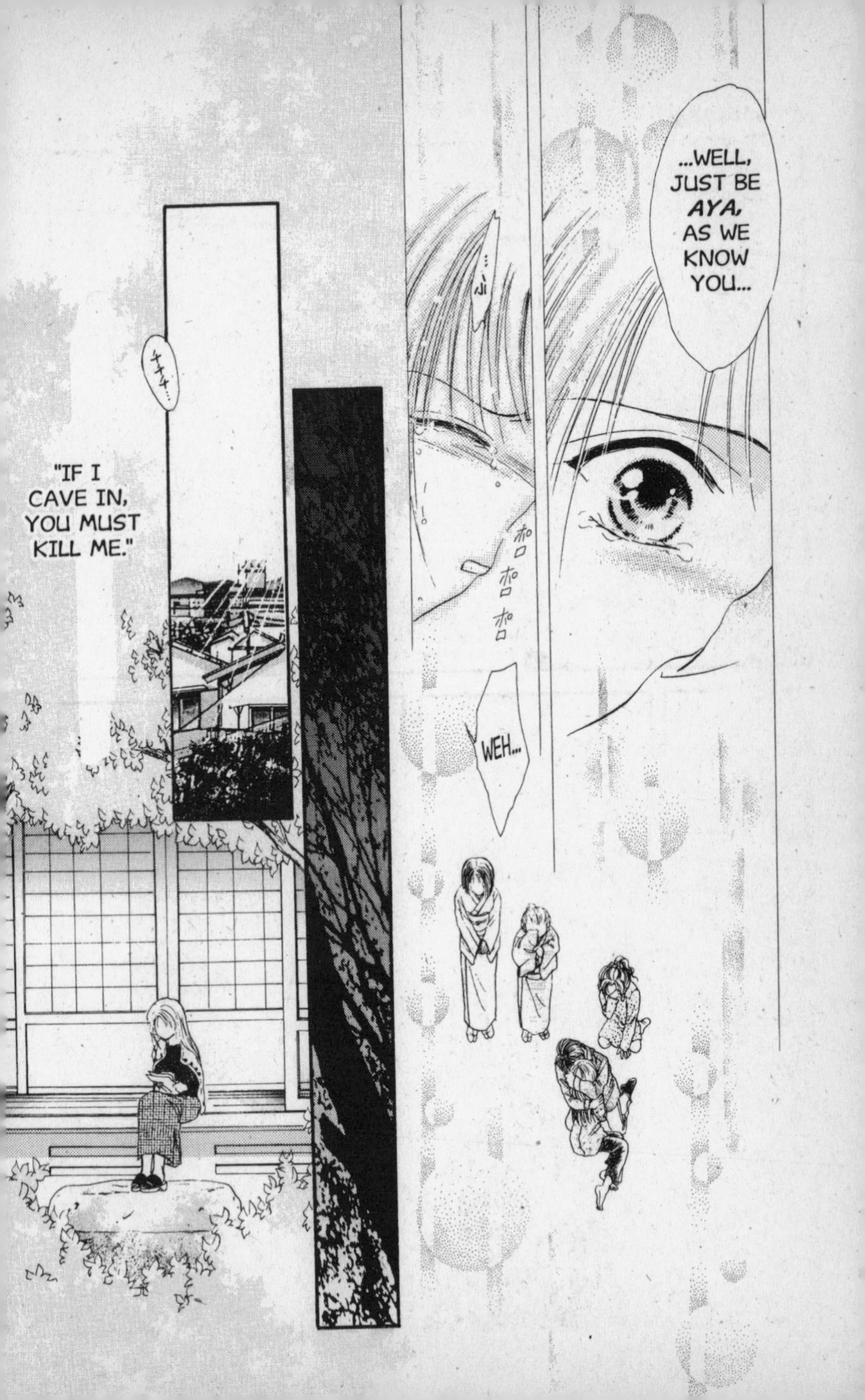
...WELL, JUST BE AYA, AS WE KNOW YOU...
ふ...
WEH...
チチチ...
"IF I CAVE IN, YOU MUST KILL ME."

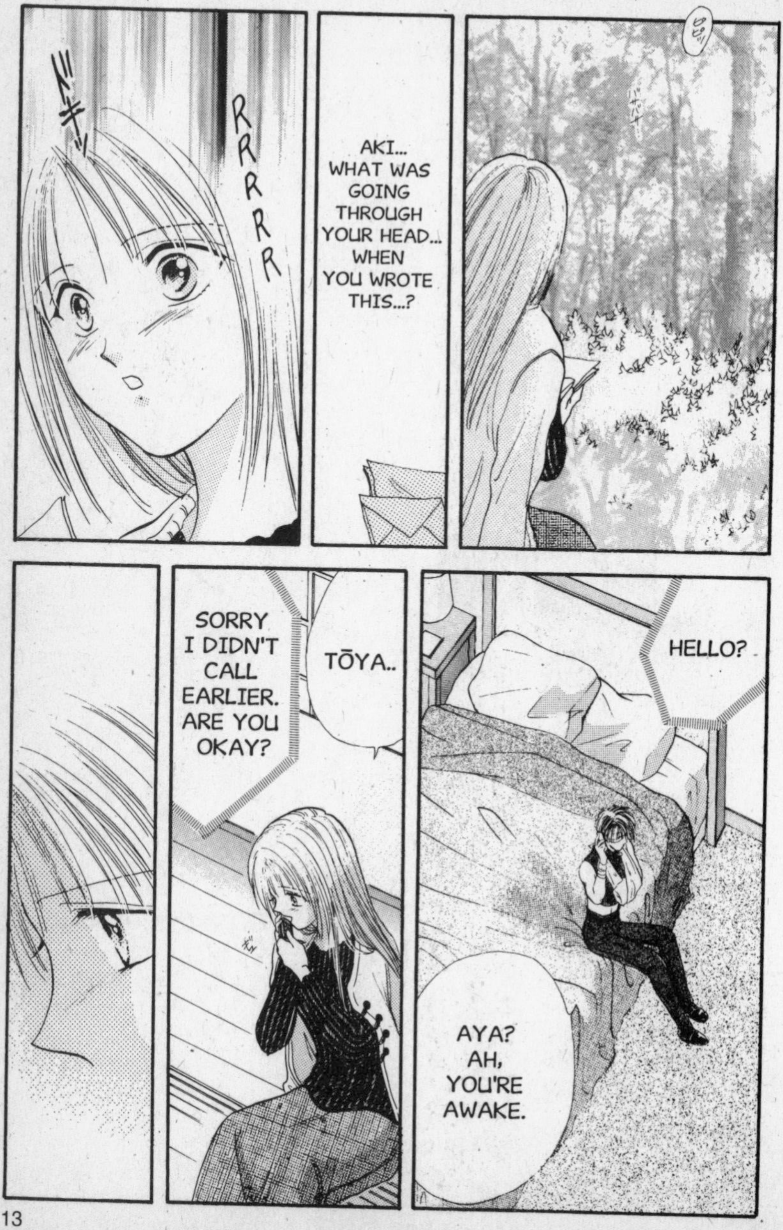
AKI... WHAT WAS GOING THROUGH YOUR HEAD... WHEN YOU WROTE THIS...?
RRRRR
ドキッ
HELLO?
AYA? AH, YOU'RE AWAKE.
TŌYA..
SORRY I DIDN'T CALL EARLIER. ARE YOU OKAY?

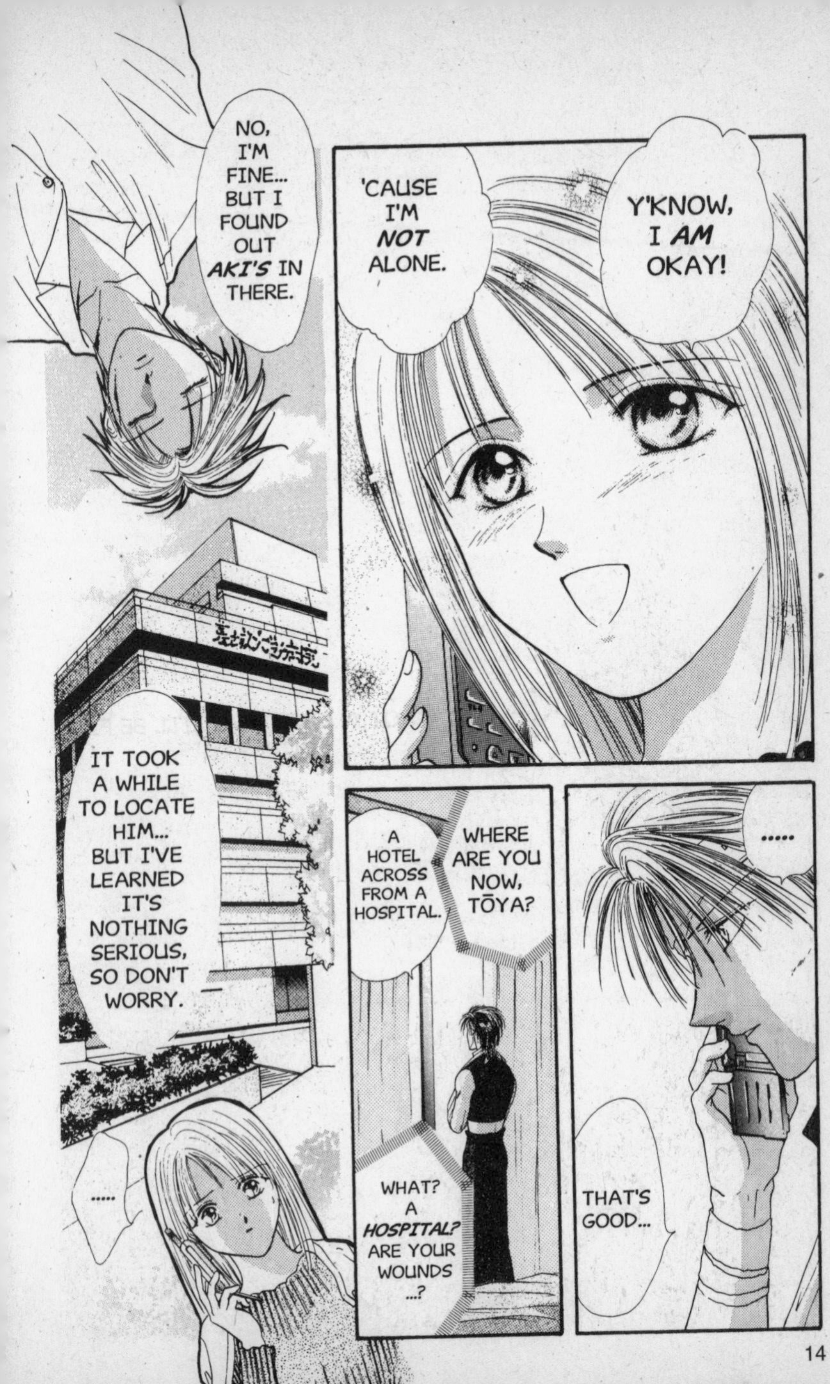
Y'KNOW, I *AM* OKAY!
'CAUSE I'M *NOT* ALONE.
.....
THAT'S GOOD...
WHERE ARE YOU NOW, TŌYA?
A HOTEL ACROSS FROM A HOSPITAL.
WHAT? A *HOSPITAL?* ARE YOUR WOUNDS ...?
NO, I'M FINE... BUT I FOUND OUT *AKI'S* IN THERE.
IT TOOK A WHILE TO LOCATE HIM... BUT I'VE LEARNED IT'S NOTHING SERIOUS, SO DON'T WORRY.
.....

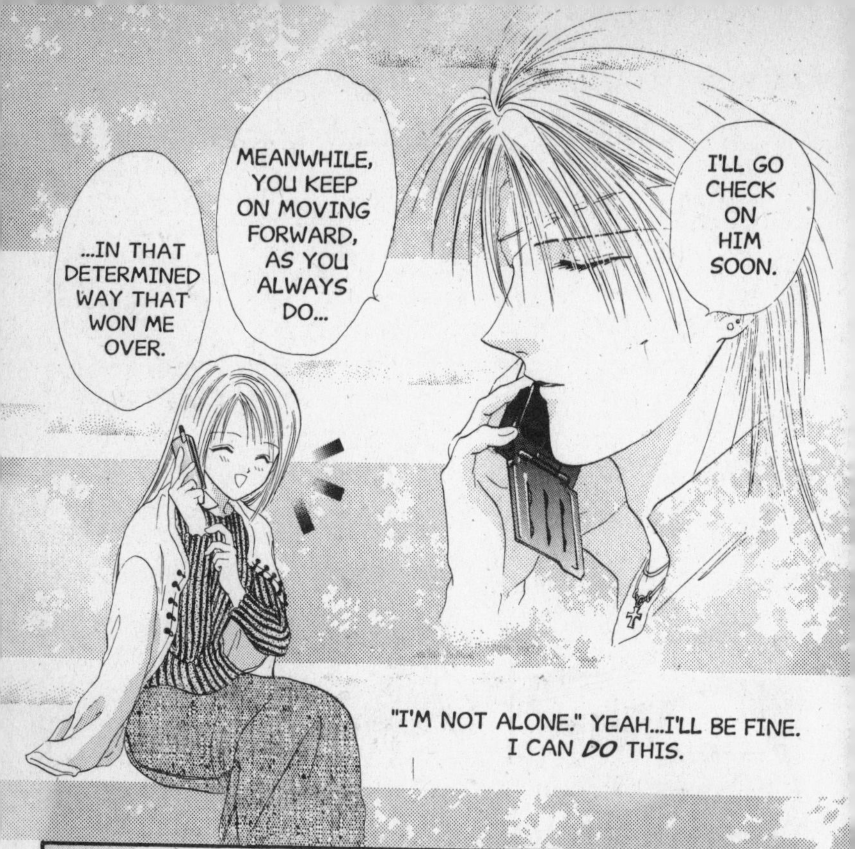
I'LL GO CHECK ON HIM SOON.
MEANWHILE, YOU KEEP ON MOVING FORWARD, AS YOU ALWAYS DO...
...IN THAT DETERMINED WAY THAT WON ME OVER.
"I'M NOT ALONE." YEAH...I'LL BE FINE. I CAN DO THIS.

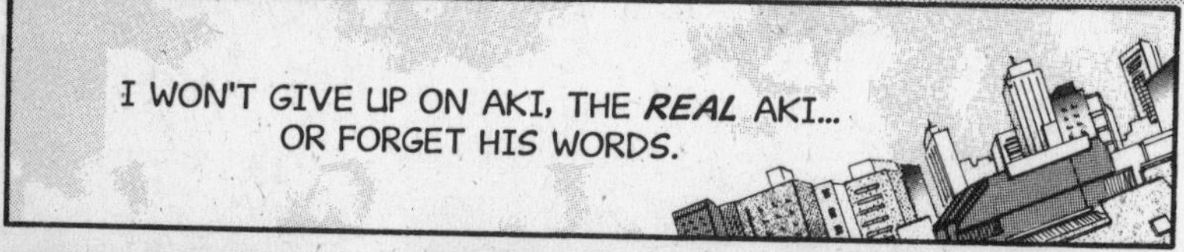
I WON'T GIVE UP ON AKI, THE REAL AKI... OR FORGET HIS WORDS.

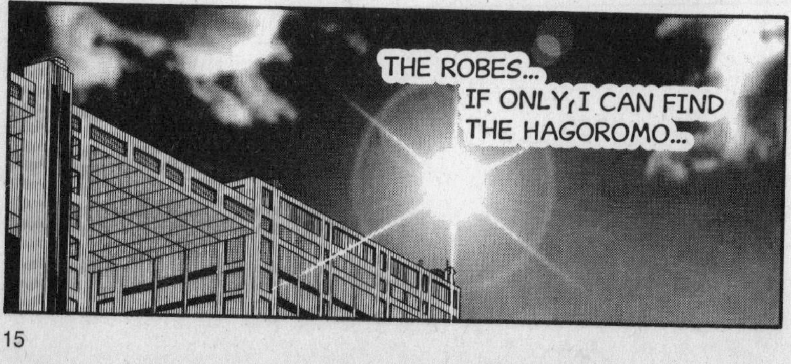
THE ROBES... IF ONLY I CAN FIND THE HAGOROMO...

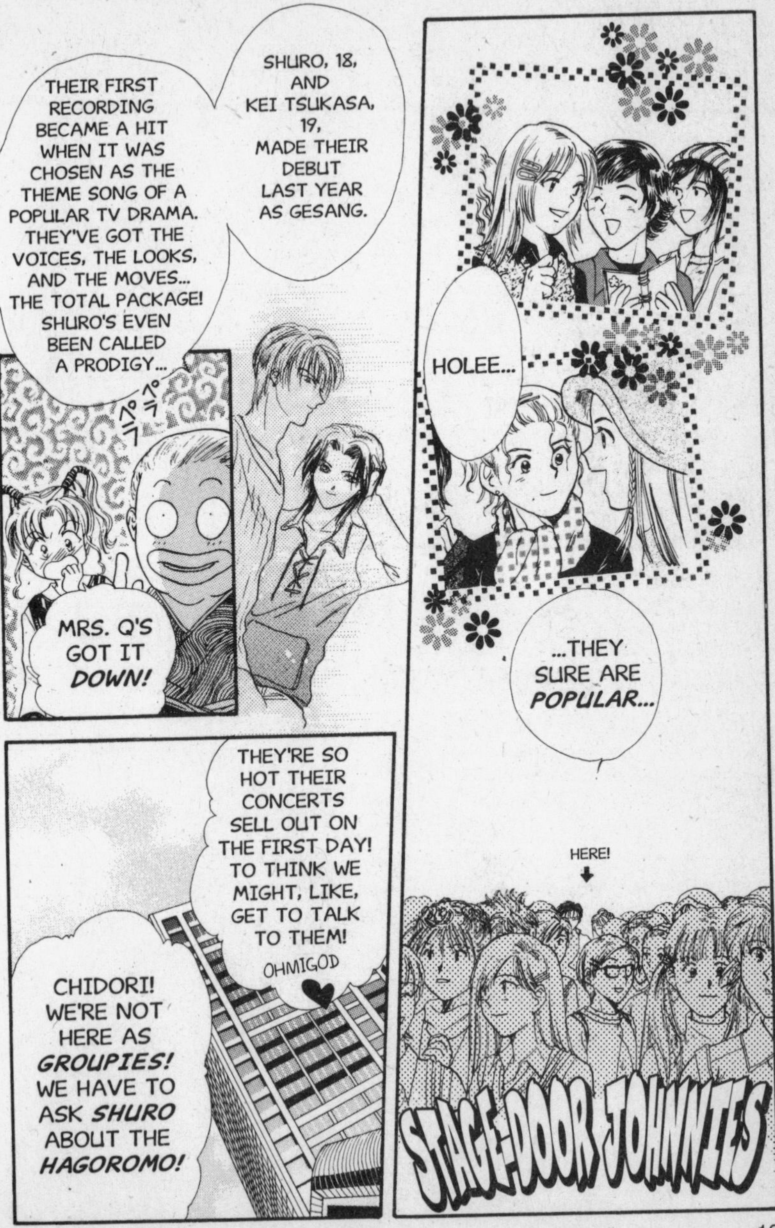
SHURO, 18, AND KEI TSUKASA, 19, MADE THEIR DEBUT LAST YEAR AS GESANG.
THEIR FIRST RECORDING BECAME A HIT WHEN IT WAS CHOSEN AS THE THEME SONG OF A POPULAR TV DRAMA. THEY'VE GOT THE VOICES, THE LOOKS, AND THE MOVES... THE TOTAL PACKAGE! SHURO'S EVEN BEEN CALLED A PRODIGY...
ペラペラ
MRS. Q'S GOT IT *DOWN!*
HOLEE...
...THEY SURE ARE *POPULAR*...
HERE!
STAGE-DOOR JOHNNIES
THEY'RE SO HOT THEIR CONCERTS SELL OUT ON THE FIRST DAY! TO THINK WE MIGHT, LIKE, GET TO TALK TO THEM!
OHMIGOD
CHIDORI! WE'RE NOT HERE AS *GROUPIES!* WE HAVE TO ASK *SHURO* ABOUT THE *HAGOROMO!*

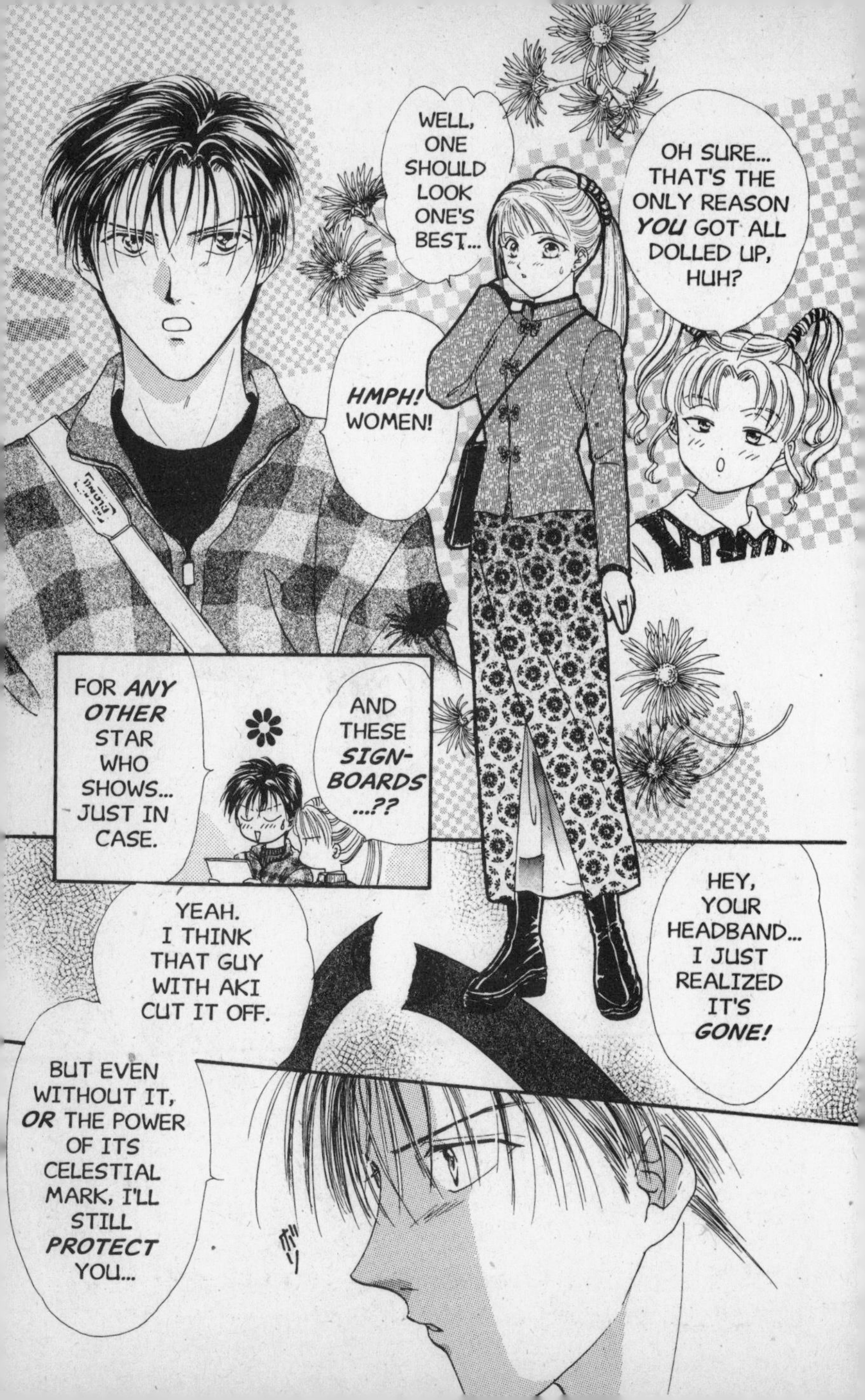
WELL, ONE SHOULD LOOK ONE'S BEST...
OH SURE... THAT'S THE ONLY REASON YOU GOT ALL DOLLED UP, HUH?
HMPH! WOMEN!
AND THESE SIGNBOARDS ...??
FOR ANY OTHER STAR WHO SHOWS... JUST IN CASE.
HEY, YOUR HEADBAND... I JUST REALIZED IT'S GONE!
YEAH. I THINK THAT GUY WITH AKI CUT IT OFF.
BUT EVEN WITHOUT IT, OR THE POWER OF ITS CELESTIAL MARK, I'LL STILL PROTECT YOU...

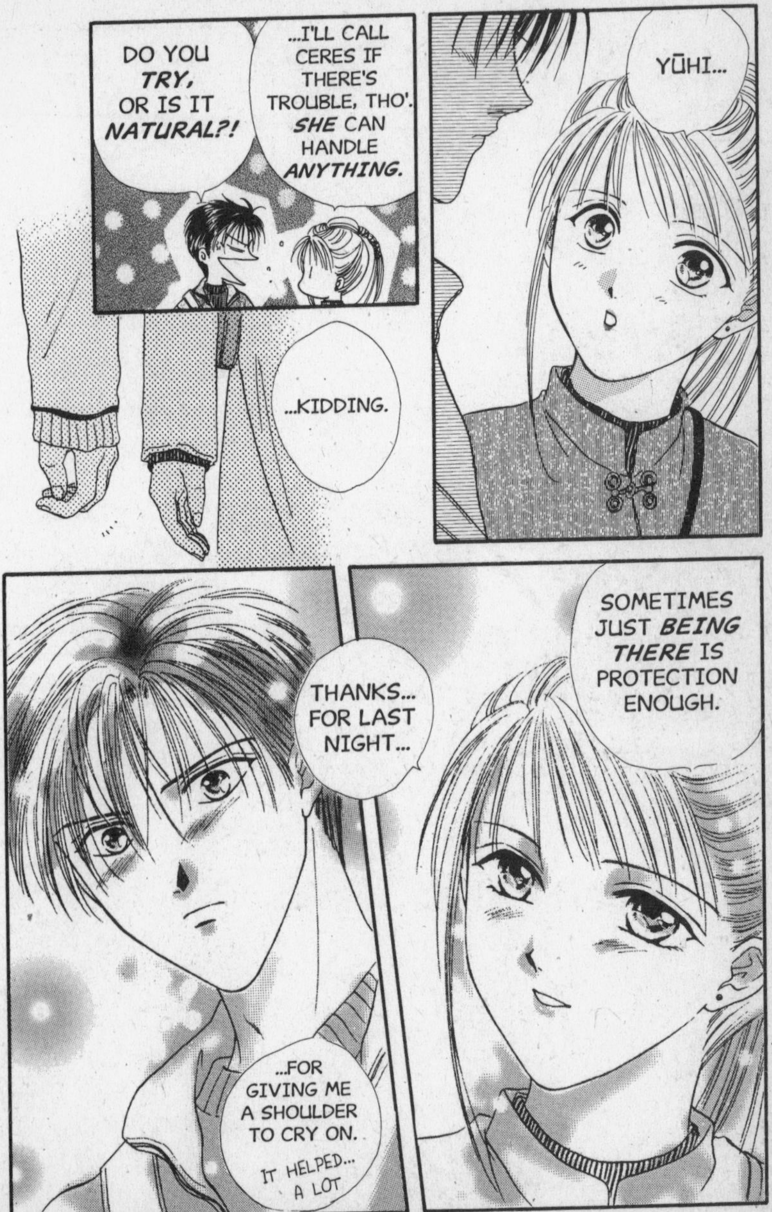
YŪHI...
...I'LL CALL CERES IF THERE'S TROUBLE, THO'. *SHE* CAN HANDLE *ANYTHING.*
DO YOU *TRY,* OR IS IT *NATURAL?!*
...KIDDING.
SOMETIMES JUST *BEING THERE* IS PROTECTION ENOUGH.
THANKS... FOR LAST NIGHT...
...FOR GIVING ME A SHOULDER TO CRY ON.
IT HELPED... A LOT

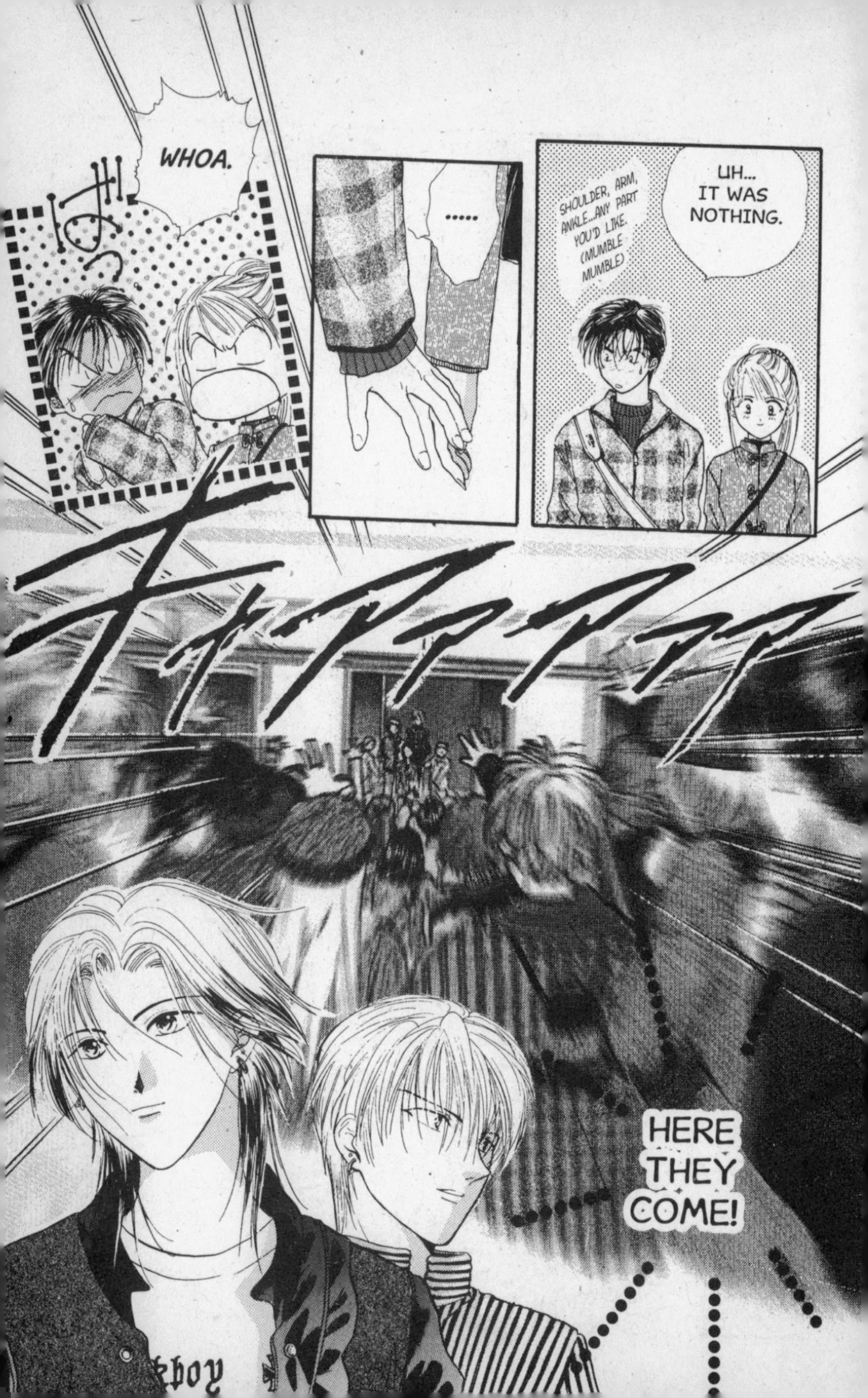
UH... IT WAS NOTHING.
SHOULDER, ARM, ANKLE...ANY PART YOU'D LIKE. (MUMBLE MUMBLE)
.....
WHOA.
HERE THEY COME!

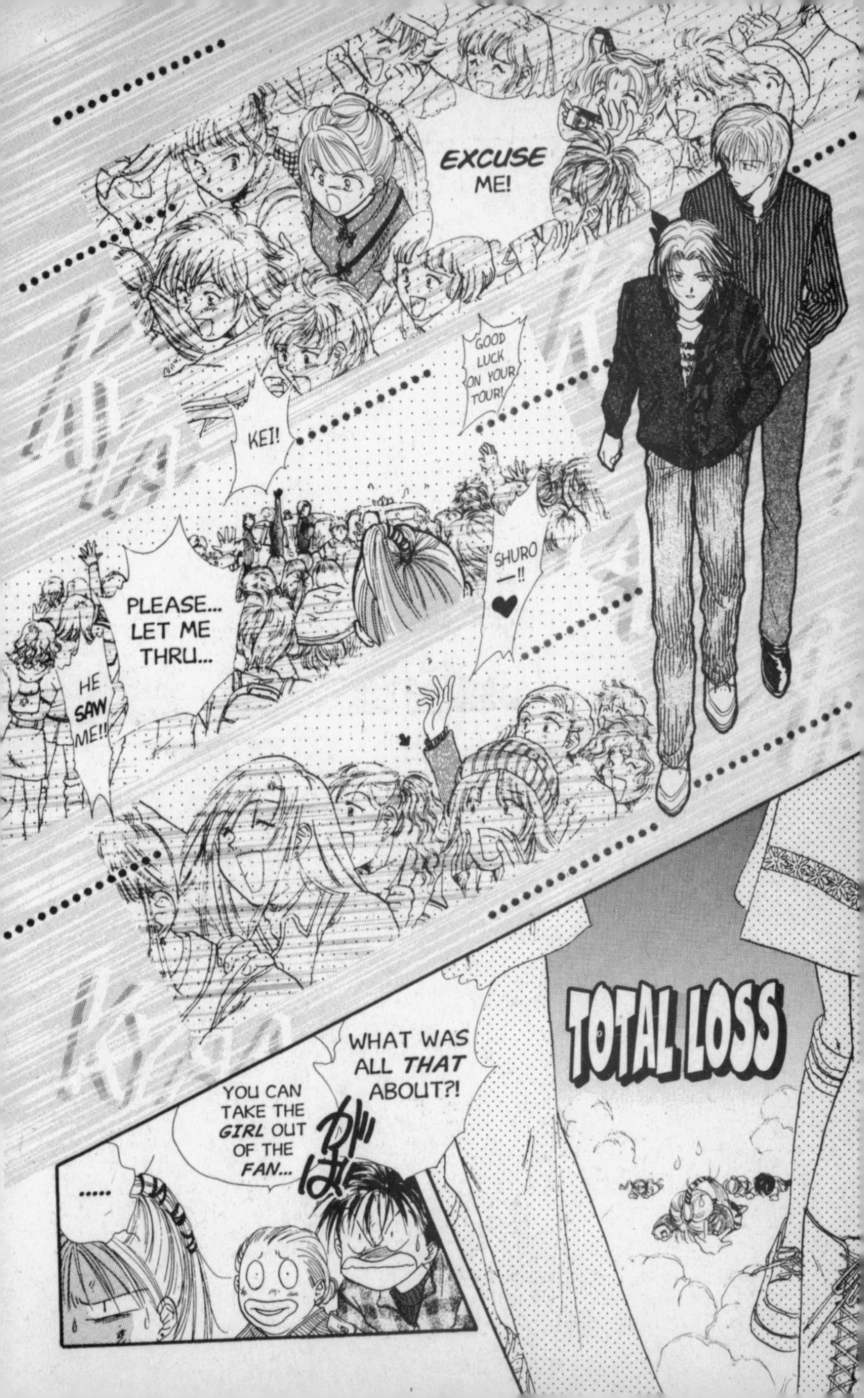
EXCUSE ME!
GOOD LUCK ON YOUR TOUR!
KEI!
SHURO—!!
PLEASE... LET ME THRU...
HE SAW ME!!
TOTAL LOSS
WHAT WAS ALL THAT ABOUT?!
YOU CAN TAKE THE GIRL OUT OF THE FAN...
.....

Ceres: 6

Hello, everyone!!
Oh my, it's the 6th volume. Aya has ended up having to wander all over Japan in search of the hagoromo, so I've been traveling myself these days for research. And then for some reason I received the "43rd Annual Shogakukan Manga Award" for Ceres
Who knows why, but there you go. This is all thanks to my devoted readers, to my editor (though it's his job) for patiently guiding me through everything, and to all the previous editors I've had, from whom I've learned so much. (That came out long.) Thank you so much.
Well, the award seems to be a big deal, so I couldn't be happier.
I'm not even close to being good enough...
I need to try and be better.
Anyway, I wonder how many people have come to really "get" the world of Ceres since the first five volumes? I do apologize—my ideas are maybe too epic. If I were to die in some tragic accident right now, it'd forever after be an unsolved mystery.
I'm full of it, aren't I.
Readers who followed my previous works have commented that the "style has completely changed," or that they thought Ceres "was by a different artist at first." (I think maybe you guys are exaggerating a bit.) I have been told by my assistants, though, that my work "looks more mature," that the way I draw now is "unlike (my) previous style." This is something I hadn't noticed myself until it was pointed out. But it is true that I wanted to make Ceres different from my previous work!
Of course, I can't call myself a professional unless I put in **something** that marks my work as being "by Watase," no matter **what** it is I end up drawing. It can't very well be "Who the heck did **this!**," right? I guess I can't resist criticizing my previous work.
A fight with the Yū Watase of yesterday...I'm my own worst rival. Or something.

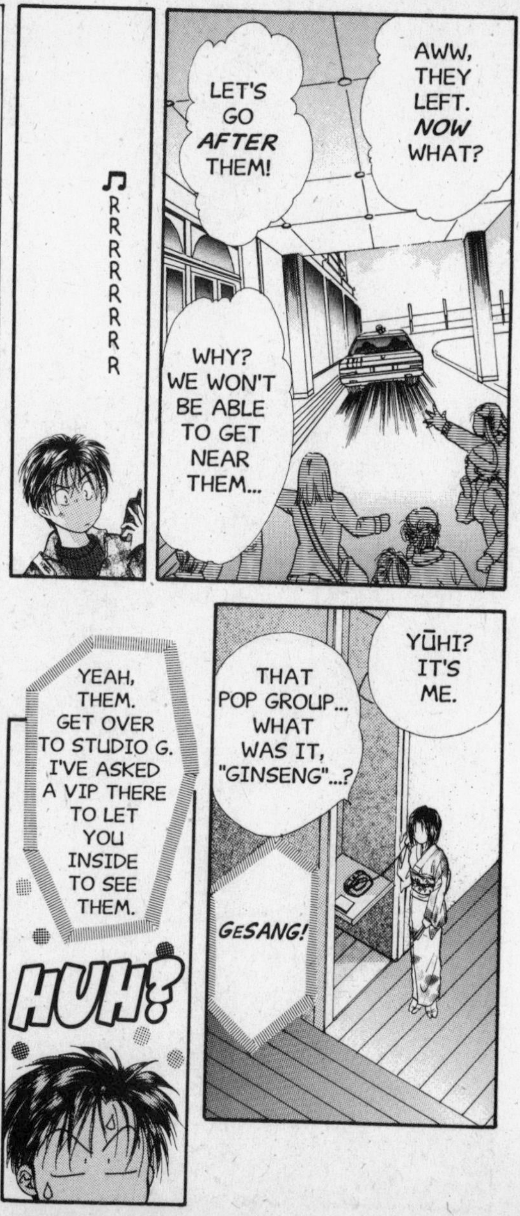
AWW, THEY LEFT. NOW WHAT?
LET'S GO AFTER THEM!
WHY? WE WON'T BE ABLE TO GET NEAR THEM...
♫ RRRRRRR
YŪHI? IT'S ME.
THAT POP GROUP... WHAT WAS IT, "GINSENG"...?
GESANG!
YEAH, THEM. GET OVER TO STUDIO G. I'VE ASKED A VIP THERE TO LET YOU INSIDE TO SEE THEM.
HUH?

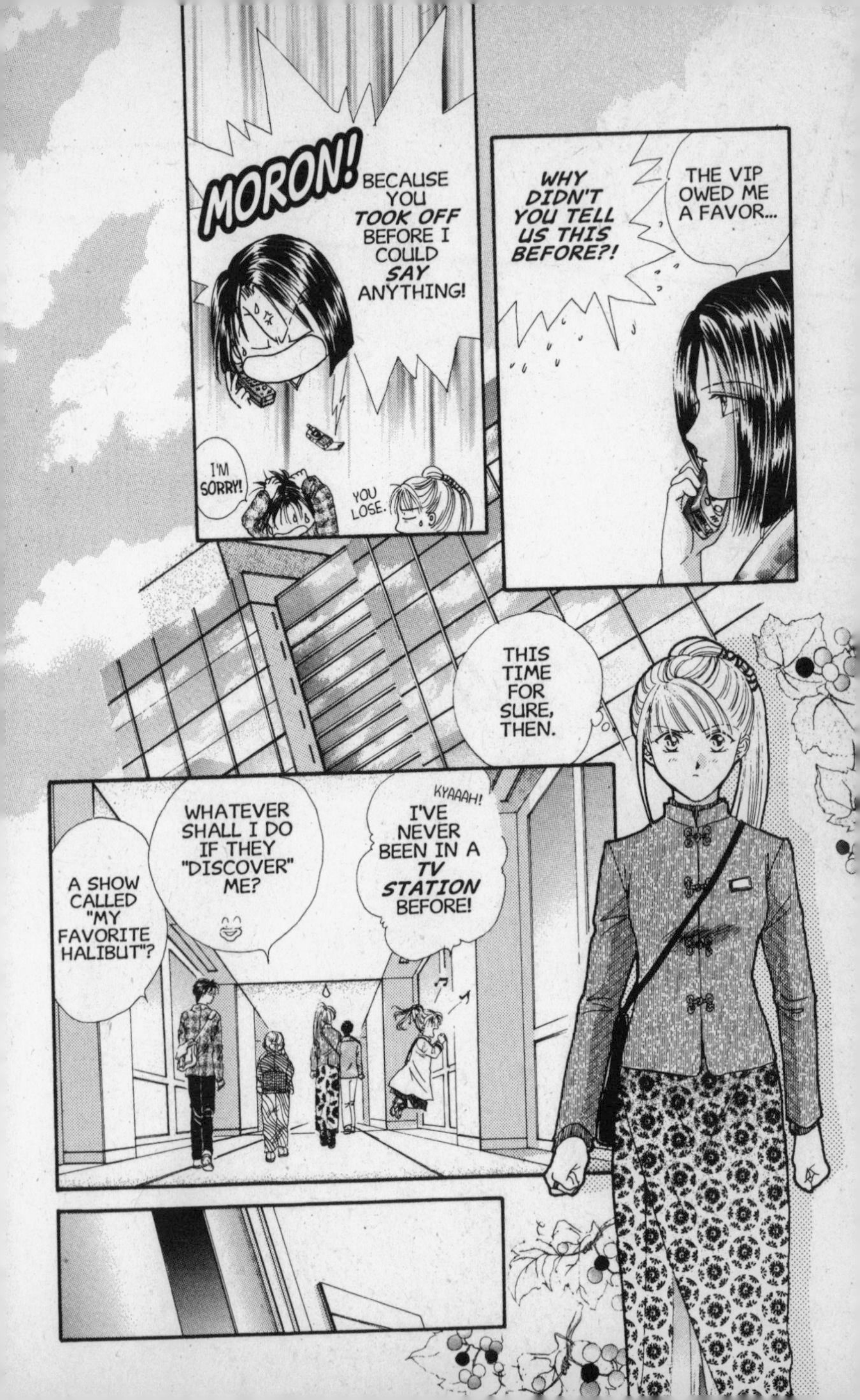
THE VIP OWED ME A FAVOR...
WHY DIDN'T YOU TELL US THIS BEFORE?!
MORON!
BECAUSE YOU TOOK OFF BEFORE I COULD SAY ANYTHING!
YOU LOSE.
I'M SORRY!
THIS TIME FOR SURE, THEN.
KYAAAH!
I'VE NEVER BEEN IN A TV STATION BEFORE!
WHATEVER SHALL I DO IF THEY "DISCOVER" ME?
A SHOW CALLED "MY FAVORITE HALIBUT"?

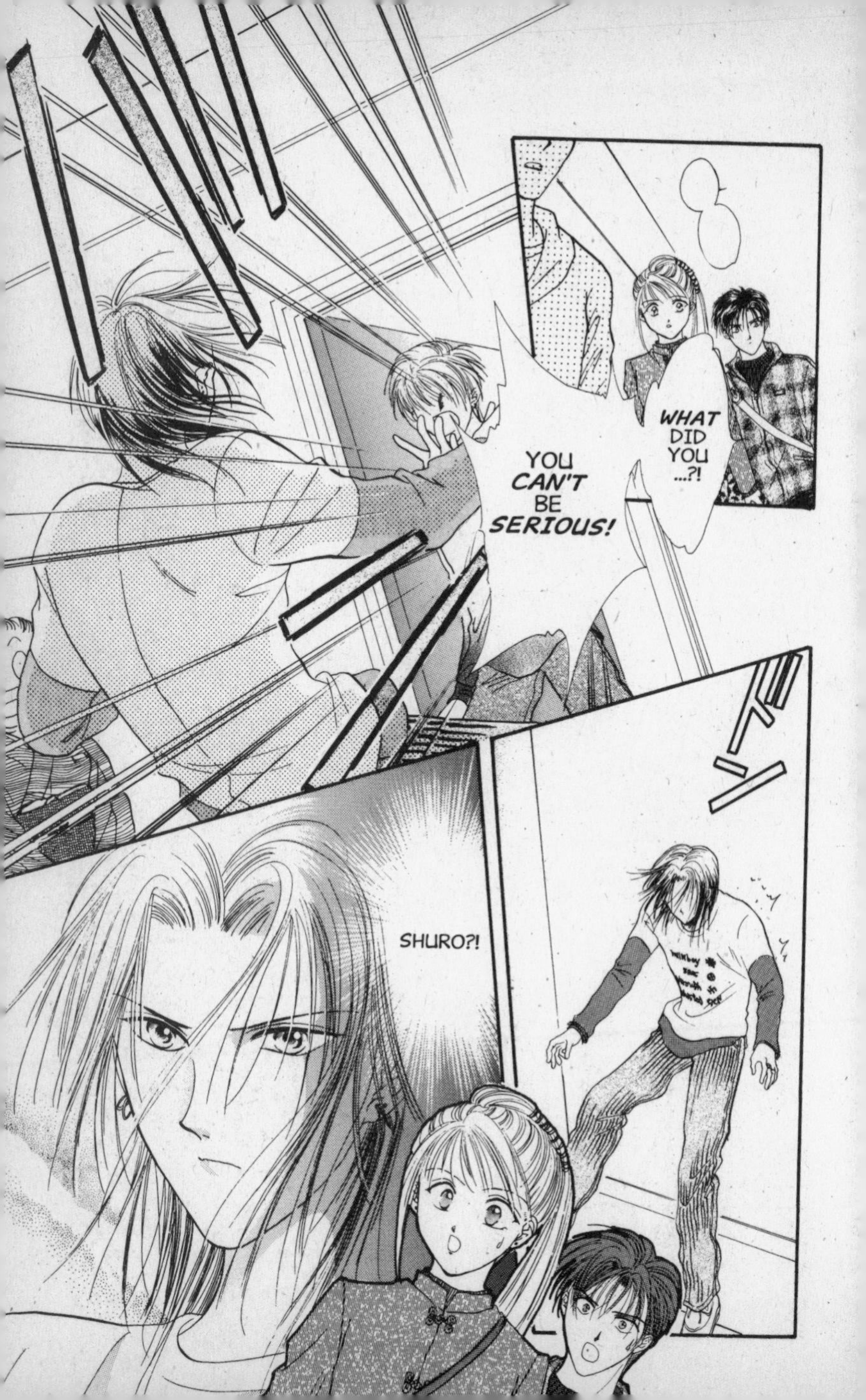
WHAT DID YOU ...?!
YOU CAN'T BE SERIOUS!
SHURO?!

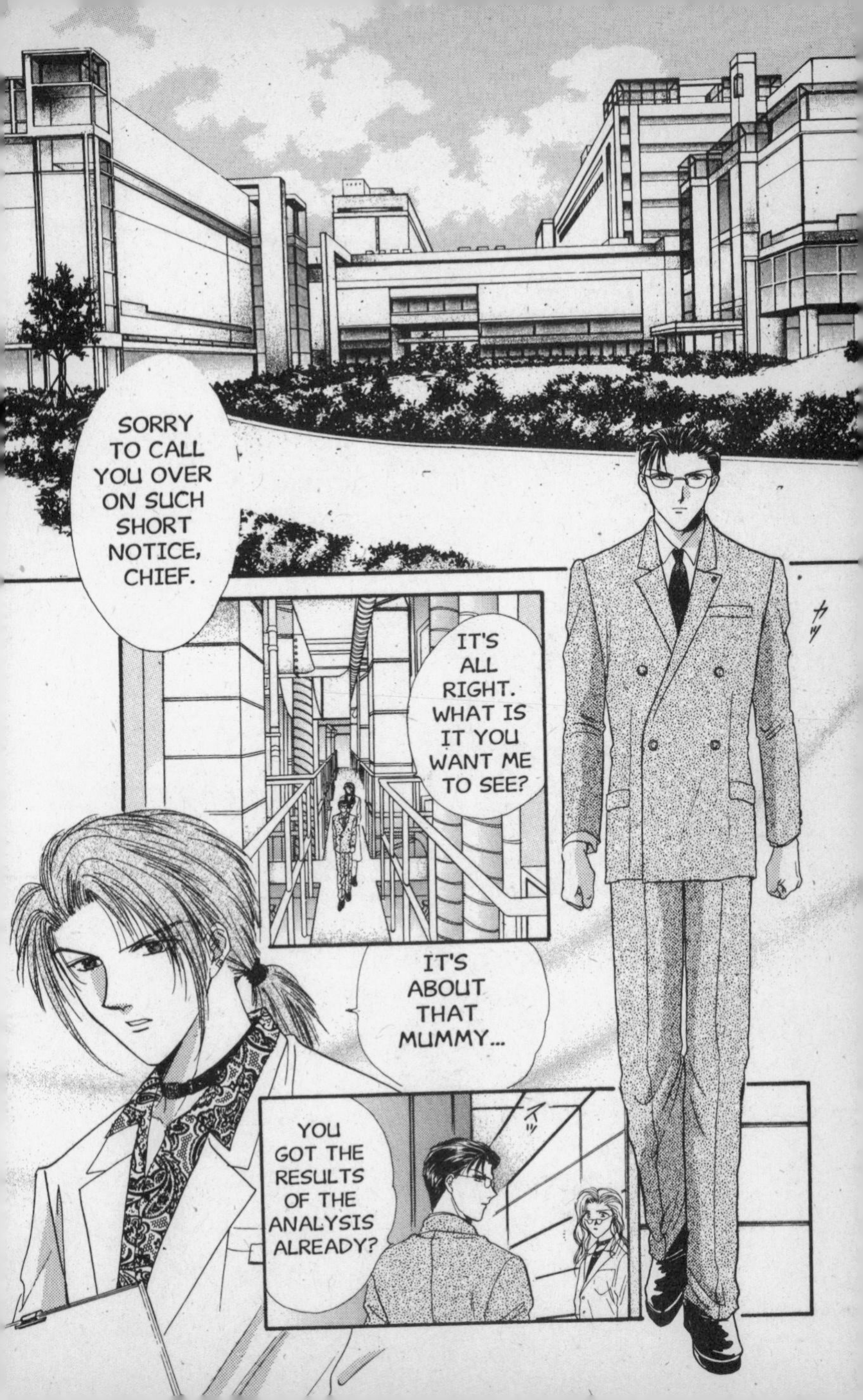
SORRY TO CALL YOU OVER ON SUCH SHORT NOTICE, CHIEF.
カッ
IT'S ALL RIGHT. WHAT IS IT YOU WANT ME TO SEE?
IT'S ABOUT THAT MUMMY...
スッ
YOU GOT THE RESULTS OF THE ANALYSIS ALREADY?

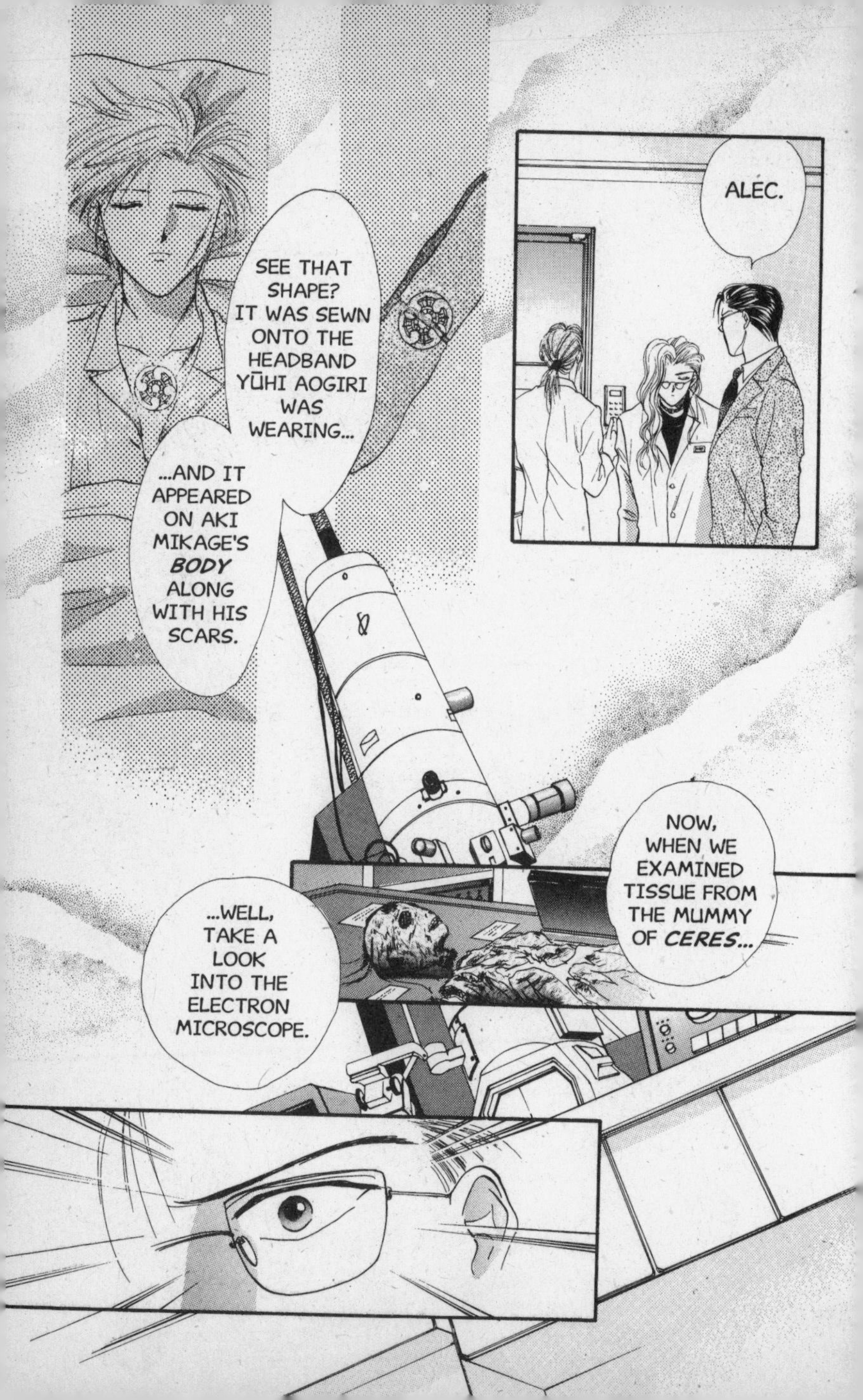
ALEC.
SEE THAT SHAPE? IT WAS SEWN ONTO THE HEADBAND YŪHI AOGIRI WAS WEARING...
...AND IT APPEARED ON AKI MIKAGE'S *BODY* ALONG WITH HIS SCARS.
NOW, WHEN WE EXAMINED TISSUE FROM THE MUMMY OF *CERES*...
...WELL, TAKE A LOOK INTO THE ELECTRON MICROSCOPE.

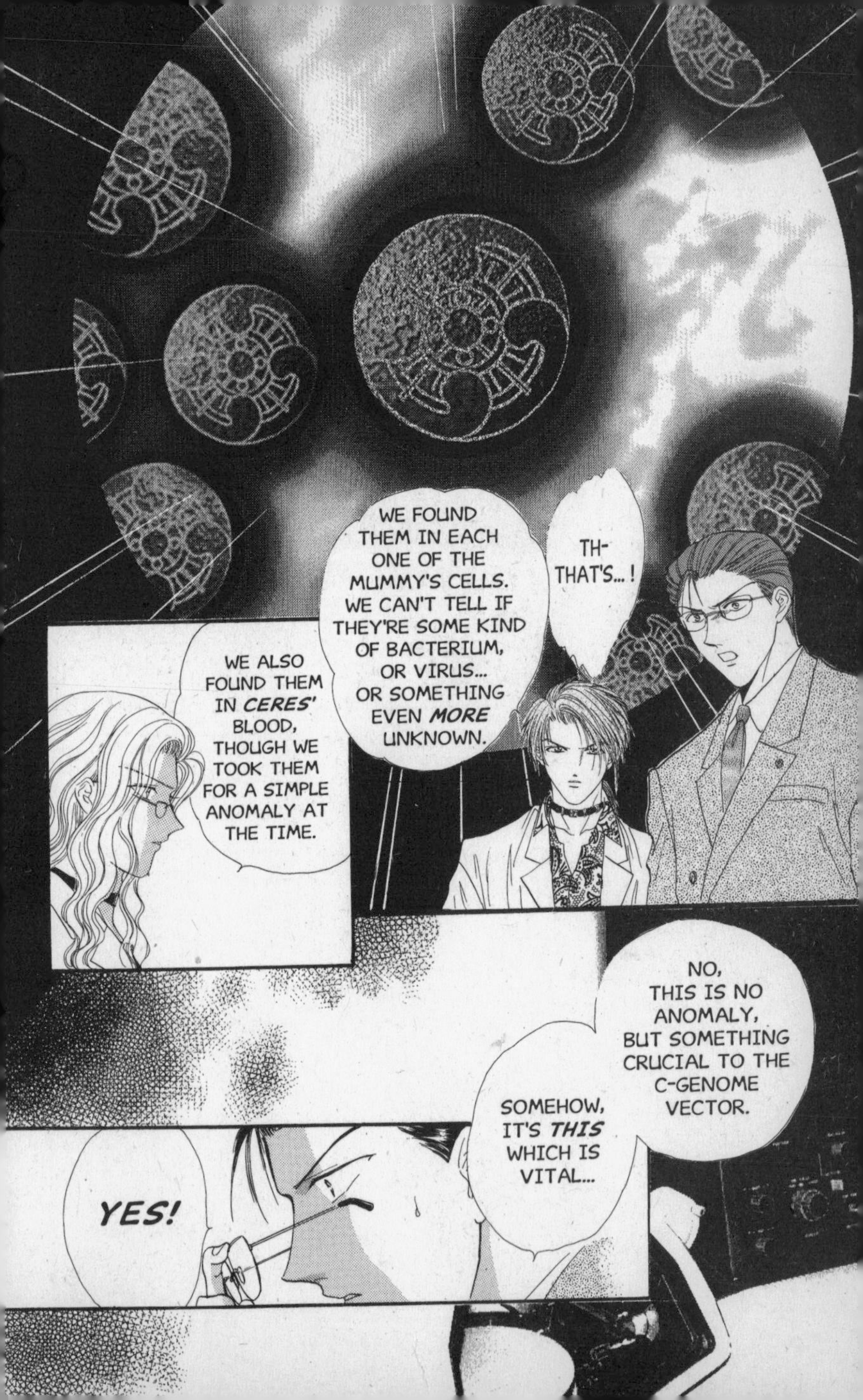
TH- THAT'S...!
WE FOUND THEM IN EACH ONE OF THE MUMMY'S CELLS. WE CAN'T TELL IF THEY'RE SOME KIND OF BACTERIUM, OR VIRUS... OR SOMETHING EVEN *MORE* UNKNOWN.
WE ALSO FOUND THEM IN *CERES'* BLOOD, THOUGH WE TOOK THEM FOR A SIMPLE ANOMALY AT THE TIME.
NO, THIS IS NO ANOMALY, BUT SOMETHING CRUCIAL TO THE C-GENOME VECTOR.
SOMEHOW, IT'S *THIS* WHICH IS VITAL...
YES!

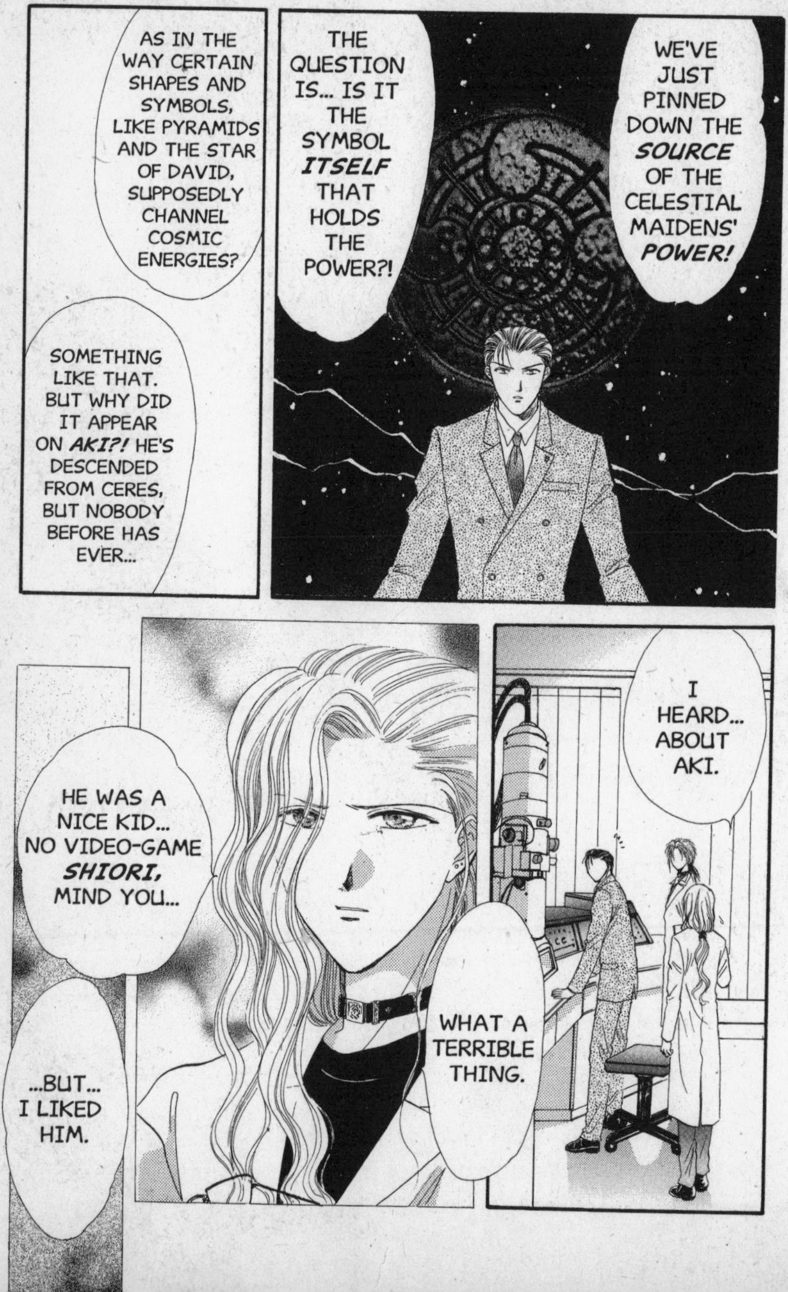
WE'VE JUST PINNED DOWN THE *SOURCE* OF THE CELESTIAL MAIDENS' *POWER!*
THE QUESTION IS... IS IT THE SYMBOL *ITSELF* THAT HOLDS THE POWER?!
AS IN THE WAY CERTAIN SHAPES AND SYMBOLS, LIKE PYRAMIDS AND THE STAR OF DAVID, SUPPOSEDLY CHANNEL COSMIC ENERGIES?
SOMETHING LIKE THAT. BUT WHY DID IT APPEAR ON *AKI?!* HE'S DESCENDED FROM CERES, BUT NOBODY BEFORE HAS EVER...
I HEARD... ABOUT AKI.
WHAT A TERRIBLE THING.
HE WAS A NICE KID... NO VIDEO-GAME *SHIORI,* MIND YOU...
...BUT... I LIKED HIM.

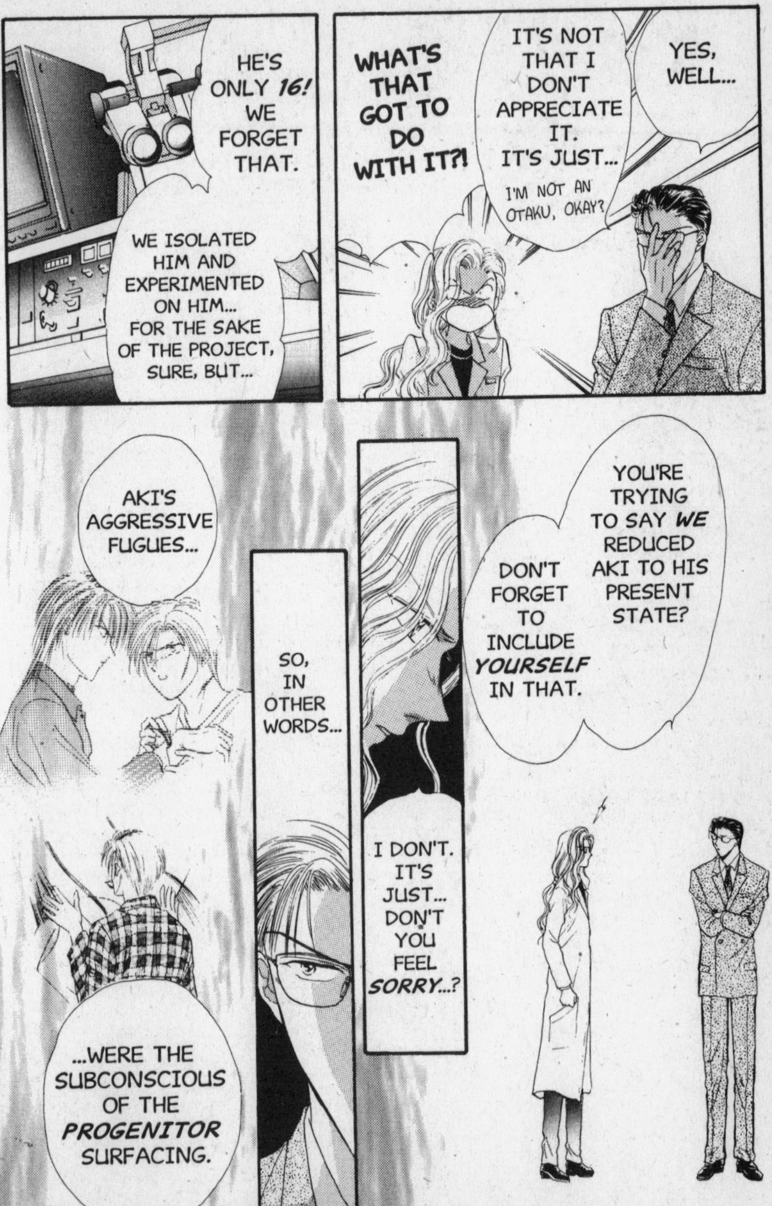
YES, WELL...
IT'S NOT THAT I DON'T APPRECIATE IT. IT'S JUST...
I'M NOT AN OTAKU, OKAY?
WHAT'S THAT GOT TO DO WITH IT?!
HE'S ONLY 16! WE FORGET THAT.
WE ISOLATED HIM AND EXPERIMENTED ON HIM... FOR THE SAKE OF THE PROJECT, SURE, BUT...
YOU'RE TRYING TO SAY WE REDUCED AKI TO HIS PRESENT STATE?
DON'T FORGET TO INCLUDE YOURSELF IN THAT.
SO, IN OTHER WORDS...
I DON'T. IT'S JUST... DON'T YOU FEEL SORRY...?
AKI'S AGGRESSIVE FUGUES...
...WERE THE SUBCONSCIOUS OF THE PROGENITOR SURFACING.

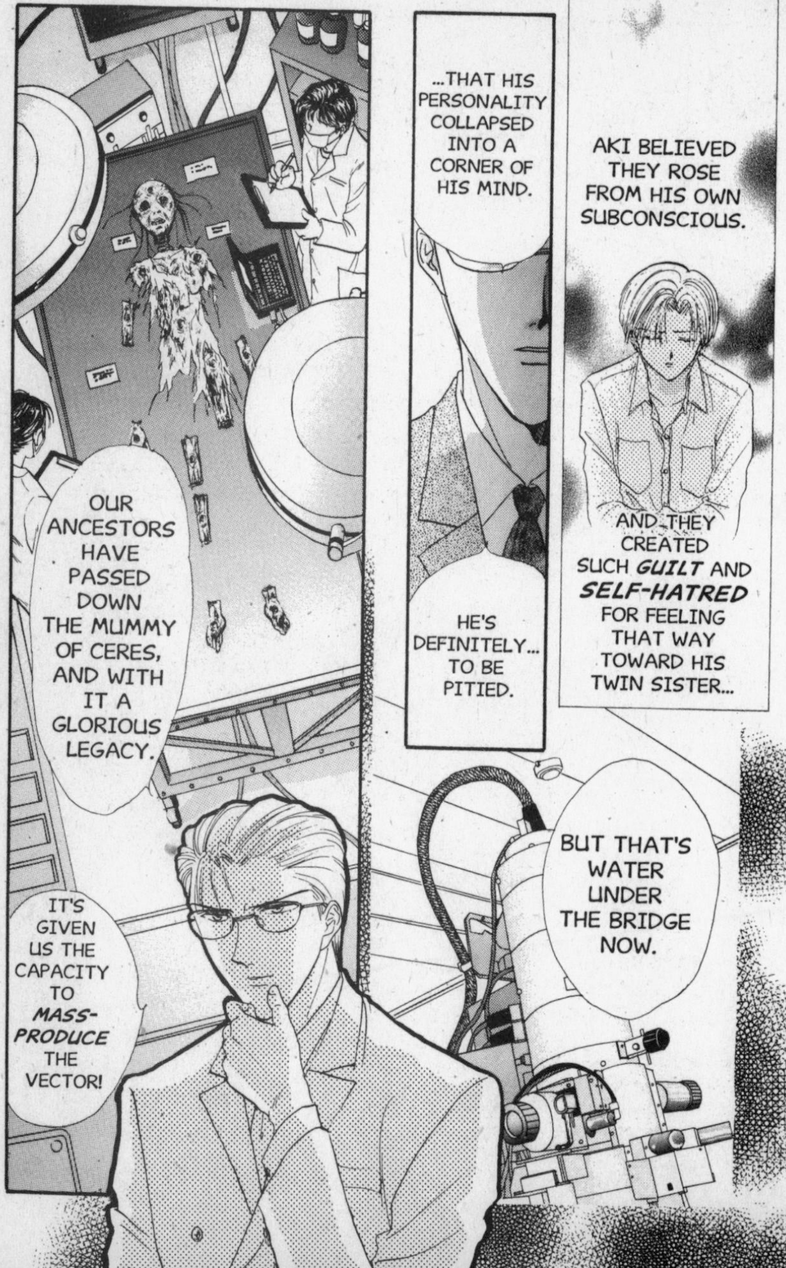
AKI BELIEVED THEY ROSE FROM HIS OWN SUBCONSCIOUS.
AND THEY CREATED SUCH *GUILT* AND *SELF-HATRED* FOR FEELING THAT WAY TOWARD HIS TWIN SISTER...
...THAT HIS PERSONALITY COLLAPSED INTO A CORNER OF HIS MIND.
HE'S DEFINITELY... TO BE PITIED.
BUT THAT'S WATER UNDER THE BRIDGE NOW.
OUR ANCESTORS HAVE PASSED DOWN THE MUMMY OF CERES, AND WITH IT A GLORIOUS LEGACY.
IT'S GIVEN US THE CAPACITY TO *MASS-PRODUCE* THE VECTOR!

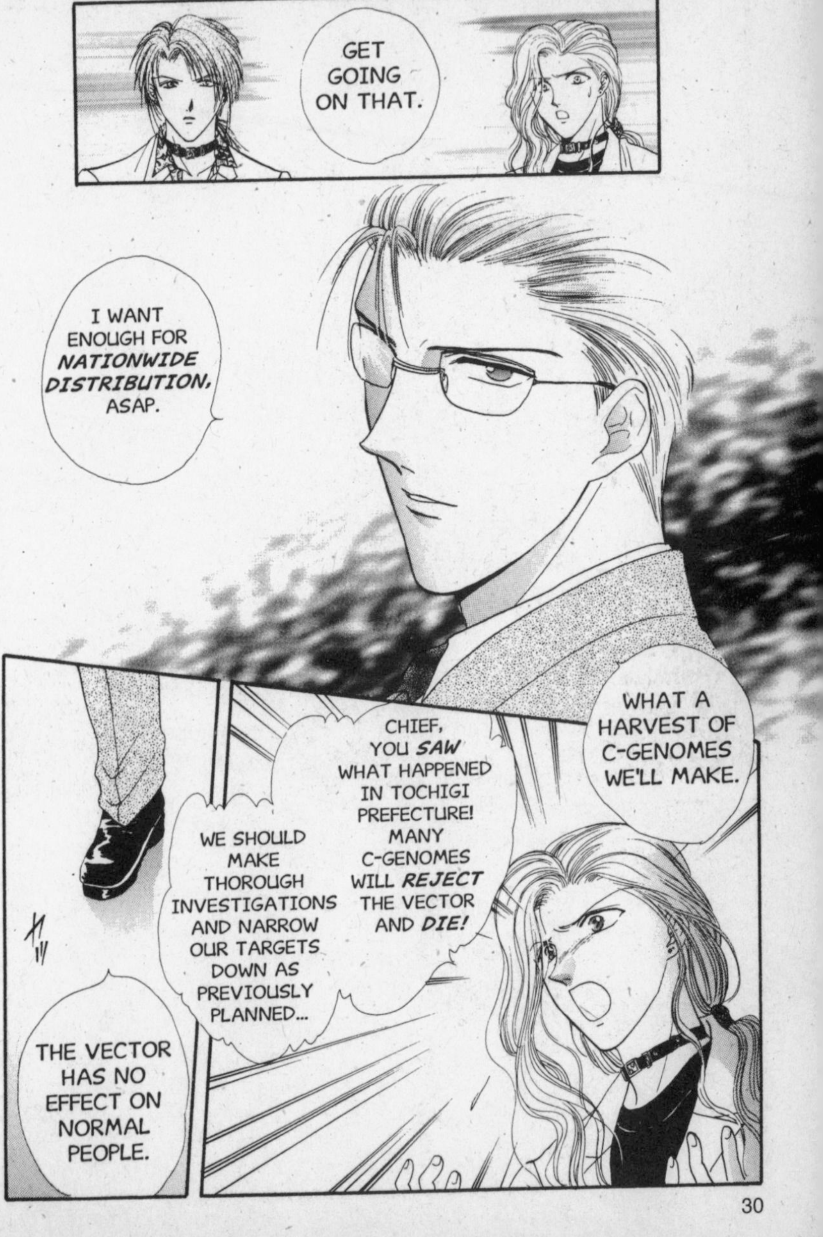
GET GOING ON THAT.
I WANT ENOUGH FOR *NATIONWIDE DISTRIBUTION,* ASAP.
WHAT A HARVEST OF C-GENOMES WE'LL MAKE.
CHIEF, YOU *SAW* WHAT HAPPENED IN TOCHIGI PREFECTURE! MANY C-GENOMES WILL *REJECT* THE VECTOR AND *DIE!*
WE SHOULD MAKE THOROUGH INVESTIGATIONS AND NARROW OUR TARGETS DOWN AS PREVIOUSLY PLANNED...
THE VECTOR HAS NO EFFECT ON NORMAL PEOPLE.

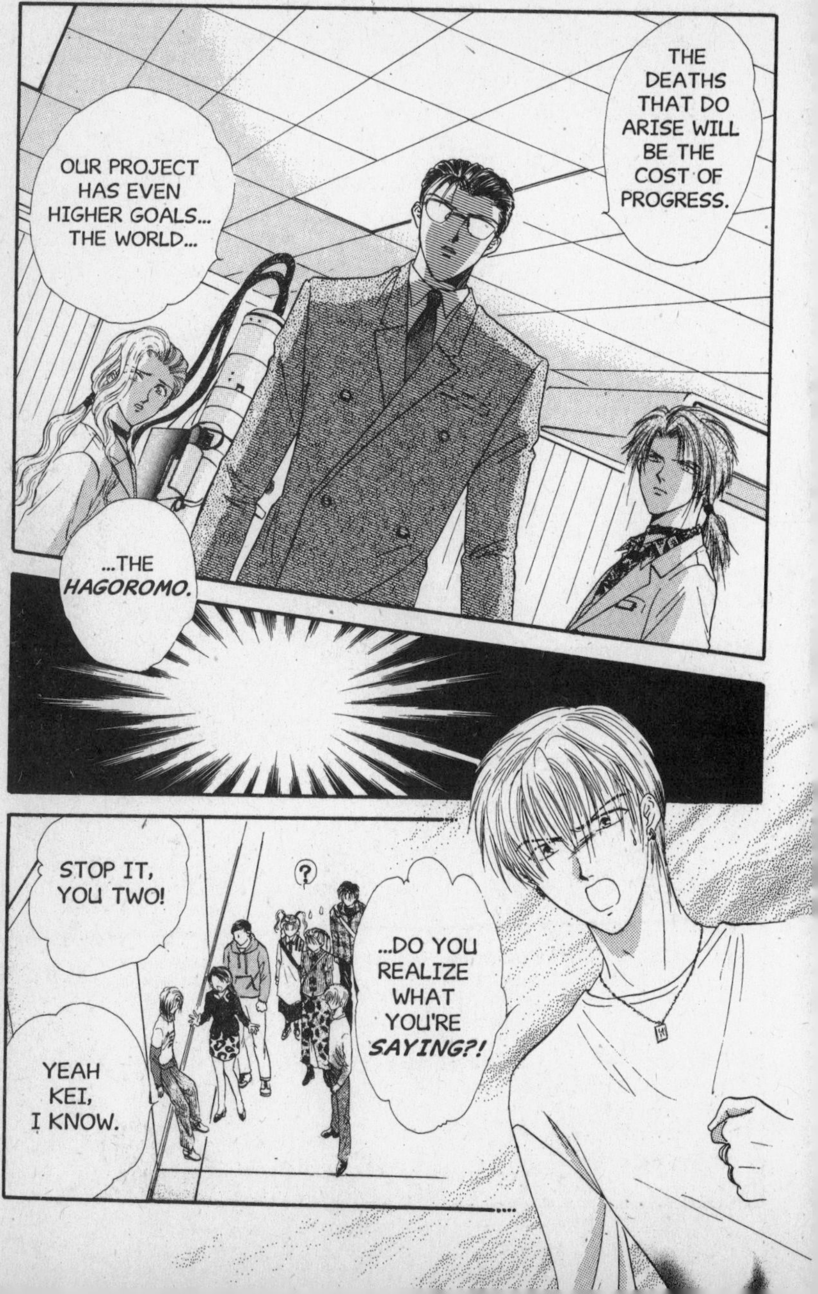
THE DEATHS THAT DO ARISE WILL BE THE COST OF PROGRESS.
OUR PROJECT HAS EVEN HIGHER GOALS... THE WORLD...
...THE *HAGOROMO.*
...DO YOU REALIZE WHAT YOU'RE *SAYING?!*
?
STOP IT, YOU TWO!
YEAH KEI, I KNOW.

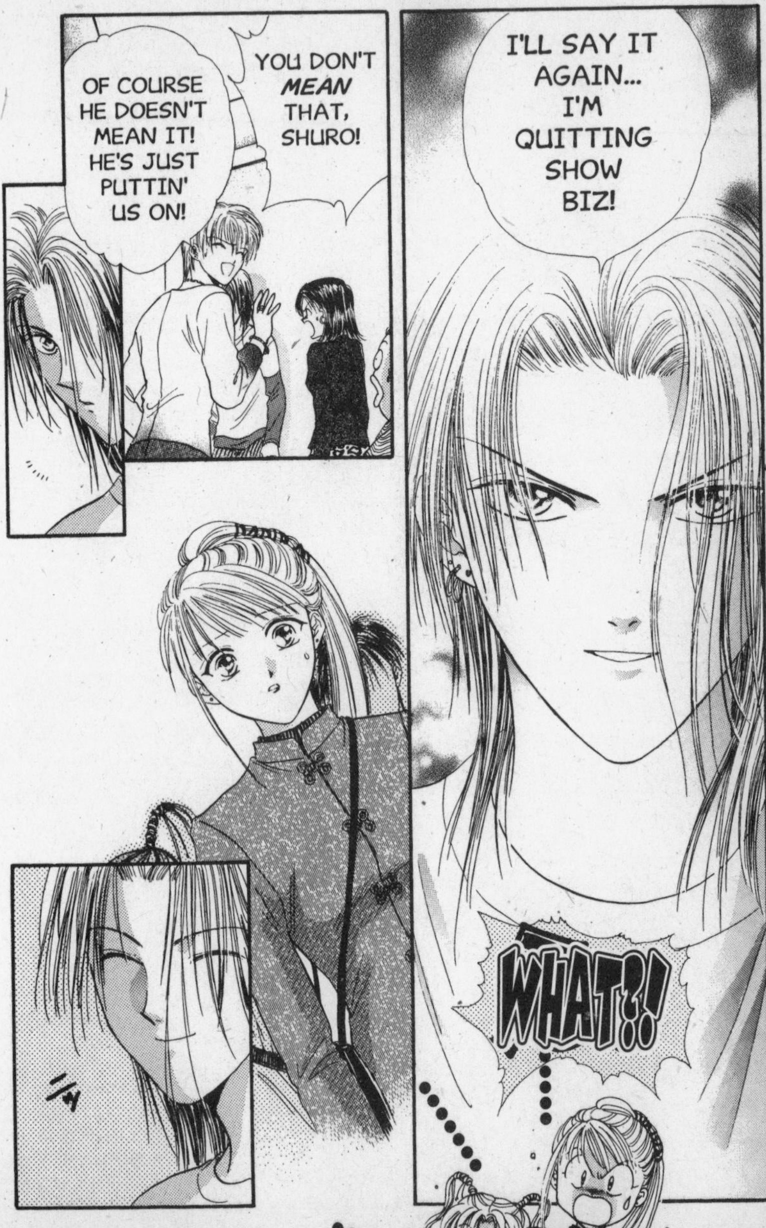
YOU DON'T *MEAN* THAT, SHURO!
OF COURSE HE DOESN'T MEAN IT! HE'S JUST PUTTIN' US ON!
I'LL SAY IT AGAIN... I'M QUITTING SHOW BIZ!
WHAT?!

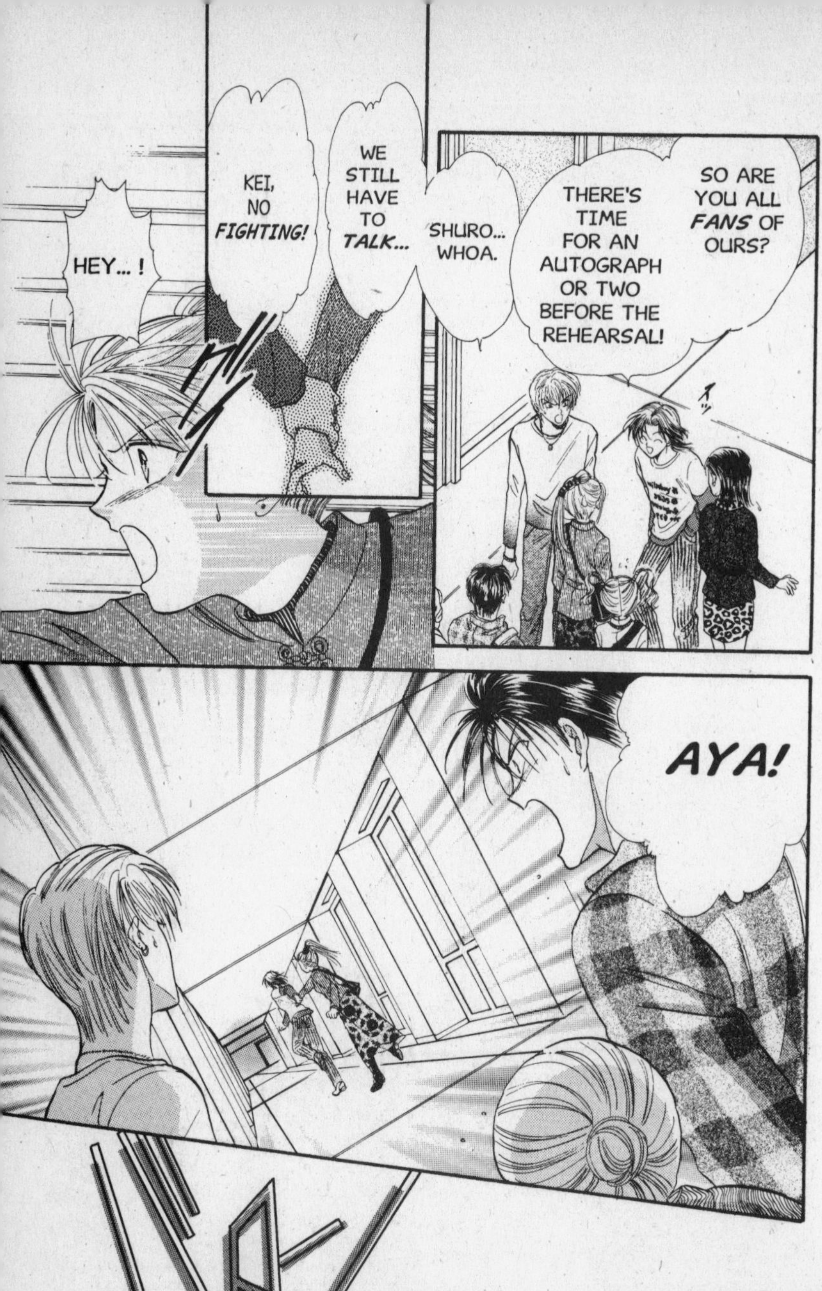
SO ARE YOU ALL FANS OF OURS?
THERE'S TIME FOR AN AUTOGRAPH OR TWO BEFORE THE REHEARSAL!
SHURO... WHOA.
WE STILL HAVE TO TALK...
KEI, NO FIGHTING!
HEY... !
AYA!

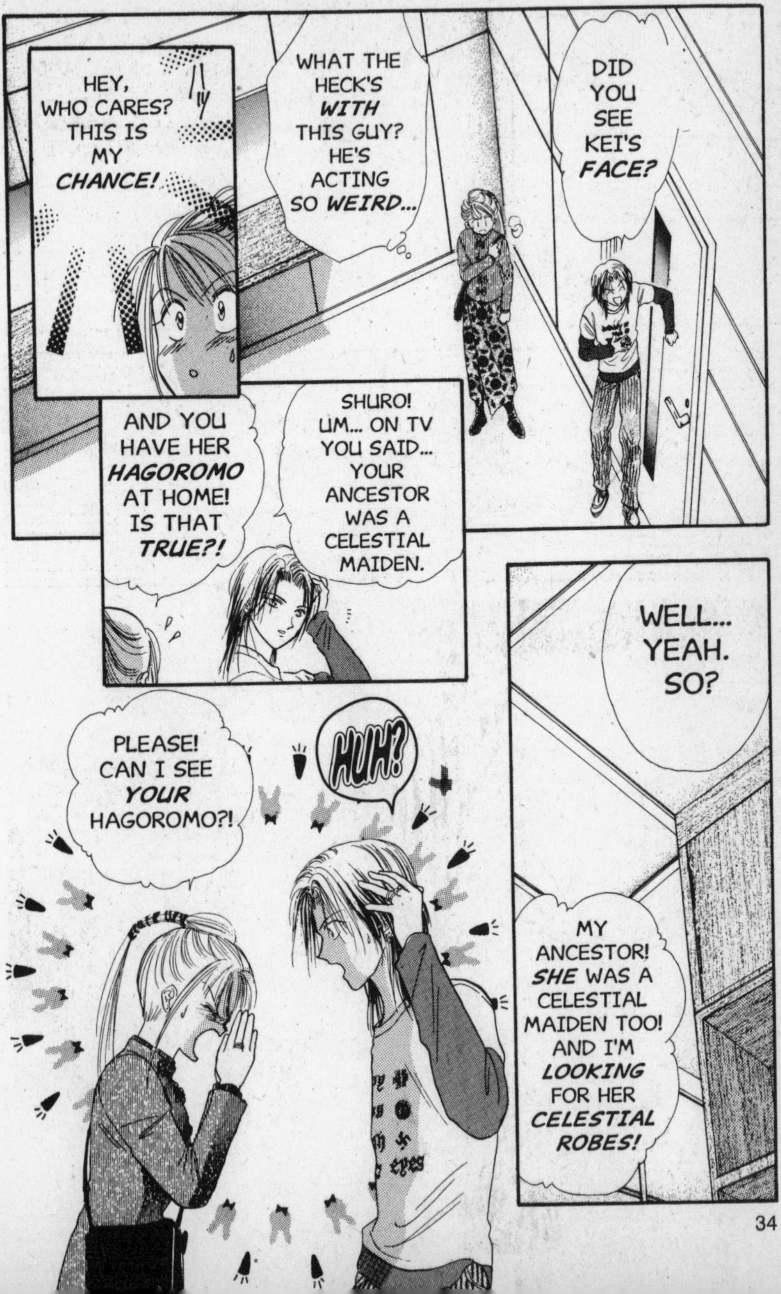
DID YOU SEE KEI'S FACE?
WHAT THE HECK'S WITH THIS GUY? HE'S ACTING SO WEIRD...
HEY, WHO CARES? THIS IS MY CHANCE!
SHURO! UM... ON TV YOU SAID... YOUR ANCESTOR WAS A CELESTIAL MAIDEN.
AND YOU HAVE HER HAGOROMO AT HOME! IS THAT TRUE?!
WELL... YEAH. SO?
MY ANCESTOR! SHE WAS A CELESTIAL MAIDEN TOO! AND I'M LOOKING FOR HER CELESTIAL ROBES!
HUH?
PLEASE! CAN I SEE YOUR HAGOROMO?!

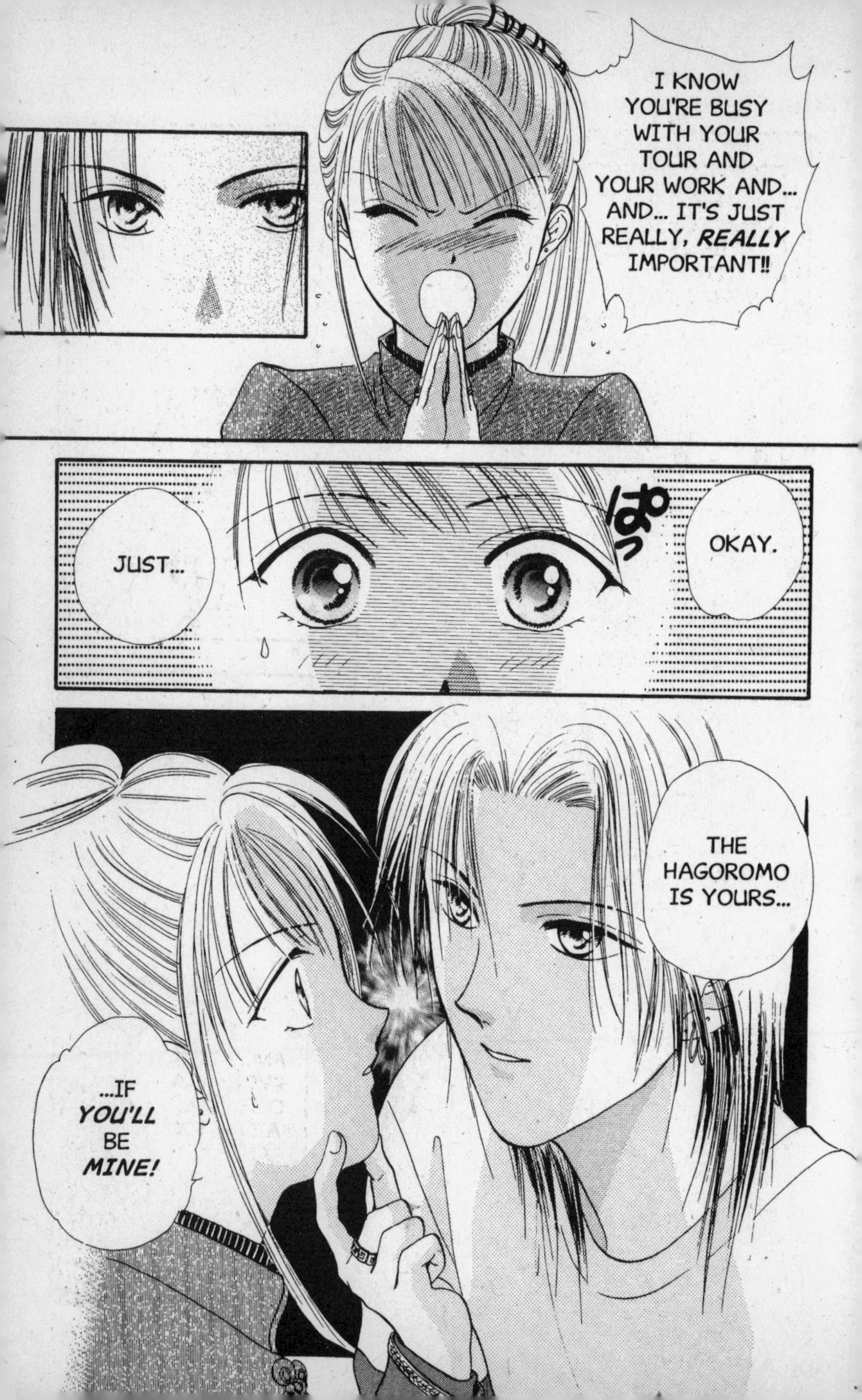
I KNOW YOU'RE BUSY WITH YOUR TOUR AND YOUR WORK AND... AND... IT'S JUST REALLY, *REALLY* IMPORTANT!!
OKAY.
ぱっ
JUST...
THE HAGOROMO IS YOURS...
...IF *YOU'LL* BE *MINE!*

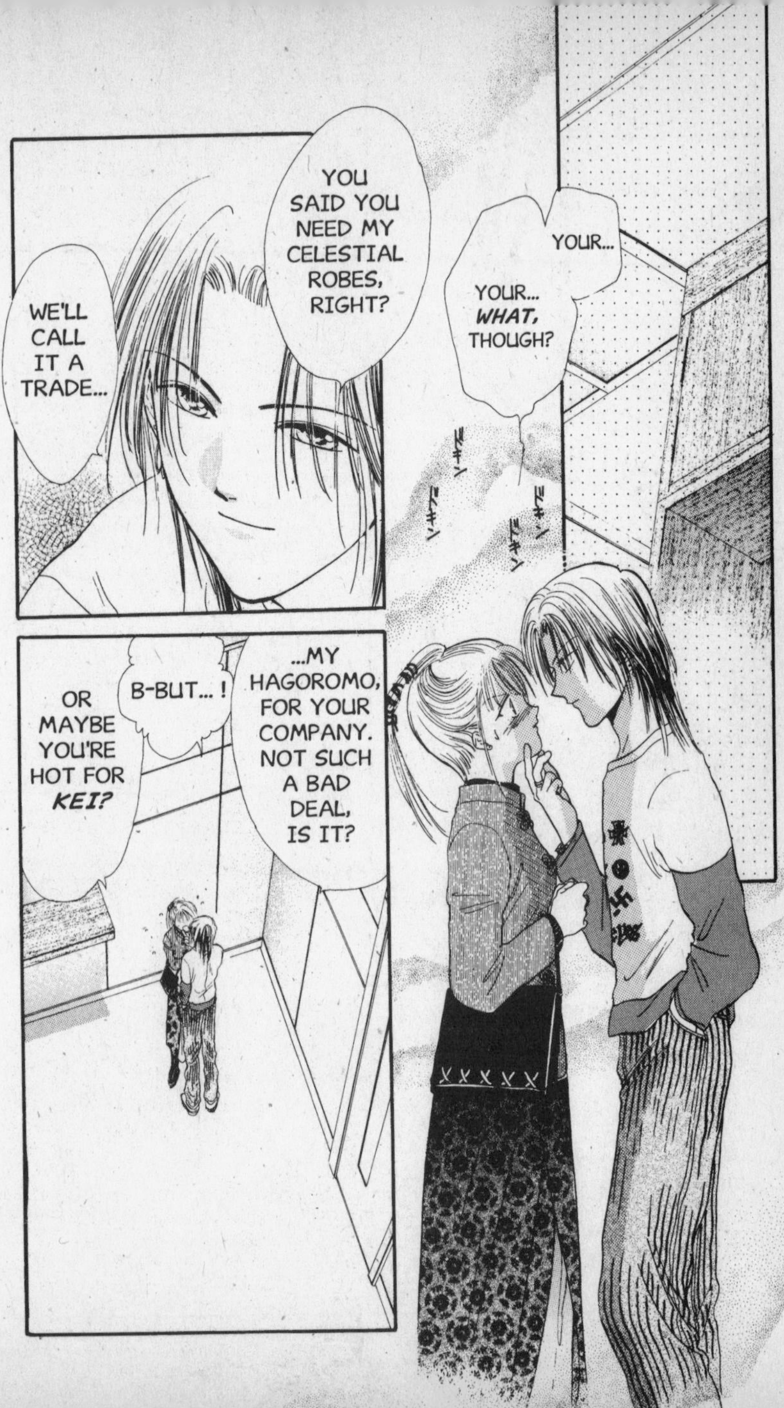
YOUR...
YOUR... WHAT, THOUGH?
YOU SAID YOU NEED MY CELESTIAL ROBES, RIGHT?
WE'LL CALL IT A TRADE...
...MY HAGOROMO, FOR YOUR COMPANY. NOT SUCH A BAD DEAL, IS IT?
B-BUT... !
OR MAYBE YOU'RE HOT FOR KEI?

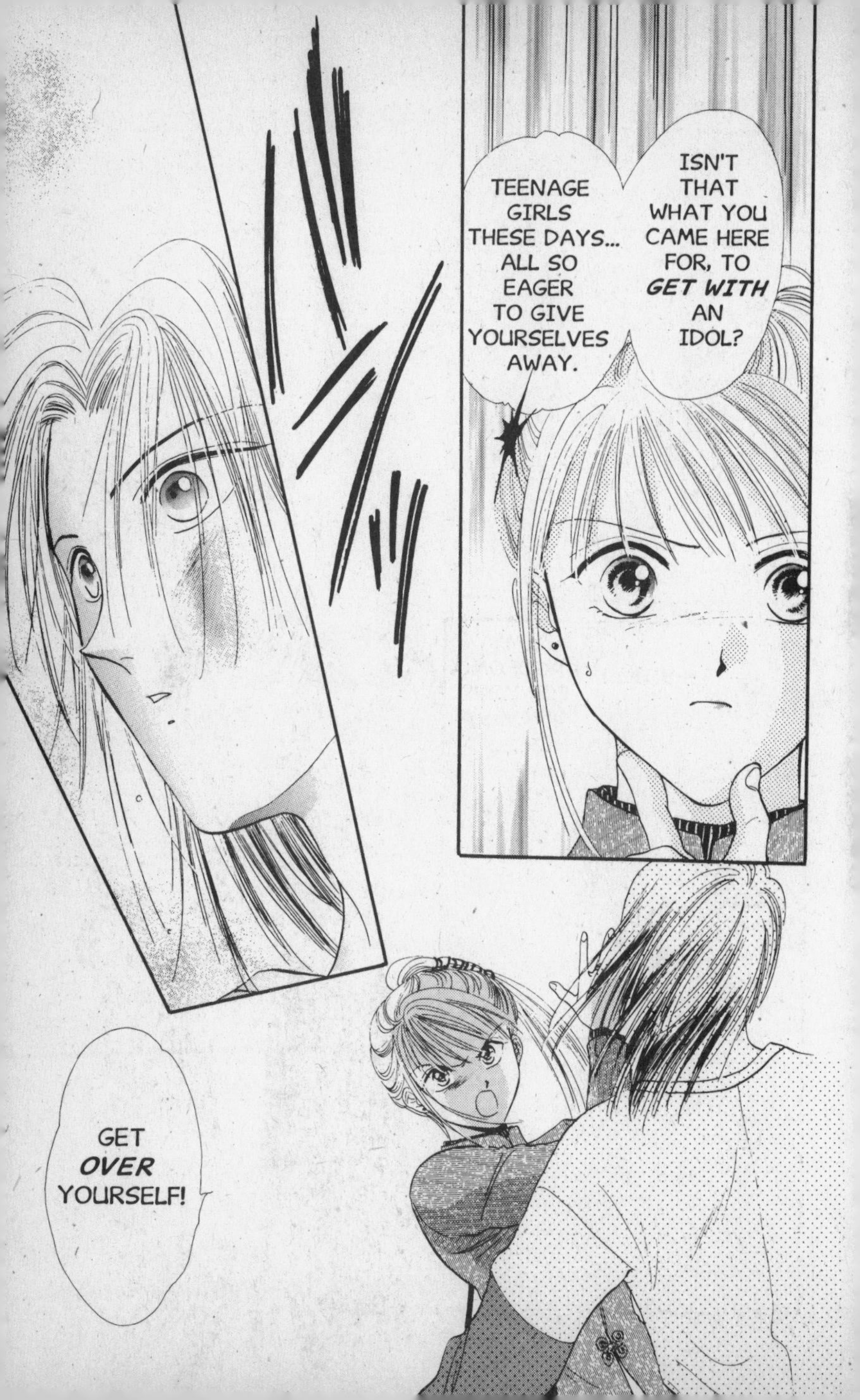
ISN'T THAT WHAT YOU CAME HERE FOR, TO *GET WITH* AN IDOL?
TEENAGE GIRLS THESE DAYS... ALL SO EAGER TO GIVE YOURSELVES AWAY.
GET *OVER* YOURSELF!

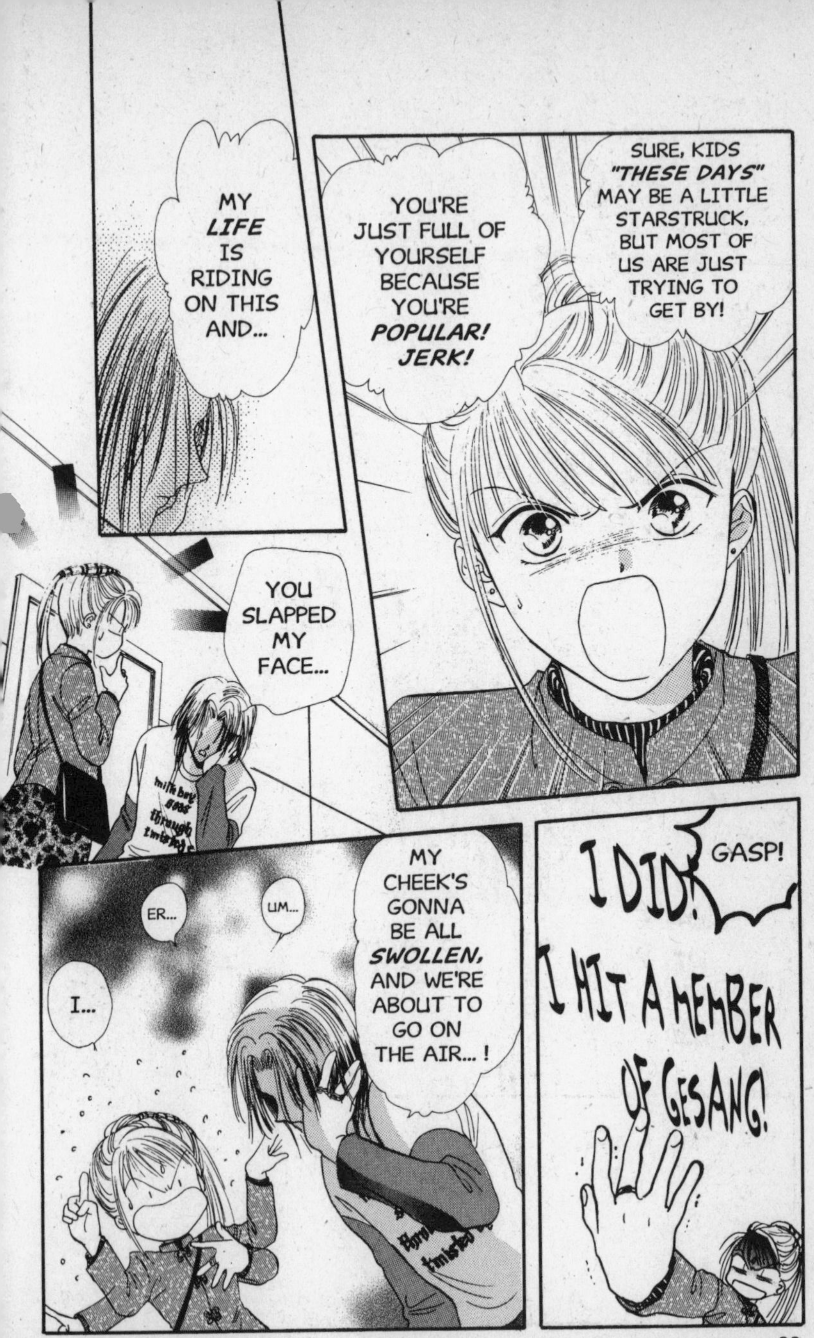
SURE, KIDS "THESE DAYS" MAY BE A LITTLE STARSTRUCK, BUT MOST OF US ARE JUST TRYING TO GET BY!
YOU'RE JUST FULL OF YOURSELF BECAUSE YOU'RE POPULAR! JERK!
MY LIFE IS RIDING ON THIS AND...
YOU SLAPPED MY FACE...
GASP!
I DID!
I HIT A MEMBER OF GESANG!
MY CHEEK'S GONNA BE ALL SWOLLEN, AND WE'RE ABOUT TO GO ON THE AIR... !
UM...
ER...
I...

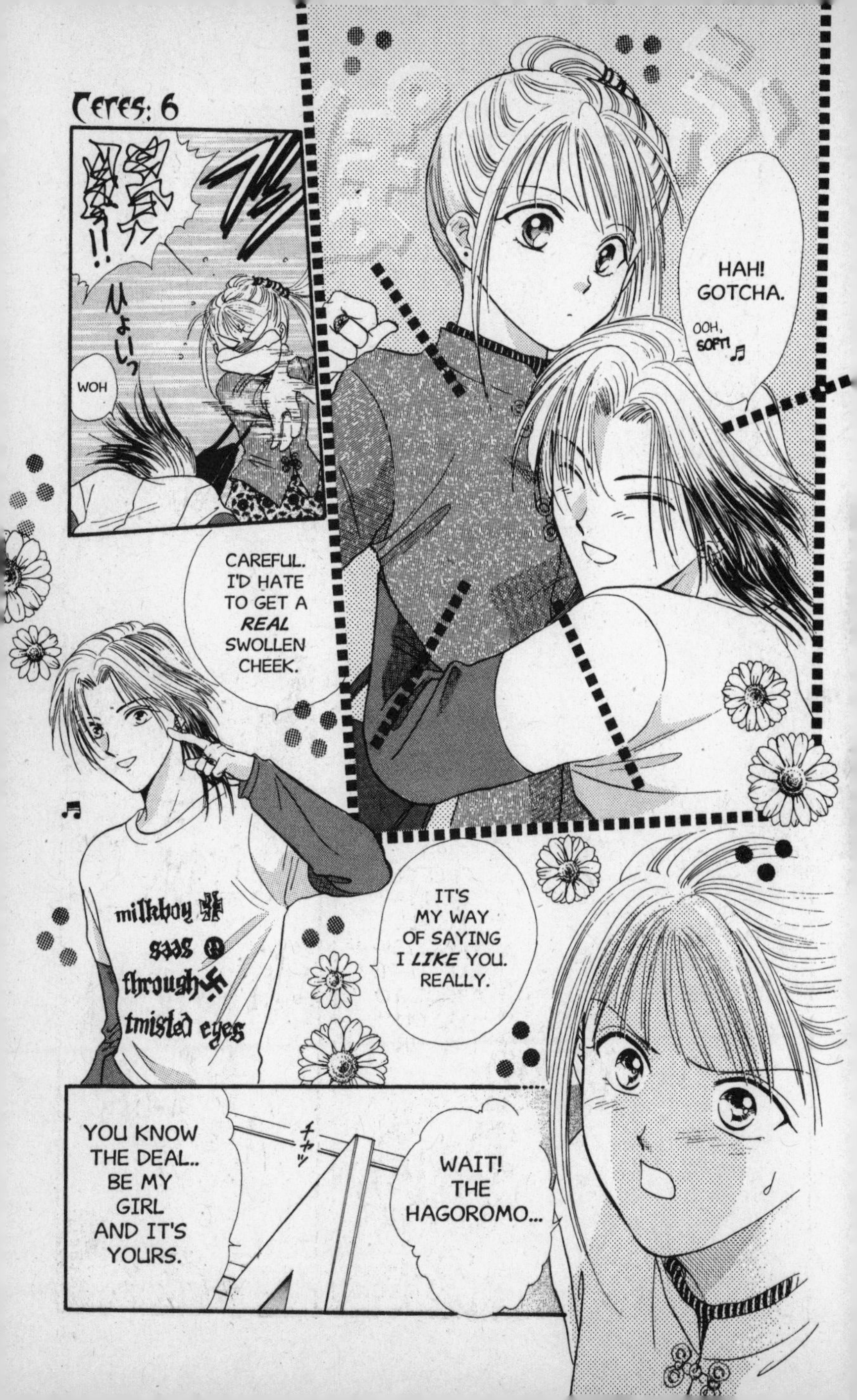
HAH! GOTCHA.
OOH, SOFT! ♫
ひょいっ
WOH
CAREFUL. I'D HATE TO GET A *REAL* SWOLLEN CHEEK.
milkboy saas through twisted eyes
IT'S MY WAY OF SAYING I *LIKE* YOU. REALLY.
WAIT! THE HAGOROMO...
チャッ
YOU KNOW THE DEAL.. BE MY GIRL AND IT'S YOURS.

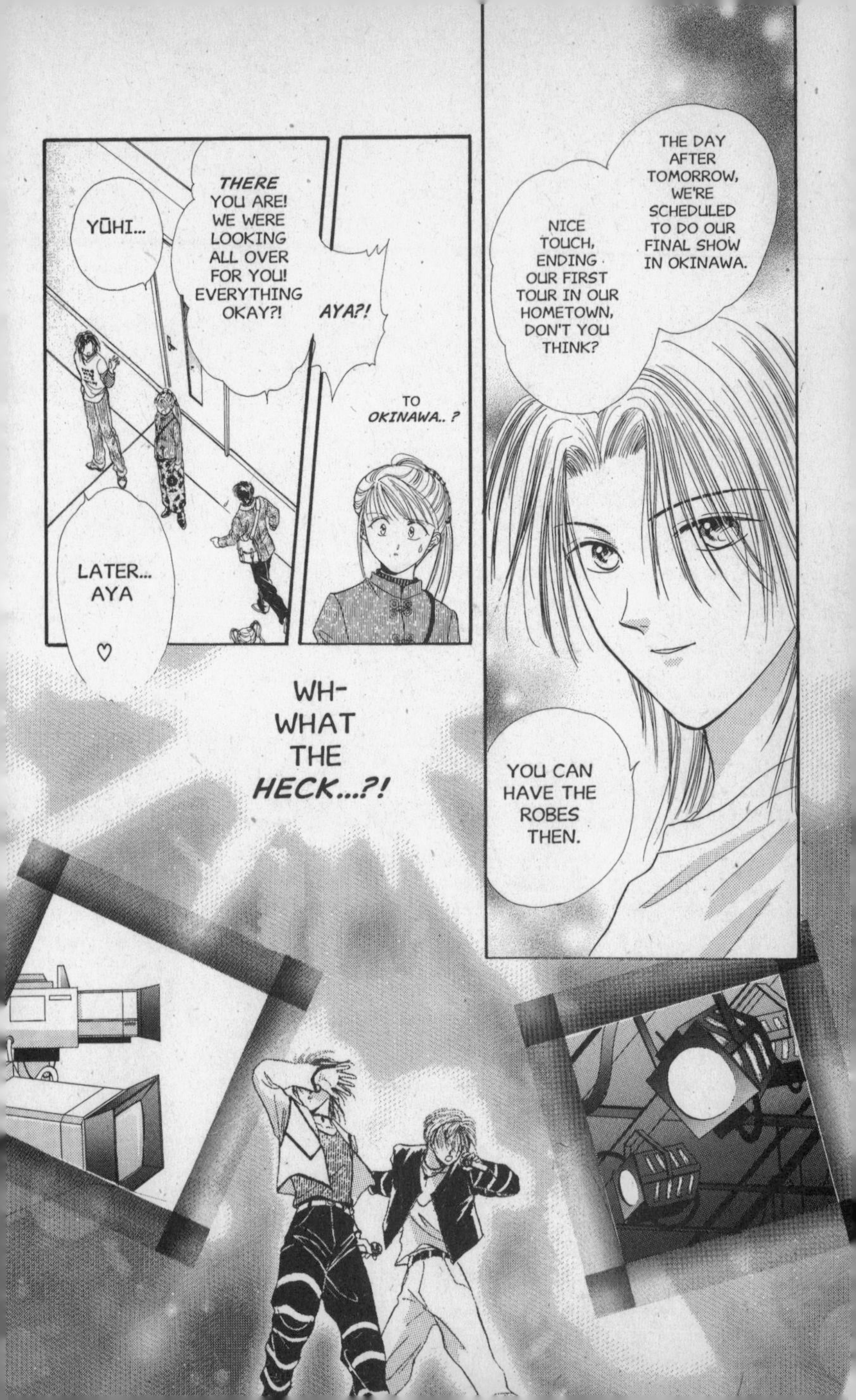
THE DAY AFTER TOMORROW, WE'RE SCHEDULED TO DO OUR FINAL SHOW IN OKINAWA.
NICE TOUCH, ENDING OUR FIRST TOUR IN OUR HOMETOWN, DON'T YOU THINK?
YOU CAN HAVE THE ROBES THEN.
AYA?!
TO OKINAWA..?
THERE YOU ARE! WE WERE LOOKING ALL OVER FOR YOU! EVERYTHING OKAY?!
YŪHI...
LATER... AYA ♡
WH- WHAT THE HECK...?!

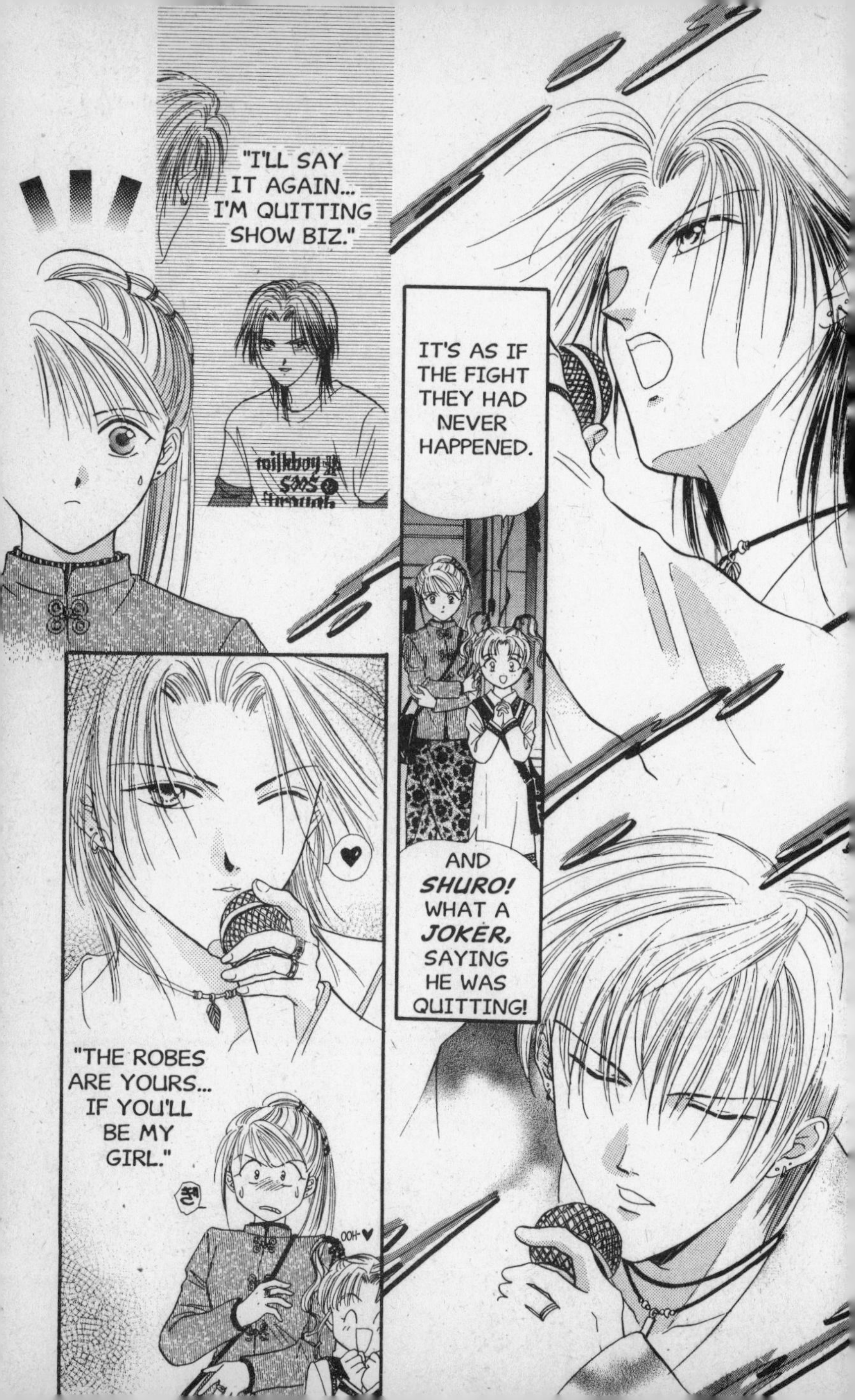
IT'S AS IF THE FIGHT THEY HAD NEVER HAPPENED.
AND *SHURO!* WHAT A *JOKER,* SAYING HE WAS QUITTING!
"I'LL SAY IT AGAIN... I'M QUITTING SHOW BIZ."
"THE ROBES ARE YOURS... IF YOU'LL BE MY GIRL."
OOH-♥

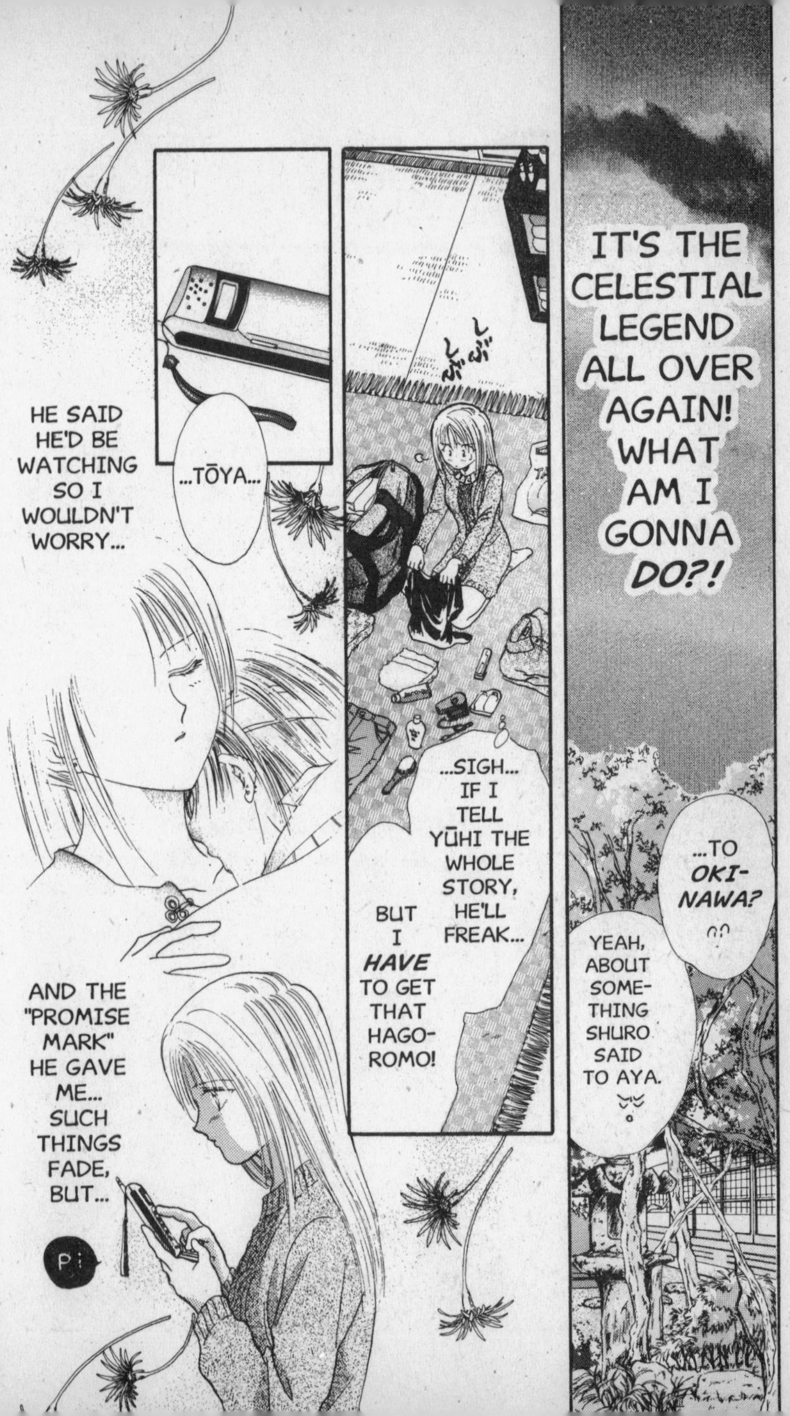
IT'S THE CELESTIAL LEGEND ALL OVER AGAIN! WHAT AM I GONNA *DO?!*
...TO *OKI-NAWA?*
YEAH, ABOUT SOME-THING SHURO SAID TO AYA.
しぶ しぶ
...SIGH... IF I TELL YŪHI THE WHOLE STORY, HE'LL FREAK...
BUT I ***HAVE*** TO GET THAT HAGO-ROMO!
...TŌYA...
HE SAID HE'D BE WATCHING SO I WOULDN'T WORRY...
AND THE "PROMISE MARK" HE GAVE ME... SUCH THINGS FADE, BUT...
Pi

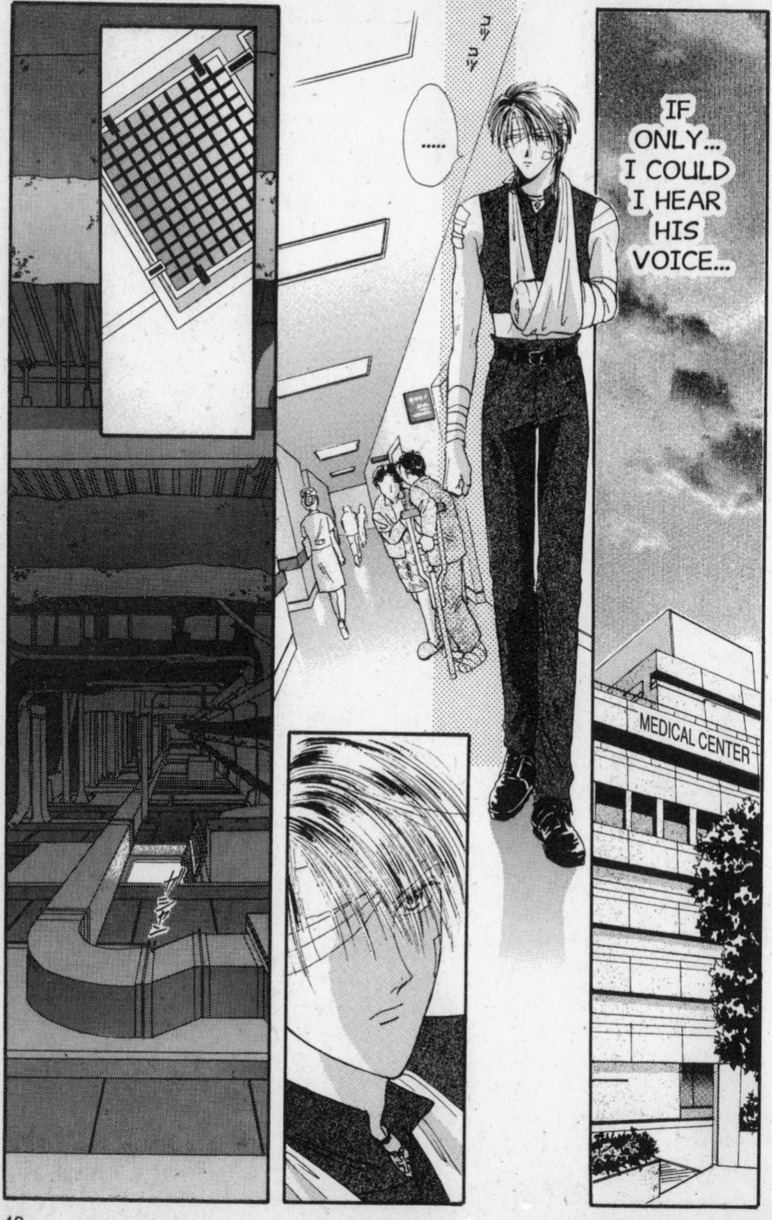
IF ONLY... I COULD I HEAR HIS VOICE...
MEDICAL CENTER
.....

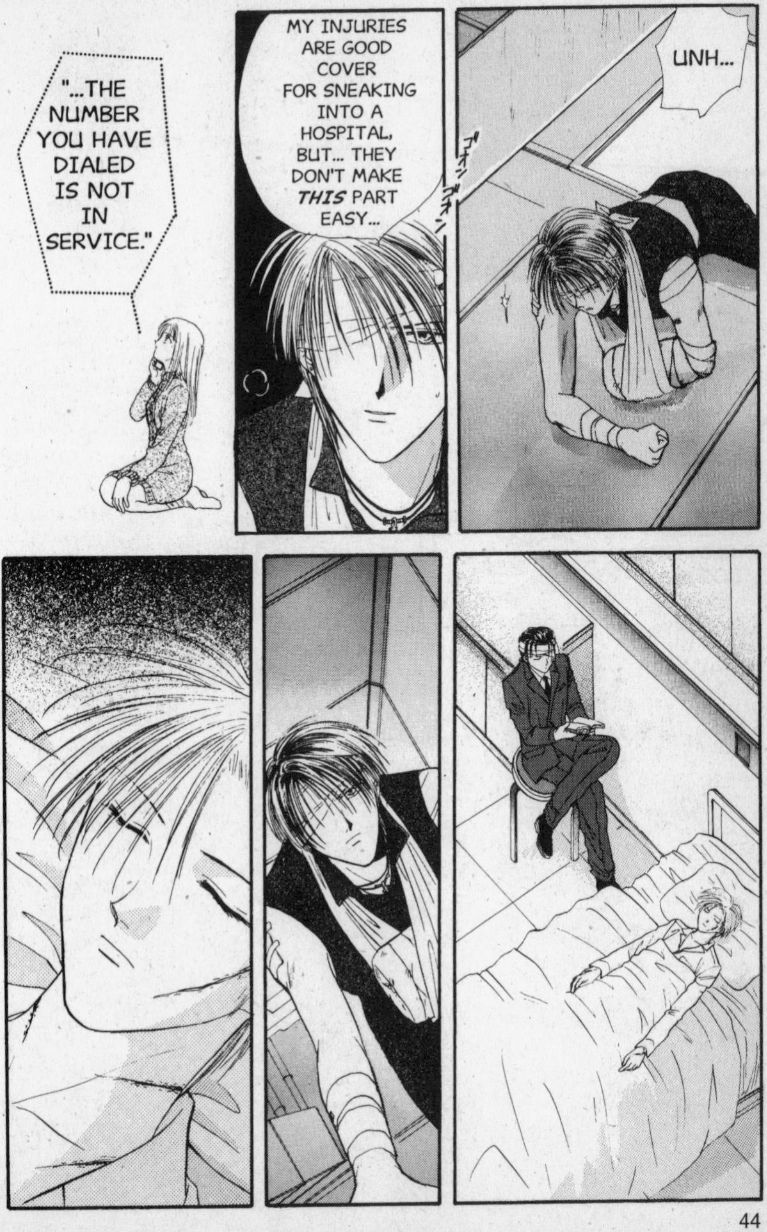
UNH...
ゴオン ゴオン
MY INJURIES ARE GOOD COVER FOR SNEAKING INTO A HOSPITAL, BUT... THEY DON'T MAKE *THIS* PART EASY...
"...THE NUMBER YOU HAVE DIALED IS NOT IN SERVICE."

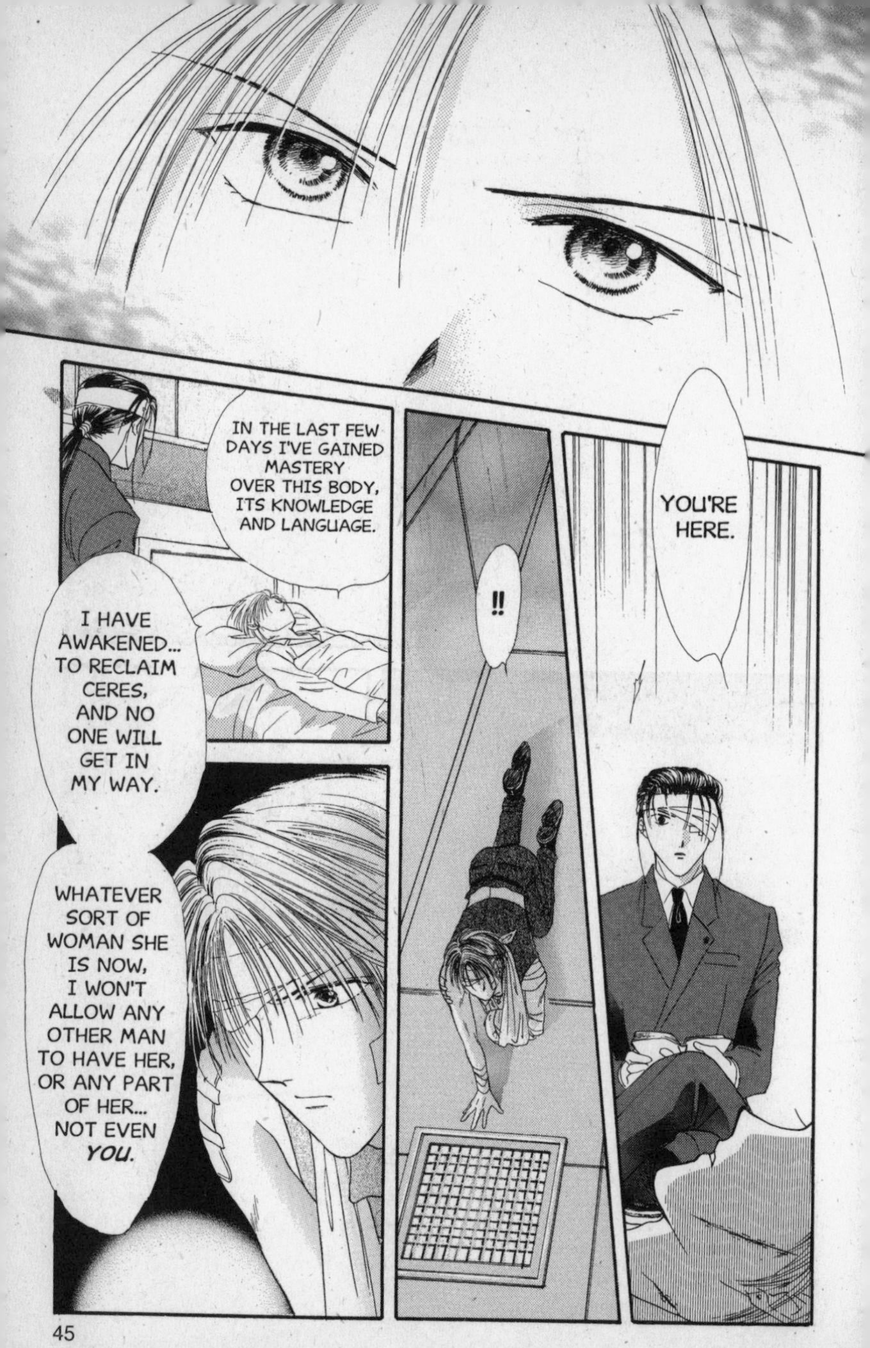
YOU'RE HERE.
!!
IN THE LAST FEW DAYS I'VE GAINED MASTERY OVER THIS BODY, ITS KNOWLEDGE AND LANGUAGE.
I HAVE AWAKENED... TO RECLAIM CERES, AND NO ONE WILL GET IN MY WAY.
WHATEVER SORT OF WOMAN SHE IS NOW, I WON'T ALLOW ANY OTHER MAN TO HAVE HER, OR ANY PART OF HER... NOT EVEN *YOU*.

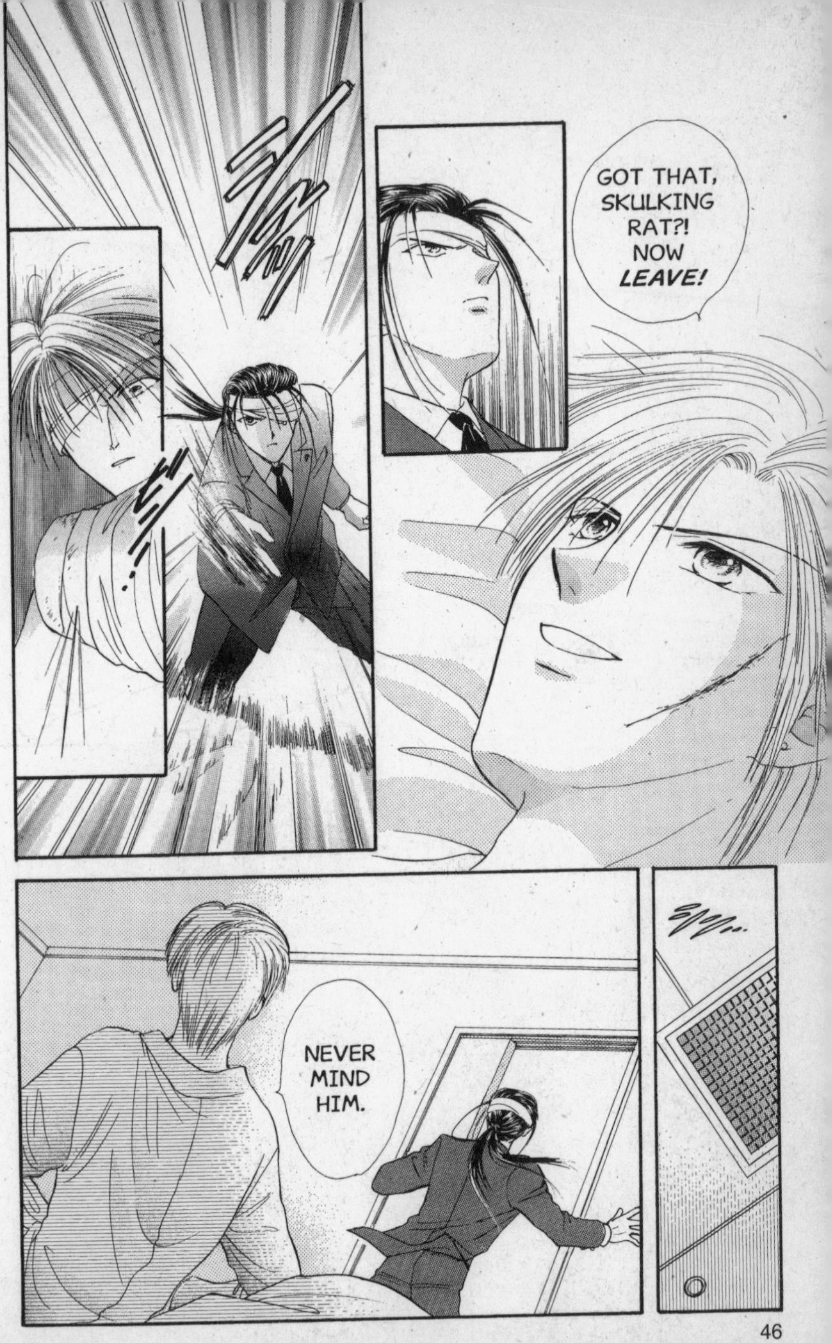
GOT THAT, SKULKING RAT?! NOW *LEAVE!*
NEVER MIND HIM.

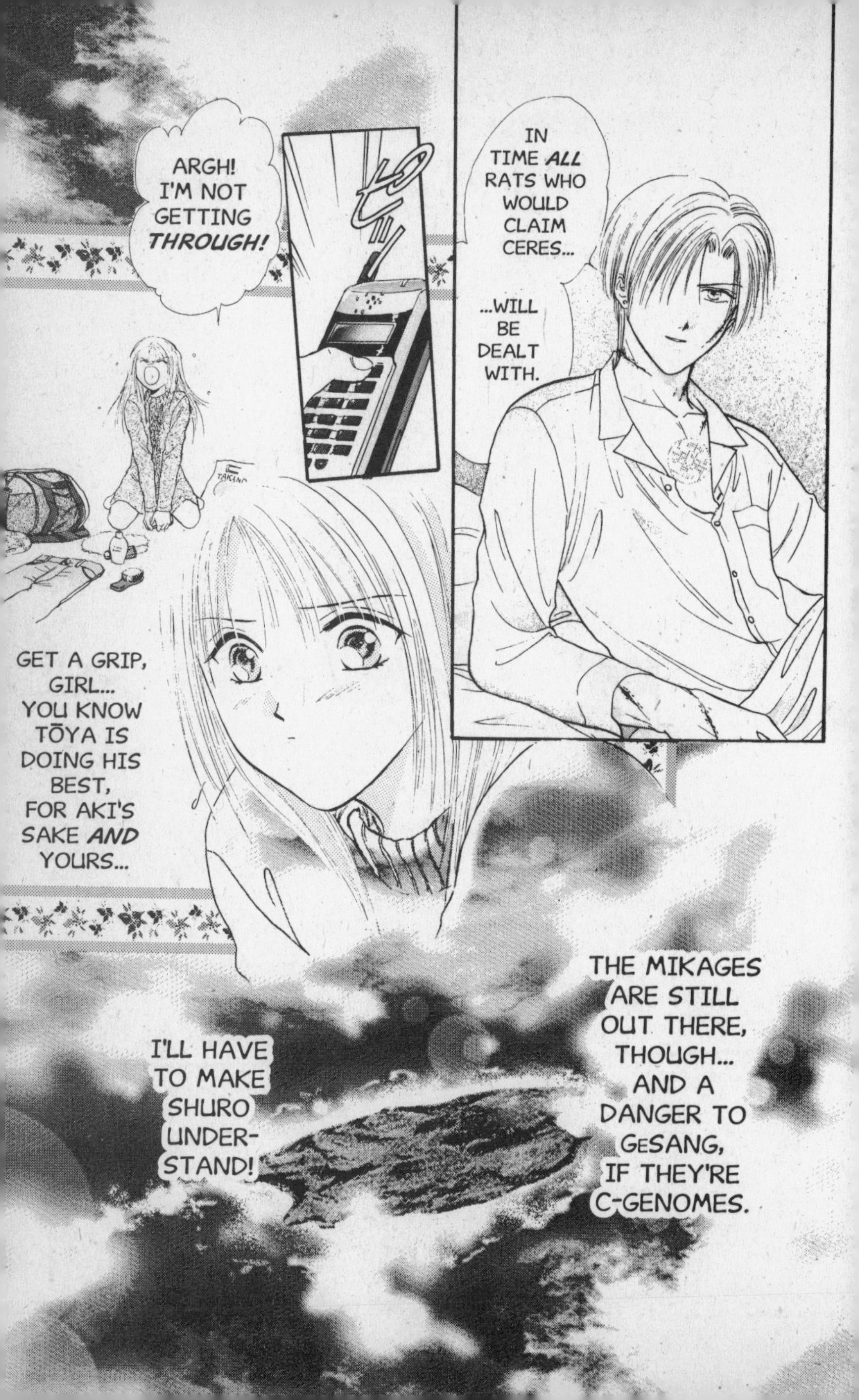
IN TIME *ALL* RATS WHO WOULD CLAIM CERES...
...WILL BE DEALT WITH.
ARGH! I'M NOT GETTING *THROUGH!*
GET A GRIP, GIRL... YOU KNOW TŌYA IS DOING HIS BEST, FOR AKI'S SAKE *AND* YOURS...
THE MIKAGES ARE STILL OUT THERE, THOUGH... AND A DANGER TO GESANG, IF THEY'RE C-GENOMES.
I'LL HAVE TO MAKE SHURO UNDER-STAND!

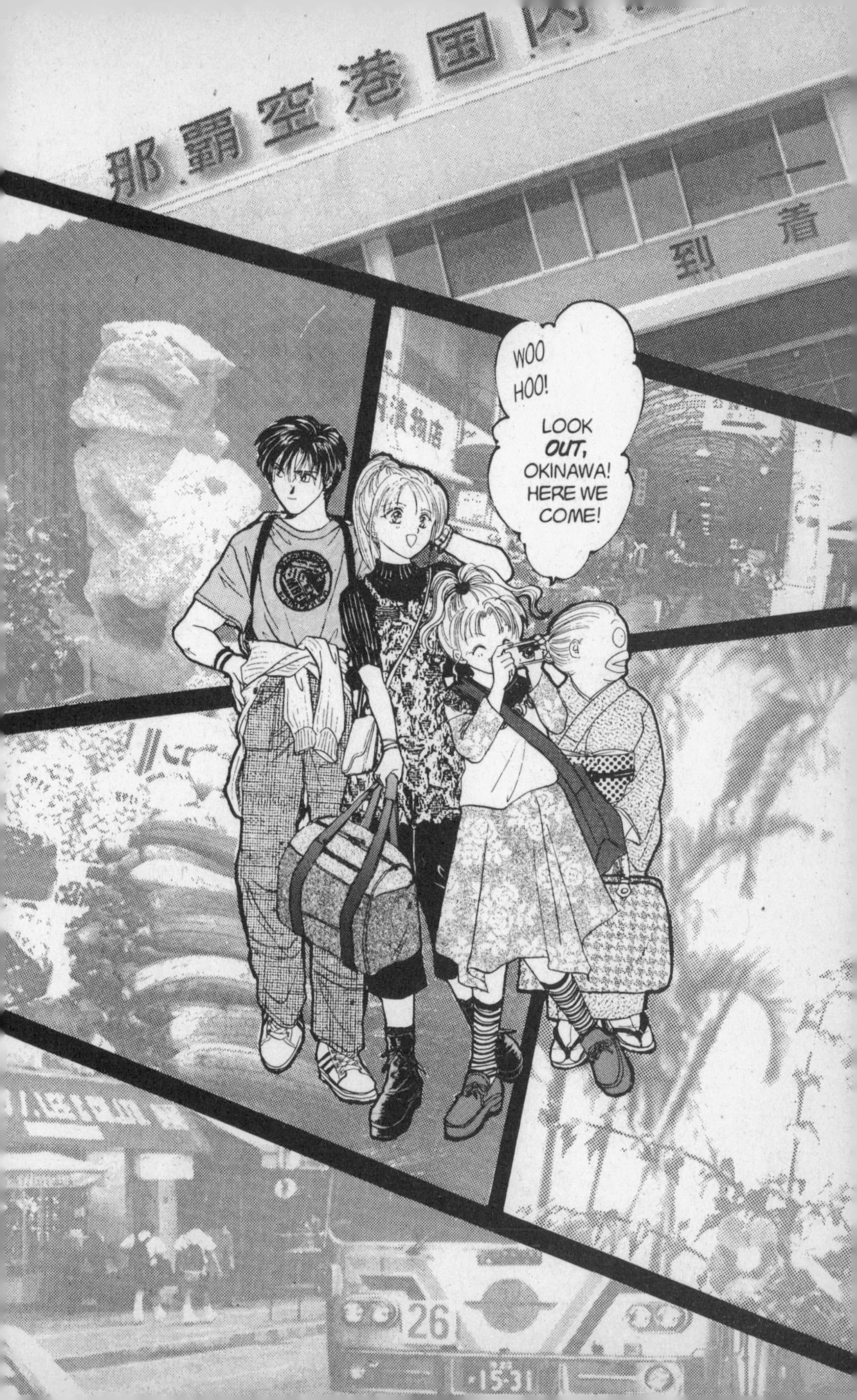
那覇空港国内
到着
WOO HOO! LOOK OUT, OKINAWA! HERE WE COME!
26

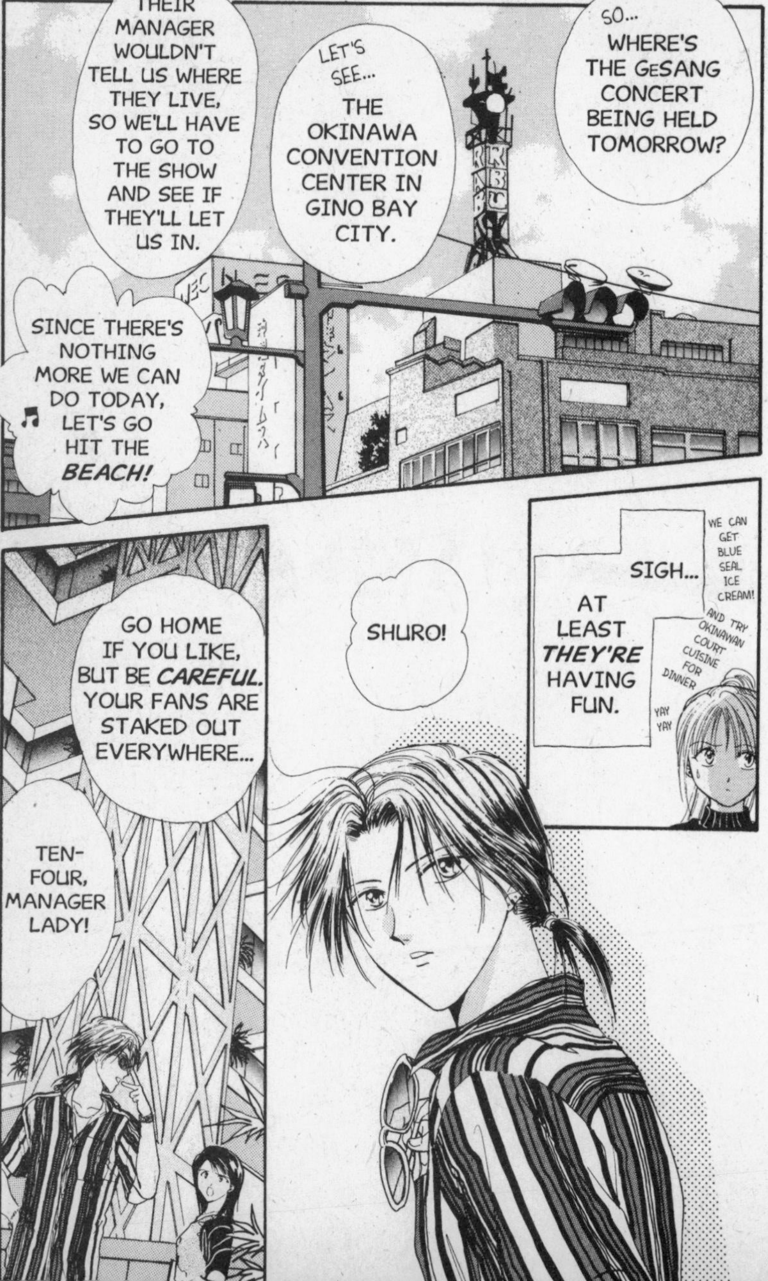
SO... WHERE'S THE GESANG CONCERT BEING HELD TOMORROW?
LET'S SEE... THE OKINAWA CONVENTION CENTER IN GINO BAY CITY.
THEIR MANAGER WOULDN'T TELL US WHERE THEY LIVE, SO WE'LL HAVE TO GO TO THE SHOW AND SEE IF THEY'LL LET US IN.
SINCE THERE'S NOTHING MORE WE CAN DO TODAY, LET'S GO HIT THE *BEACH!*
SIGH...
AT LEAST *THEY'RE* HAVING FUN.
WE CAN GET BLUE SEAL ICE CREAM!
AND TRY OKINAWAN COURT CUISINE FOR DINNER
YAY YAY
SHURO!
GO HOME IF YOU LIKE, BUT BE *CAREFUL.* YOUR FANS ARE STAKED OUT EVERYWHERE...
TEN-FOUR, MANAGER LADY!

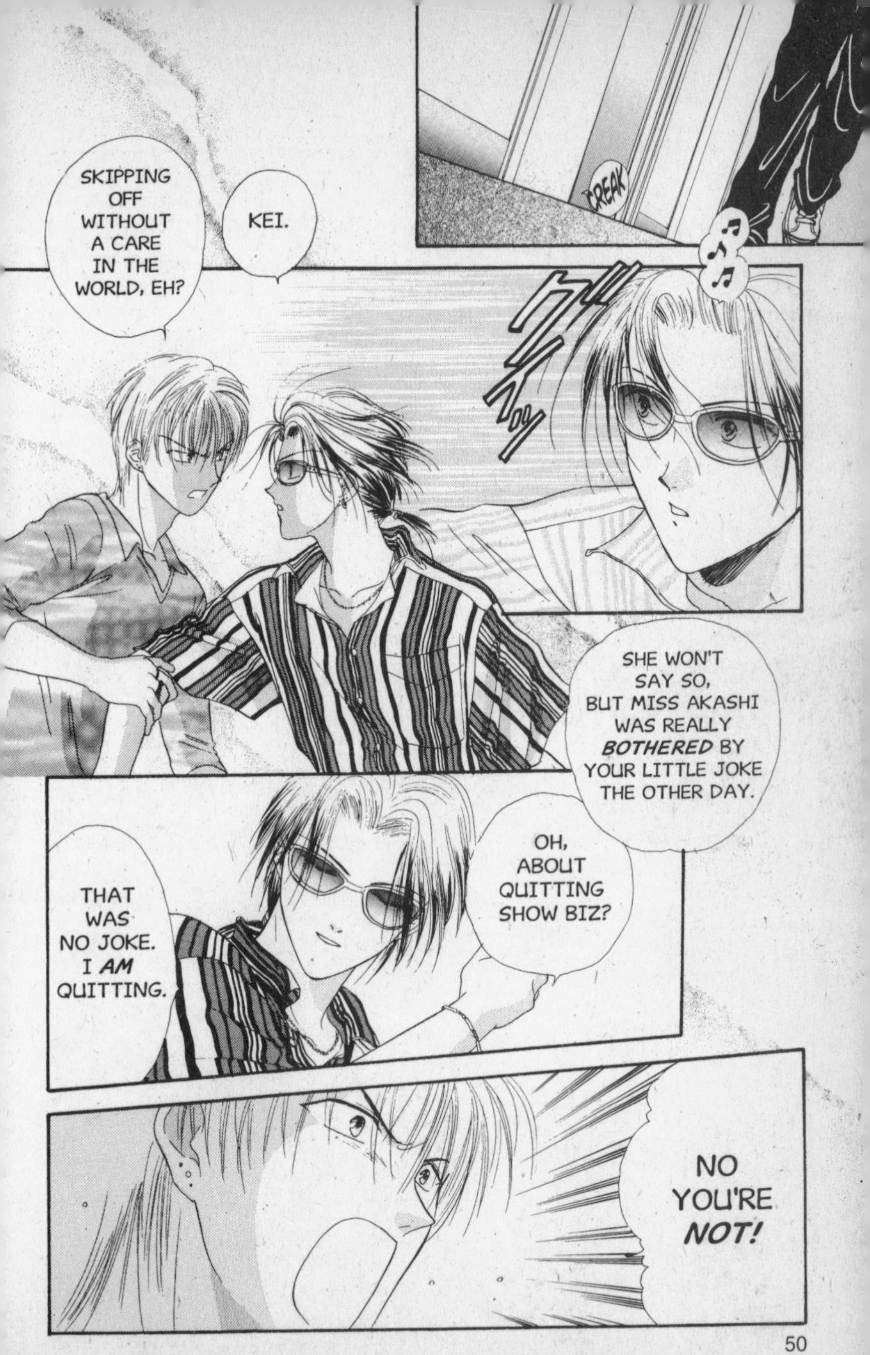
CREAK
KEI.
SKIPPING OFF WITHOUT A CARE IN THE WORLD, EH?
SHE WON'T SAY SO, BUT MISS AKASHI WAS REALLY *BOTHERED* BY YOUR LITTLE JOKE THE OTHER DAY.
OH, ABOUT QUITTING SHOW BIZ?
THAT WAS NO JOKE. I *AM* QUITTING.
NO YOU'RE *NOT!*

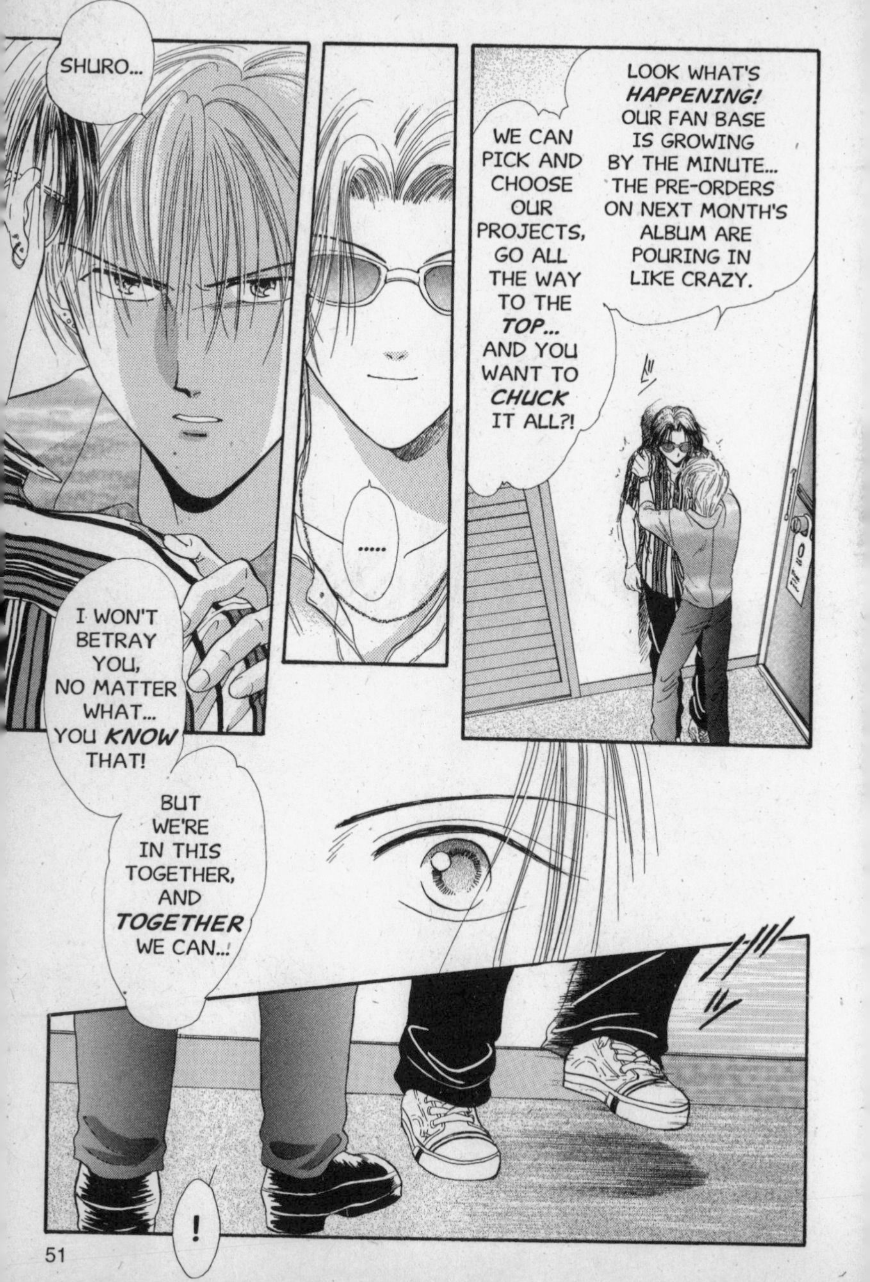
LOOK WHAT'S HAPPENING! OUR FAN BASE IS GROWING BY THE MINUTE... THE PRE-ORDERS ON NEXT MONTH'S ALBUM ARE POURING IN LIKE CRAZY.
WE CAN PICK AND CHOOSE OUR PROJECTS, GO ALL THE WAY TO THE TOP... AND YOU WANT TO CHUCK IT ALL?!
......
SHURO...
I WON'T BETRAY YOU, NO MATTER WHAT... YOU KNOW THAT!
BUT WE'RE IN THIS TOGETHER, AND TOGETHER WE CAN...!
!

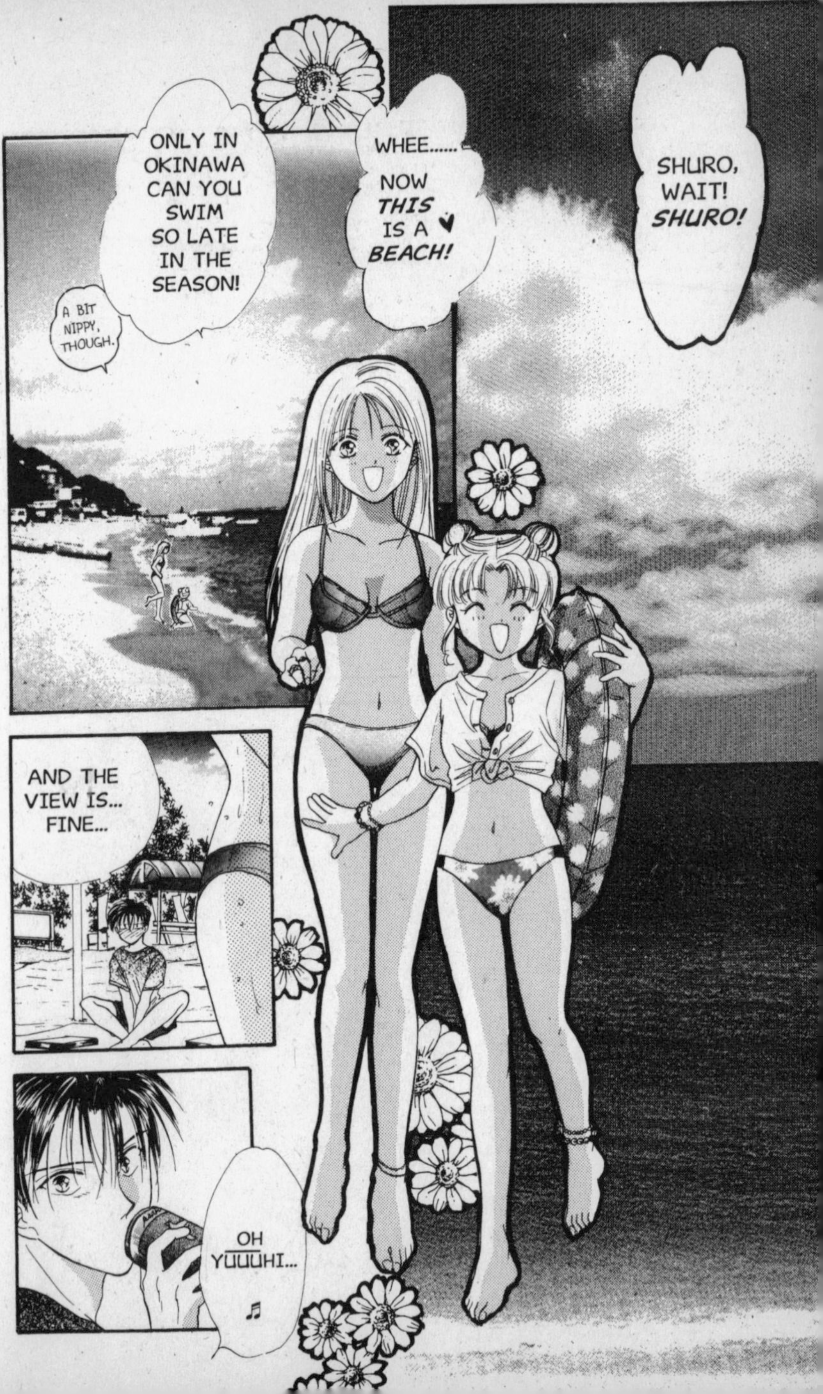
SHURO, WAIT! SHURO!
WHEE...... NOW THIS IS A BEACH! ♥
ONLY IN OKINAWA CAN YOU SWIM SO LATE IN THE SEASON!
A BIT NIPPY, THOUGH.
AND THE VIEW IS... FINE...
OH YUUUHI... ♪

Ceres: 6

Some people have said that there aren't enough "H" (sexy) scenes in Ceres. :-) Shame on you. If you think the only kind of "H" scene is a bedroom scene... you've got a lot to learn! If you ask my assistants, the "H" scene in Ceres is the entire **series.** "Subtly sexy," is what they say. You'll understand when you're older. (You think?) Sexuality **is** a big part of the story, and there's always the chance it'll get more and more graphic as time goes by—or so we can hope. :-) Seriously, though. I'm looking at sex from a biological and psychological angle!! I wonder how other people see me looking at it. It's not like I'm offering up the series as any kind of **sex ed,** though. :-)
Mm, I **do** want to make it harsh, though. (I hear that from people, as well.) Not that I only like totally dark stories that focus only on the negative. Humans have a weakness where they're easily tempted by the dark, but at the same time, they have an awesome power to be positive. The battle repeats itself over and over. I've come to the realization lately that I'm a passionate person, while also being aloof. But that's all part of being human! Ceres is maybe a manga that expresses that aloof side. Not to say that it isn't also plenty passionate!
I'm not trying to be a conservative here (a bad Japanese habit). I saw a lot of movies last year, and was deeply impressed not by the plots, but by the underlying ideas, especially Princess Mononoke. I went on opening day, and again in October, but I cried more the second time around. The depth of it isn't something you necessarily get just from the plot. It may be something only writers/creators understand; I won't keep going on about it. It does seem there's been a lot of impact, and power, in the movies I saw last year. There was stuff that really invigorated me, too. My hope is that I can keep drawing stories that are "cries from the heart" as well—even if they do turn out a little incomprehensible, or even out-and-out failures. Onward!! I've ended up rambling, haven't I.

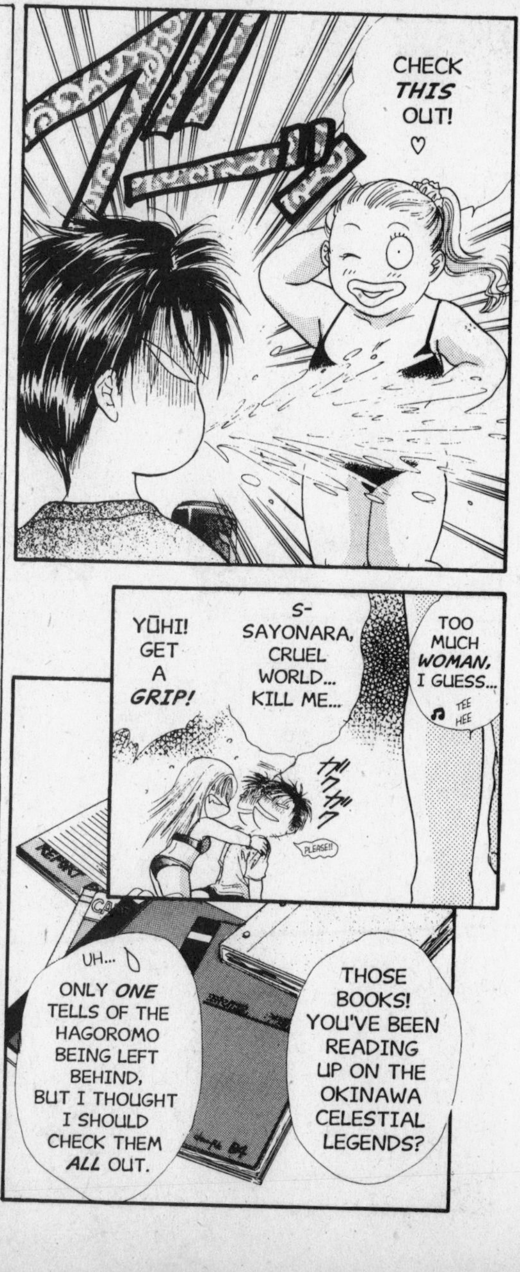
CHECK *THIS* OUT! ♡
TOO MUCH *WOMAN,* I GUESS...
♪ TEE HEE
S-SAYONARA, CRUEL WORLD... KILL ME...
YŪHI! GET A *GRIP!*
PLEASE!!
THOSE BOOKS! YOU'VE BEEN READING UP ON THE OKINAWA CELESTIAL LEGENDS?
UH...
ONLY *ONE* TELLS OF THE HAGOROMO BEING LEFT BEHIND, BUT I THOUGHT I SHOULD CHECK THEM *ALL* OUT.

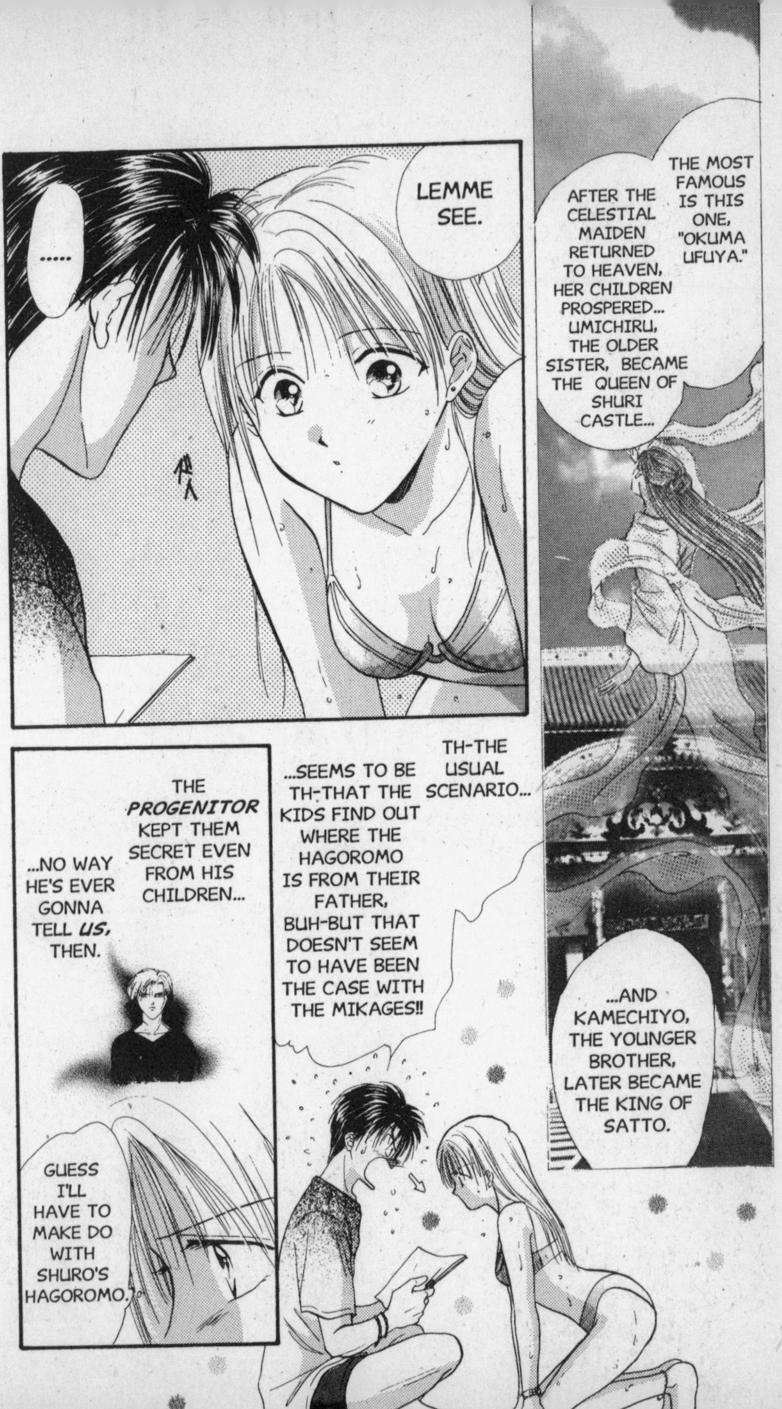
THE MOST FAMOUS IS THIS ONE, "OKUMA UFUYA."
AFTER THE CELESTIAL MAIDEN RETURNED TO HEAVEN, HER CHILDREN PROSPERED... UMICHIRU, THE OLDER SISTER, BECAME THE QUEEN OF SHURI CASTLE...
...AND KAMECHIYO, THE YOUNGER BROTHER, LATER BECAME THE KING OF SATTO.
LEMME SEE.
......
TH-THE USUAL SCENARIO...
...SEEMS TO BE TH-THAT THE KIDS FIND OUT WHERE THE HAGOROMO IS FROM THEIR FATHER, BUH-BUT THAT DOESN'T SEEM TO HAVE BEEN THE CASE WITH THE MIKAGES!!
THE *PROGENITOR* KEPT THEM SECRET EVEN FROM HIS CHILDREN...
...NO WAY HE'S EVER GONNA TELL *US,* THEN.
GUESS I'LL HAVE TO MAKE DO WITH SHURO'S HAGOROMO.

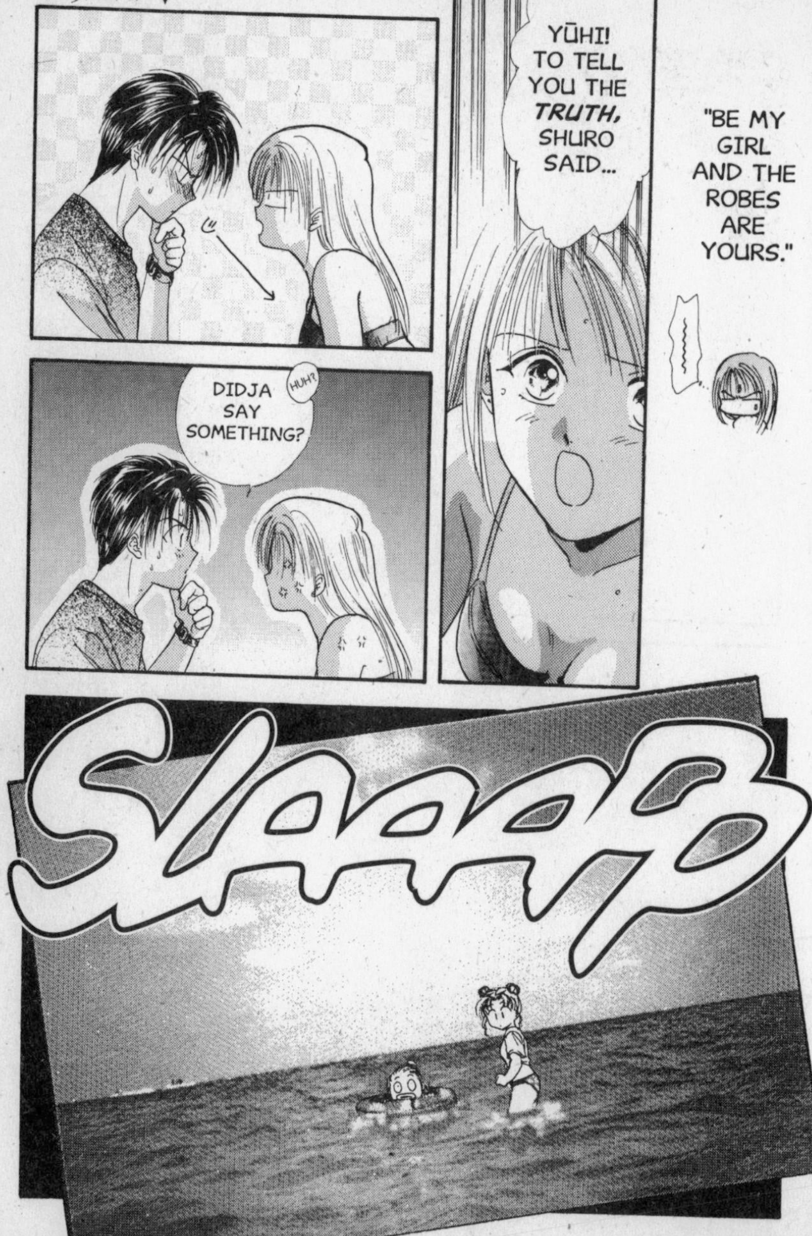
DIDJA SAY SOMETHING?
HUH?
YŪHI! TO TELL YOU THE *TRUTH,* SHURO SAID...
"BE MY GIRL AND THE ROBES ARE YOURS."
SLAAAP

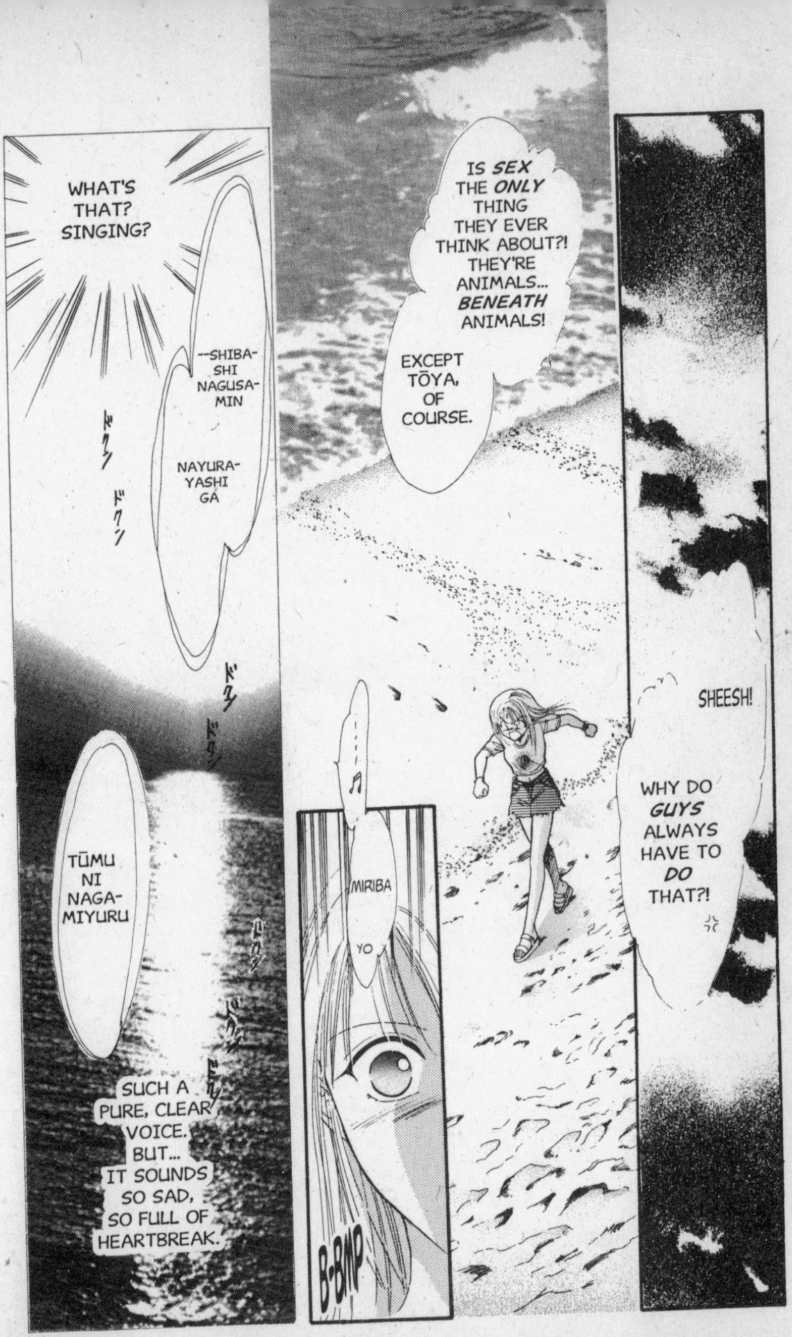
SHEESH!
WHY DO *GUYS* ALWAYS HAVE TO *DO* THAT?!
IS *SEX* THE *ONLY* THING THEY EVER THINK ABOUT?! THEY'RE ANIMALS... ***BENEATH*** ANIMALS!
EXCEPT TŌYA, OF COURSE.
♪
MIRIBA YO
B-BMP
WHAT'S THAT? SINGING?
--SHIBA-SHI NAGUSA-MIN
NAYURA-YASHI GA
ドクン
ドクン
TŪMU NI NAGA-MIYURU
SUCH A PURE, CLEAR VOICE. BUT... IT SOUNDS SO SAD, SO FULL OF HEARTBREAK.

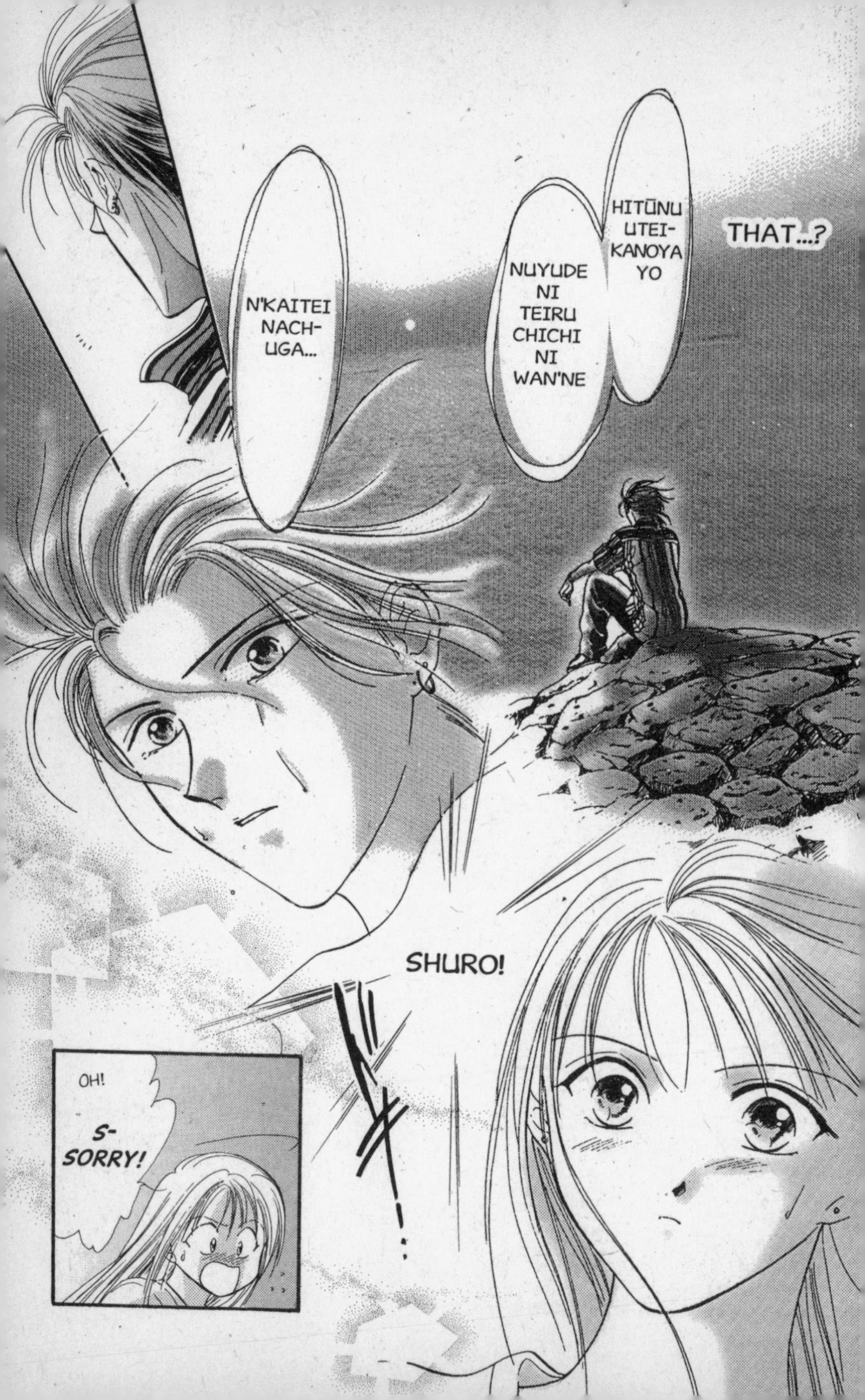
HITŪNU UTEI-KANOYA YO
NUYUDE NI TEIRU CHICHI NI WAN'NE
N'KAITEI NACH-UGA...
THAT...?
SHURO!
OH!
S-SORRY!

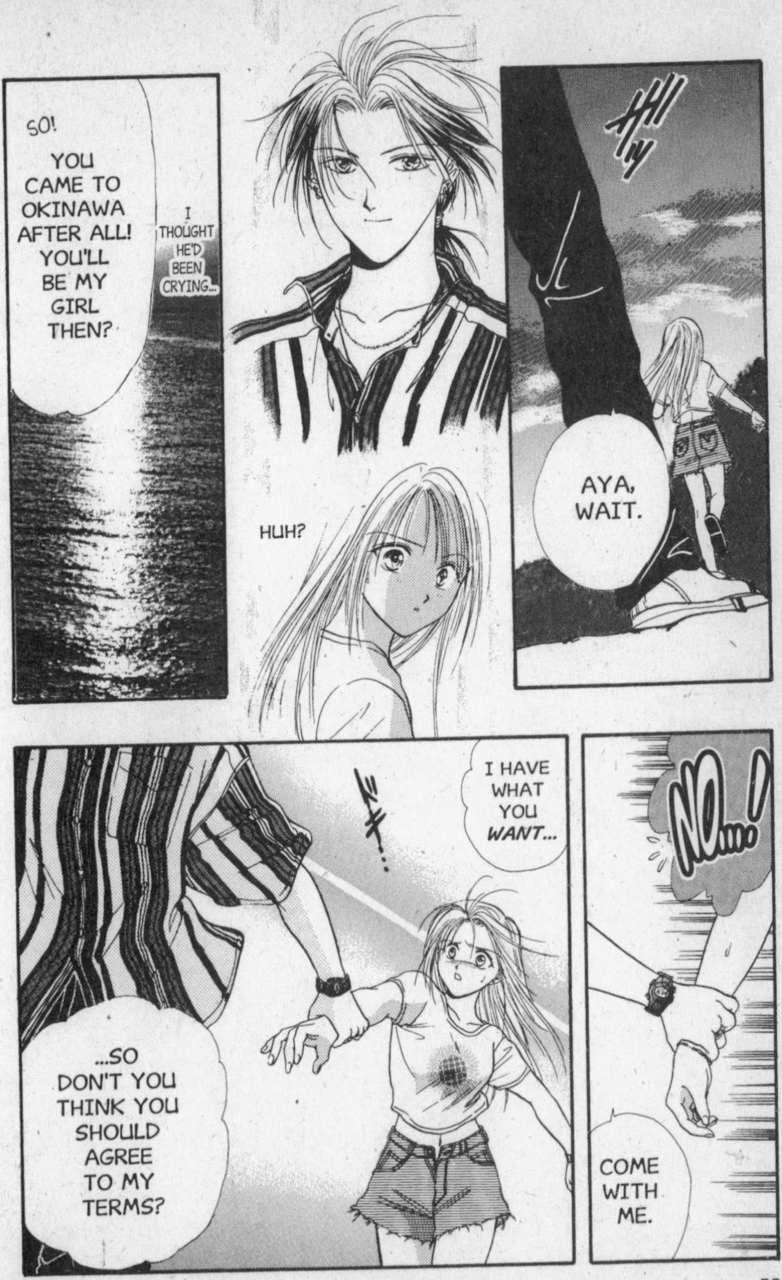
AYA, WAIT.
HUH?
SO!
YOU CAME TO OKINAWA AFTER ALL! YOU'LL BE MY GIRL THEN?
I THOUGHT HE'D BEEN CRYING...
NO...!
COME WITH ME.
I HAVE WHAT YOU *WANT*...
...SO DON'T YOU THINK YOU SHOULD AGREE TO MY TERMS?

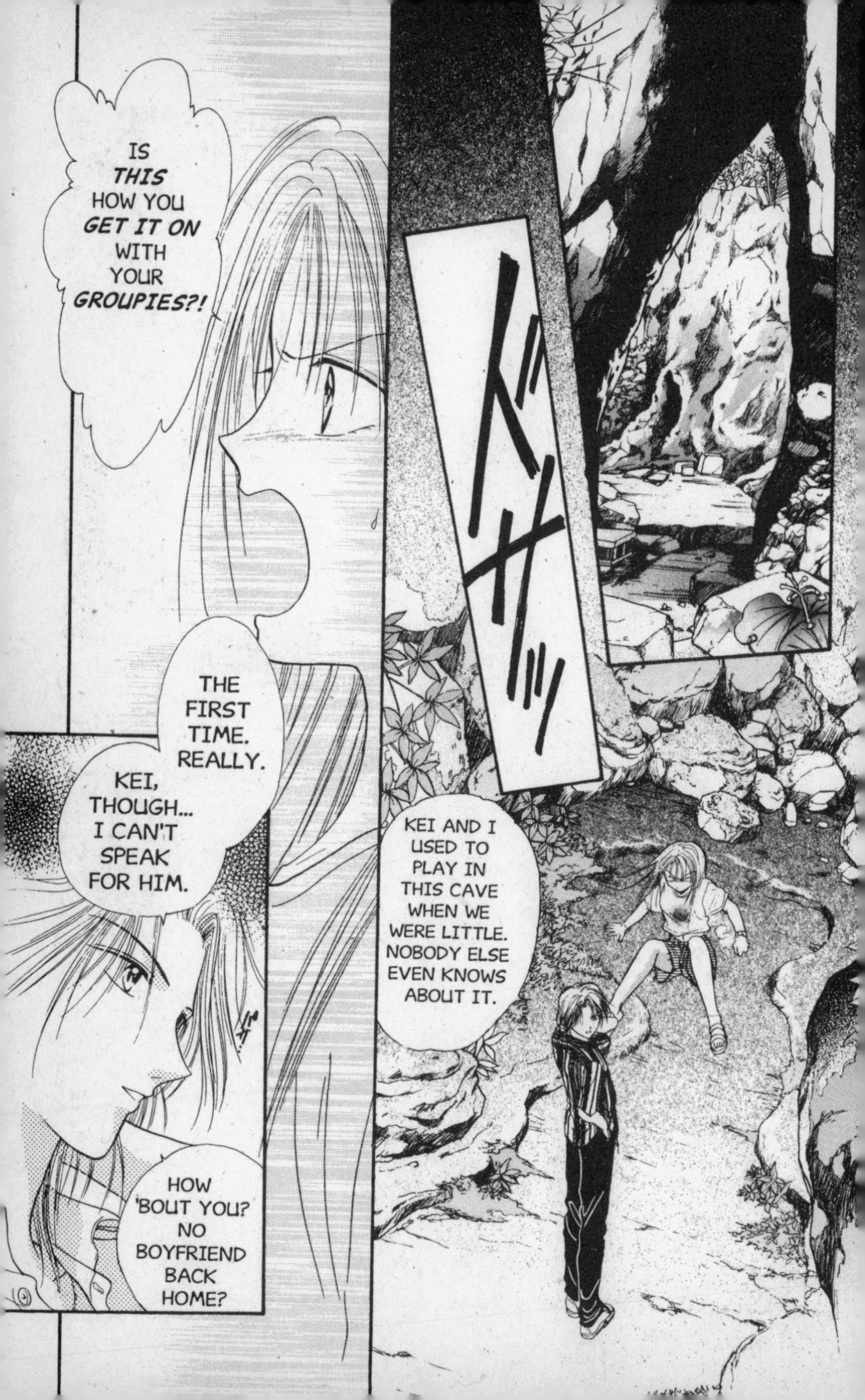
KEI AND I USED TO PLAY IN THIS CAVE WHEN WE WERE LITTLE. NOBODY ELSE EVEN KNOWS ABOUT IT.
IS *THIS* HOW YOU *GET IT ON* WITH YOUR *GROUPIES?!*
THE FIRST TIME. REALLY.
KEI, THOUGH... I CAN'T SPEAK FOR HIM.
HOW 'BOUT YOU? NO BOYFRIEND BACK HOME?

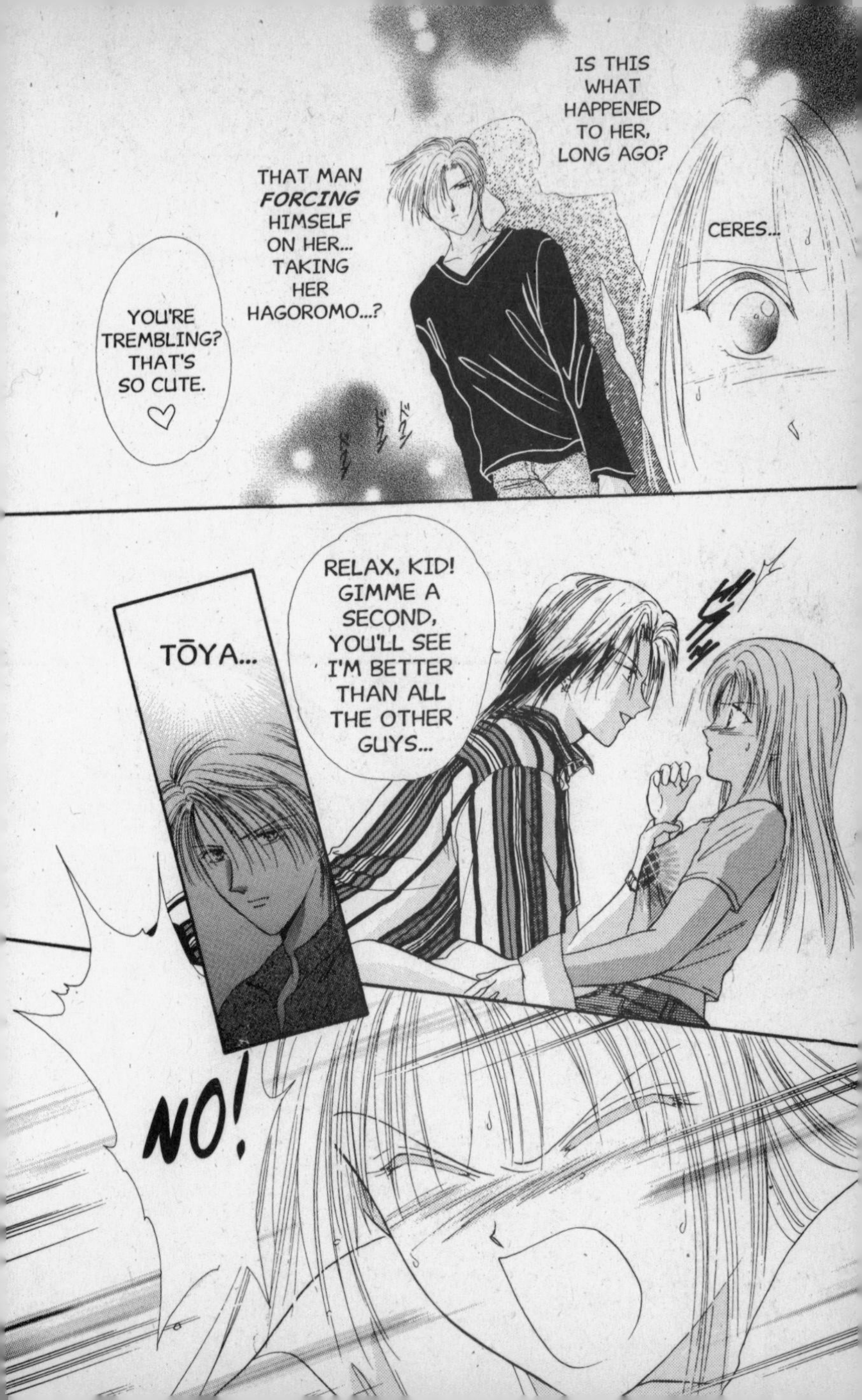
IS THIS WHAT HAPPENED TO HER, LONG AGO?
CERES...
THAT MAN *FORCING* HIMSELF ON HER... TAKING HER HAGOROMO...?
YOU'RE TREMBLING? THAT'S SO CUTE. ♡
RELAX, KID! GIMME A SECOND, YOU'LL SEE I'M BETTER THAN ALL THE OTHER GUYS...
TŌYA...
NO!

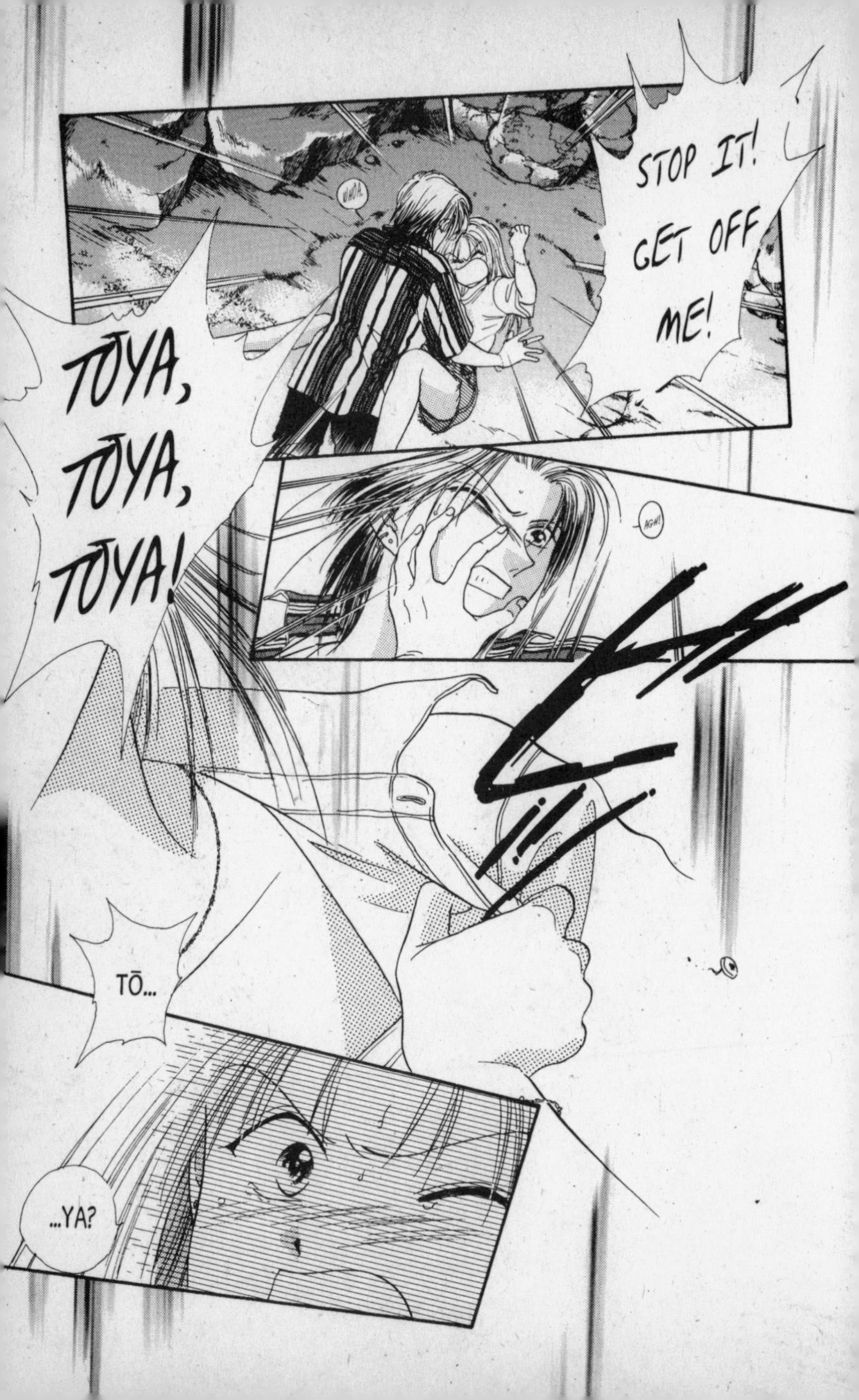
STOP IT! GET OFF ME!
WHOA.
TŌYA, TŌYA, TŌYA!
AGH!
TŌ...
...YA?

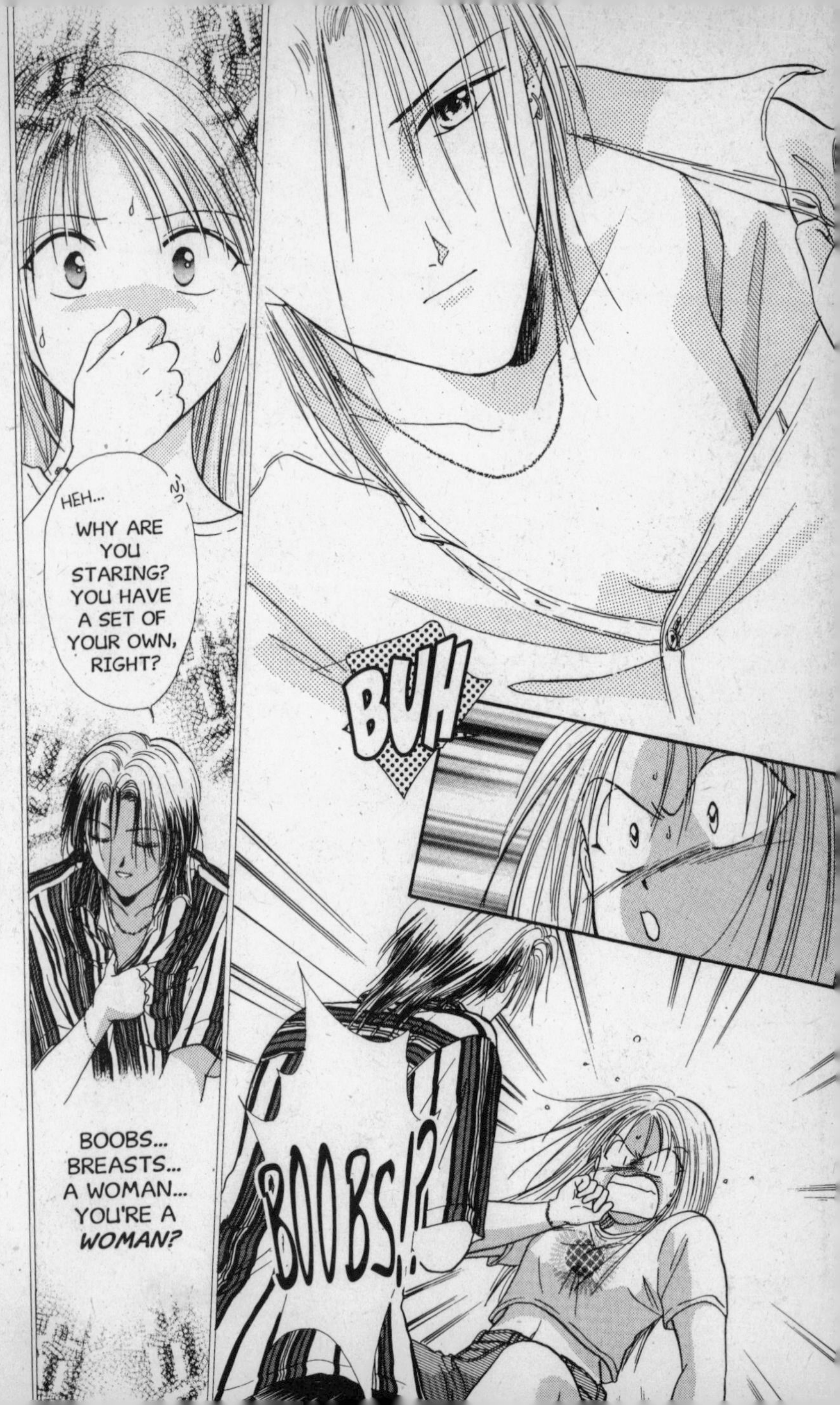
HEH... WHY ARE YOU STARING? YOU HAVE A SET OF YOUR OWN, RIGHT?
BUH
BOOBS!?
BOOBS... BREASTS... A WOMAN... YOU'RE A *WOMAN?*

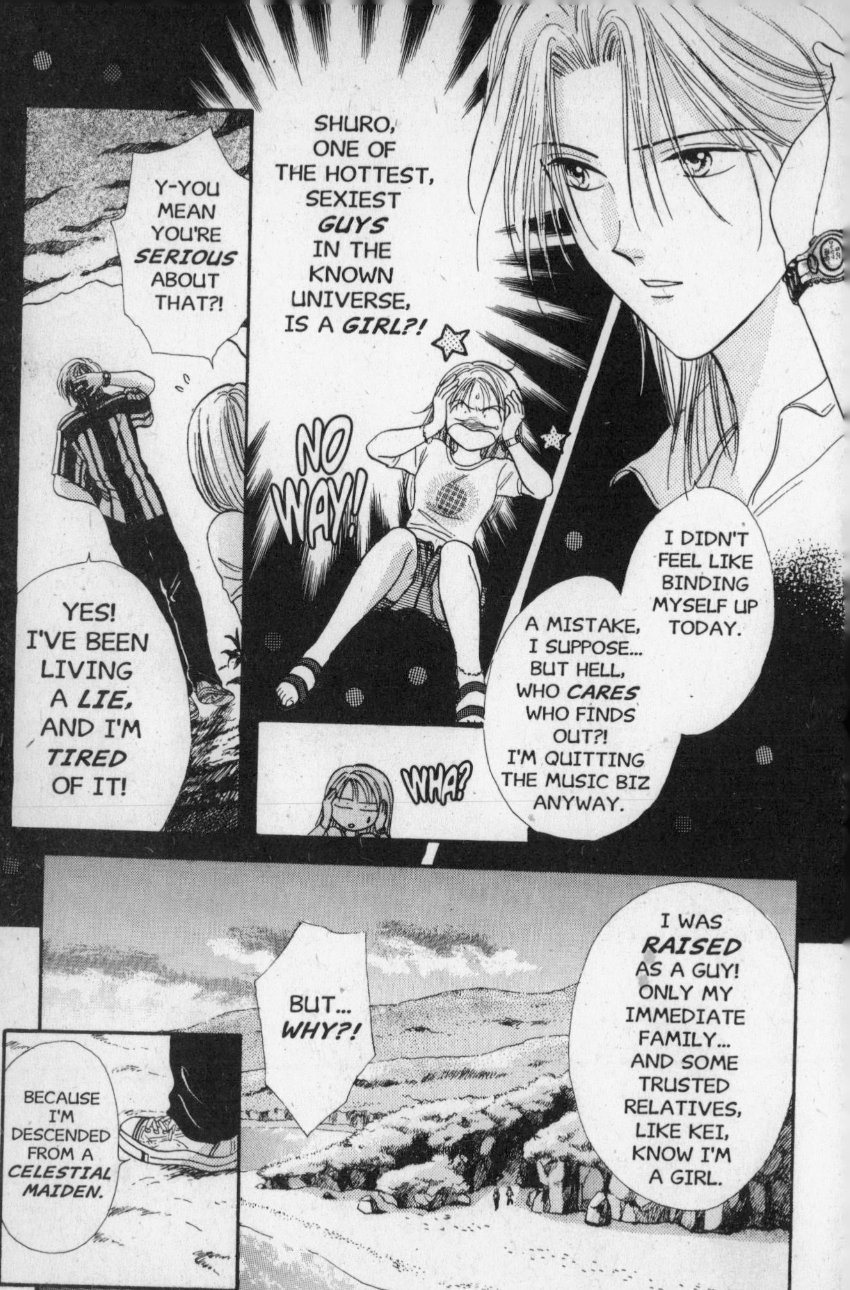
I DIDN'T FEEL LIKE BINDING MYSELF UP TODAY.
A MISTAKE, I SUPPOSE... BUT HELL, WHO CARES WHO FINDS OUT?! I'M QUITTING THE MUSIC BIZ ANYWAY.
SHURO, ONE OF THE HOTTEST, SEXIEST GUYS IN THE KNOWN UNIVERSE, IS A GIRL?!
NO WAY!
WHA?
Y-YOU MEAN YOU'RE SERIOUS ABOUT THAT?!
YES! I'VE BEEN LIVING A LIE, AND I'M TIRED OF IT!
I WAS RAISED AS A GUY! ONLY MY IMMEDIATE FAMILY... AND SOME TRUSTED RELATIVES, LIKE KEI, KNOW I'M A GIRL.
BUT... WHY?!
BECAUSE I'M DESCENDED FROM A CELESTIAL MAIDEN.

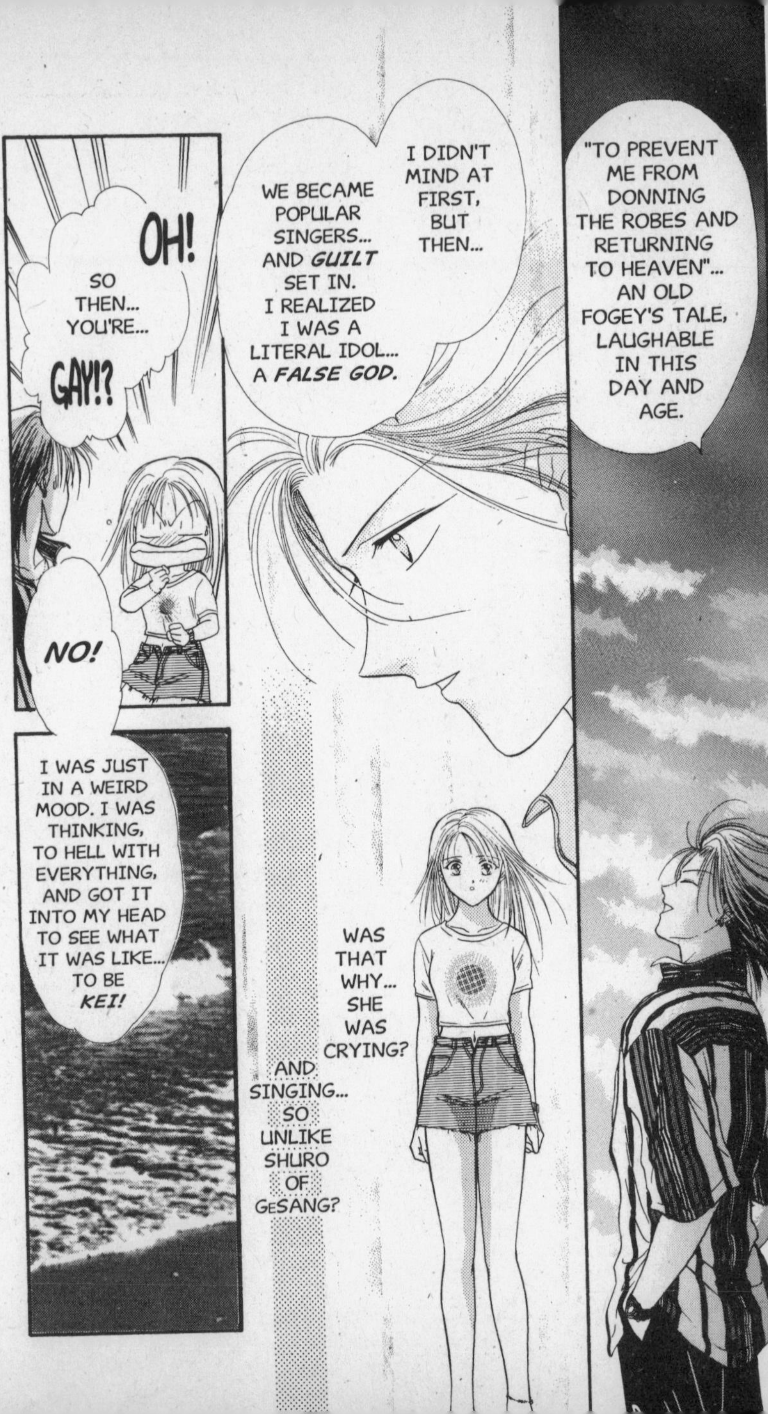
"TO PREVENT ME FROM DONNING THE ROBES AND RETURNING TO HEAVEN"... AN OLD FOGEY'S TALE, LAUGHABLE IN THIS DAY AND AGE.
I DIDN'T MIND AT FIRST, BUT THEN...
WE BECAME POPULAR SINGERS... AND *GUILT* SET IN. I REALIZED I WAS A LITERAL IDOL... A *FALSE GOD.*
WAS THAT WHY... SHE WAS CRYING?
AND SINGING... SO UNLIKE SHURO OF GESANG?
OH!
SO THEN... YOU'RE... GAY!?
NO!
I WAS JUST IN A WEIRD MOOD. I WAS THINKING, TO HELL WITH EVERYTHING, AND GOT IT INTO MY HEAD TO SEE WHAT IT WAS LIKE... TO BE *KEI!*

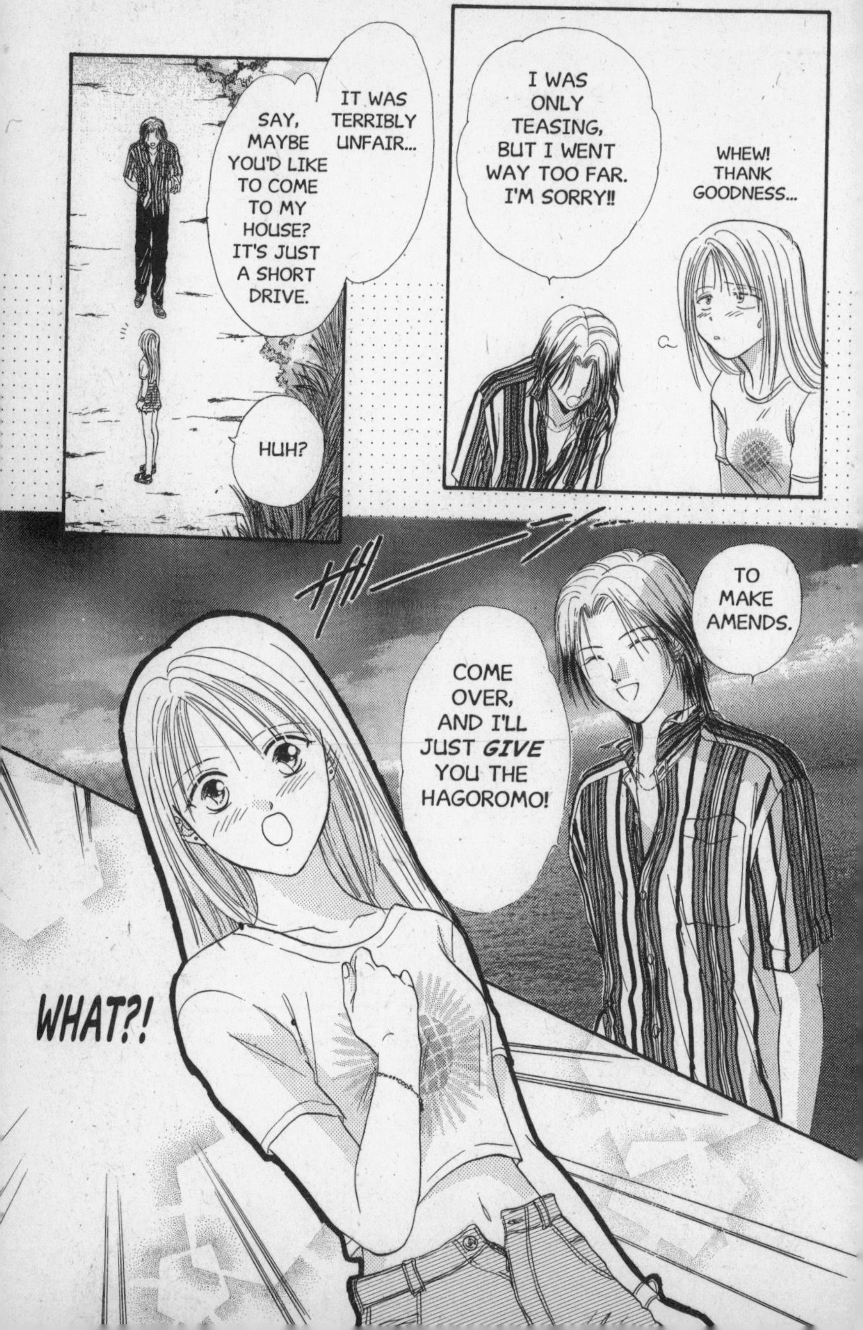
I WAS ONLY TEASING, BUT I WENT WAY TOO FAR. I'M SORRY!!
WHEW! THANK GOODNESS...
IT WAS TERRIBLY UNFAIR...
SAY, MAYBE YOU'D LIKE TO COME TO MY HOUSE? IT'S JUST A SHORT DRIVE.
HUH?
TO MAKE AMENDS.
COME OVER, AND I'LL JUST *GIVE* YOU THE HAGOROMO!
WHAT?!

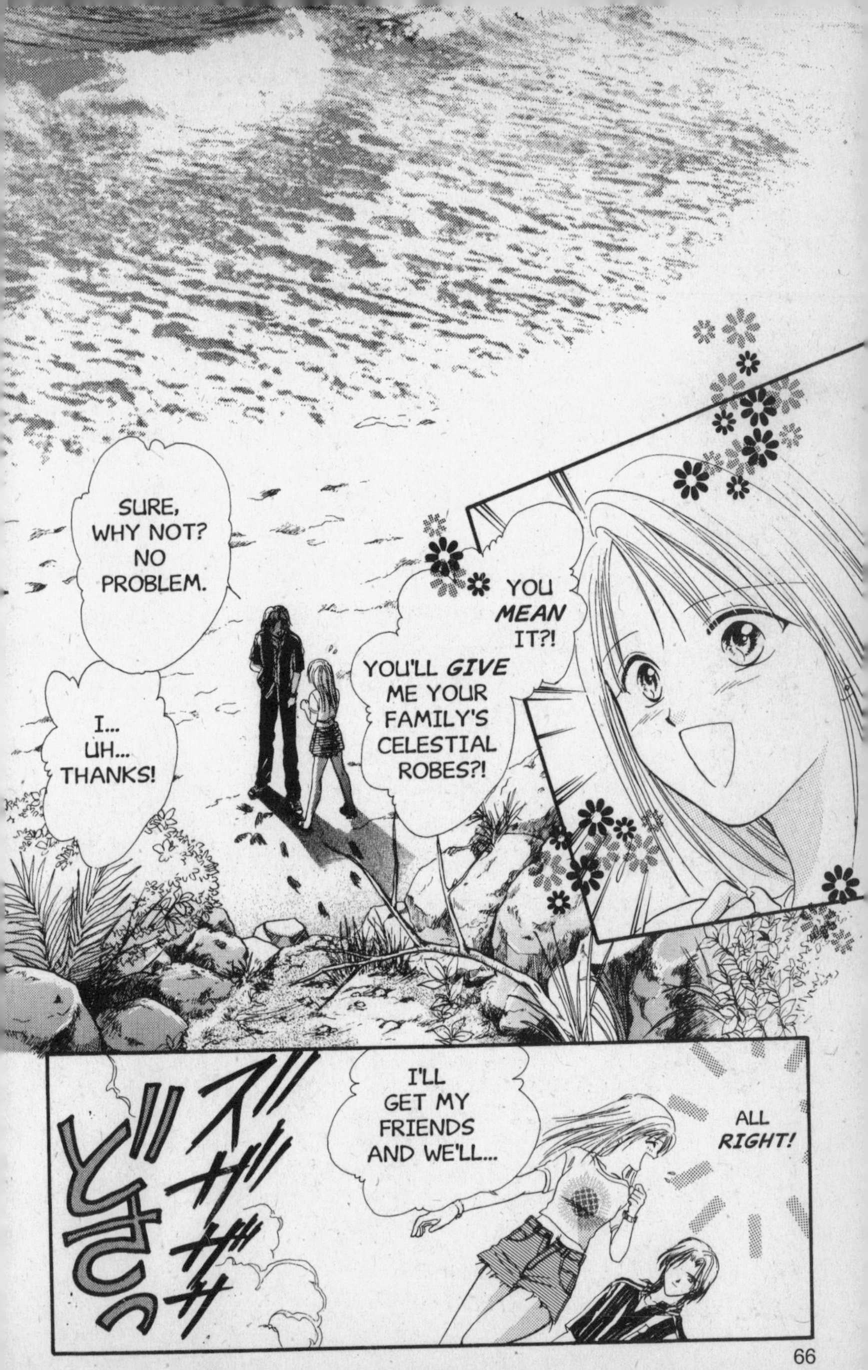
YOU MEAN IT?!
YOU'LL GIVE ME YOUR FAMILY'S CELESTIAL ROBES?!
SURE, WHY NOT? NO PROBLEM.
I... UH... THANKS!
ALL RIGHT!
I'LL GET MY FRIENDS AND WE'LL...
どさっ

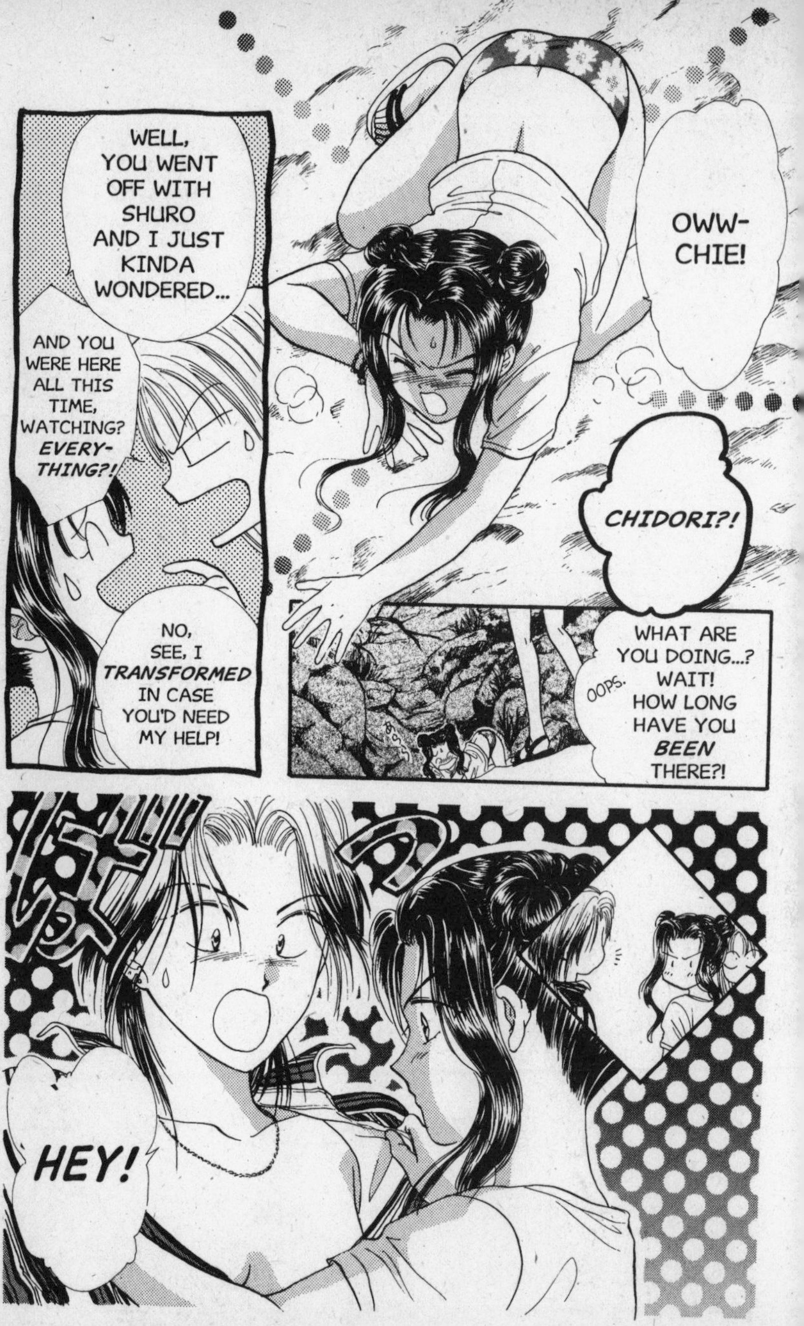
OWW-CHIE!
CHIDORI?!
WHAT ARE YOU DOING...? WAIT! HOW LONG HAVE YOU BEEN THERE?!
OOPS.
WELL, YOU WENT OFF WITH SHURO AND I JUST KINDA WONDERED...
AND YOU WERE HERE ALL THIS TIME, WATCHING? EVERY-THING?!
NO, SEE, I TRANSFORMED IN CASE YOU'D NEED MY HELP!
HEY!

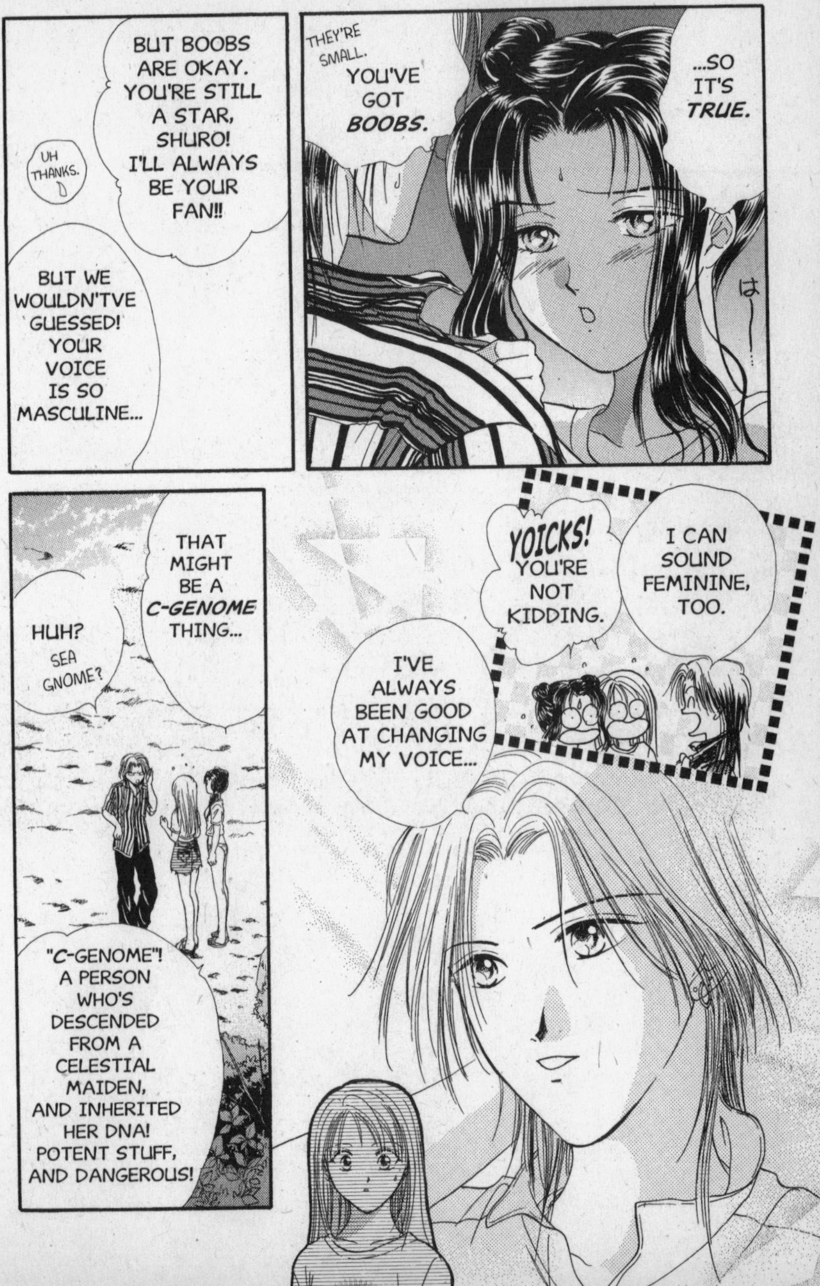
...SO IT'S *TRUE.*
THEY'RE SMALL.
YOU'VE GOT *BOOBS.*
は―…
BUT BOOBS ARE OKAY. YOU'RE STILL A STAR, SHURO! I'LL ALWAYS BE YOUR FAN!!
UH THANKS.
BUT WE WOULDN'TVE GUESSED! YOUR VOICE IS SO MASCULINE...
I'VE ALWAYS BEEN GOOD AT CHANGING MY VOICE...
I CAN SOUND FEMININE, TOO.
YOICKS! YOU'RE NOT KIDDING.
THAT MIGHT BE A *C-GENOME* THING...
HUH?
SEA GNOME?
"C-GENOME"! A PERSON WHO'S DESCENDED FROM A CELESTIAL MAIDEN, AND INHERITED HER DNA! POTENT STUFF, AND DANGEROUS!

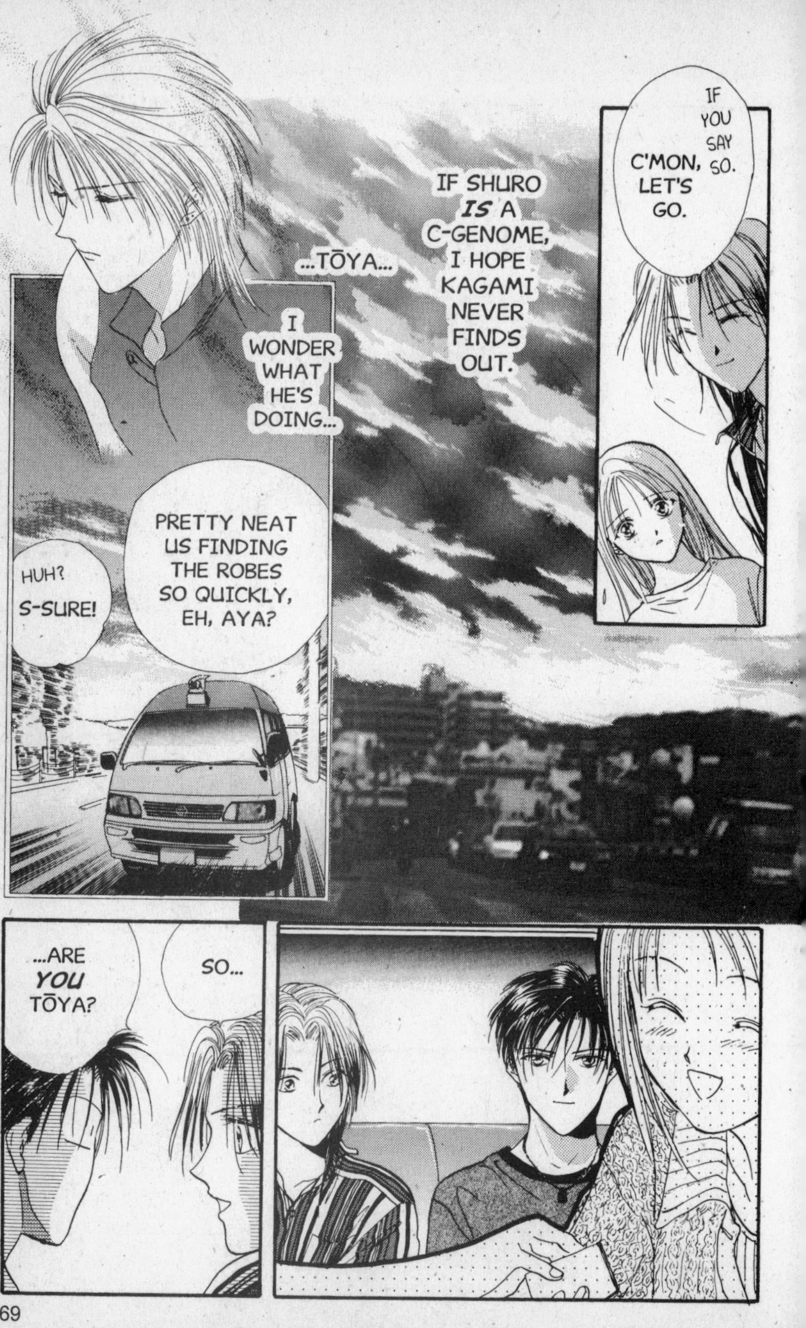
IF YOU SAY SO.
C'MON, LET'S GO.
IF SHURO *IS* A C-GENOME, I HOPE KAGAMI NEVER FINDS OUT.
...TŌYA...
I WONDER WHAT HE'S DOING...
PRETTY NEAT US FINDING THE ROBES SO QUICKLY, EH, AYA?
HUH? S-SURE!
SO...
...ARE *YOU* TŌYA?

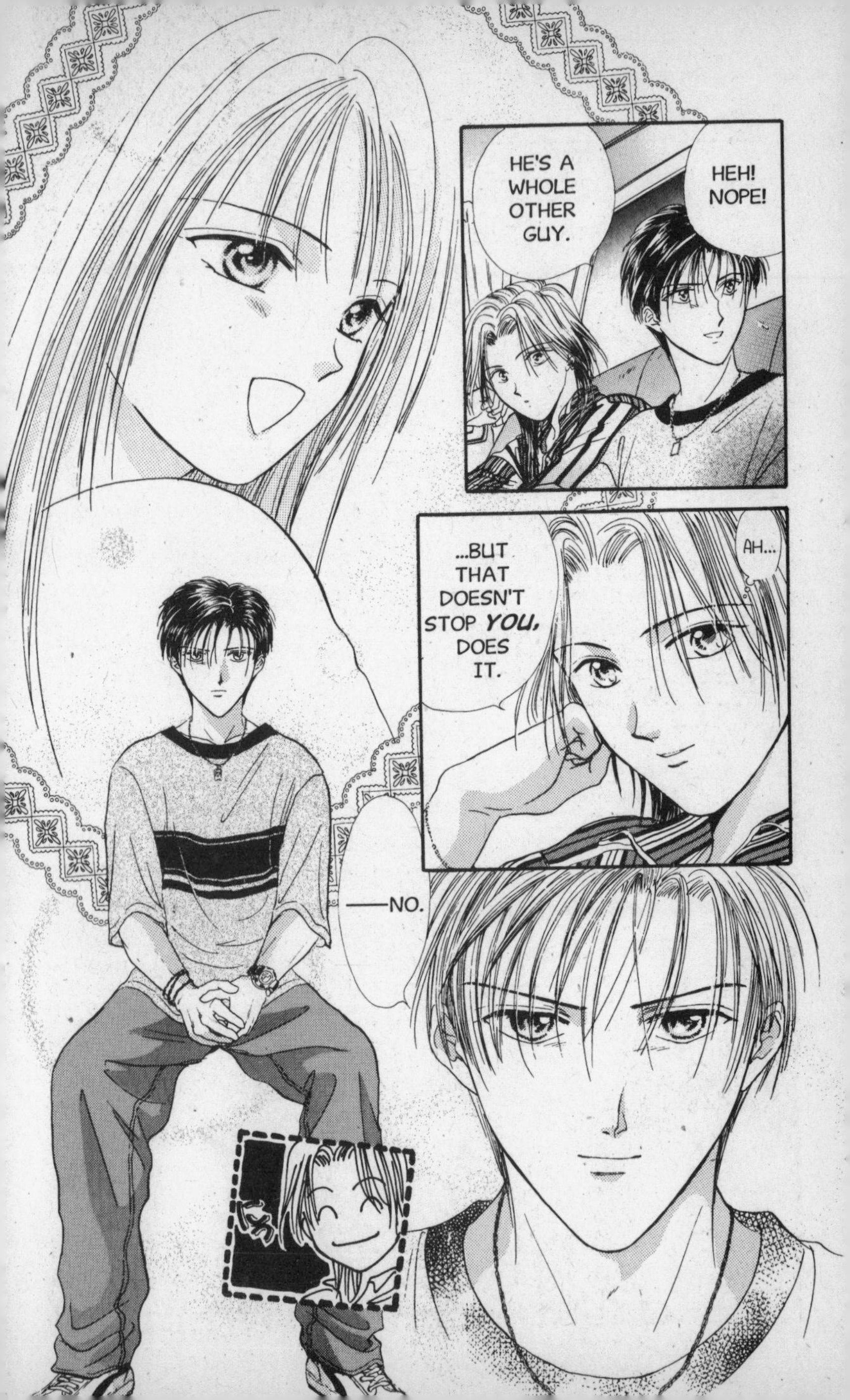
HEH! NOPE!
HE'S A WHOLE OTHER GUY.
AH...
...BUT THAT DOESN'T STOP YOU, DOES IT.
——NO.

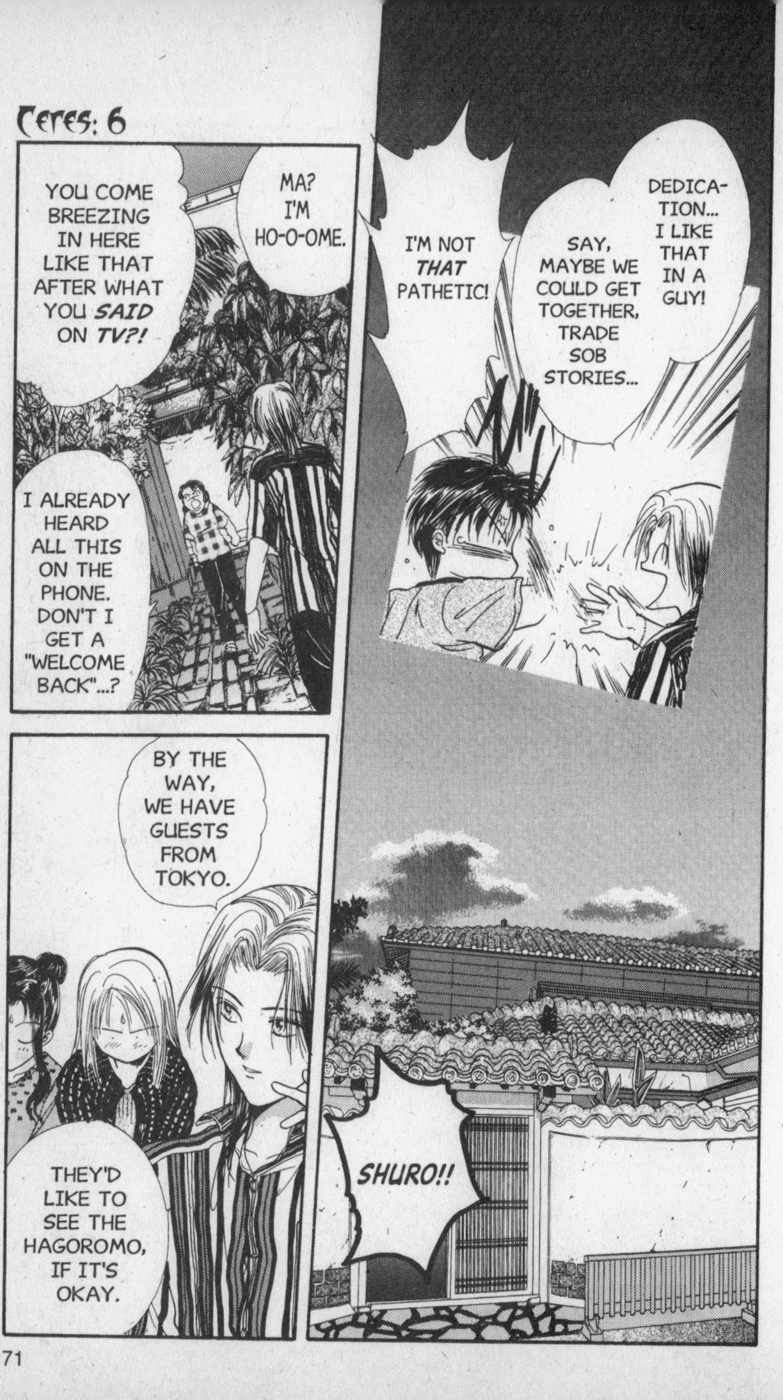
DEDICATION... I LIKE THAT IN A GUY!
SAY, MAYBE WE COULD GET TOGETHER, TRADE SOB STORIES...
I'M NOT THAT PATHETIC!
SHURO!!
MA? I'M HO-O-OME.
YOU COME BREEZING IN HERE LIKE THAT AFTER WHAT YOU SAID ON TV?!
I ALREADY HEARD ALL THIS ON THE PHONE. DON'T I GET A "WELCOME BACK"...?
BY THE WAY, WE HAVE GUESTS FROM TOKYO.
THEY'D LIKE TO SEE THE HAGOROMO, IF IT'S OKAY.

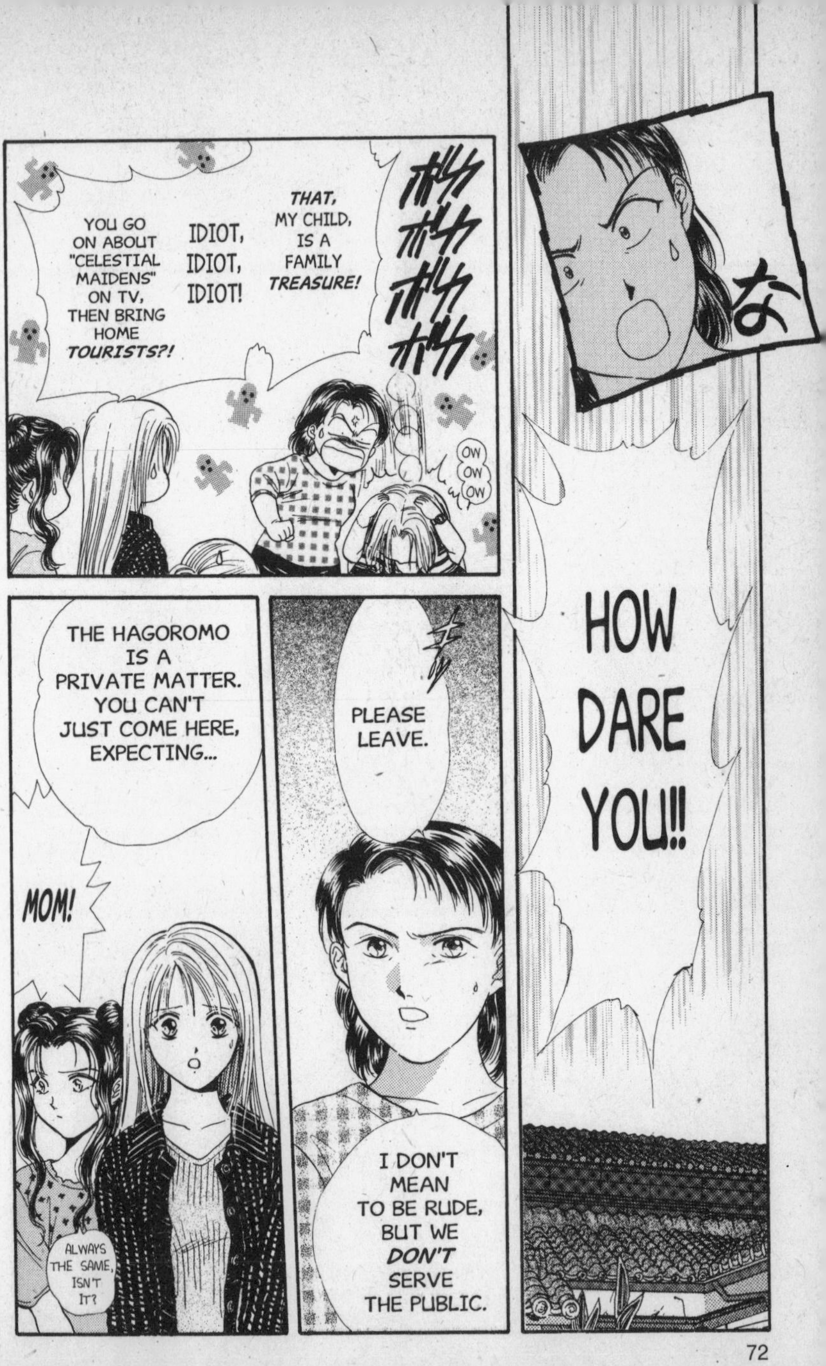
THAT, MY CHILD, IS A FAMILY *TREASURE!*
ボカ ボカ ボカ ボカ
IDIOT, IDIOT, IDIOT!
YOU GO ON ABOUT "CELESTIAL MAIDENS" ON TV, THEN BRING HOME *TOURISTS?!*
OW OW OW
PLEASE LEAVE.
I DON'T MEAN TO BE RUDE, BUT WE *DON'T* SERVE THE PUBLIC.
THE HAGOROMO IS A PRIVATE MATTER. YOU CAN'T JUST COME HERE, EXPECTING...
MOM!
ALWAYS THE SAME, ISN'T IT?
な
HOW DARE YOU!!

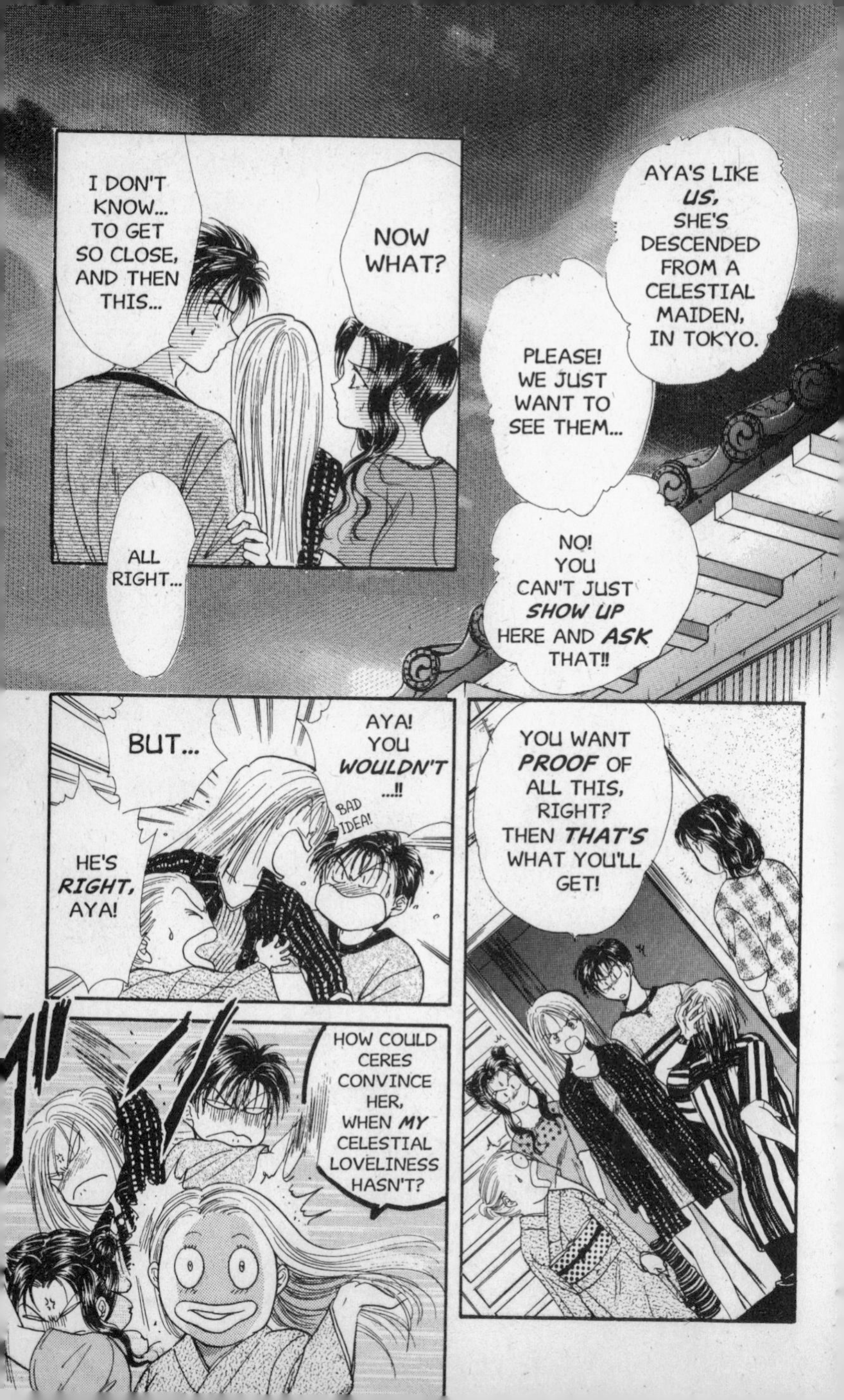
AYA'S LIKE US, SHE'S DESCENDED FROM A CELESTIAL MAIDEN, IN TOKYO.
PLEASE! WE JUST WANT TO SEE THEM...
NO! YOU CAN'T JUST SHOW UP HERE AND ASK THAT!!
NOW WHAT?
I DON'T KNOW... TO GET SO CLOSE, AND THEN THIS...
ALL RIGHT...
YOU WANT PROOF OF ALL THIS, RIGHT? THEN THAT'S WHAT YOU'LL GET!
AYA! YOU WOULDN'T ...!!
BAD IDEA!
BUT...
HE'S RIGHT, AYA!
HOW COULD CERES CONVINCE HER, WHEN MY CELESTIAL LOVELINESS HASN'T?

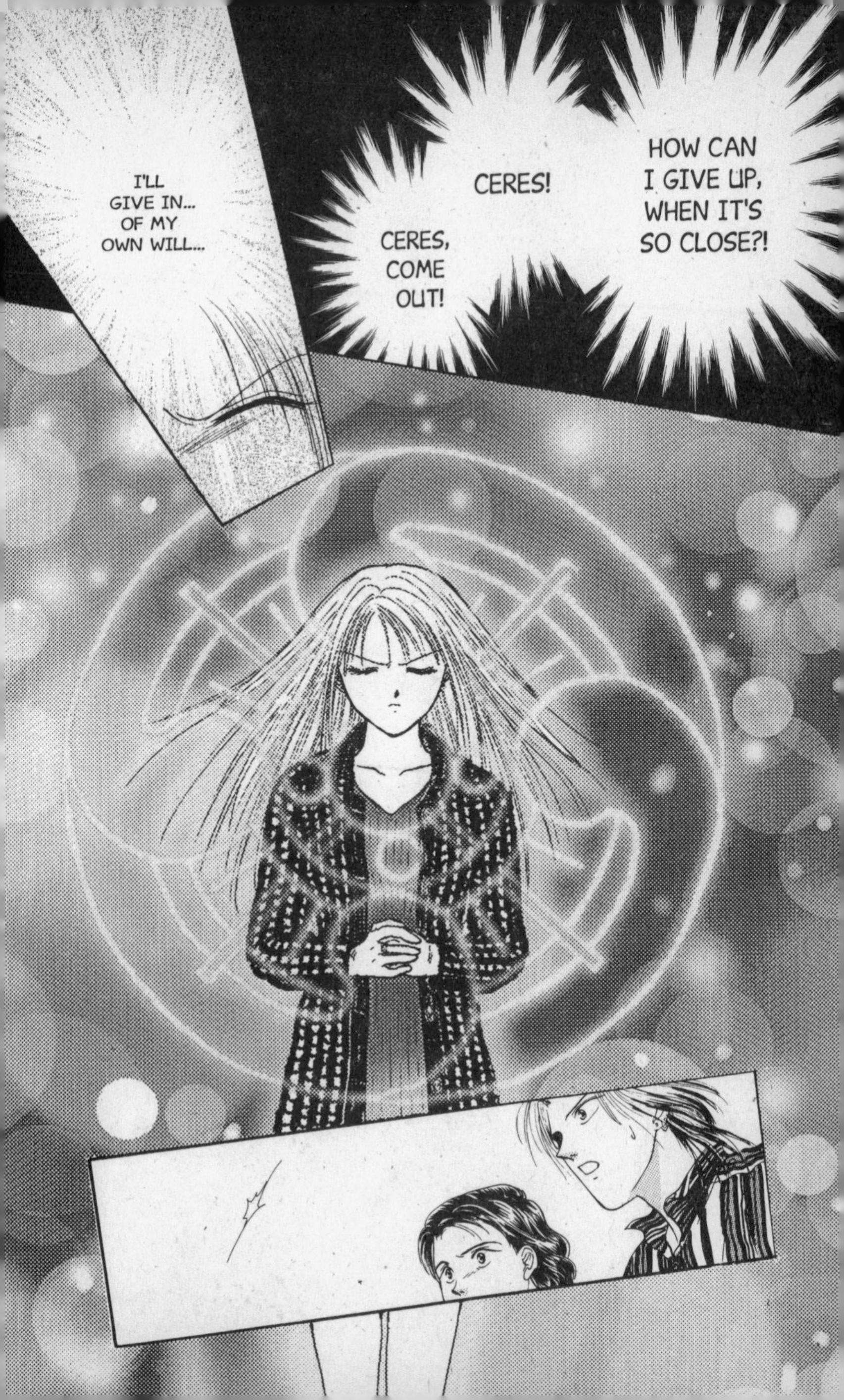
HOW CAN I GIVE UP, WHEN IT'S SO CLOSE?!
CERES!
CERES, COME OUT!
I'LL GIVE IN... OF MY OWN WILL...

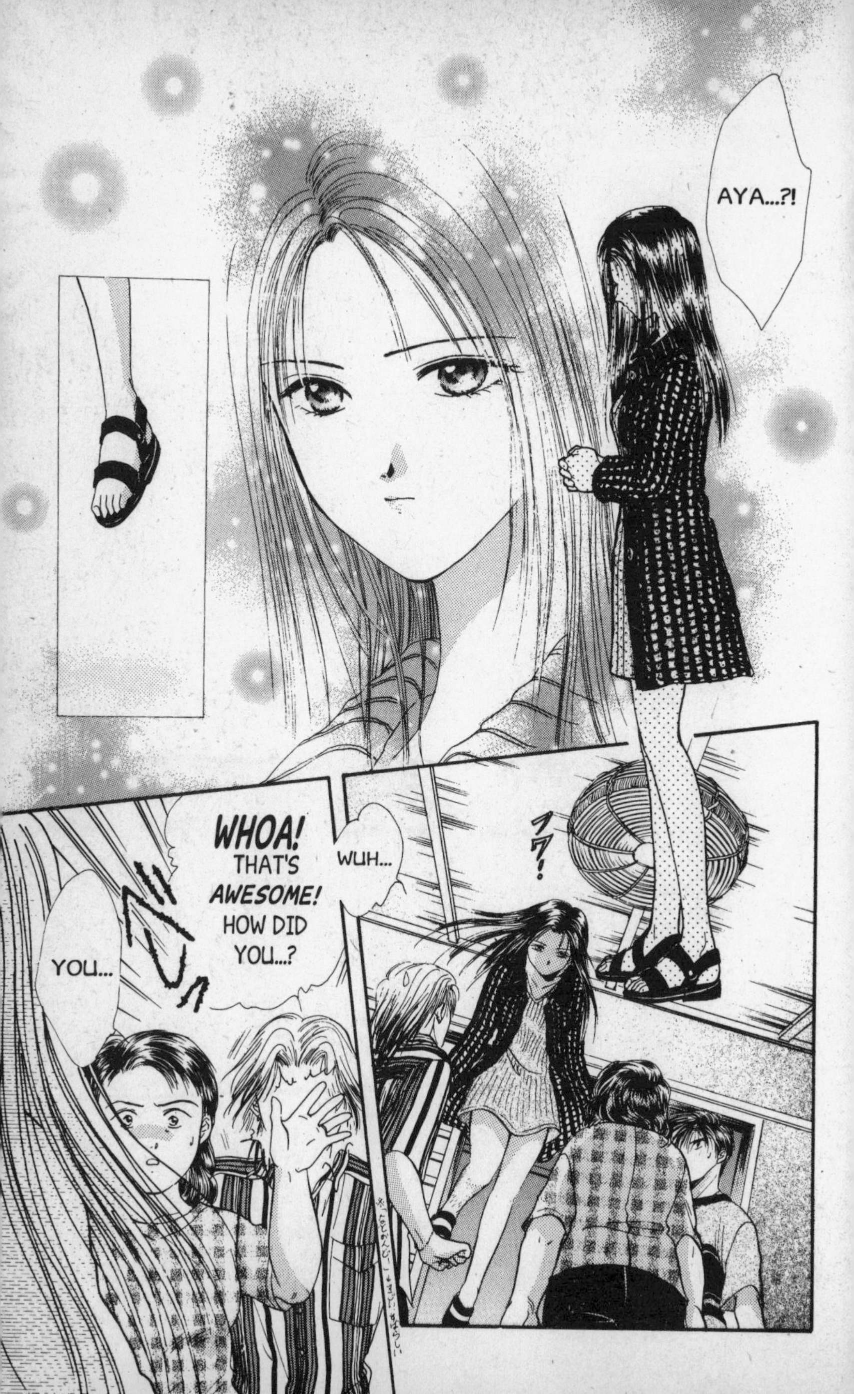
AYA...?!
フワ!
WUH...
WHOA! THAT'S AWESOME! HOW DID YOU...?
YOU...

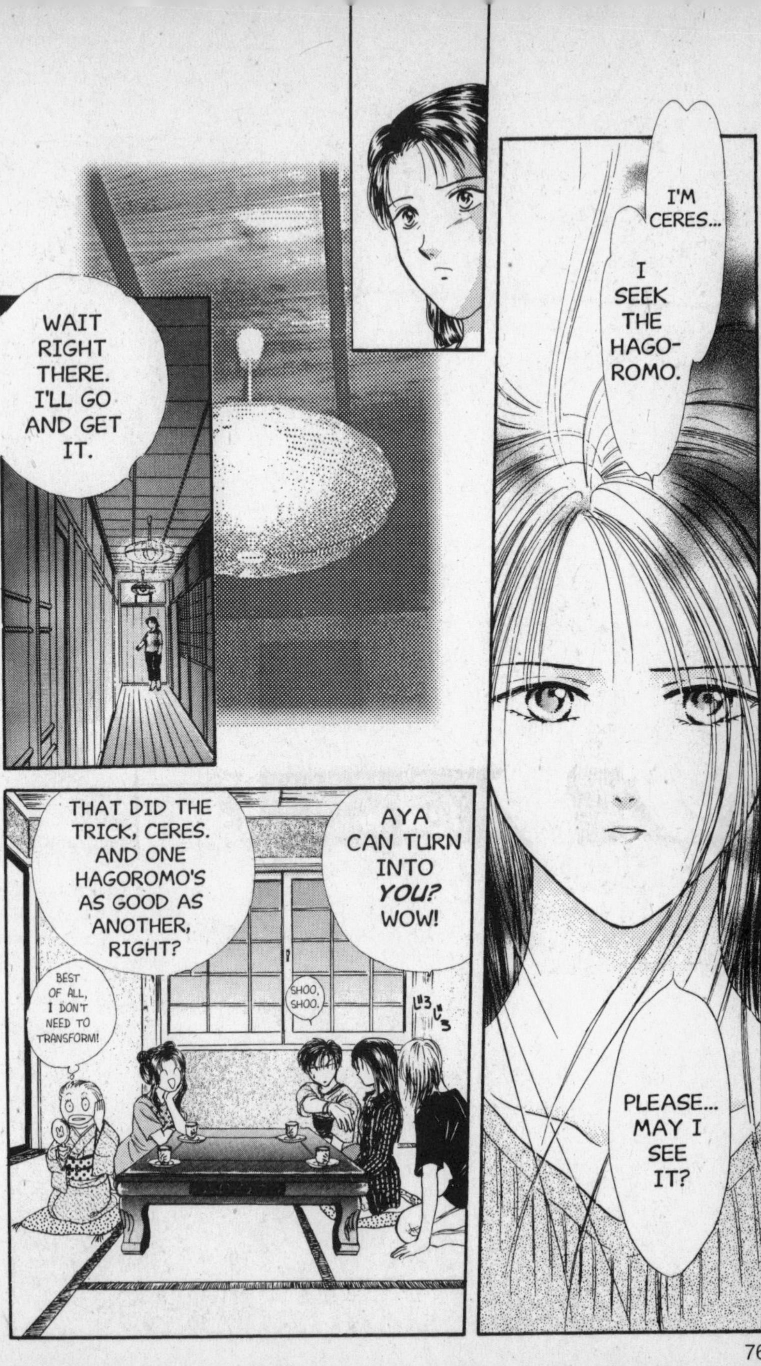
I'M CERES...
I SEEK THE HAGO-ROMO.
PLEASE... MAY I SEE IT?
WAIT RIGHT THERE. I'LL GO AND GET IT.
AYA CAN TURN INTO *YOU?* WOW!
THAT DID THE TRICK, CERES. AND ONE HAGOROMO'S AS GOOD AS ANOTHER, RIGHT?
じろ じろ
SHOO, SHOO.
BEST OF ALL, I DON'T NEED TO TRANSFORM!

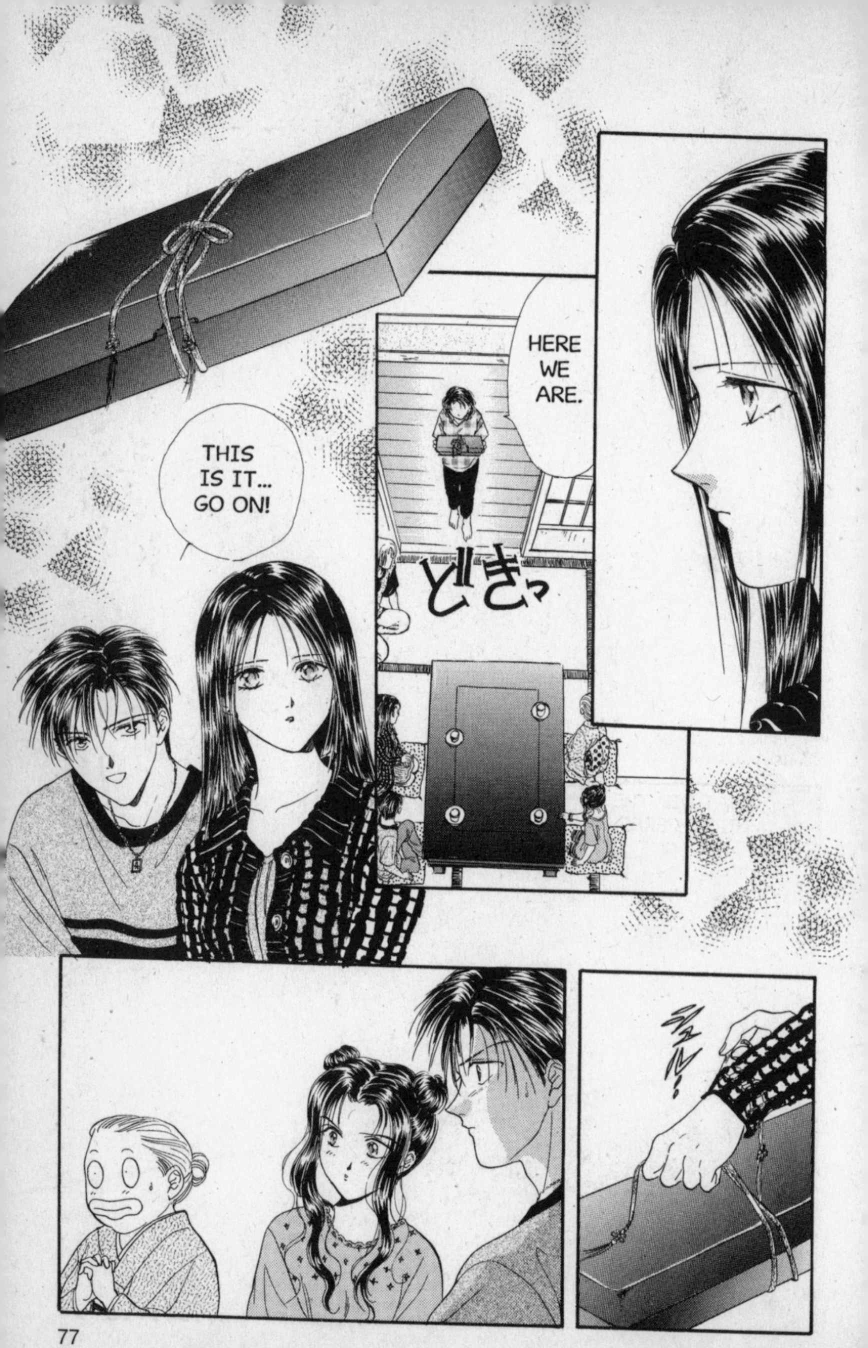
HERE WE ARE.
どきっ
THIS IS IT... GO ON!
シュル

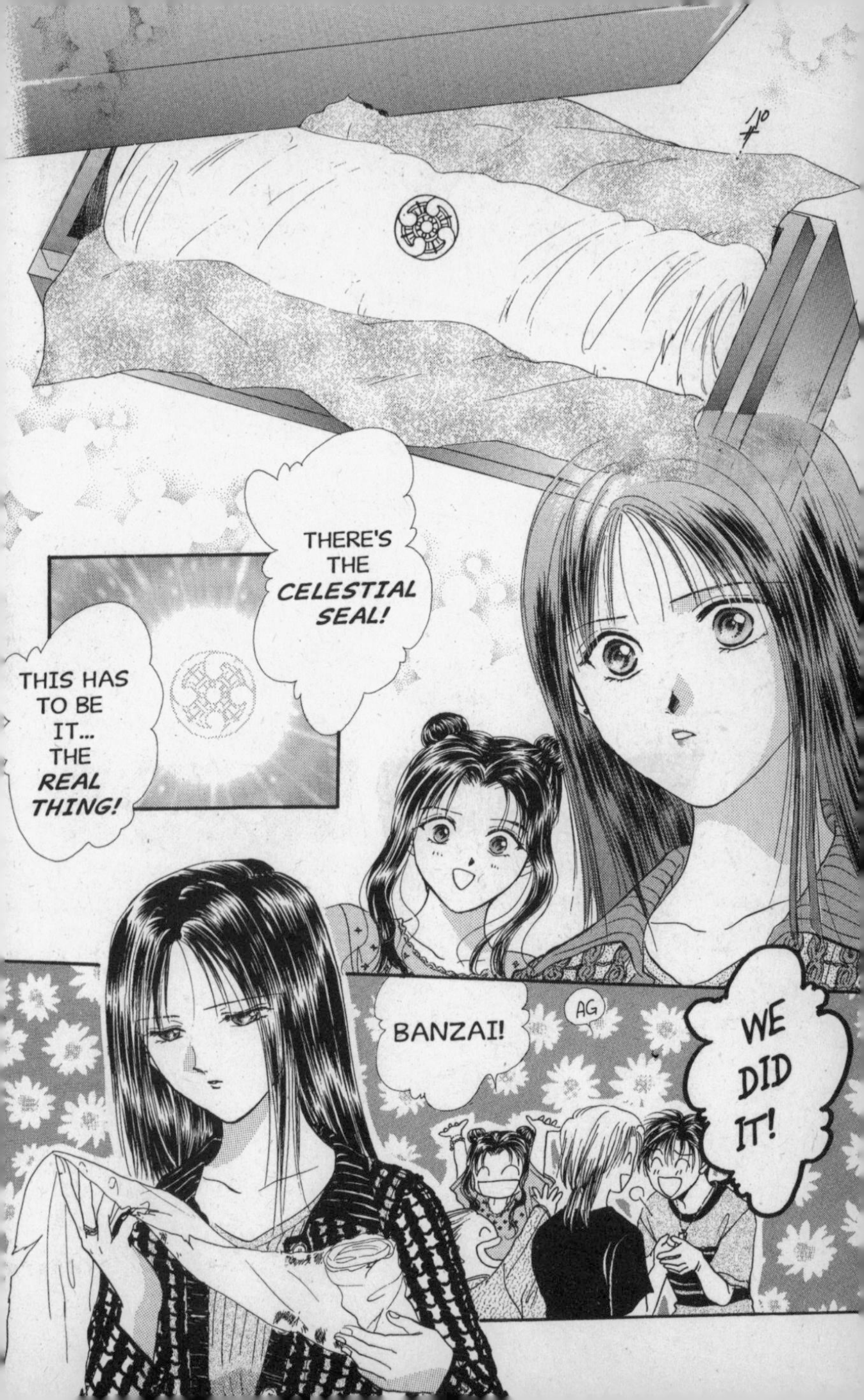
THERE'S THE CELESTIAL SEAL!
THIS HAS TO BE IT... THE REAL THING!
WE DID IT!
AG
BANZAI!

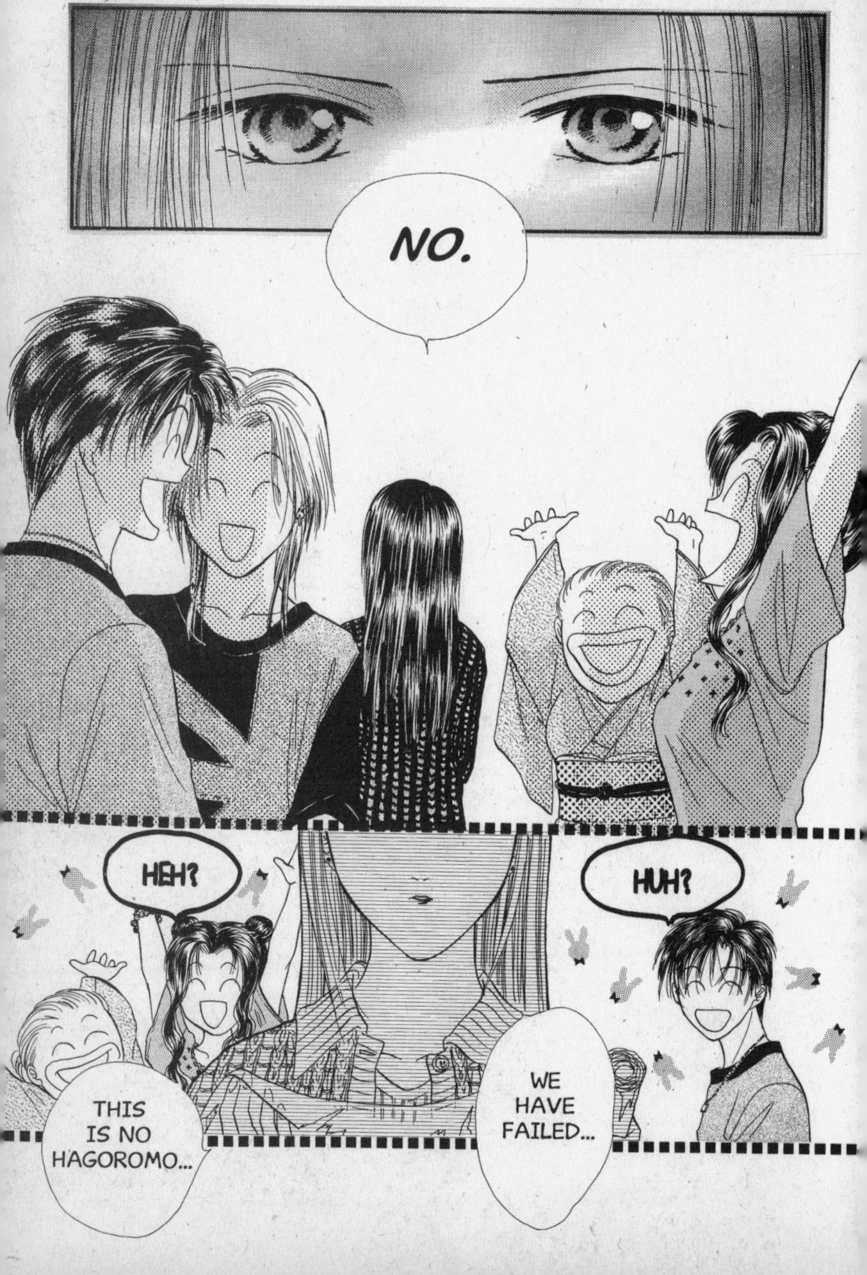
NO.
HUH?
HEH?
WE HAVE FAILED...
THIS IS NO HAGOROMO...

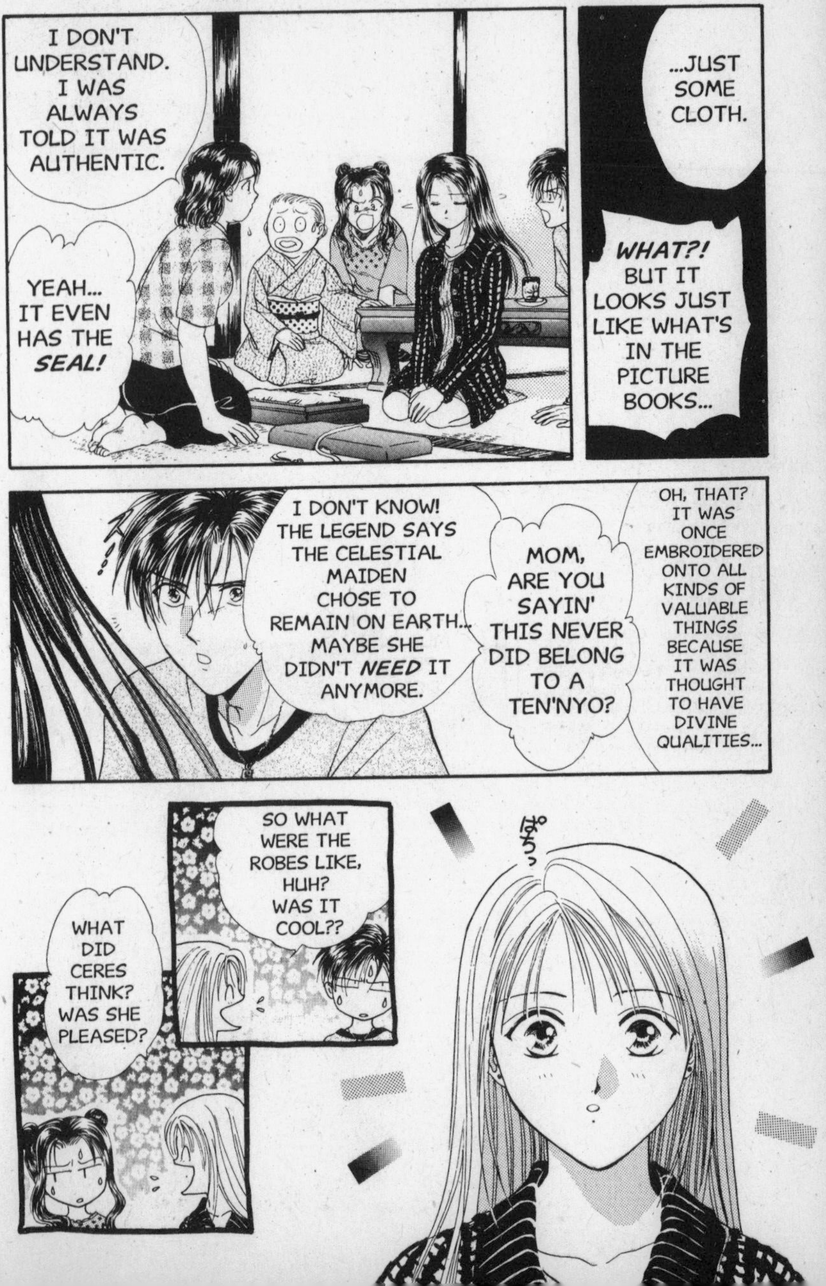
...JUST SOME CLOTH.
WHAT?! BUT IT LOOKS JUST LIKE WHAT'S IN THE PICTURE BOOKS...
I DON'T UNDERSTAND. I WAS ALWAYS TOLD IT WAS AUTHENTIC.
YEAH... IT EVEN HAS THE SEAL!
OH, THAT? IT WAS ONCE EMBROIDERED ONTO ALL KINDS OF VALUABLE THINGS BECAUSE IT WAS THOUGHT TO HAVE DIVINE QUALITIES...
MOM, ARE YOU SAYIN' THIS NEVER DID BELONG TO A TEN'NYO?
I DON'T KNOW! THE LEGEND SAYS THE CELESTIAL MAIDEN CHOSE TO REMAIN ON EARTH... MAYBE SHE DIDN'T NEED IT ANYMORE.
ぱちっ
SO WHAT WERE THE ROBES LIKE, HUH? WAS IT COOL??
WHAT DID CERES THINK? WAS SHE PLEASED?

Ceres: 6

...When will I learn to stop getting myself in trouble? :-) My assistants tell me my "personality really comes through" in these little sidebars of mine. Is it that obvious?
Even in my other graphic novels, though, these sidebars are "just my opinion." If you don't agree, that's **your** opinion. People have different ideas about things. Just because someone doesn't share yours, doesn't make them wrong. Unless they're totally on crack. With Ceres, more so than with any of my previous works, I've really made an effort. "**This** is what I think! **This,** we should think about! **This** bugs me! What'll we do about **this?!**" What do **you** guys think about this stuff? **That's** what I wanna know. Do I, though? Guess I'll be "waiting for your letters," as they say. Just send them to my publisher.
Oh, yeah. On another note...I finished FFVII (here she goes again, huh?). Just gotta get it out. :-) At a friend's house, she had a copy of her memory card. I played the ending with it...it was **incredible.** Her characters were, like, Level 99. With 9,999 HP. And 9,999 MP! What th—?! All her "Materia" were maxed out. A lot of them were "mastered" ...and I hadn't even **known** about some of them. Her Chocobo was "gold," the spells were all "ultimate"—so were the "limit breaks" (even for Aeris)—it was a piece of cake to finish. (**Duh,** right?) To play the final battle at Level 99, it took like 10 minutes, but the best part was that I could do it without breaking a sweat. I got to see all the "summonings," too...it was amazing, I totally had so much respect for her. I couldn't've managed it, not even if I'd had the rest of my life. (Says the girl who plays with another person's memory card.) Maybe I'll go for "Tales of Destiny" next... Waah, if I only had more **time**...but that's all I **ever** say, isn't it.

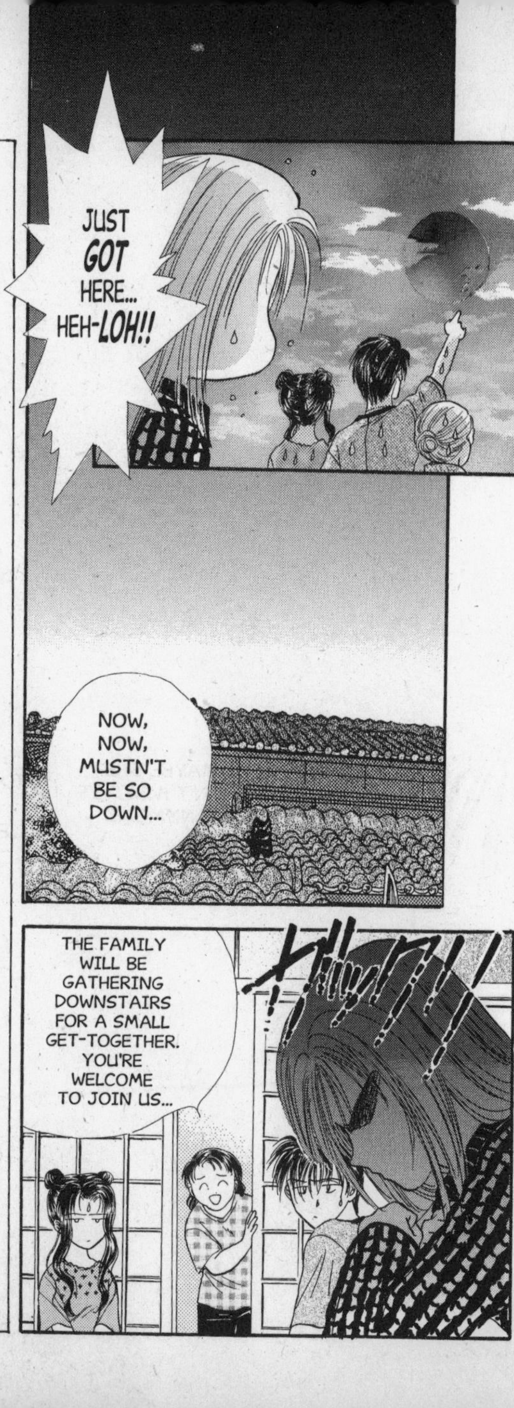
JUST GOT HERE... HEH-LOH!!
NOW, NOW, MUSTN'T BE SO DOWN...
THE FAMILY WILL BE GATHERING DOWNSTAIRS FOR A SMALL GET-TOGETHER. YOU'RE WELCOME TO JOIN US...

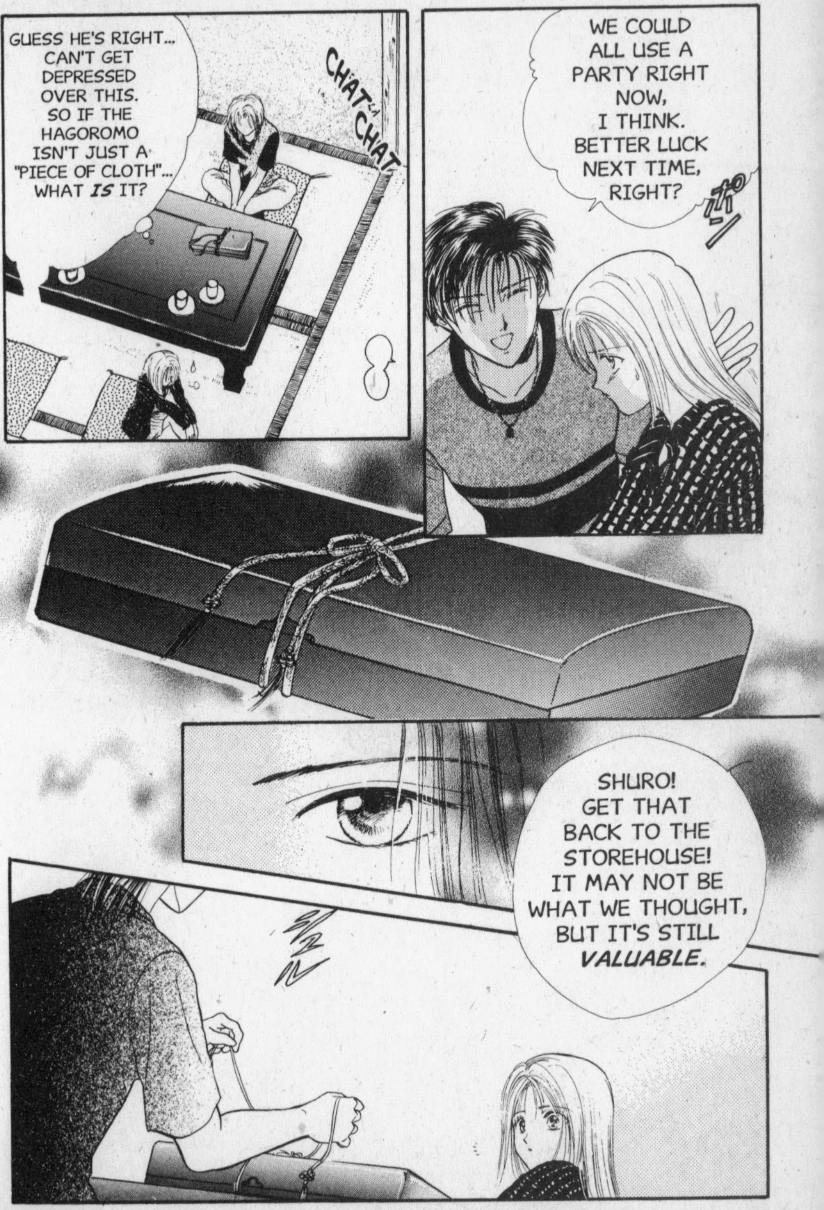
WE COULD ALL USE A PARTY RIGHT NOW, I THINK. BETTER LUCK NEXT TIME, RIGHT?
GUESS HE'S RIGHT... CAN'T GET DEPRESSED OVER THIS. SO IF THE HAGOROMO ISN'T JUST A "PIECE OF CLOTH"... WHAT *IS* IT?
CHAT CHAT
SHURO! GET THAT BACK TO THE STOREHOUSE! IT MAY NOT BE WHAT WE THOUGHT, BUT IT'S STILL ***VALUABLE.***

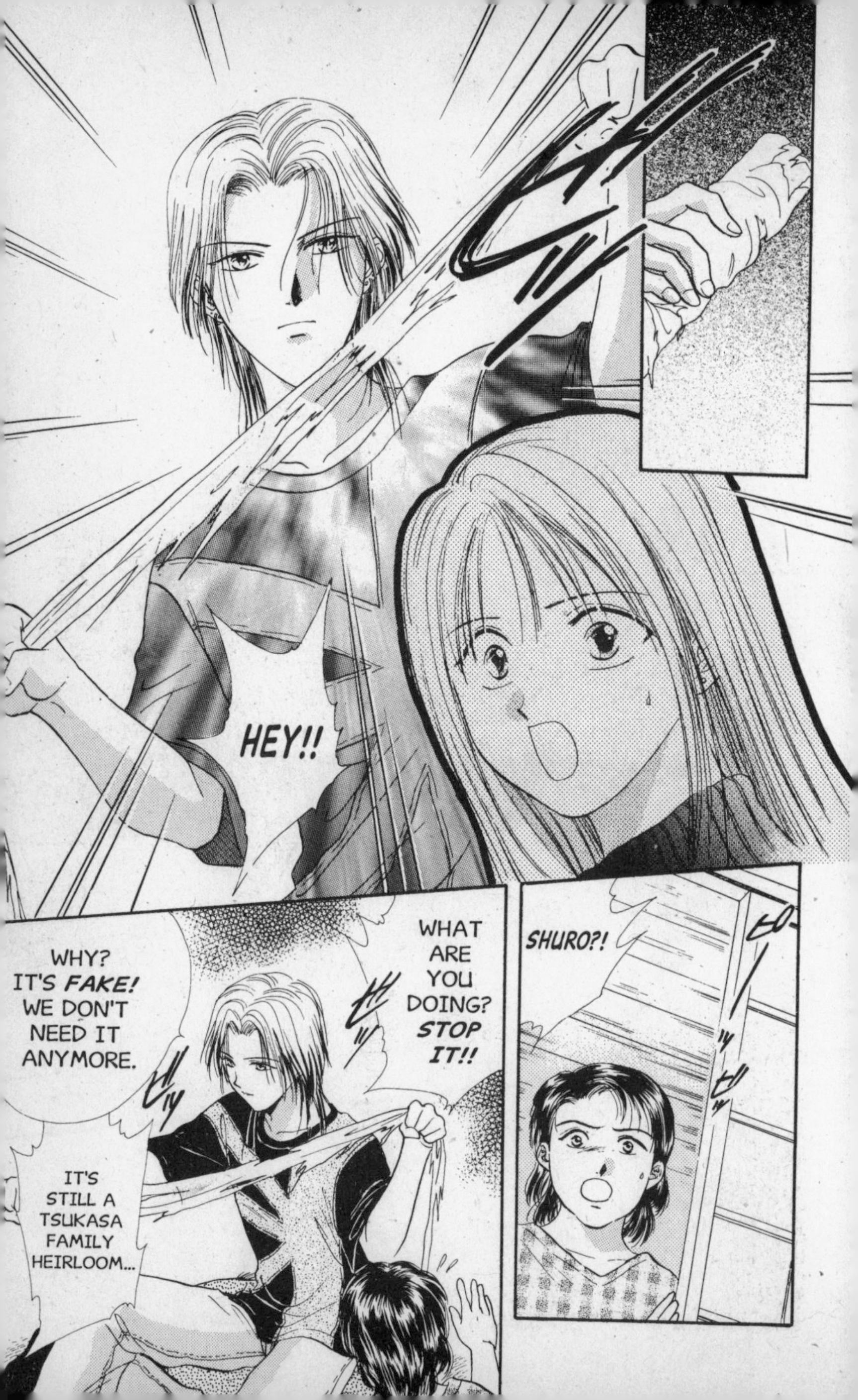
HEY!!
SHURO?!
WHAT ARE YOU DOING? STOP IT!!
WHY? IT'S FAKE! WE DON'T NEED IT ANYMORE.
IT'S STILL A TSUKASA FAMILY HEIRLOOM...

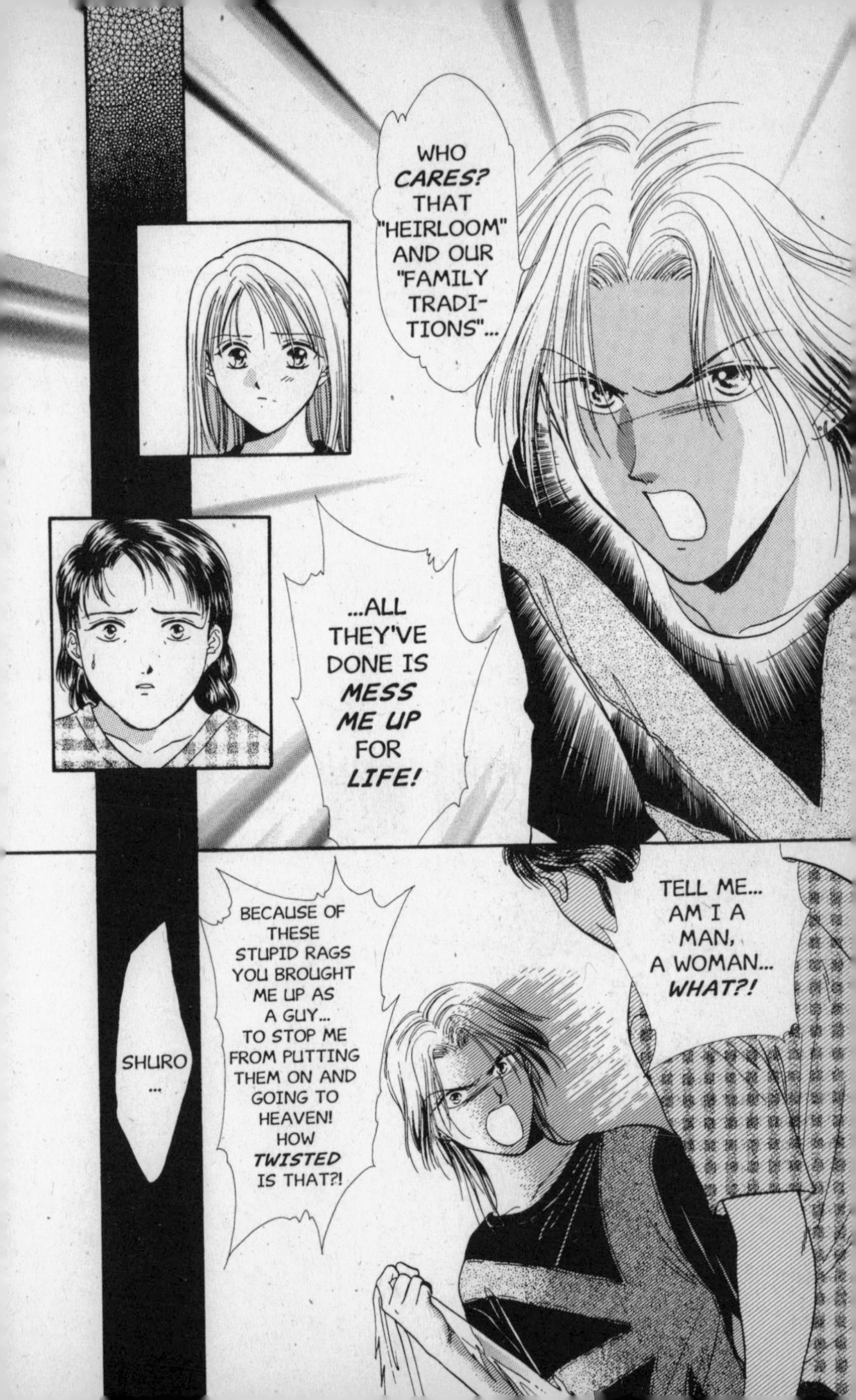
WHO *CARES?* THAT "HEIRLOOM" AND OUR "FAMILY TRADI-TIONS"...
...ALL THEY'VE DONE IS *MESS ME UP* FOR *LIFE!*
TELL ME... AM I A MAN, A WOMAN... *WHAT?!*
BECAUSE OF THESE STUPID RAGS YOU BROUGHT ME UP AS A GUY... TO STOP ME FROM PUTTING THEM ON AND GOING TO HEAVEN! HOW *TWISTED* IS THAT?!
SHURO ...

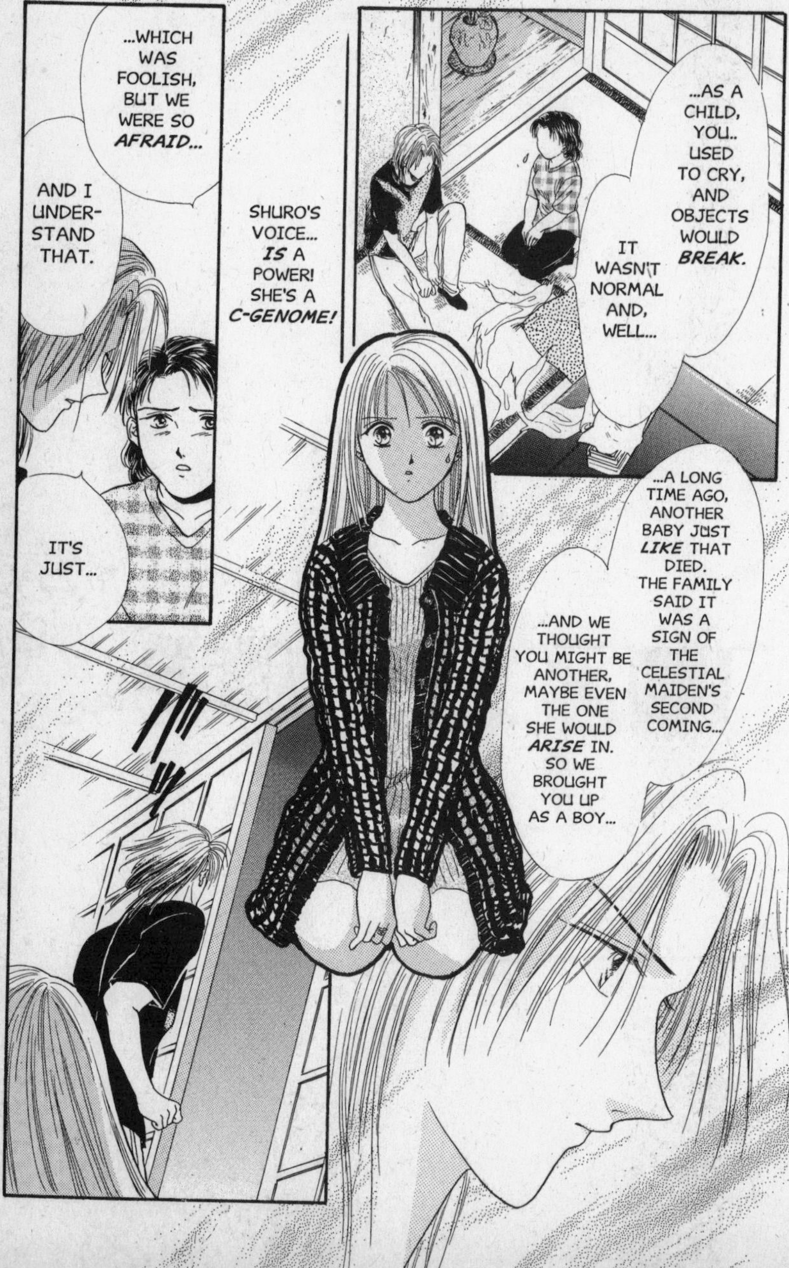
...AS A CHILD, YOU.. USED TO CRY, AND OBJECTS WOULD BREAK.
IT WASN'T NORMAL AND, WELL...
...A LONG TIME AGO, ANOTHER BABY JUST LIKE THAT DIED. THE FAMILY SAID IT WAS A SIGN OF THE CELESTIAL MAIDEN'S SECOND COMING...
...AND WE THOUGHT YOU MIGHT BE ANOTHER, MAYBE EVEN THE ONE SHE WOULD ARISE IN. SO WE BROUGHT YOU UP AS A BOY...
...WHICH WAS FOOLISH, BUT WE WERE SO AFRAID...
AND I UNDERSTAND THAT.
IT'S JUST...
SHURO'S VOICE... IS A POWER! SHE'S A C-GENOME!

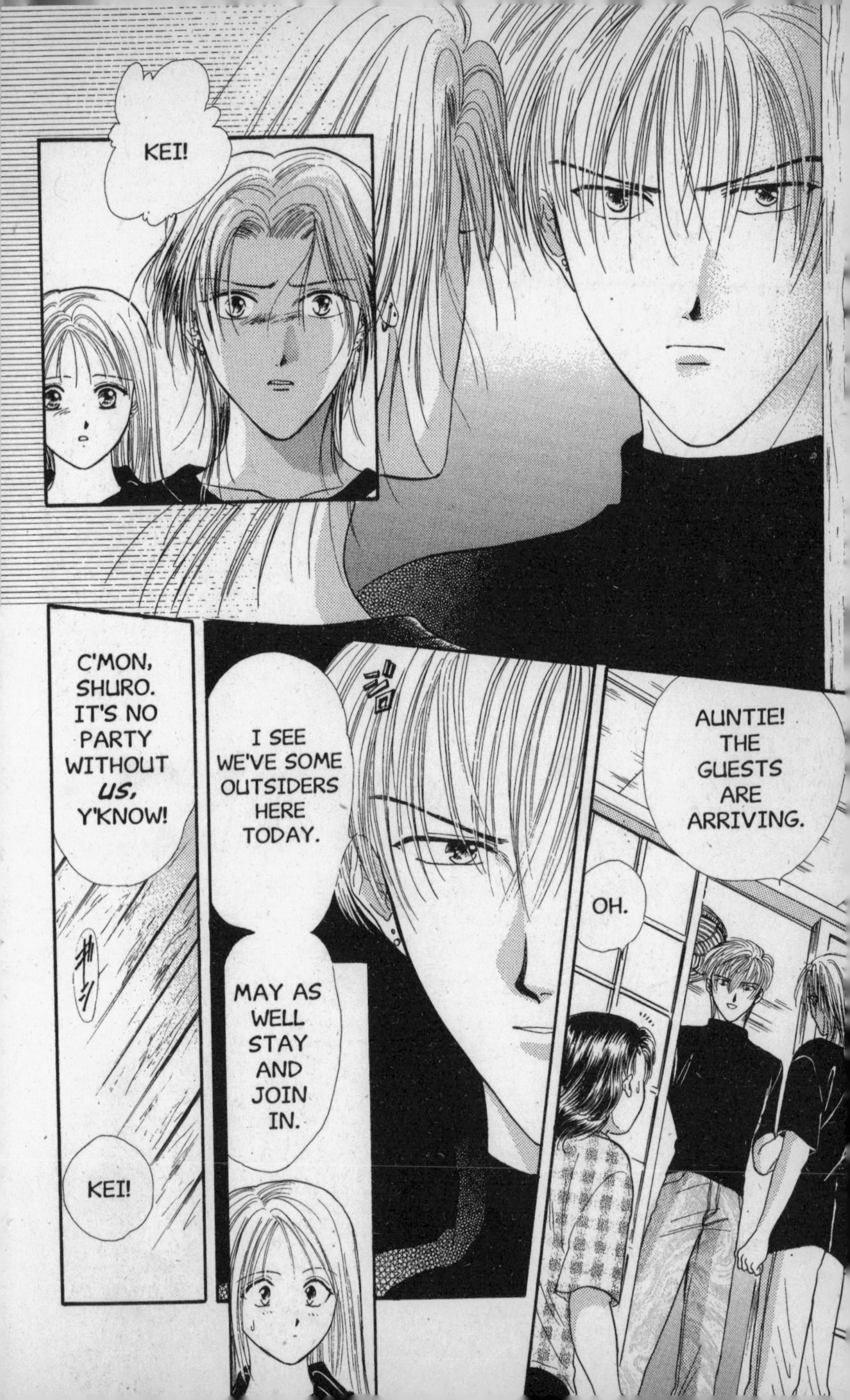
KEI!
AUNTIE! THE GUESTS ARE ARRIVING.
OH.
I SEE WE'VE SOME OUTSIDERS HERE TODAY.
MAY AS WELL STAY AND JOIN IN.
C'MON, SHURO. IT'S NO PARTY WITHOUT US, Y'KNOW!
KEI!

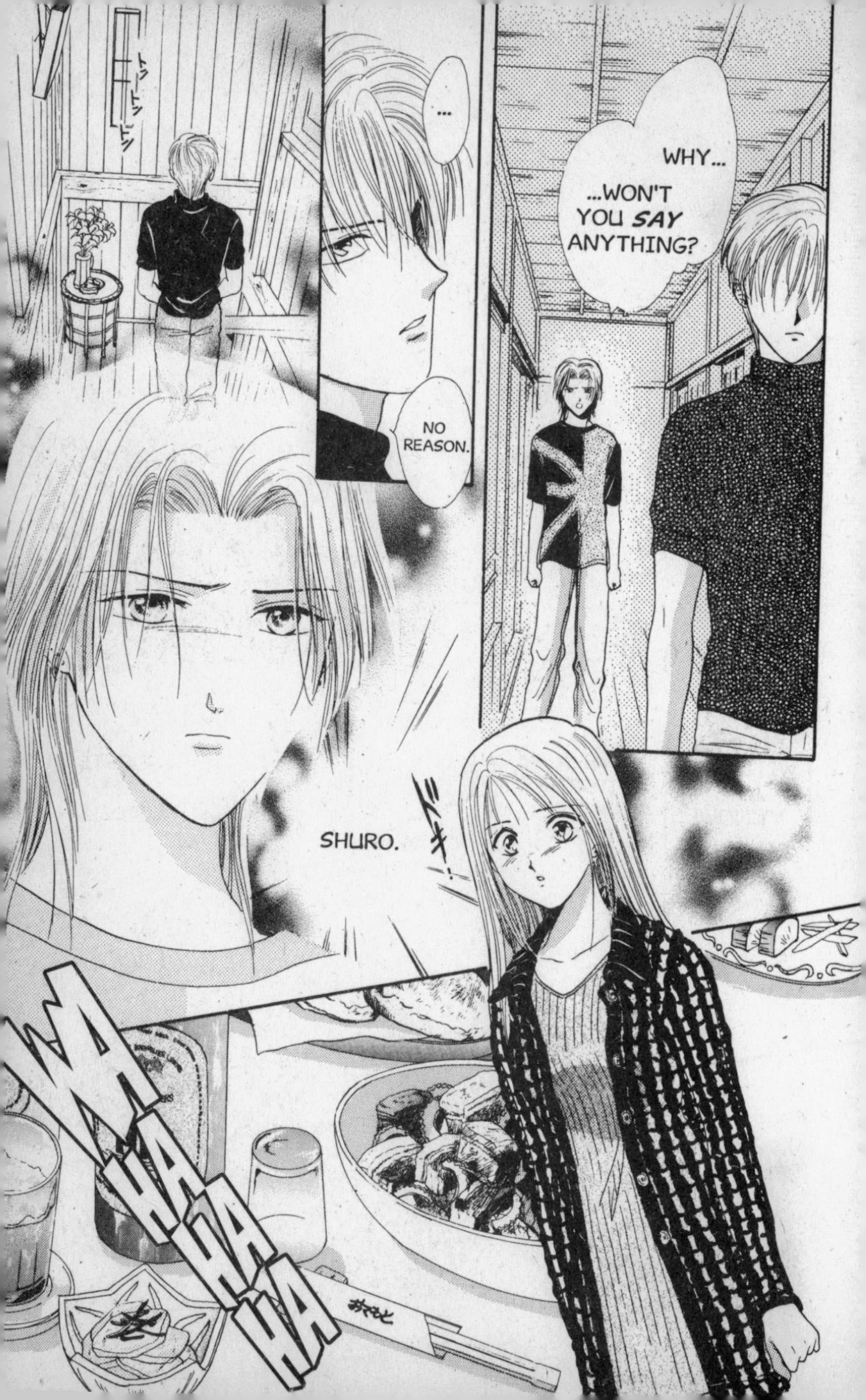
WHY...
...WON'T YOU *SAY* ANYTHING?
...
NO REASON.
SHURO.
WAHAHAHA

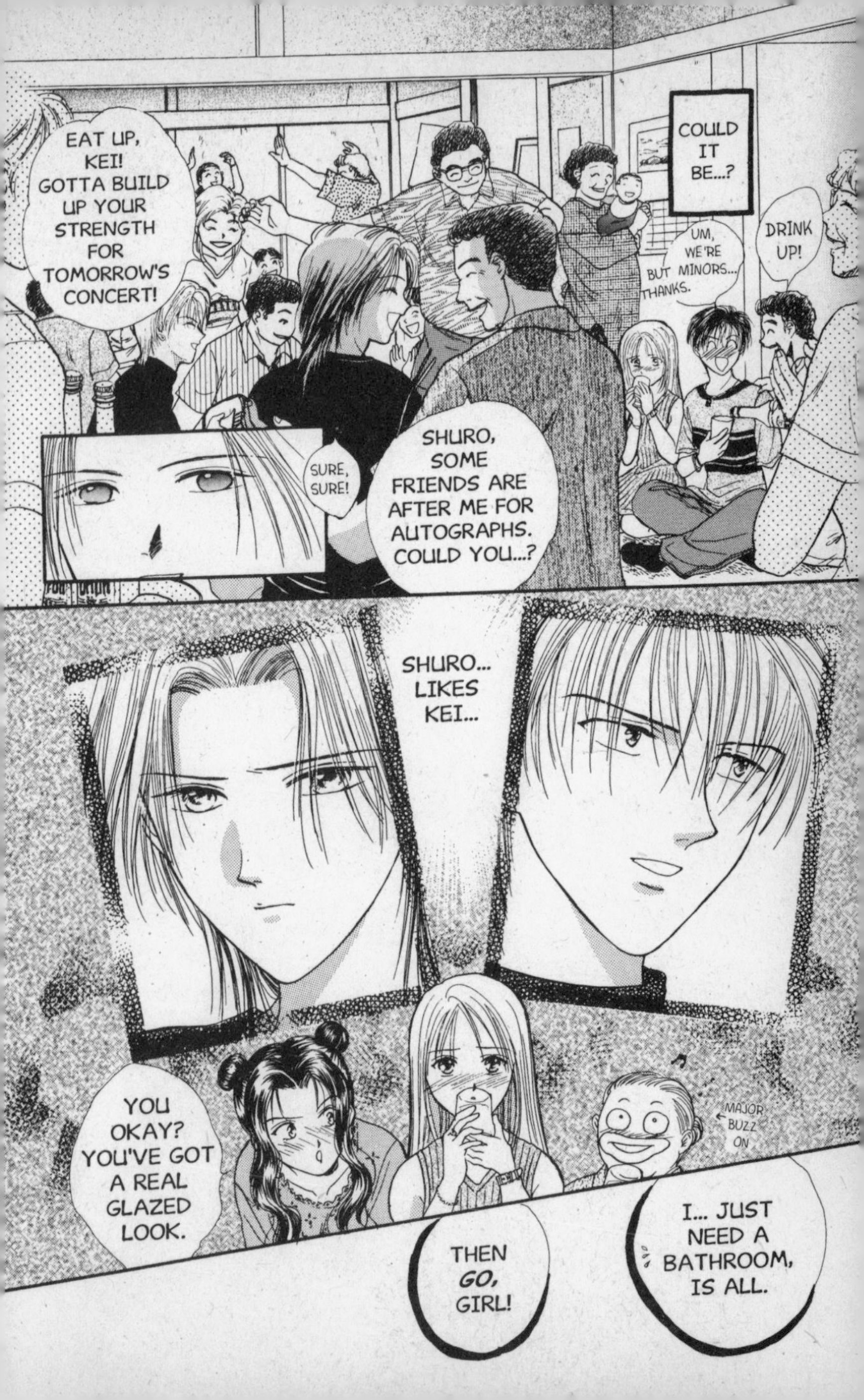
COULD IT BE...?
DRINK UP!
UM, WE'RE MINORS... BUT THANKS.
EAT UP, KEI! GOTTA BUILD UP YOUR STRENGTH FOR TOMORROW'S CONCERT!
SHURO, SOME FRIENDS ARE AFTER ME FOR AUTOGRAPHS. COULD YOU...?
SURE, SURE!
SHURO... LIKES KEI...
YOU OKAY? YOU'VE GOT A REAL GLAZED LOOK.
MAJOR BUZZ ON
I... JUST NEED A BATHROOM, IS ALL.
THEN *GO*, GIRL!

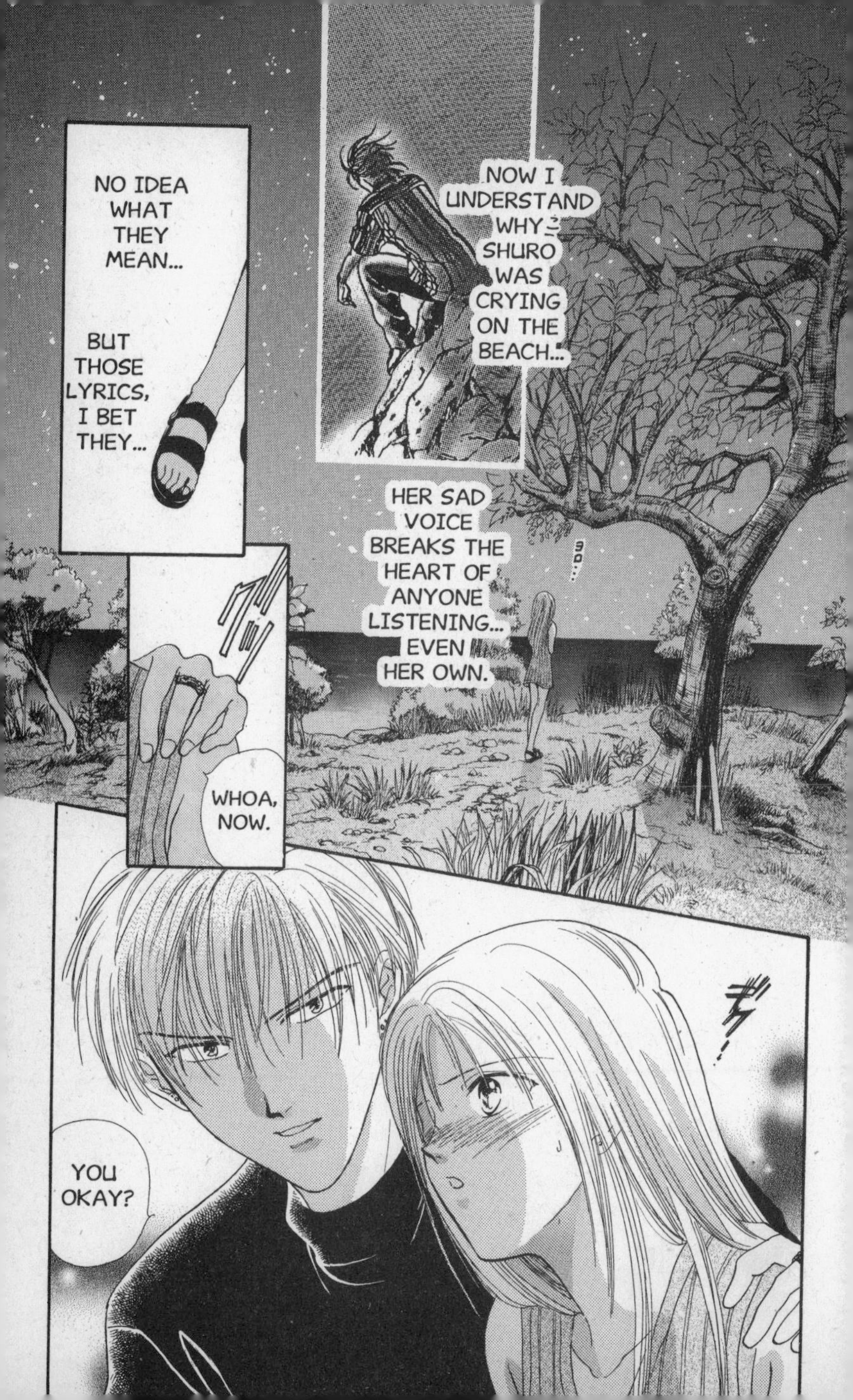
NOW I UNDERSTAND WHY SHURO WAS CRYING ON THE BEACH...
HER SAD VOICE BREAKS THE HEART OF ANYONE LISTENING... EVEN HER OWN.
NO IDEA WHAT THEY MEAN...
BUT THOSE LYRICS, I BET THEY...
WHOA, NOW.
YOU OKAY?

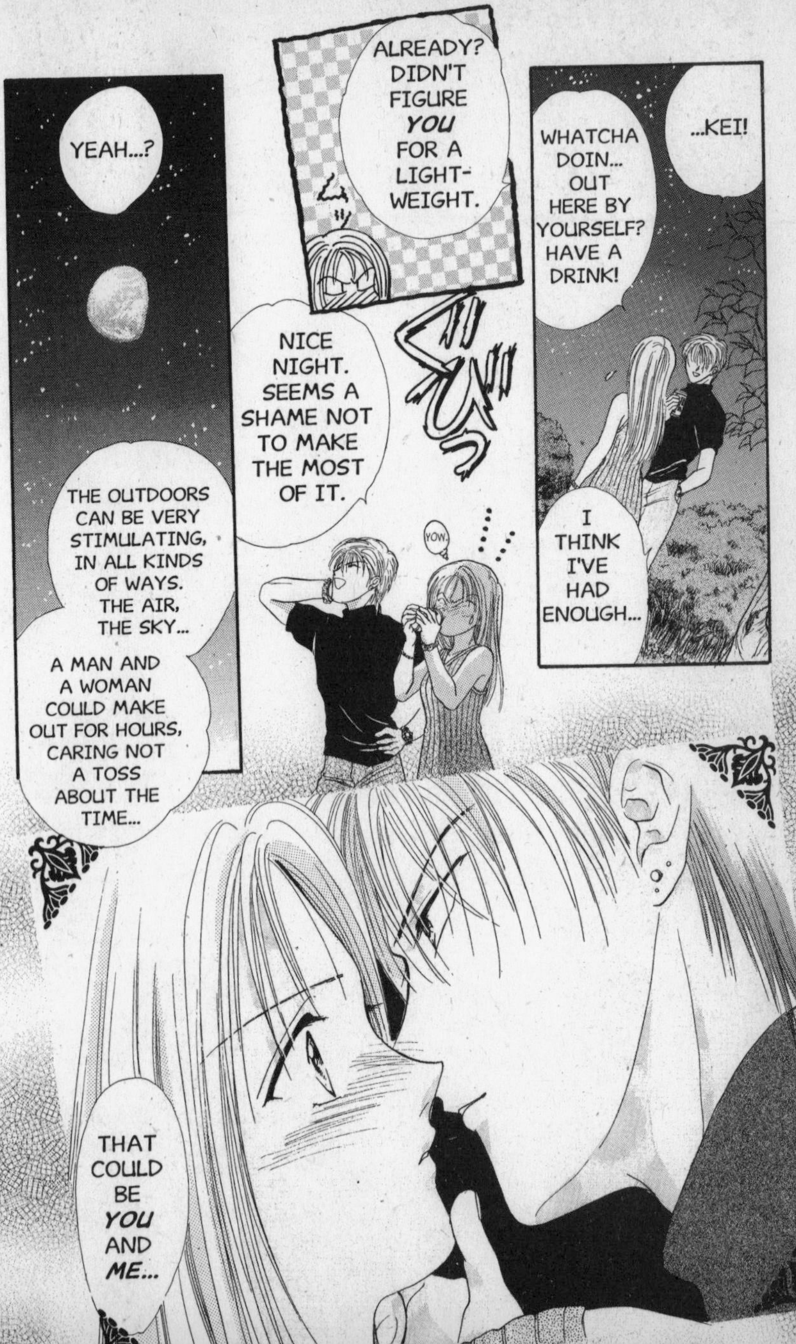
...KEI!
WHATCHA DOIN... OUT HERE BY YOURSELF? HAVE A DRINK!
I THINK I'VE HAD ENOUGH...
ALREADY? DIDN'T FIGURE *YOU* FOR A LIGHT-WEIGHT.
YOW.
NICE NIGHT. SEEMS A SHAME NOT TO MAKE THE MOST OF IT.
YEAH...?
THE OUTDOORS CAN BE VERY STIMULATING, IN ALL KINDS OF WAYS. THE AIR, THE SKY...
A MAN AND A WOMAN COULD MAKE OUT FOR HOURS, CARING NOT A TOSS ABOUT THE TIME...
THAT COULD BE *YOU* AND *ME*...

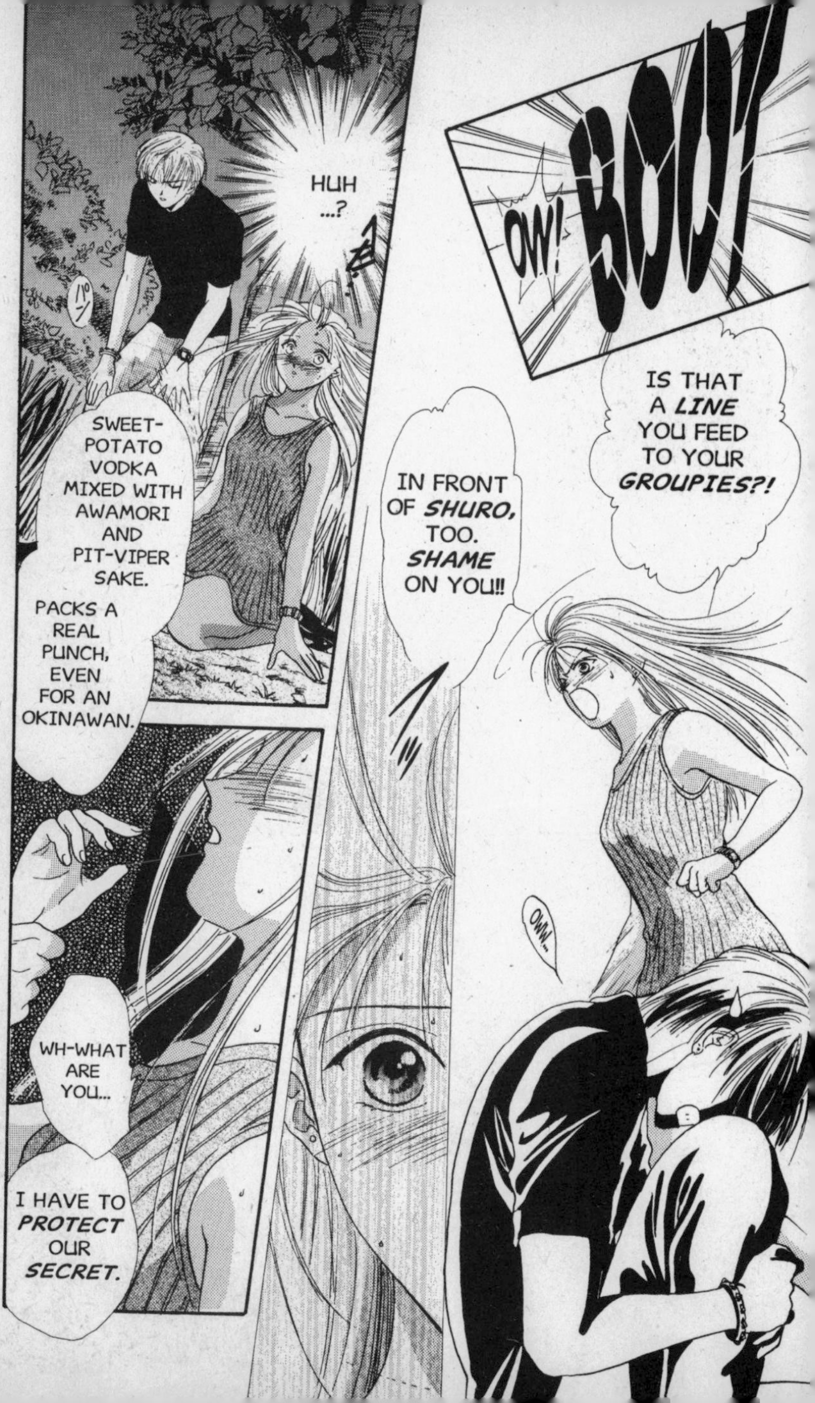
BOOT
OW!
IS THAT A *LINE* YOU FEED TO YOUR *GROUPIES?!*
IN FRONT OF *SHURO,* TOO. *SHAME* ON YOU!!
OWW...
HUH ...?
SWEET-POTATO VODKA MIXED WITH AWAMORI AND PIT-VIPER SAKE.
PACKS A REAL PUNCH, EVEN FOR AN OKINAWAN.
WH-WHAT ARE YOU...
I HAVE TO *PROTECT* OUR *SECRET.*

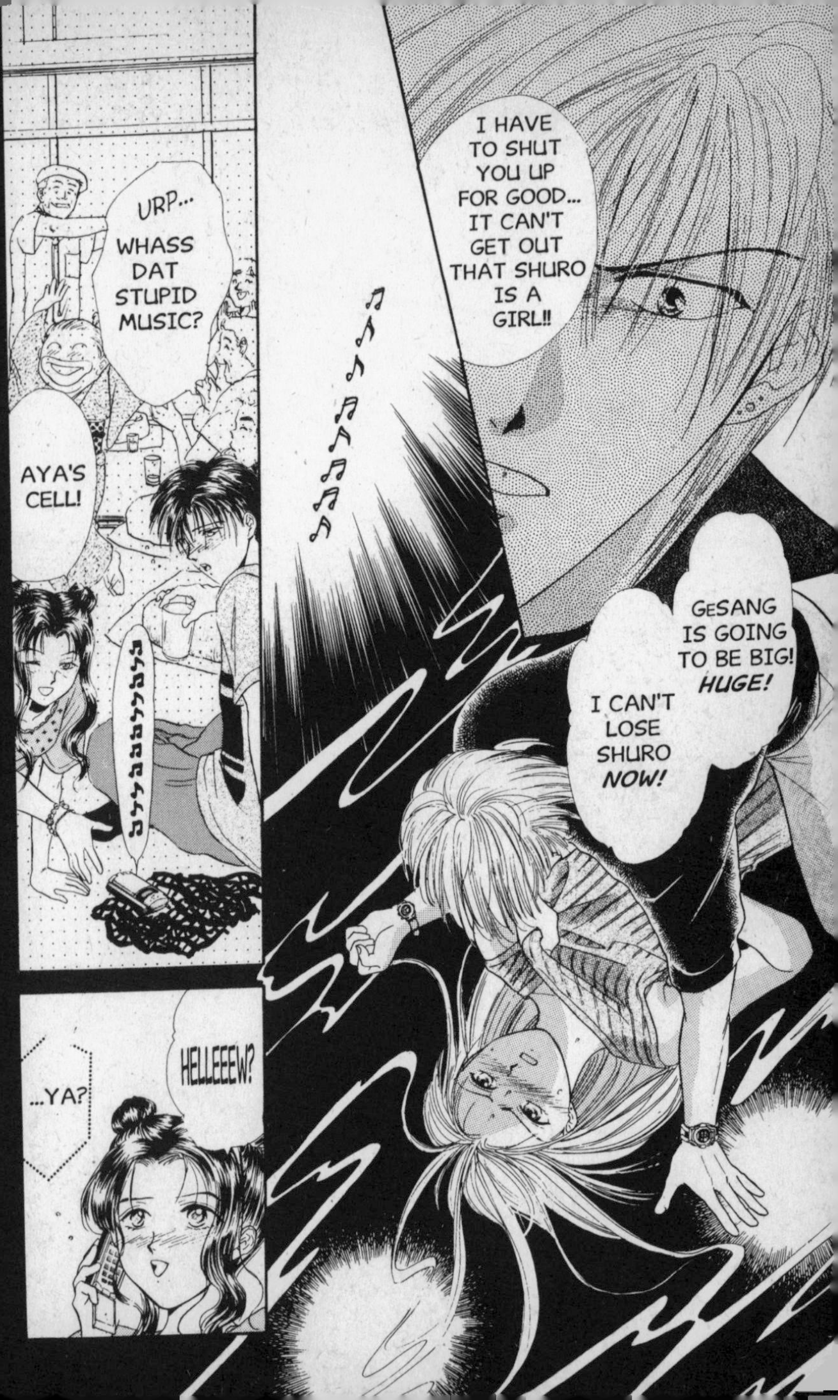
I HAVE TO SHUT YOU UP FOR GOOD... IT CAN'T GET OUT THAT SHURO IS A GIRL!!
GESANG IS GOING TO BE BIG! *HUGE!*
I CAN'T LOSE SHURO *NOW!*
URP... WHASS DAT STUPID MUSIC?
AYA'S CELL!
HELLEEEW?
...YA?

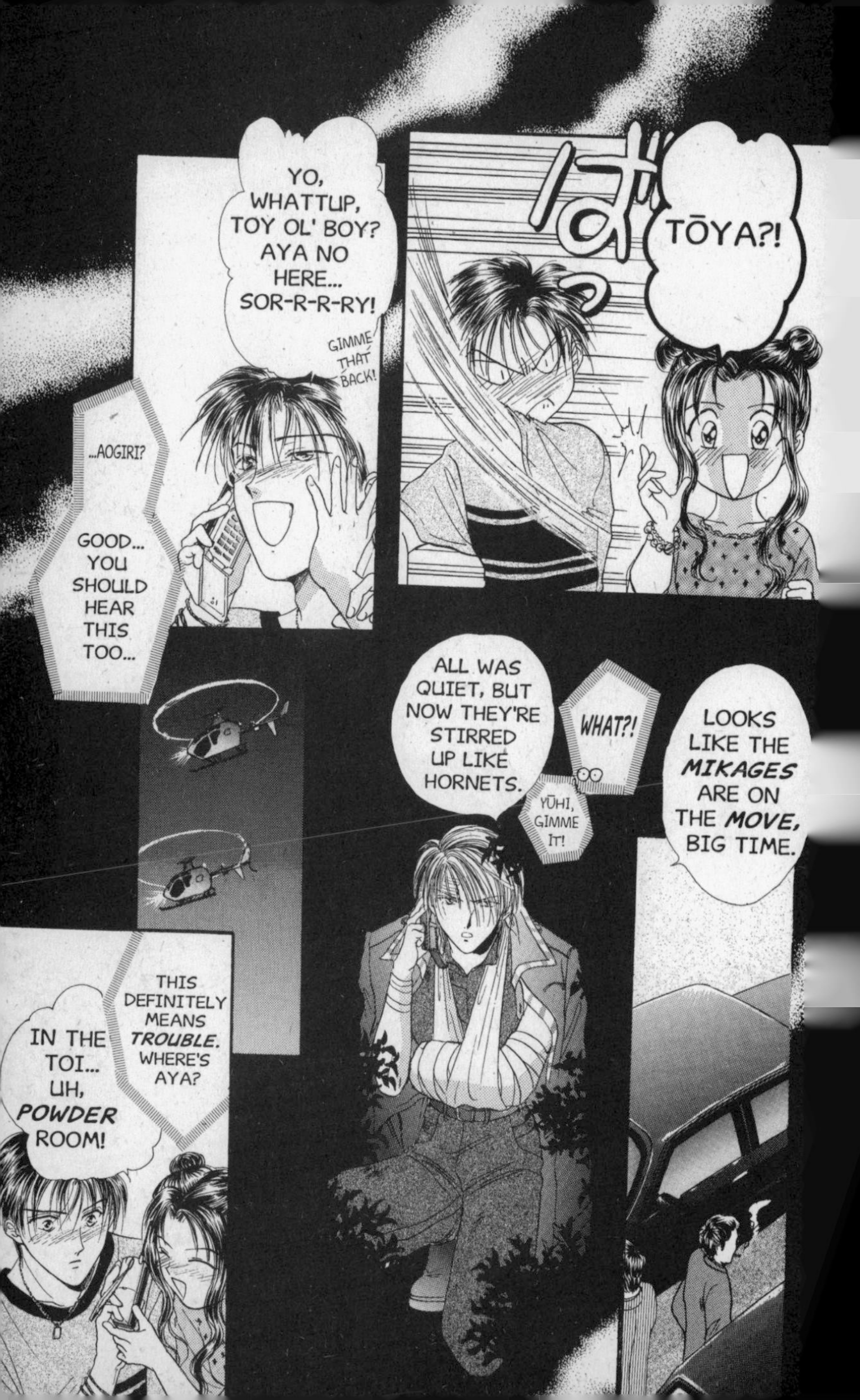

ぱっ
TŌYA?!
YO, WHATTUP, TOY OL' BOY? AYA NO HERE... SOR-R-R-RY!
GIMME THAT BACK!
...AOGIRI?
GOOD... YOU SHOULD HEAR THIS TOO...
LOOKS LIKE THE MIKAGES ARE ON THE MOVE, BIG TIME.
WHAT?!
ALL WAS QUIET, BUT NOW THEY'RE STIRRED UP LIKE HORNETS.
YŪHI, GIMME IT!
THIS DEFINITELY MEANS TROUBLE. WHERE'S AYA?
IN THE TOI... UH, POWDER ROOM!

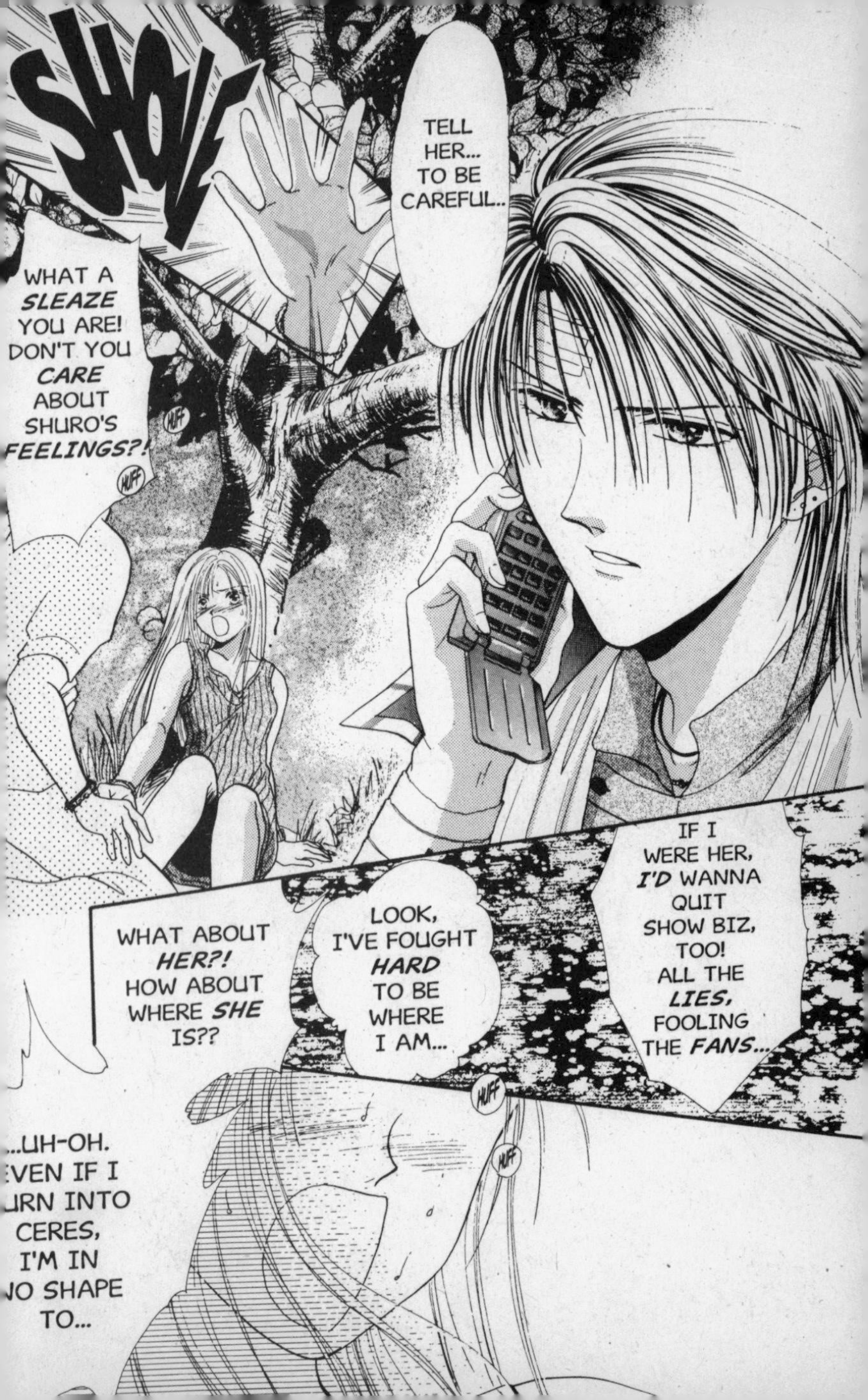

TELL HER... TO BE CAREFUL...
SHOVE
WHAT A SLEAZE YOU ARE! DON'T YOU CARE ABOUT SHURO'S FEELINGS?!
HUFF
HUFF
IF I WERE HER, I'D WANNA QUIT SHOW BIZ, TOO! ALL THE LIES, FOOLING THE FANS...
LOOK, I'VE FOUGHT HARD TO BE WHERE I AM...
WHAT ABOUT HER?! HOW ABOUT WHERE SHE IS??
HUFF
HUFF
...UH-OH. VEN IF I URN INTO CERES, I'M IN O SHAPE TO...

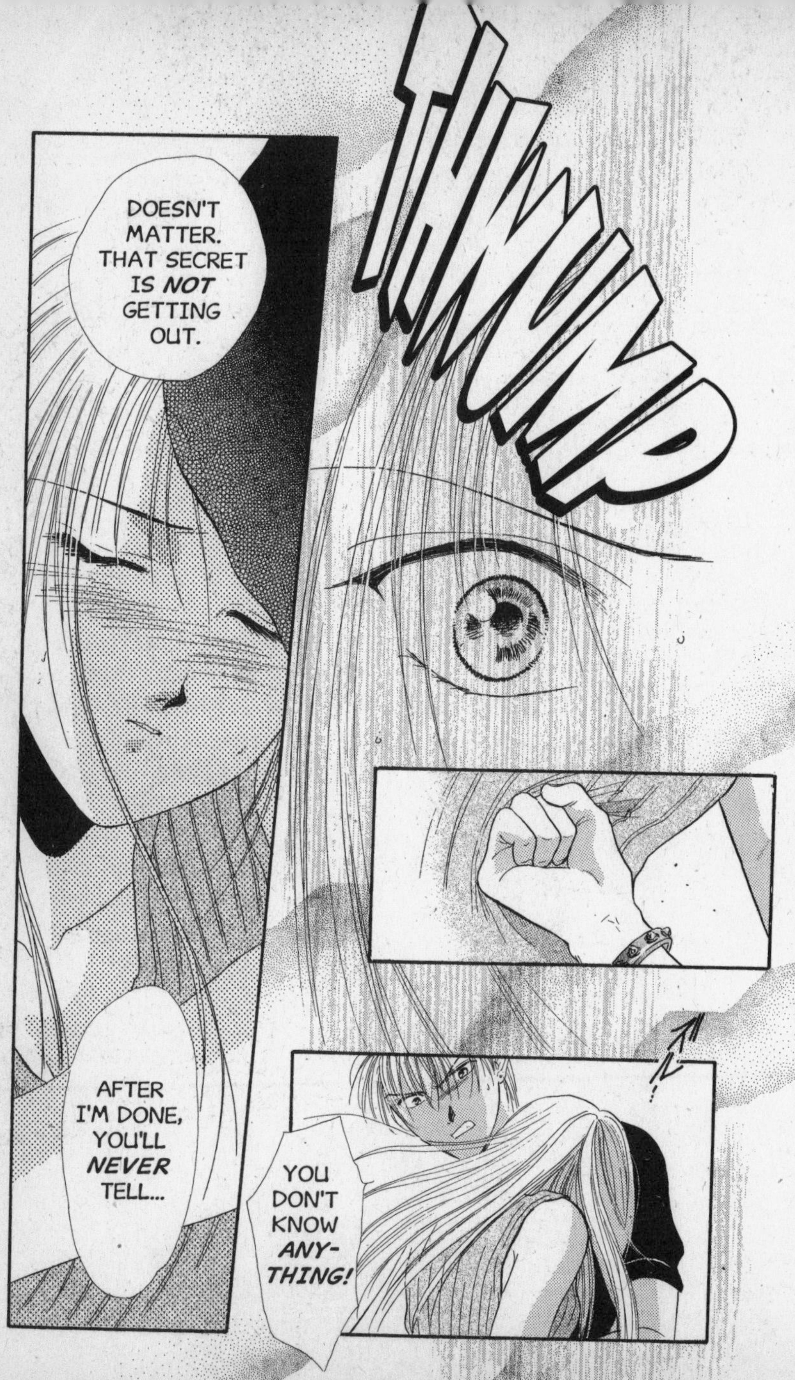
THWUMP
YOU DON'T KNOW ANYTHING!
DOESN'T MATTER. THAT SECRET IS NOT GETTING OUT.
AFTER I'M DONE, YOU'LL NEVER TELL...

BIRTHDAY October 8,   Libra (30)

BLOOD TYPE   AB

T. 183"   HOBBY Classical music

Fluent in 12 languages. Indisputable polymath.

Engaged to the daughter
of a major bank president

KAGAMI MIKAGE

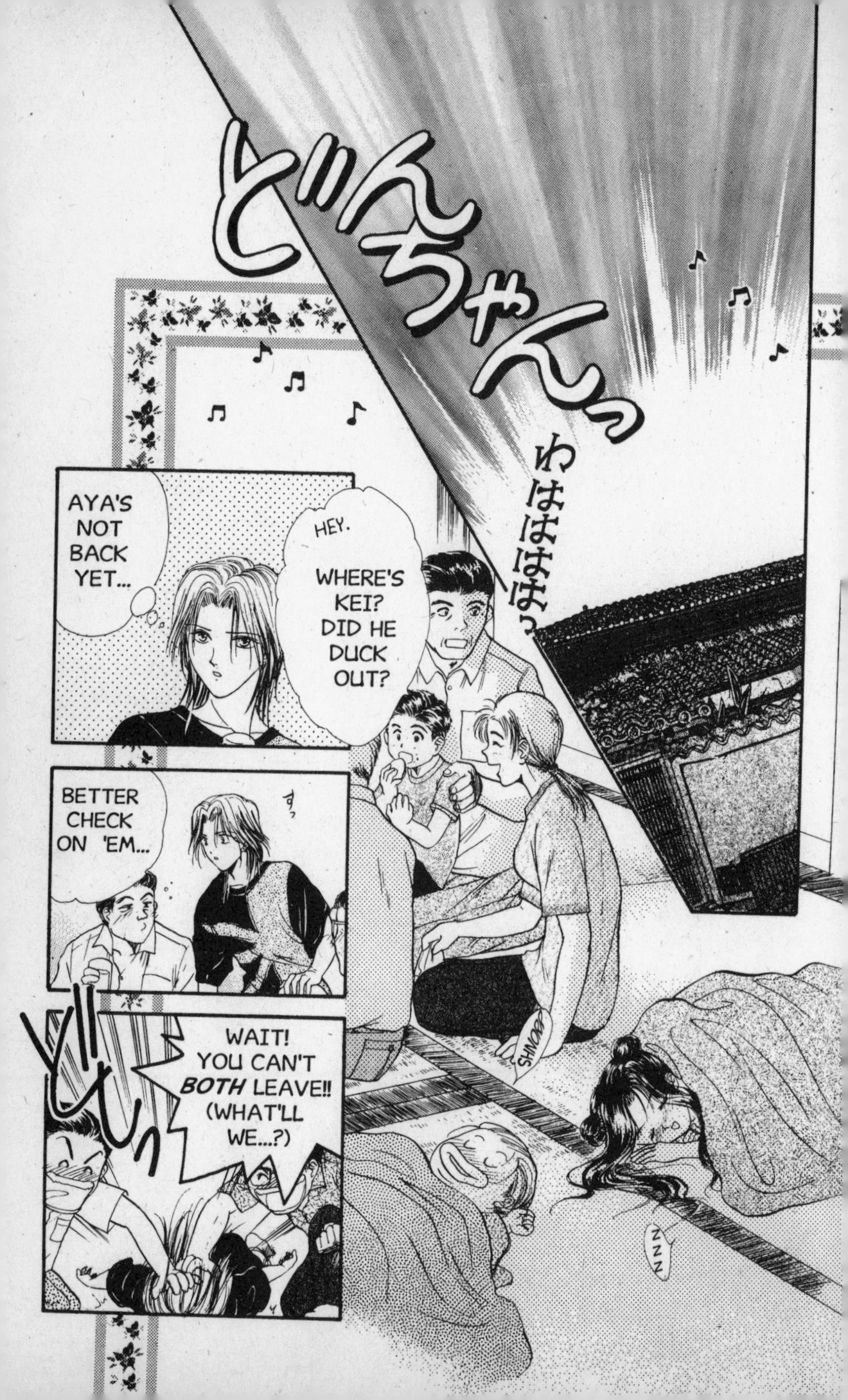
どんちゃんっ
わはははっ
SHNORR
NNN
HEY. WHERE'S KEI? DID HE DUCK OUT?
AYA'S NOT BACK YET...
すっ
BETTER CHECK ON 'EM...
WAIT! YOU CAN'T *BOTH* LEAVE!! (WHAT'LL WE...?)

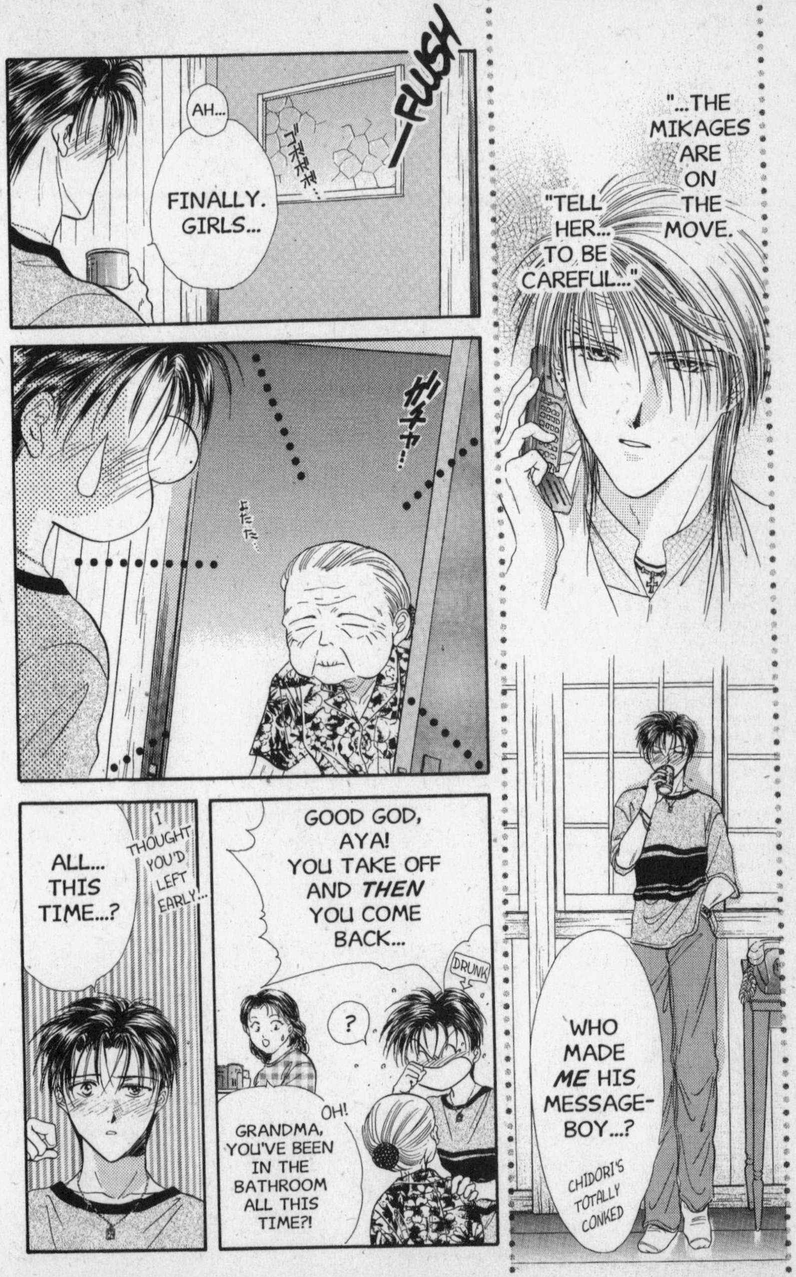
"...THE MIKAGES ARE ON THE MOVE.
"TELL HER... TO BE CAREFUL..."
WHO MADE ME HIS MESSAGE-BOY...?
CHIDORI'S TOTALLY CONKED
FLUSH
AH...
FINALLY. GIRLS...
ガチャ…
よたた…
GOOD GOD, AYA! YOU TAKE OFF AND *THEN* YOU COME BACK...
DRUNK
?
OH!
GRANDMA, YOU'VE BEEN IN THE BATHROOM ALL THIS TIME?!
ALL... THIS TIME...?
I THOUGHT YOU'D LEFT EARLY...

✦ Shuro ✦

Now for a review...or, maybe not. Still, I'd like to talk about the characters a bit, so we can all get a better idea where they're coming from.

First our main character, Aya. Perhaps you got the early impression that Aya's different from previous Watase characters—she's so the typical, teenage girl of her time. She bleaches her hair, wears loose socks, has pierced ears, loves karaoke, and has overall too much time on her hands.
She doesn't do the fake tan thing, though.
Until Aya, a lot of my characters were more like manga caricatures (good at all sports, able to eat massive amounts of food). None of that for her, though. She's just a little rough in her language, and is a bit outrageous (not that turning into Ceres isn't itself outrageous enough...). I wanted her to be someone you'd see walking on the street. If I were in her class, I might have steered clear of her—maybe not someone I'd have been friends with. Readers have written to say that they don't like her because she **is** so much the trend-following teen. Eventually, though, I think they've come not only to feel for her, but to root for her, as well. :-)

Not to say Aya doesn't have her pride. She's had her fun, yeah, but she's basically a good girl. She's innocent, in a sense.

What I **didn't** want for her was to be the stereotypical "main character," the kind who goes beyond being simply "nice," approaching "in your face," instead. My assistant pointed out how quickly Aya backed off when (in Volume 3) Urakawa snubbed her—she felt that had been realistic. A typical main character might have persisted anyway, but I don't care for that. Aya's not apathetic, but she's no save-the-world type, either. When she bum-rushed that purse-snatcher back at the beginning, it was because letting him get away with it was unthinkable. She's her own person.
People have said she's like "Yui" from Fushigi Yûgi that way.

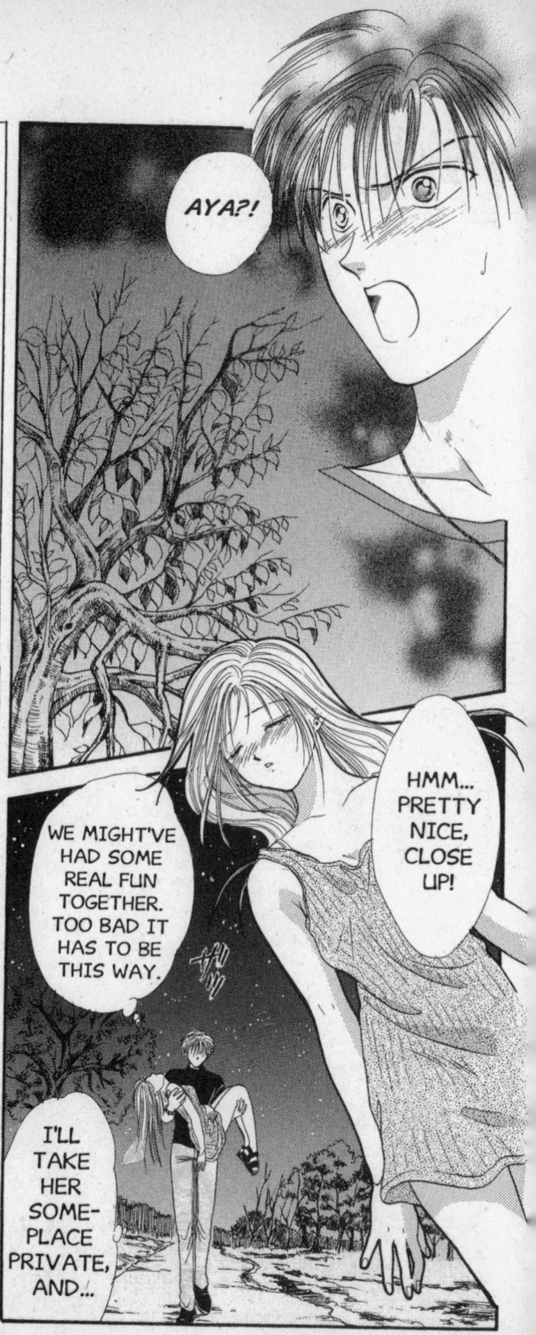
AYA?!
HMM... PRETTY NICE, CLOSE UP!
WE MIGHT'VE HAD SOME REAL FUN TOGETHER. TOO BAD IT HAS TO BE THIS WAY.
I'LL TAKE HER SOME-PLACE PRIVATE, AND...

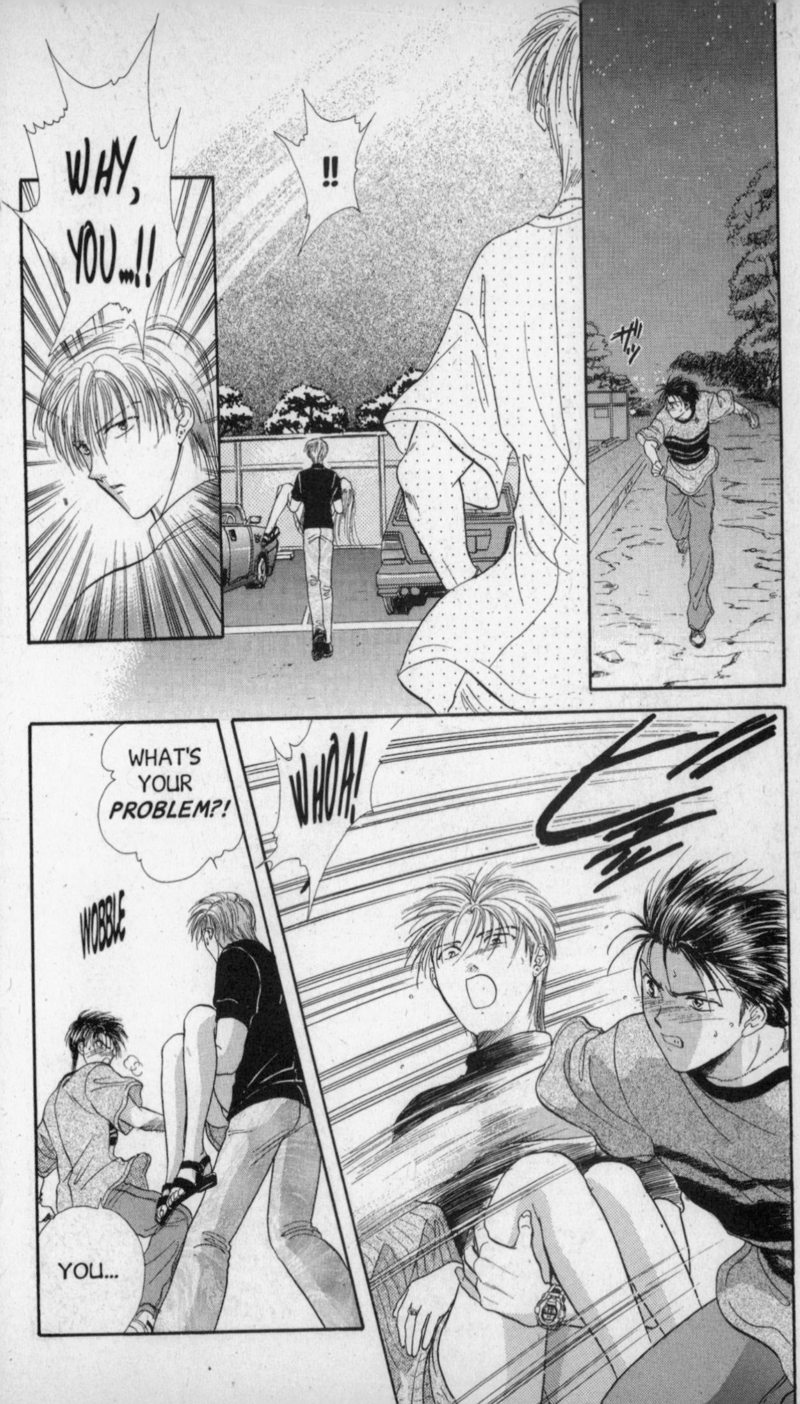
!!
WHY, YOU...!!
WHOA!
WHAT'S YOUR PROBLEM?!
WOBBLE
YOU...

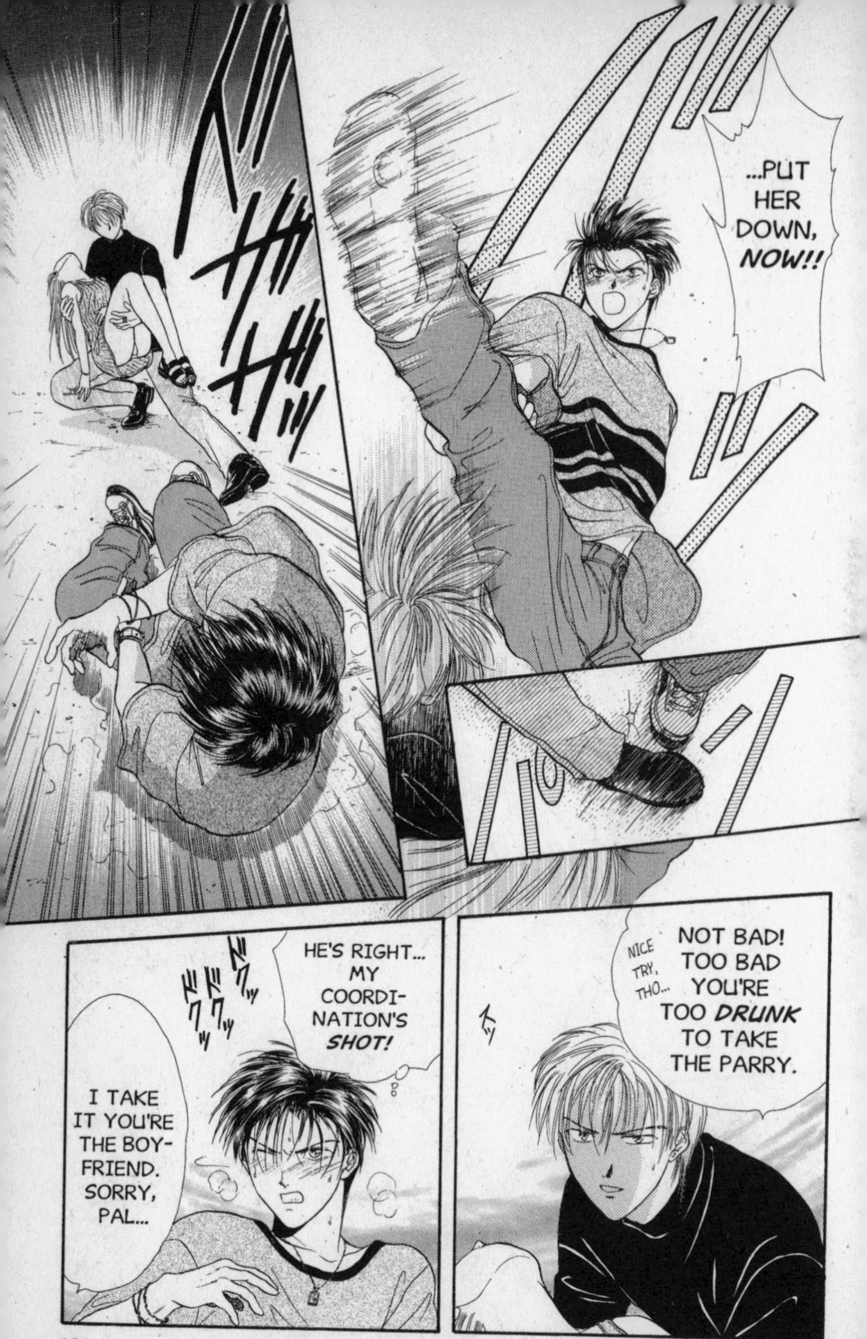
...PUT HER DOWN, *NOW!!*
NOT BAD! TOO BAD YOU'RE TOO *DRUNK* TO TAKE THE PARRY.
NICE TRY, THO...
HE'S RIGHT... MY COORDINATION'S *SHOT!*
I TAKE IT YOU'RE THE BOYFRIEND. SORRY, PAL...

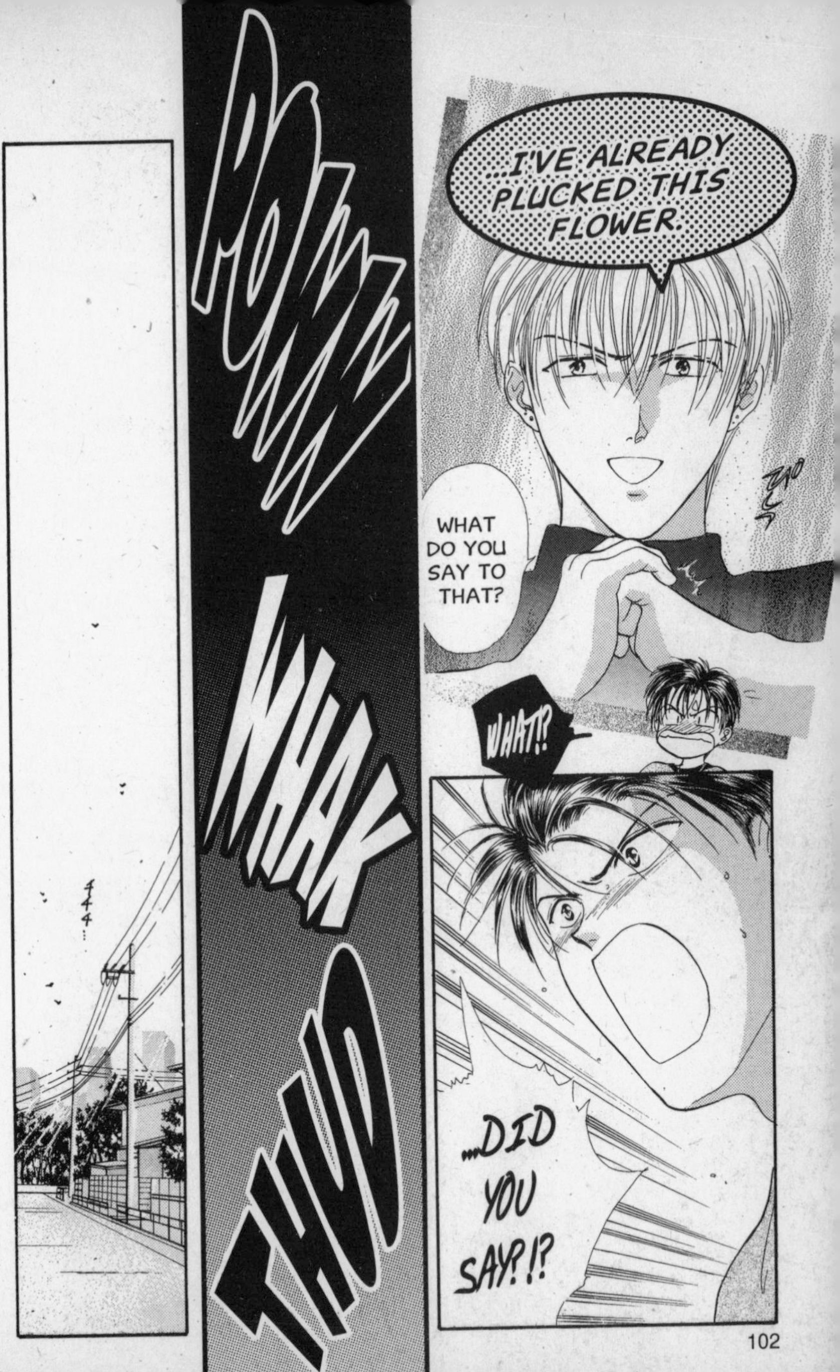
...I'VE ALREADY PLUCKED THIS FLOWER.
WHAT DO YOU SAY TO THAT?
WHAT!?
...DID YOU SAY?!?
POW
WHAK
THUD

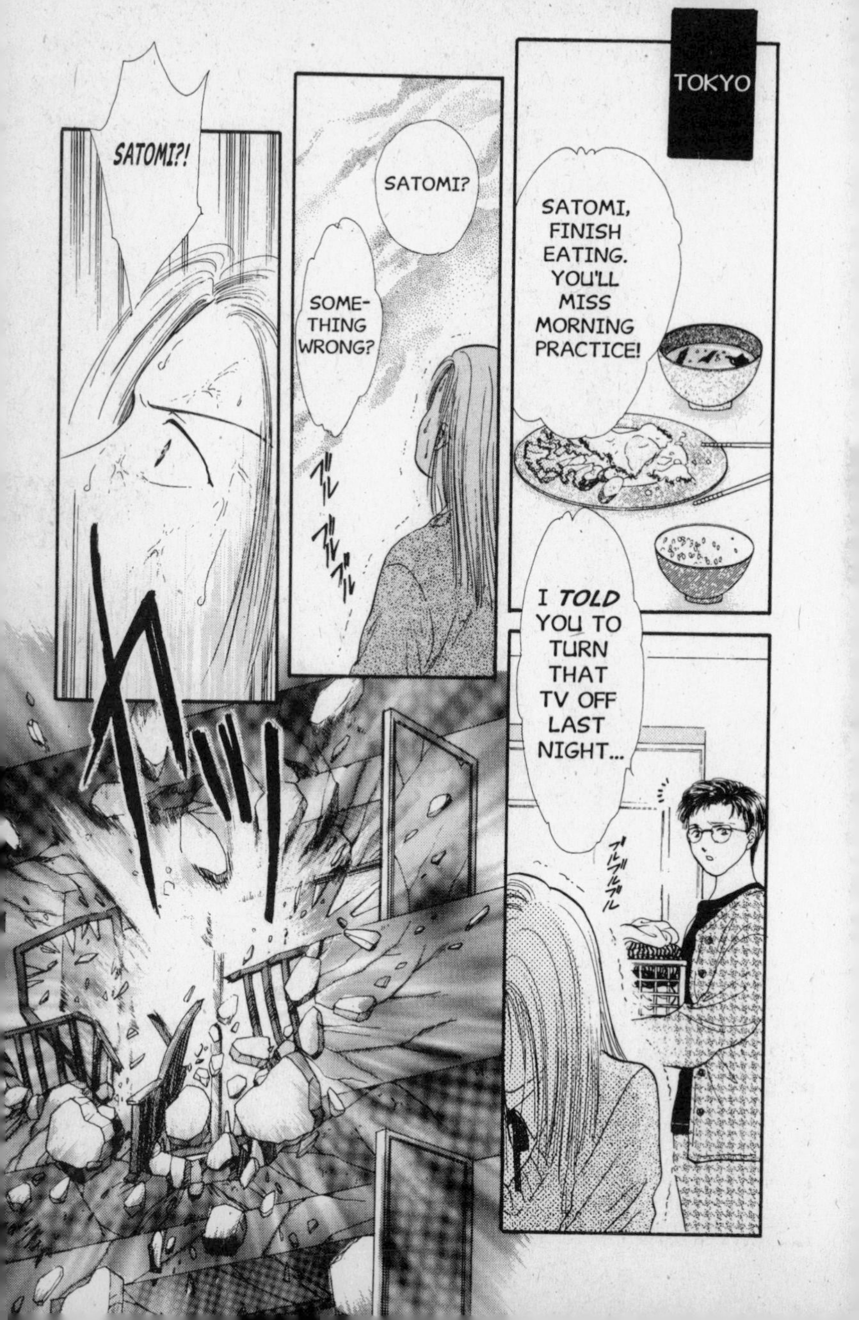
TOKYO
SATOMI, FINISH EATING. YOU'LL MISS MORNING PRACTICE!
I *TOLD* YOU TO TURN THAT TV OFF LAST NIGHT...
ブルブルブル
SATOMI?
SOME-THING WRONG?
ブルブルブル
SATOMI?!

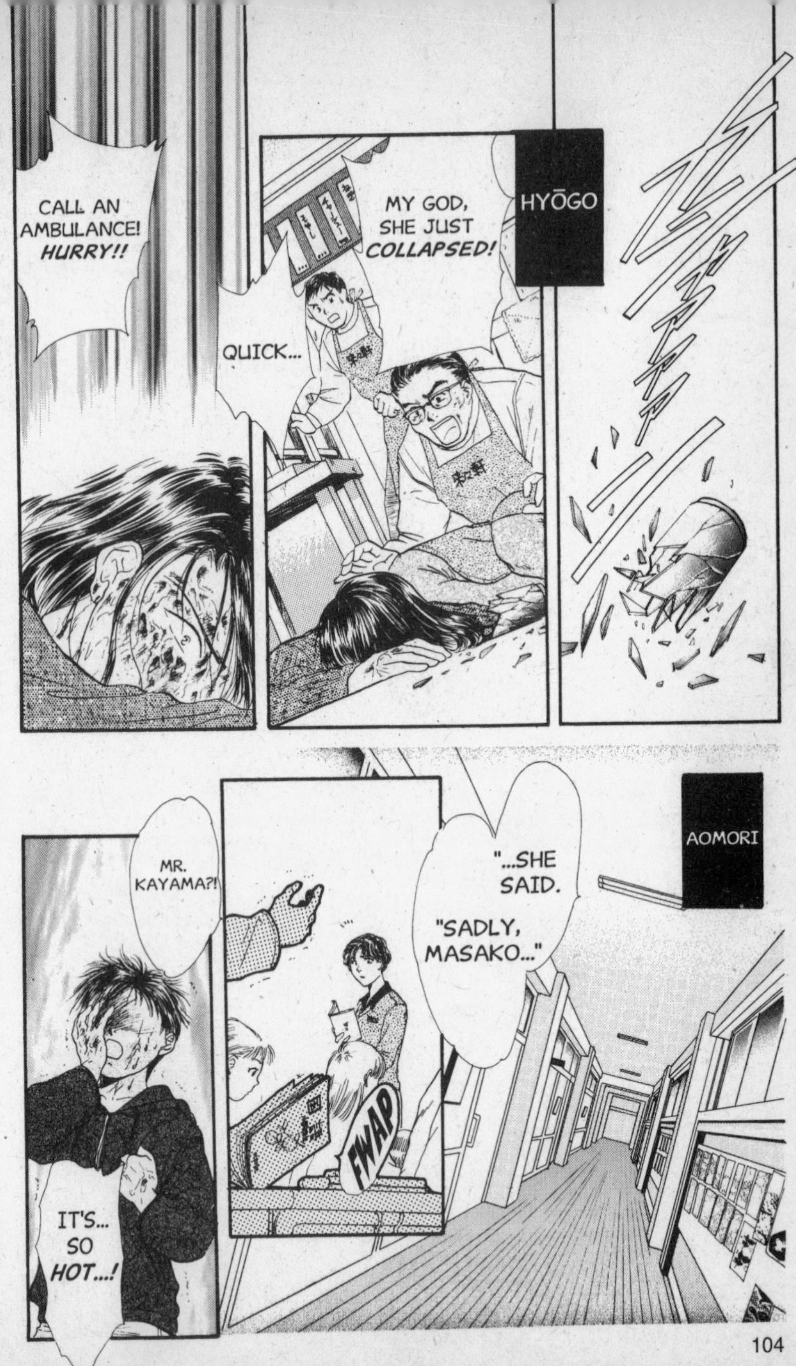
HYŌGO
MY GOD, SHE JUST *COLLAPSED!*
QUICK...
CALL AN AMBULANCE! *HURRY!!*
AOMORI
"...SHE SAID.
"SADLY, MASAKO..."
FWAP
MR. KAYAMA?!
IT'S... SO *HOT...!*

Ceres: 6

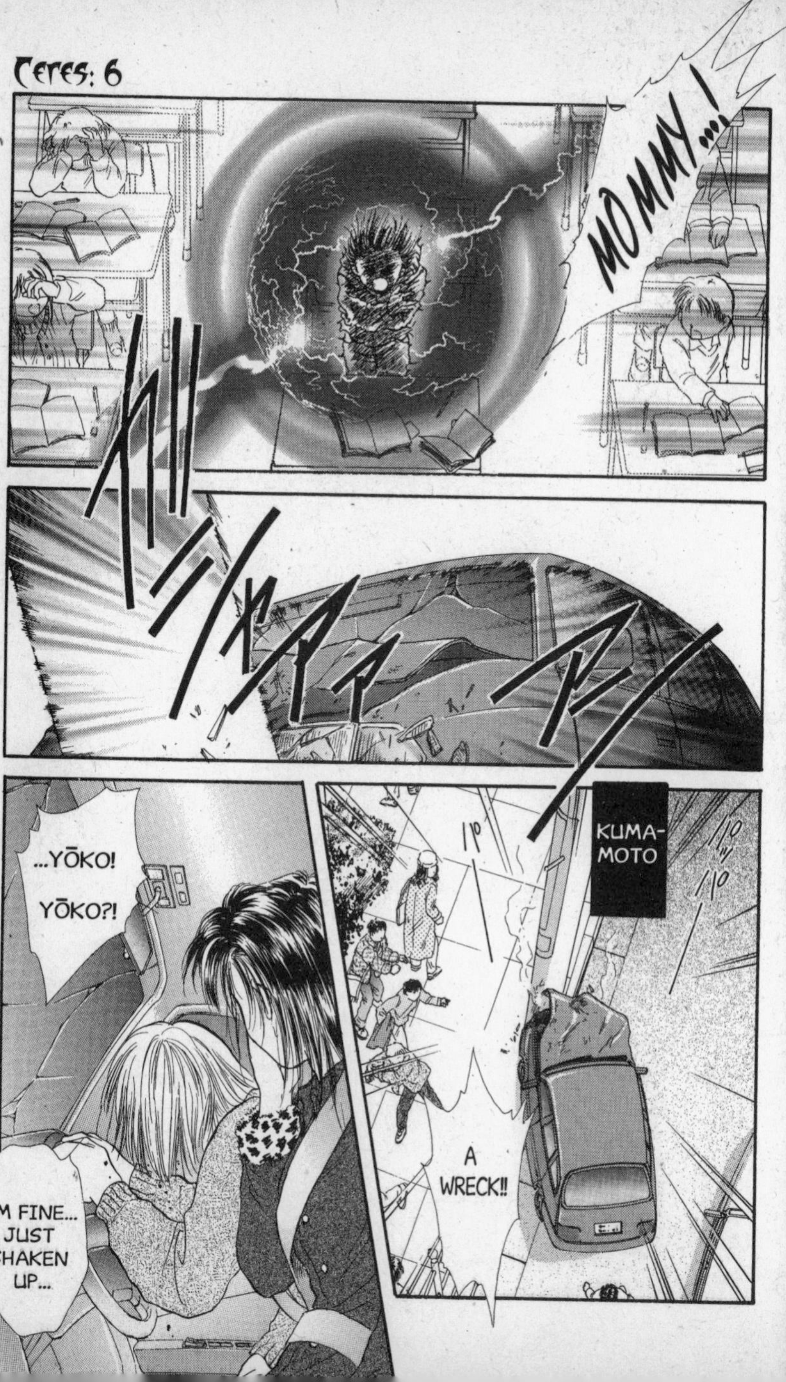
MOMMY...!
KUMAMOTO
A WRECK!!
...YŌKO!
YŌKO?!
I'M FINE... JUST SHAKEN UP...

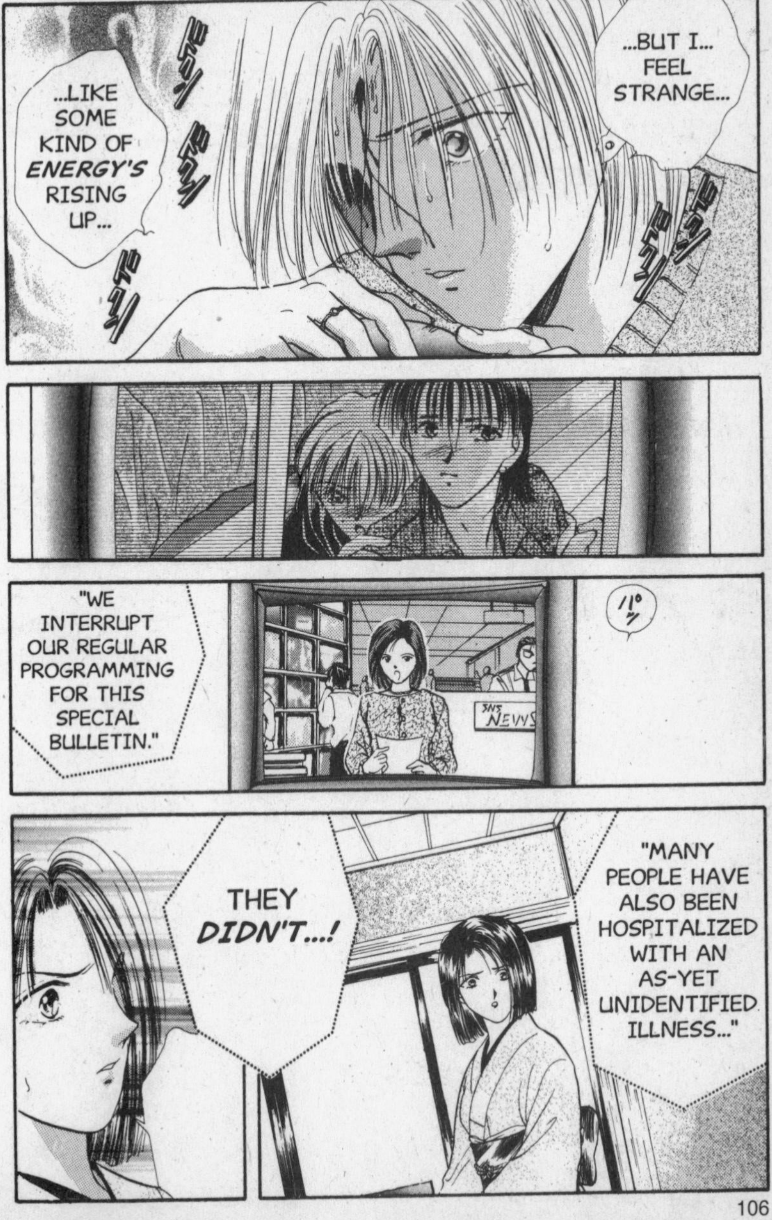
...BUT I... FEEL STRANGE...
...LIKE SOME KIND OF *ENERGY'S* RISING UP...
パッ
"WE INTERRUPT OUR REGULAR PROGRAMMING FOR THIS SPECIAL BULLETIN."
"MANY PEOPLE HAVE ALSO BEEN HOSPITALIZED WITH AN AS-YET UNIDENTIFIED ILLNESS..."
THEY *DIDN'T*...!

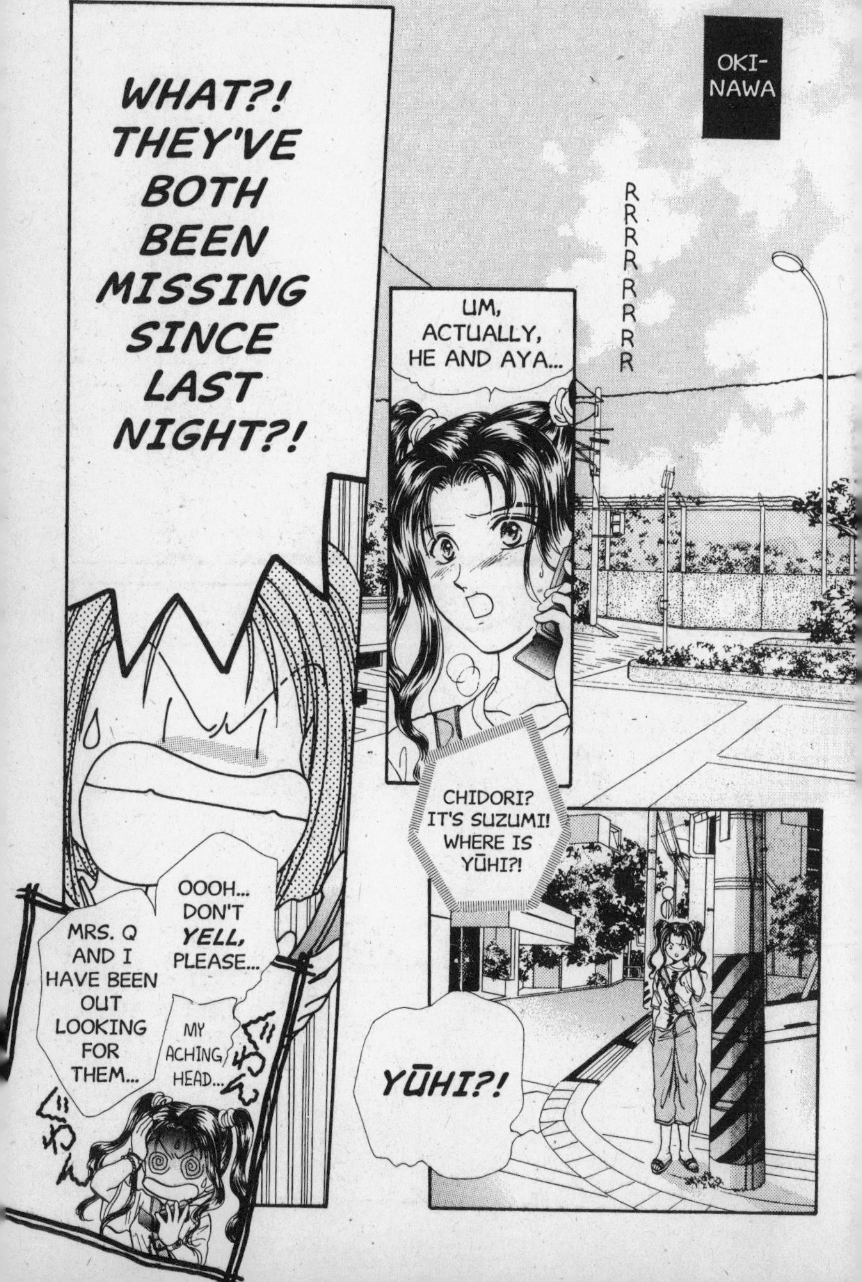
OKI-
NAWA
RRRRRRR
CHIDORI? IT'S SUZUMI! WHERE IS YŪHI?!
YŪHI?!
UM, ACTUALLY, HE AND AYA...
WHAT?! THEY'VE BOTH BEEN MISSING SINCE LAST NIGHT?!
OOOH... DON'T YELL, PLEASE...
MRS. Q AND I HAVE BEEN OUT LOOKING FOR THEM...
MY ACHING HEAD...

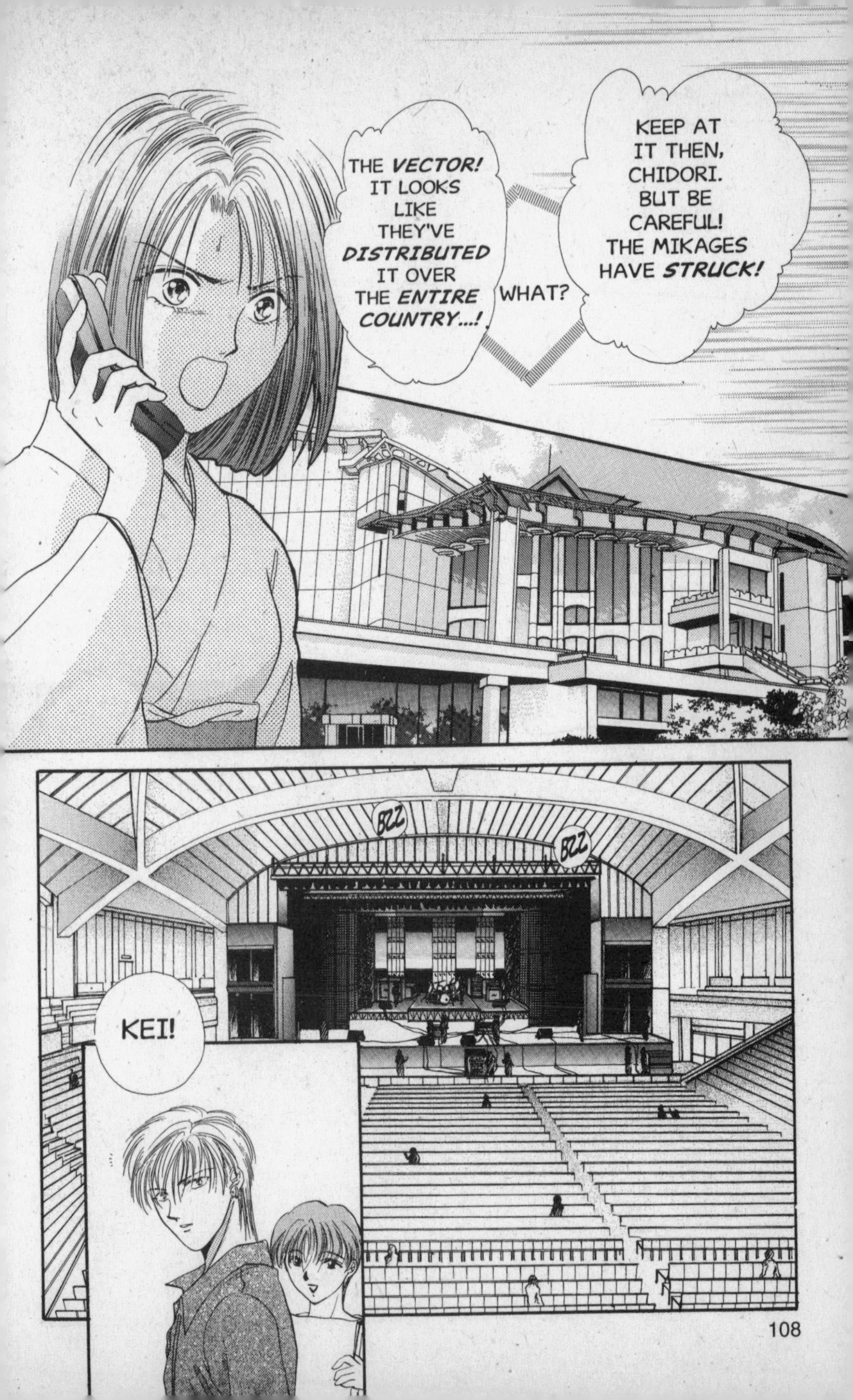
KEEP AT IT THEN, CHIDORI. BUT BE CAREFUL! THE MIKAGES HAVE STRUCK!
WHAT?
THE VECTOR! IT LOOKS LIKE THEY'VE DISTRIBUTED IT OVER THE ENTIRE COUNTRY...!
BZZ
BZZ
KEI!

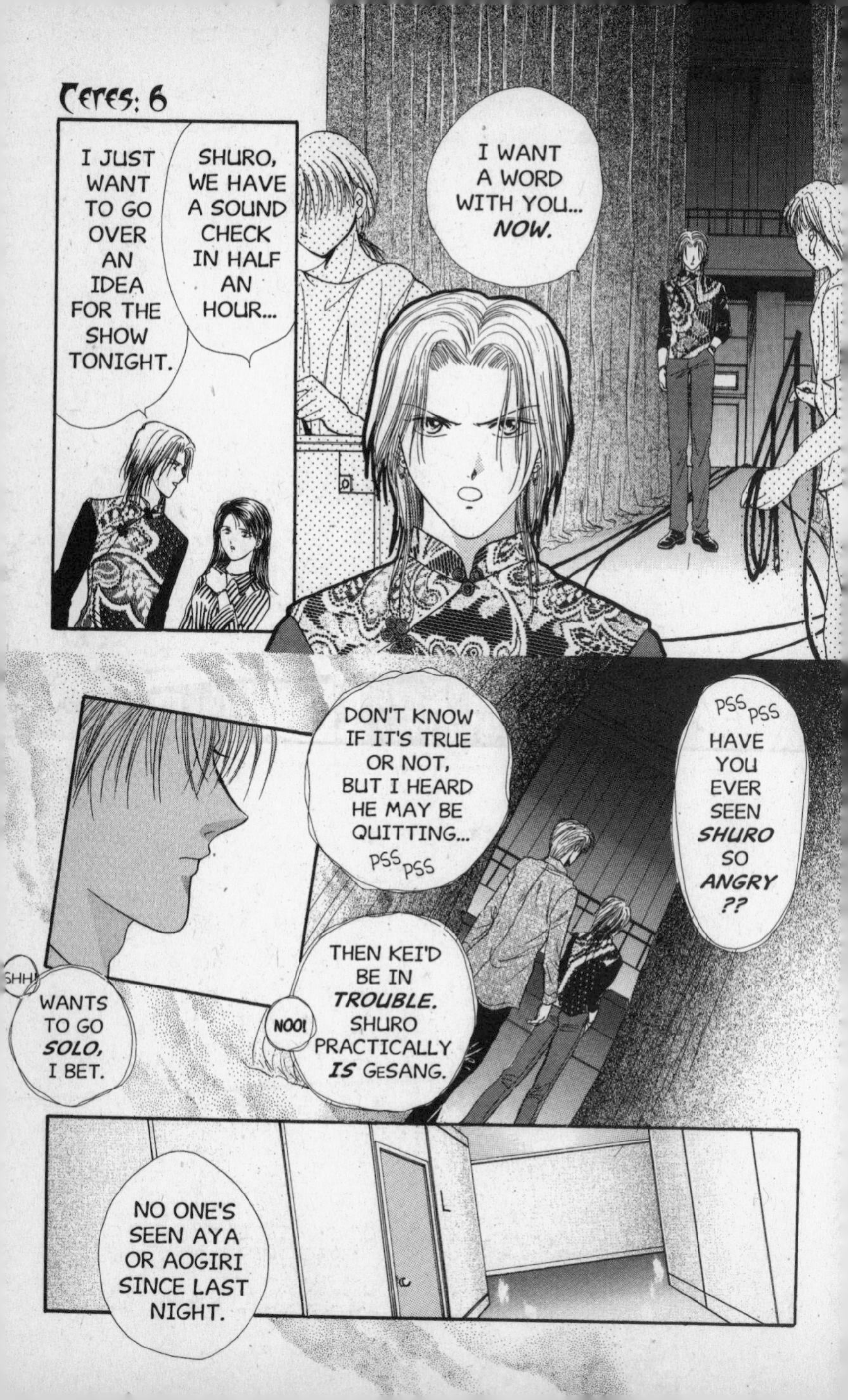
I WANT A WORD WITH YOU... NOW.
SHURO, WE HAVE A SOUND CHECK IN HALF AN HOUR...
I JUST WANT TO GO OVER AN IDEA FOR THE SHOW TONIGHT.
PSS PSS
HAVE YOU EVER SEEN SHURO SO ANGRY??
DON'T KNOW IF IT'S TRUE OR NOT, BUT I HEARD HE MAY BE QUITTING...
PSS PSS
THEN KEI'D BE IN TROUBLE. SHURO PRACTICALLY IS GESANG.
NOO!
SHH!
WANTS TO GO SOLO, I BET.
NO ONE'S SEEN AYA OR AOGIRI SINCE LAST NIGHT.

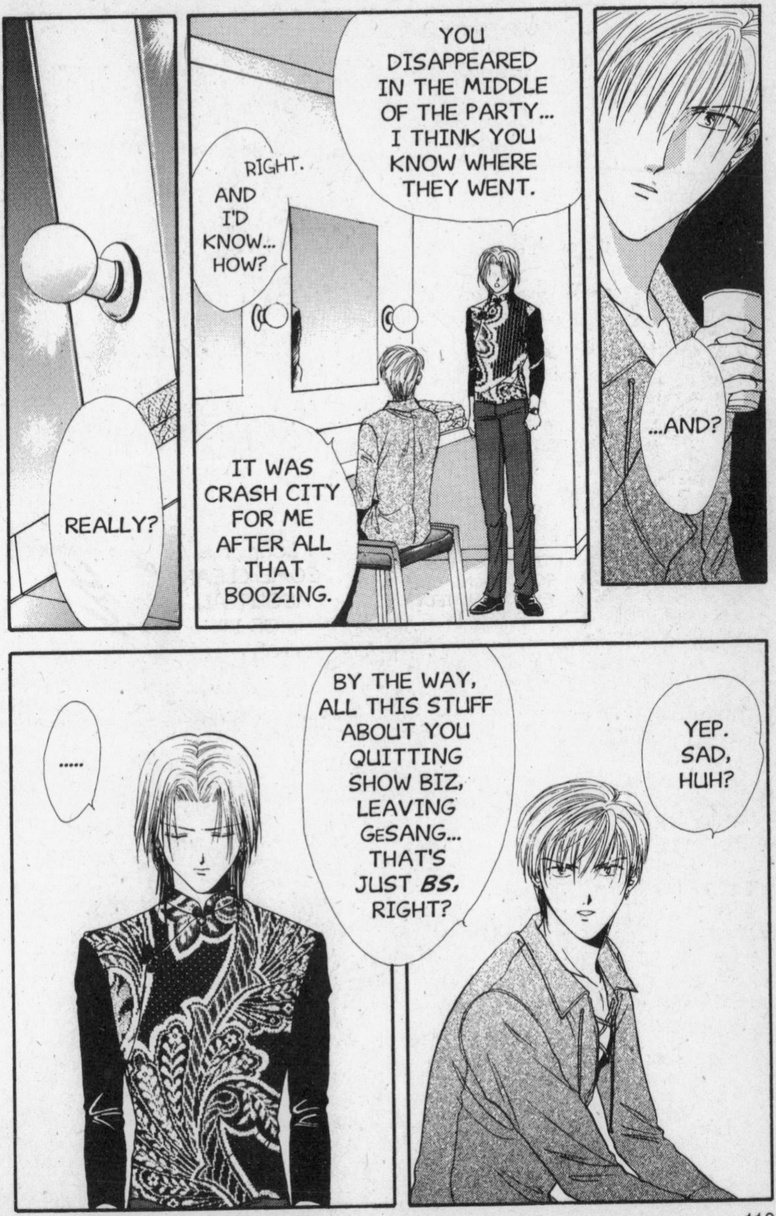
...AND?
YOU DISAPPEARED IN THE MIDDLE OF THE PARTY... I THINK YOU KNOW WHERE THEY WENT.
RIGHT. AND I'D KNOW... HOW?
IT WAS CRASH CITY FOR ME AFTER ALL THAT BOOZING.
REALLY?
YEP. SAD, HUH?
BY THE WAY, ALL THIS STUFF ABOUT YOU QUITTING SHOW BIZ, LEAVING GESANG... THAT'S JUST *BS,* RIGHT?
.....

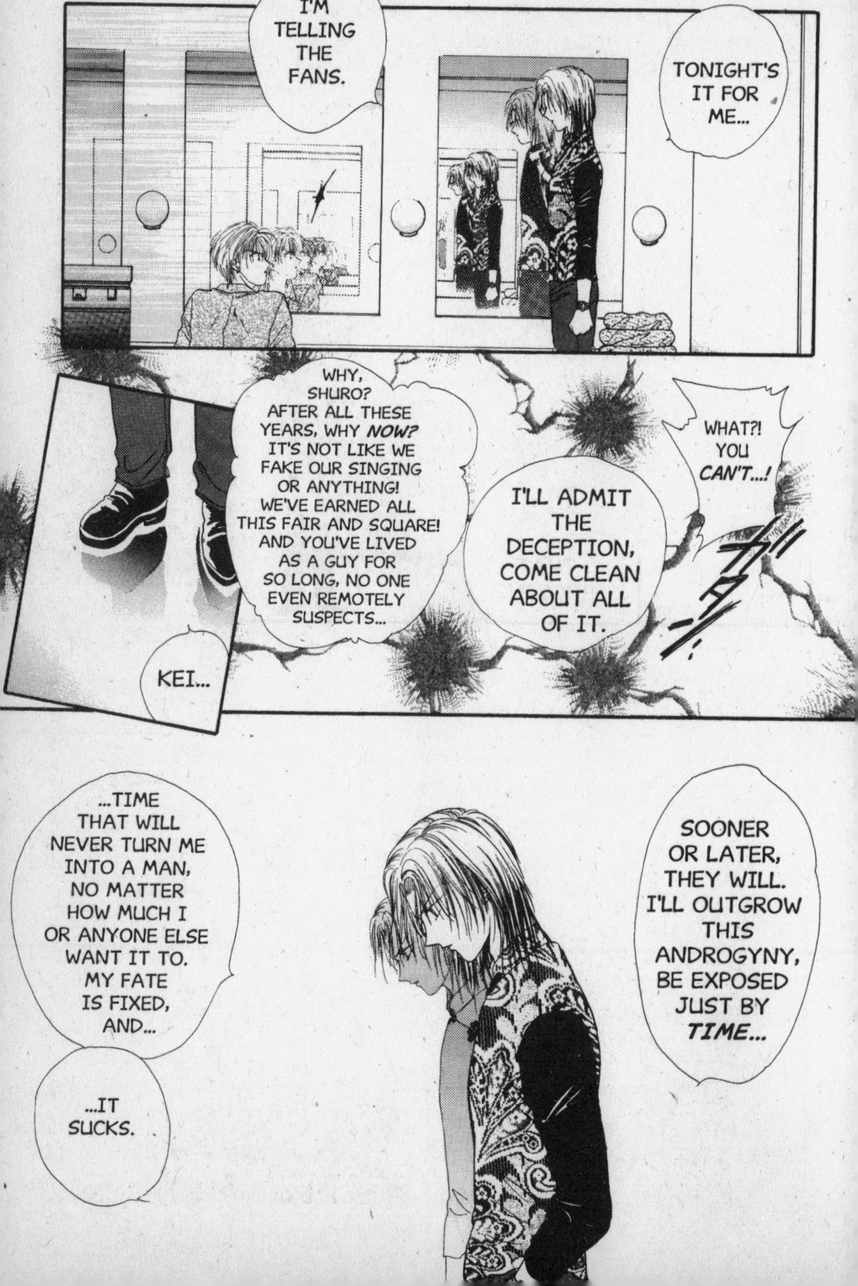
TONIGHT'S IT FOR ME...
I'M TELLING THE FANS.
WHAT?! YOU *CAN'T...!*
I'LL ADMIT THE DECEPTION, COME CLEAN ABOUT ALL OF IT.
WHY, SHURO? AFTER ALL THESE YEARS, WHY *NOW?* IT'S NOT LIKE WE FAKE OUR SINGING OR ANYTHING! WE'VE EARNED ALL THIS FAIR AND SQUARE! AND YOU'VE LIVED AS A GUY FOR SO LONG, NO ONE EVEN REMOTELY SUSPECTS...
KEI...
SOONER OR LATER, THEY WILL. I'LL OUTGROW THIS ANDROGYNY, BE EXPOSED JUST BY *TIME...*
...TIME THAT WILL NEVER TURN ME INTO A MAN, NO MATTER HOW MUCH I OR ANYONE ELSE WANT IT TO. MY FATE IS FIXED, AND...
...IT SUCKS.

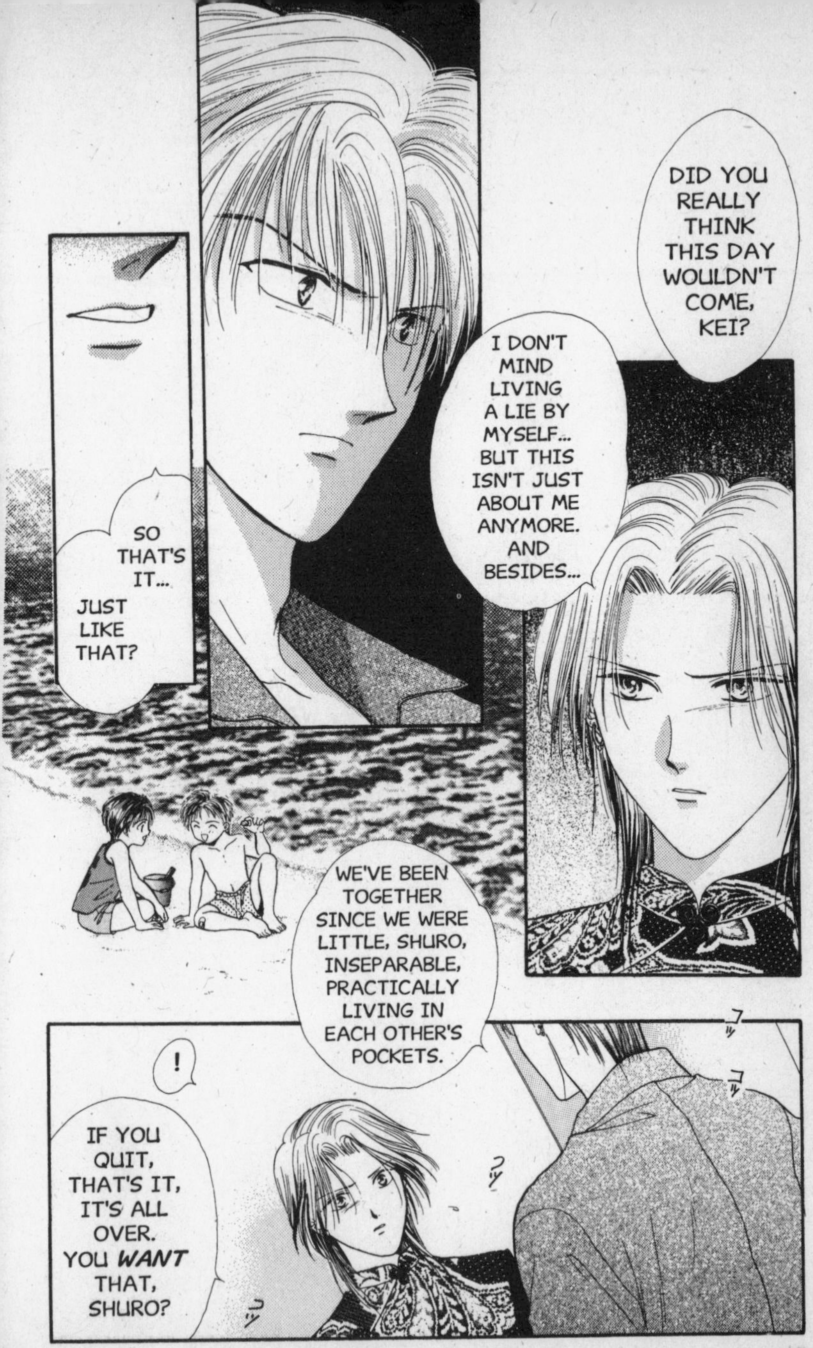
DID YOU REALLY THINK THIS DAY WOULDN'T COME, KEI?
I DON'T MIND LIVING A LIE BY MYSELF... BUT THIS ISN'T JUST ABOUT ME ANYMORE. AND BESIDES...
SO THAT'S IT... JUST LIKE THAT?
WE'VE BEEN TOGETHER SINCE WE WERE LITTLE, SHURO, INSEPARABLE, PRACTICALLY LIVING IN EACH OTHER'S POCKETS.
!
IF YOU QUIT, THAT'S IT, IT'S ALL OVER. YOU *WANT* THAT, SHURO?

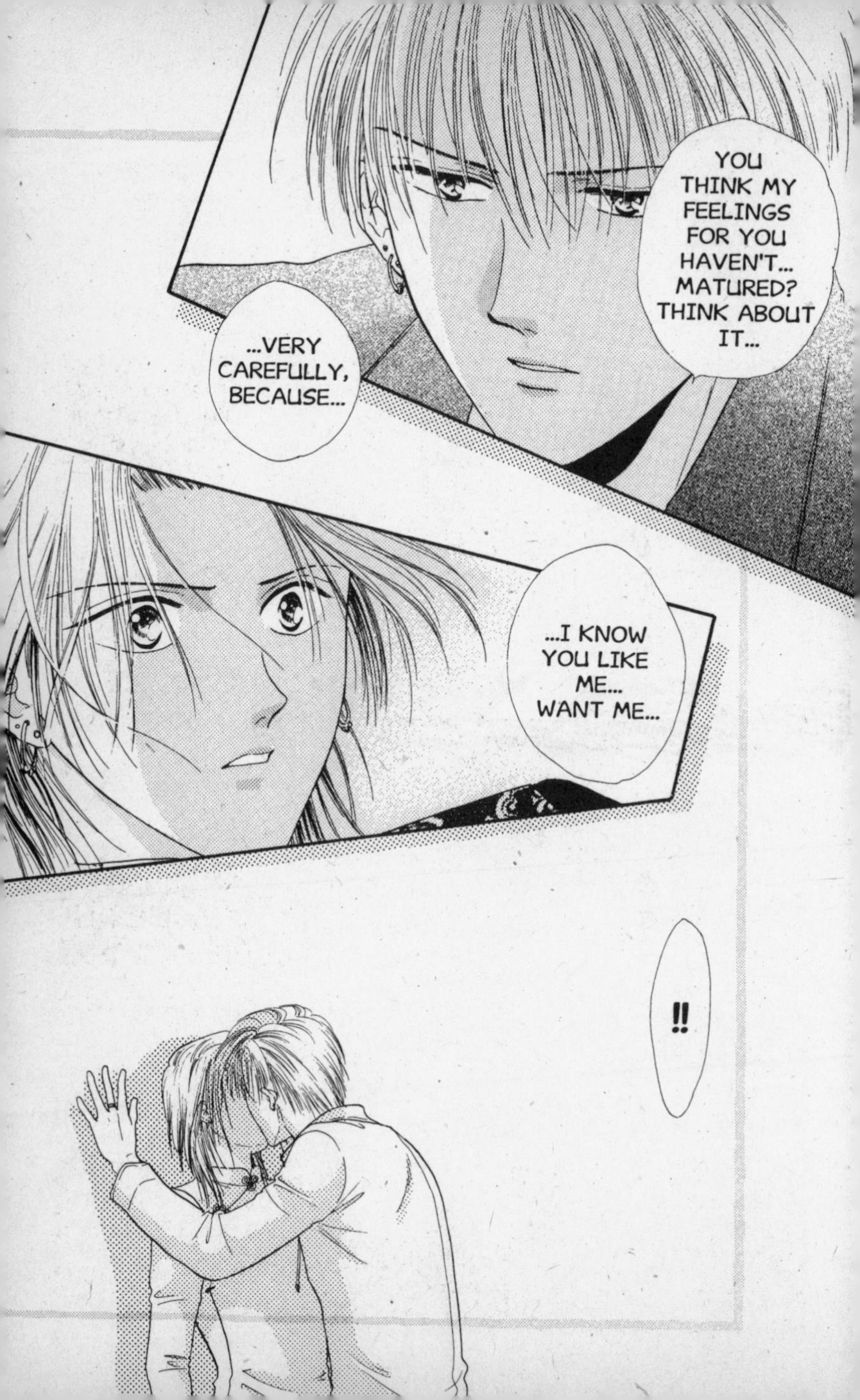
YOU THINK MY FEELINGS FOR YOU HAVEN'T... MATURED? THINK ABOUT IT...
...VERY CAREFULLY, BECAUSE...
...I KNOW YOU LIKE ME... WANT ME...
!!

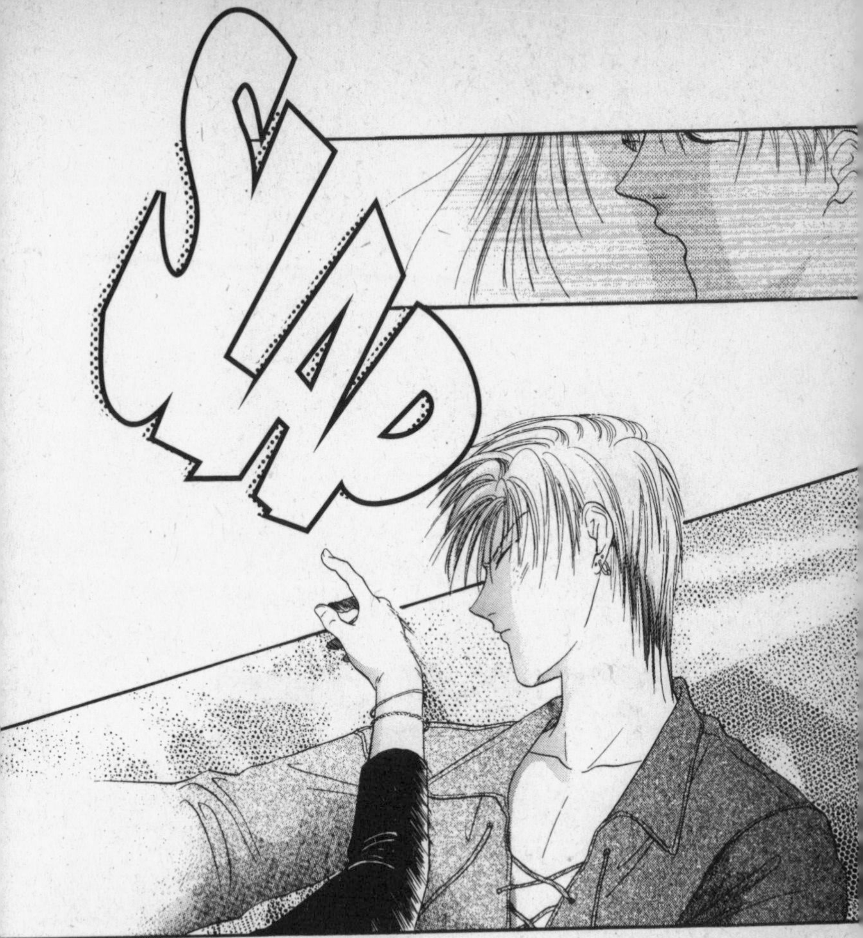
SLAP
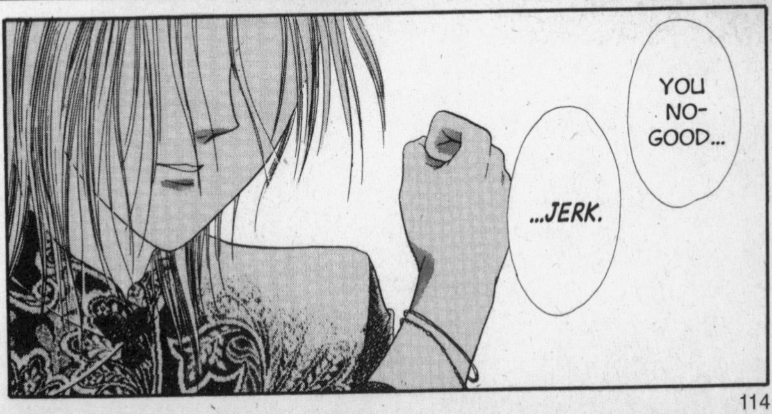
YOU NO-GOOD...
...JERK.

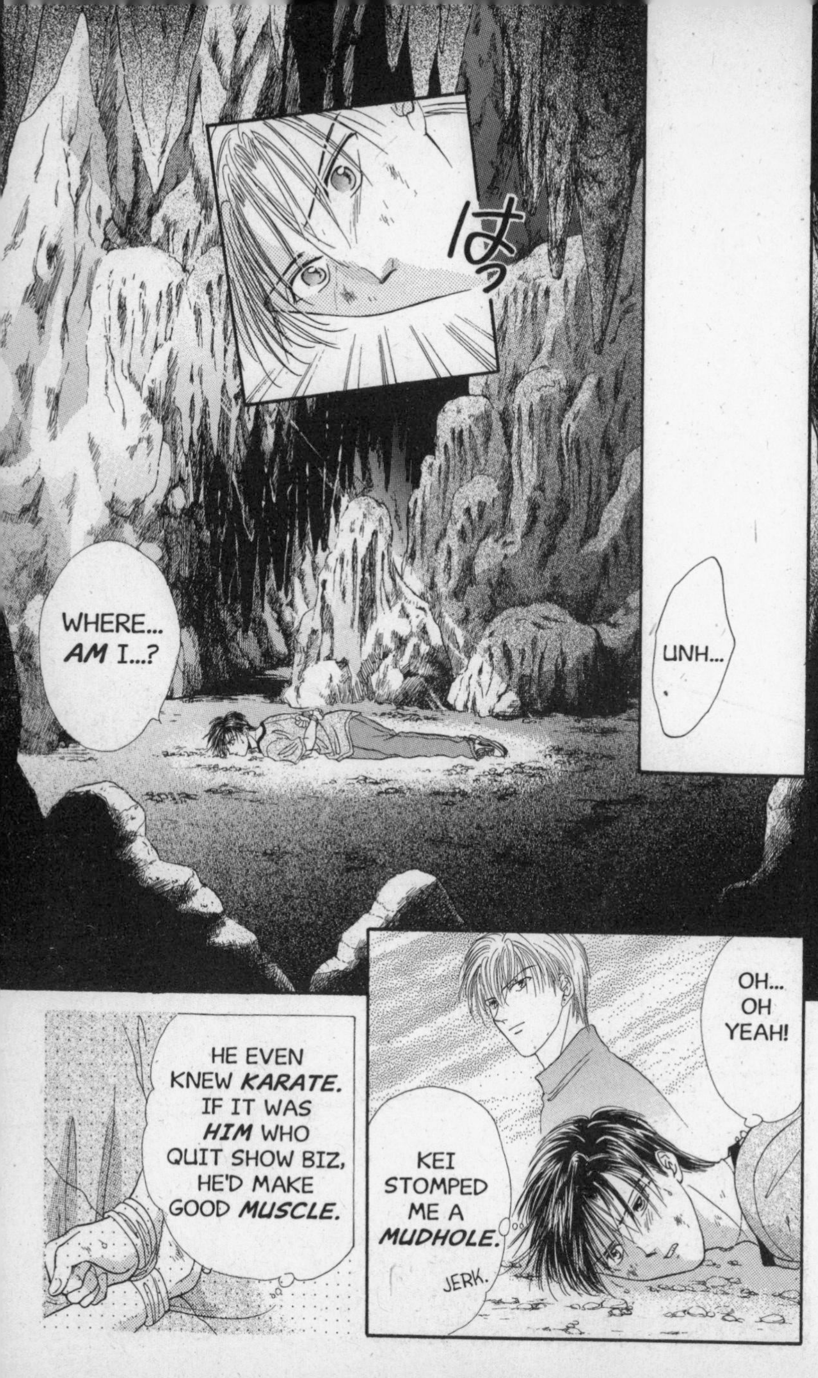
UNH...
はっ
WHERE... AM I...?
OH... OH YEAH!
KEI STOMPED ME A MUDHOLE.
JERK.
HE EVEN KNEW KARATE. IF IT WAS HIM WHO QUIT SHOW BIZ, HE'D MAKE GOOD MUSCLE.

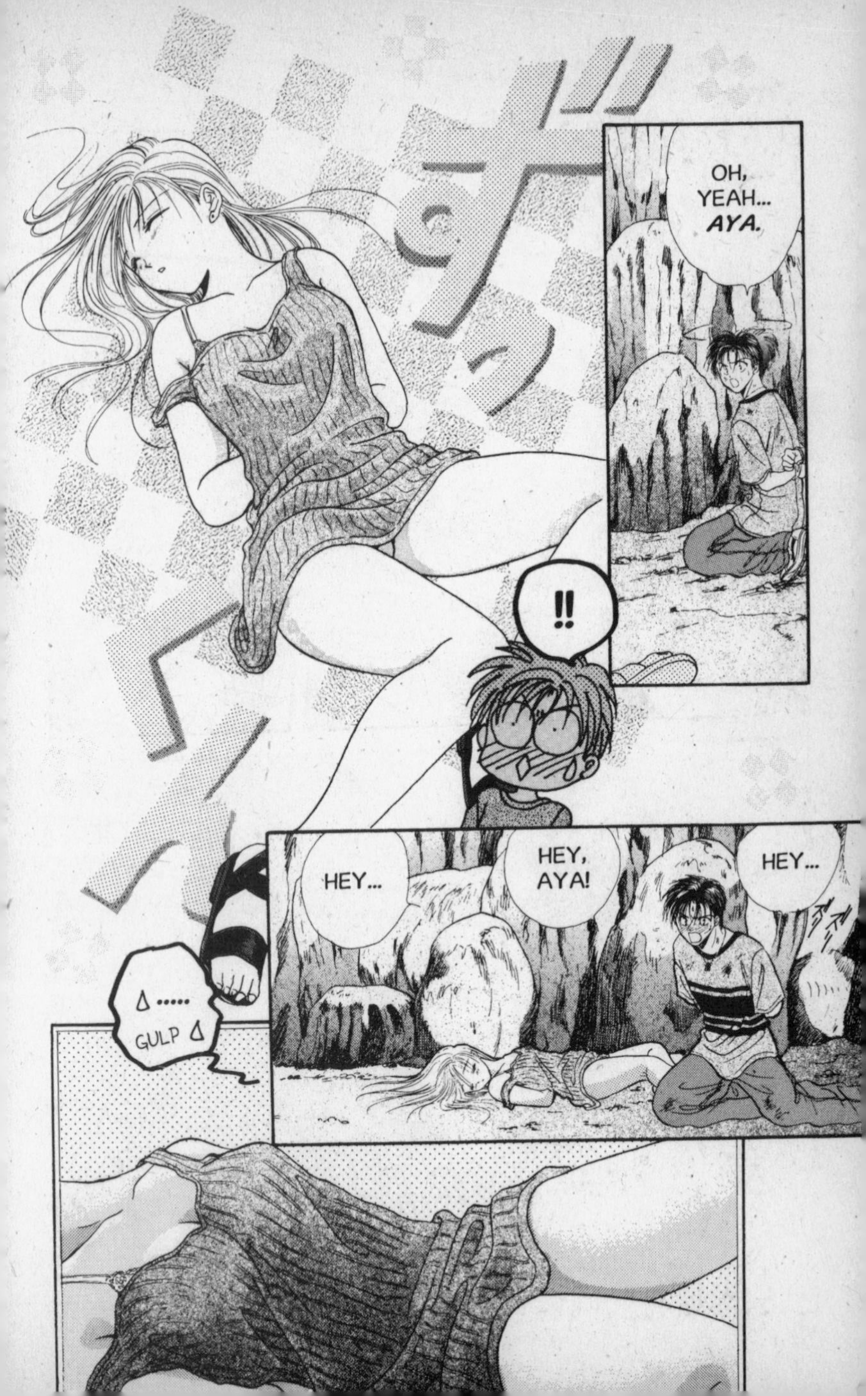
OH, YEAH... *AYA.*
!!
HEY...
HEY, AYA!
HEY...
......
GULP

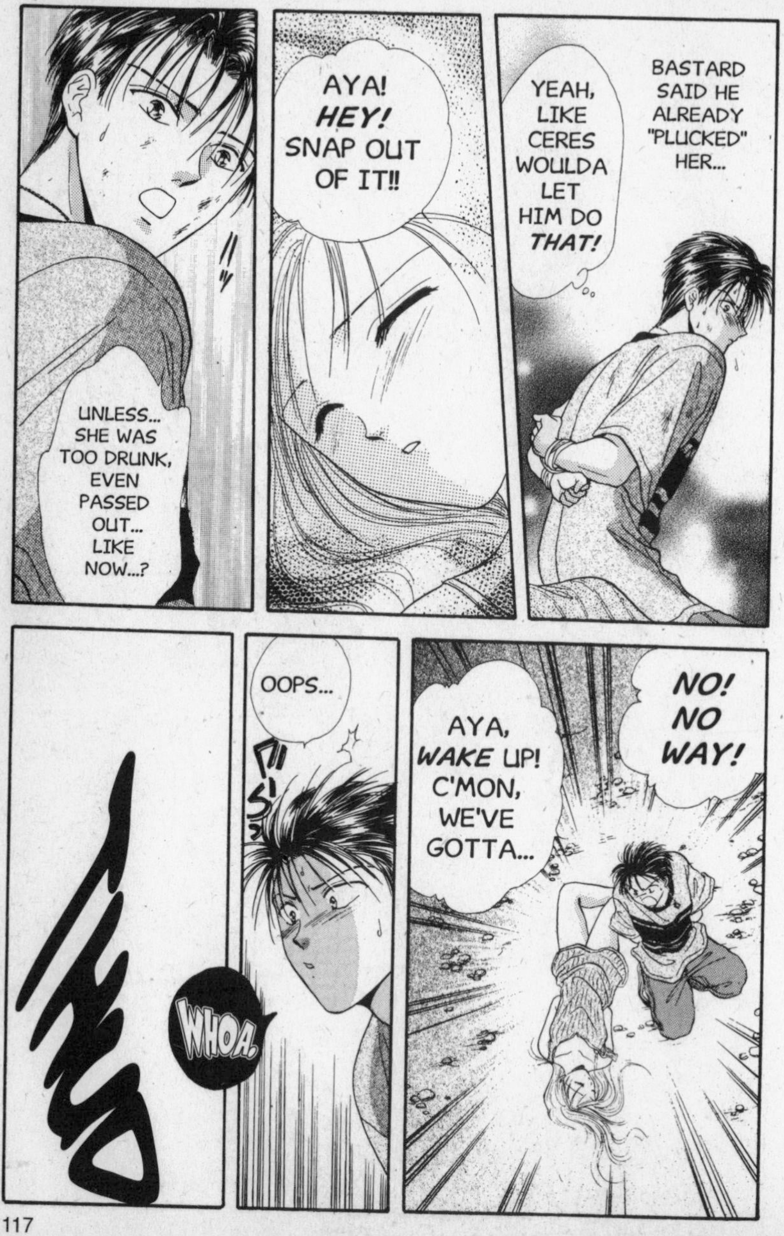
BASTARD SAID HE ALREADY "PLUCKED" HER...
YEAH, LIKE CERES WOULDA LET HIM DO *THAT!*
AYA! *HEY!* SNAP OUT OF IT!!
UNLESS... SHE WAS TOO DRUNK, EVEN PASSED OUT... LIKE NOW...?
NO! NO WAY!
AYA, *WAKE* UP! C'MON, WE'VE GOTTA...
OOPS...
WHOA.

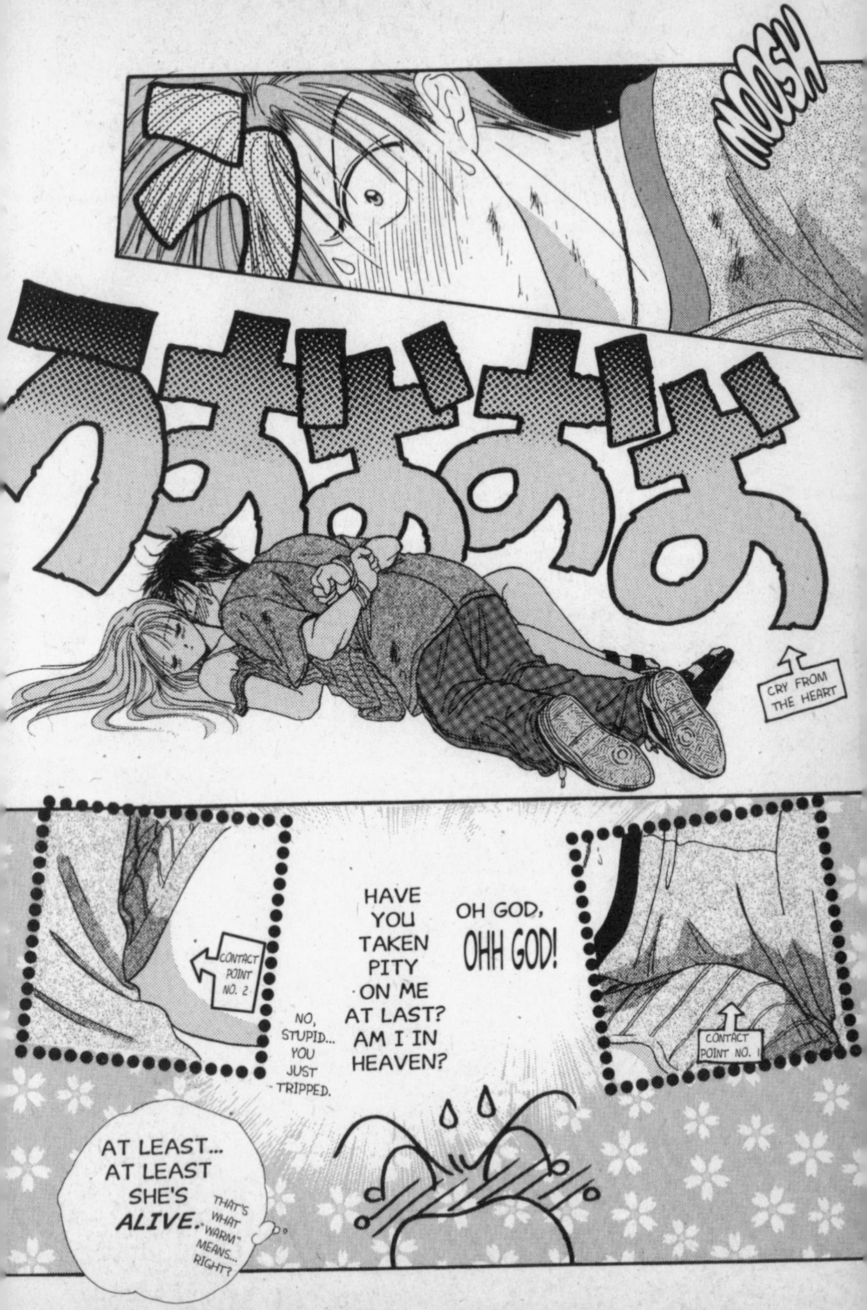
WHOOSH!
CRY FROM THE HEART
CONTACT POINT NO. 1
OH GOD, OHH GOD!
HAVE YOU TAKEN PITY ON ME AT LAST? AM I IN HEAVEN?
NO, STUPID... YOU JUST TRIPPED.
CONTACT POINT NO. 2
AT LEAST... AT LEAST SHE'S *ALIVE*.
THAT'S WHAT "WARM" MEANS... RIGHT?

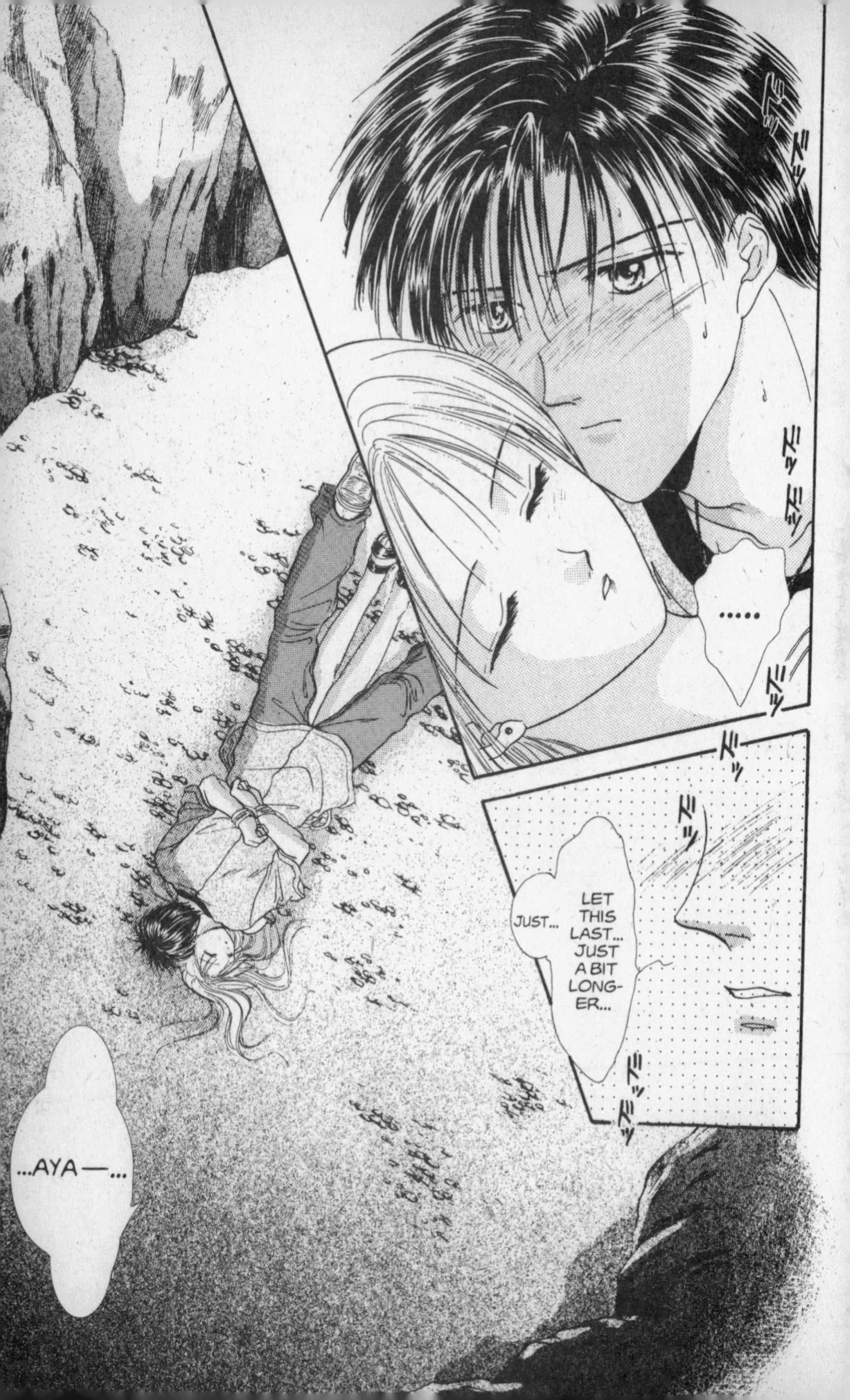
.....
JUST...
LET THIS LAST... JUST A BIT LONGER...
...AYA—...

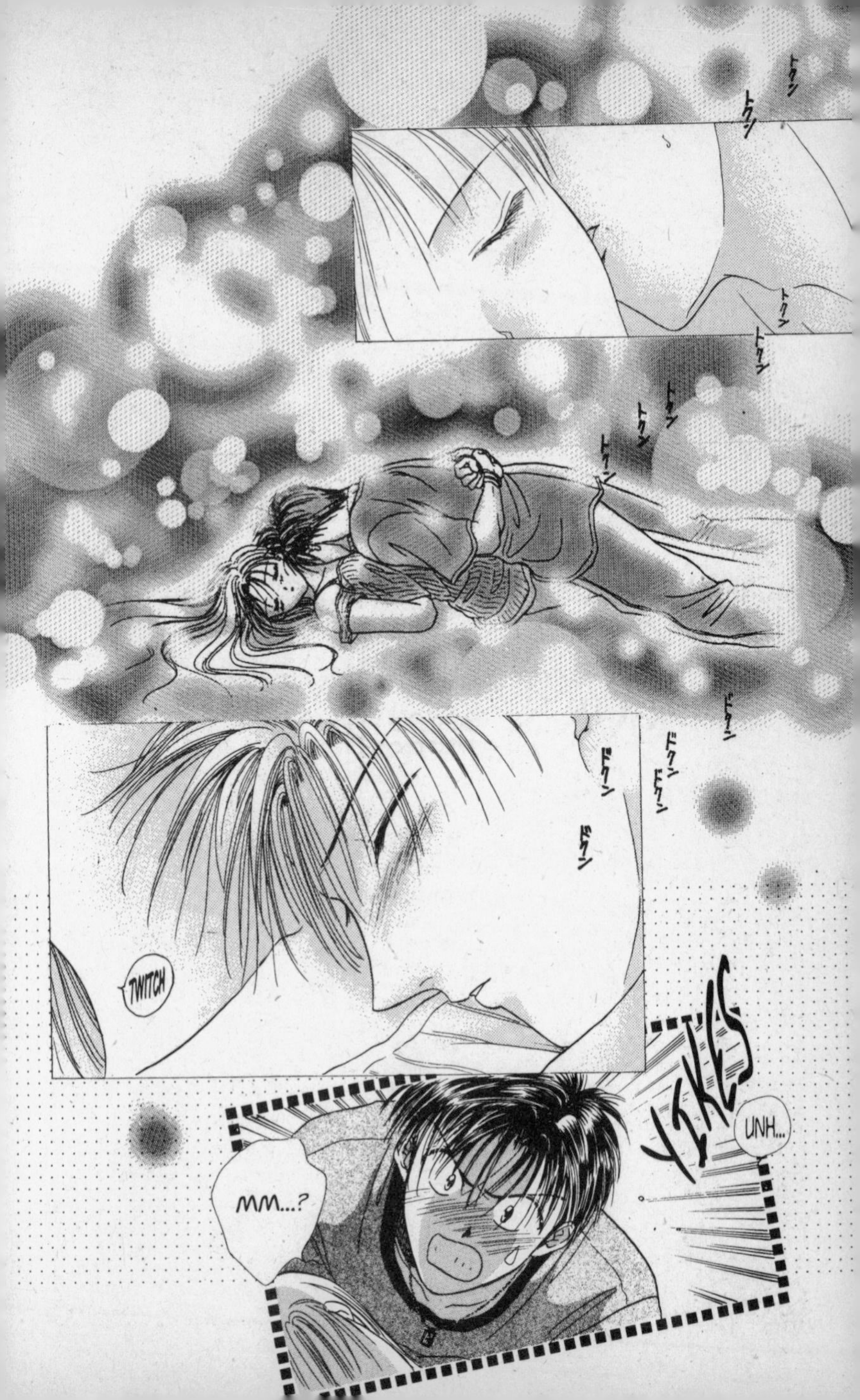
トクン
ドクン
TWITCH
YIKES
UNH...
MM...?

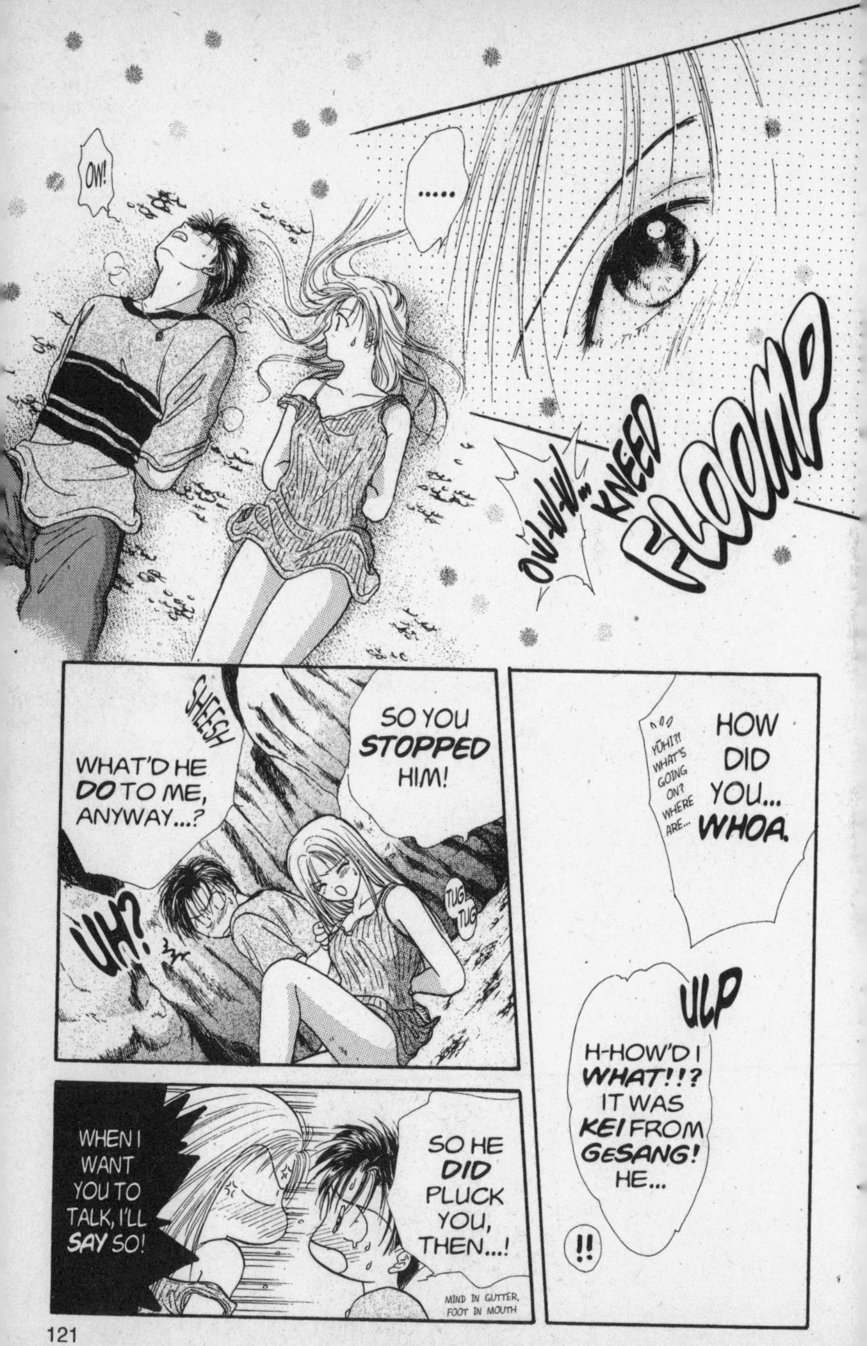
FLOOMP
KNEED
OW-W-W...
......
OW!
HOW DID YOU... WHOA.
YŪHI?! WHAT'S GOING ON? WHERE ARE...
ULP
H-HOW'D I WHAT!!? IT WAS KEI FROM GESANG! HE...
!!
SO YOU STOPPED HIM!
SHEESH
WHAT'D HE DO TO ME, ANYWAY...?
TUG TUG
UH?
SO HE DID PLUCK YOU, THEN...!
WHEN I WANT YOU TO TALK, I'LL SAY SO!
MIND IN GUTTER, FOOT IN MOUTH

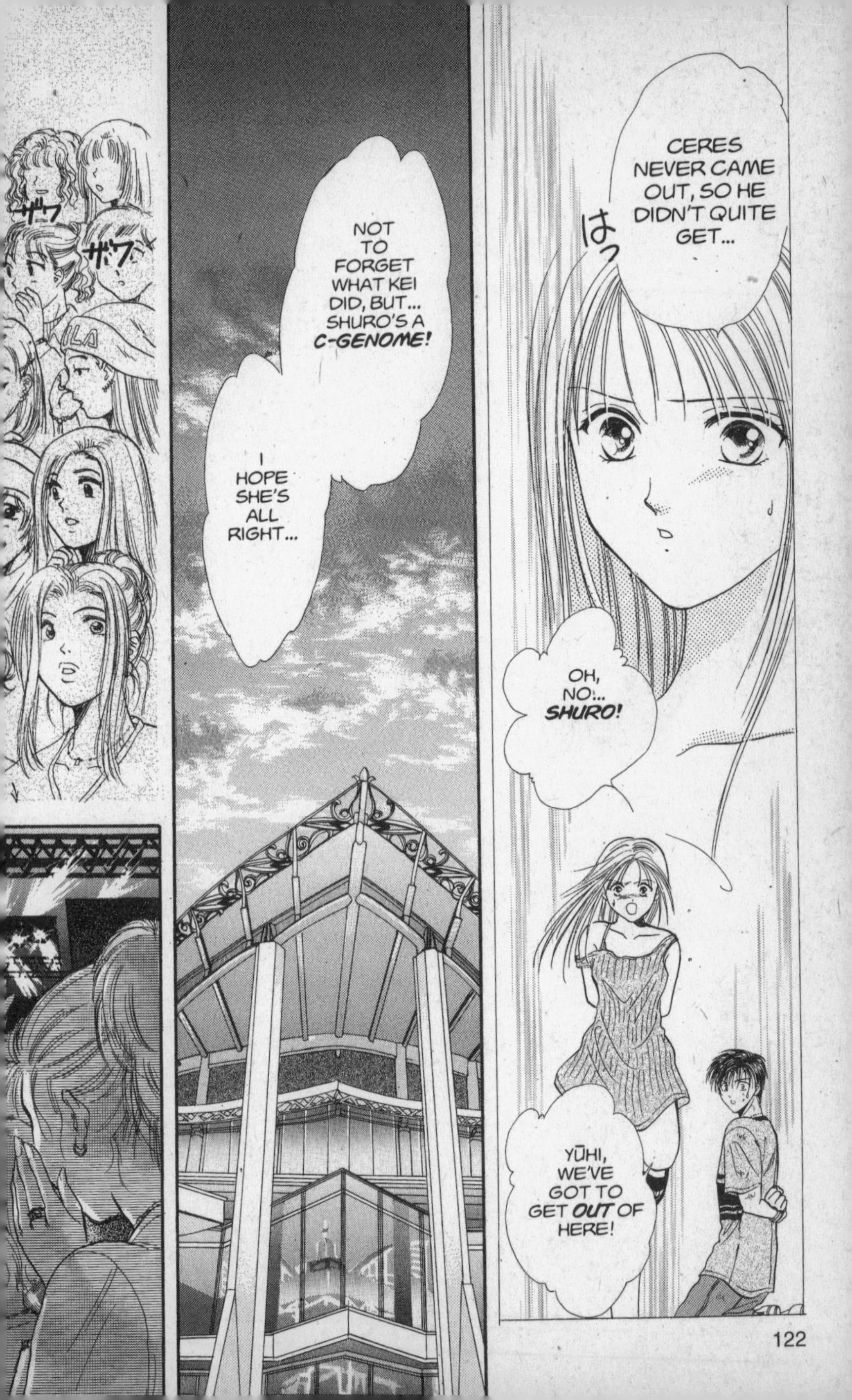
CERES NEVER CAME OUT, SO HE DIDN'T QUITE GET...
はっ
OH, NO... SHURO!
YŪHI, WE'VE GOT TO GET OUT OF HERE!
NOT TO FORGET WHAT KEI DID, BUT... SHURO'S A C-GENOME!
I HOPE SHE'S ALL RIGHT...
ザワ
ザワ

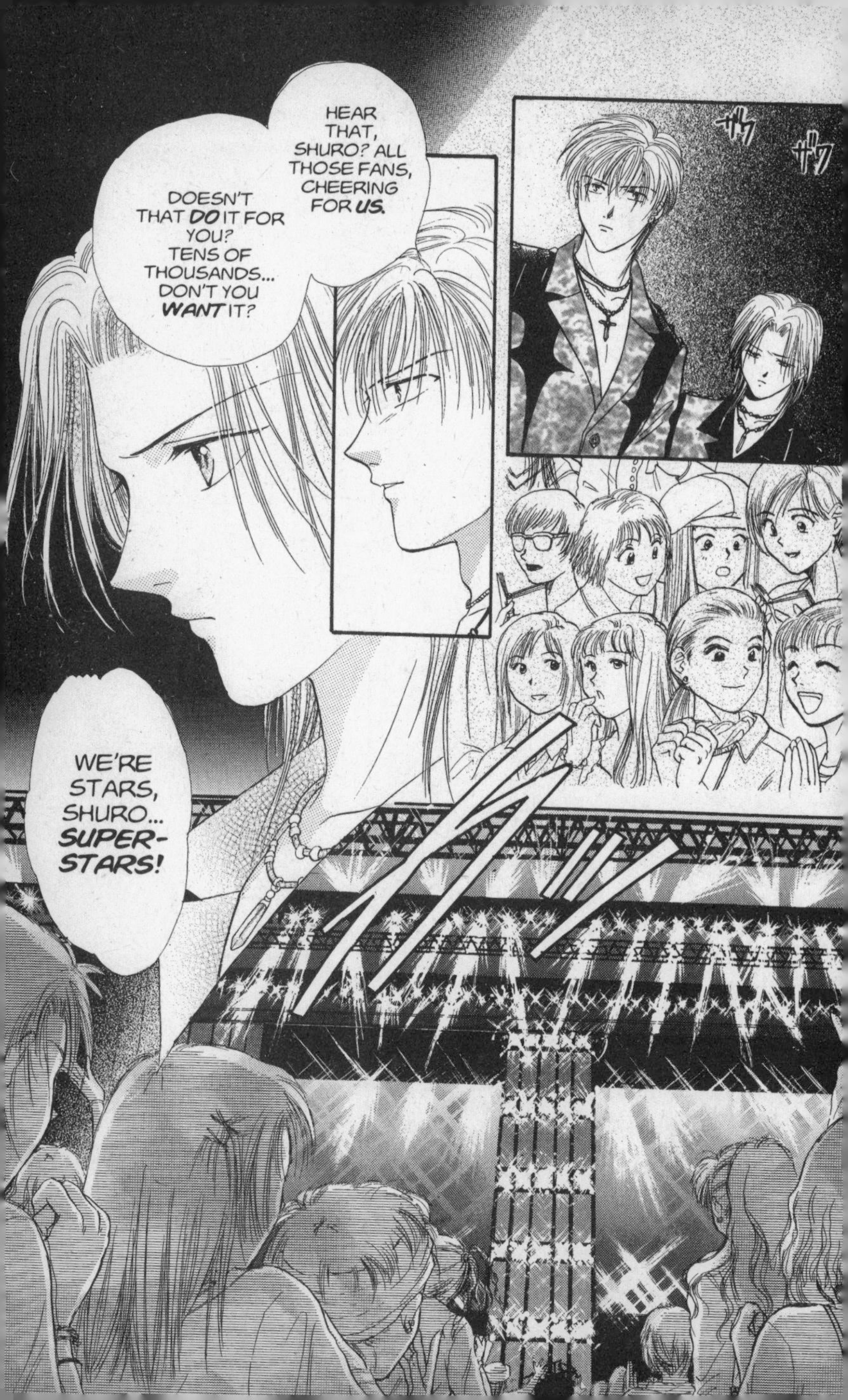
ザワ ザワ
HEAR THAT, SHURO? ALL THOSE FANS, CHEERING FOR *US.*
DOESN'T THAT ***DO*** IT FOR YOU? TENS OF THOUSANDS... DON'T YOU ***WANT*** IT?
WE'RE STARS, SHURO... **SUPER-STARS!**

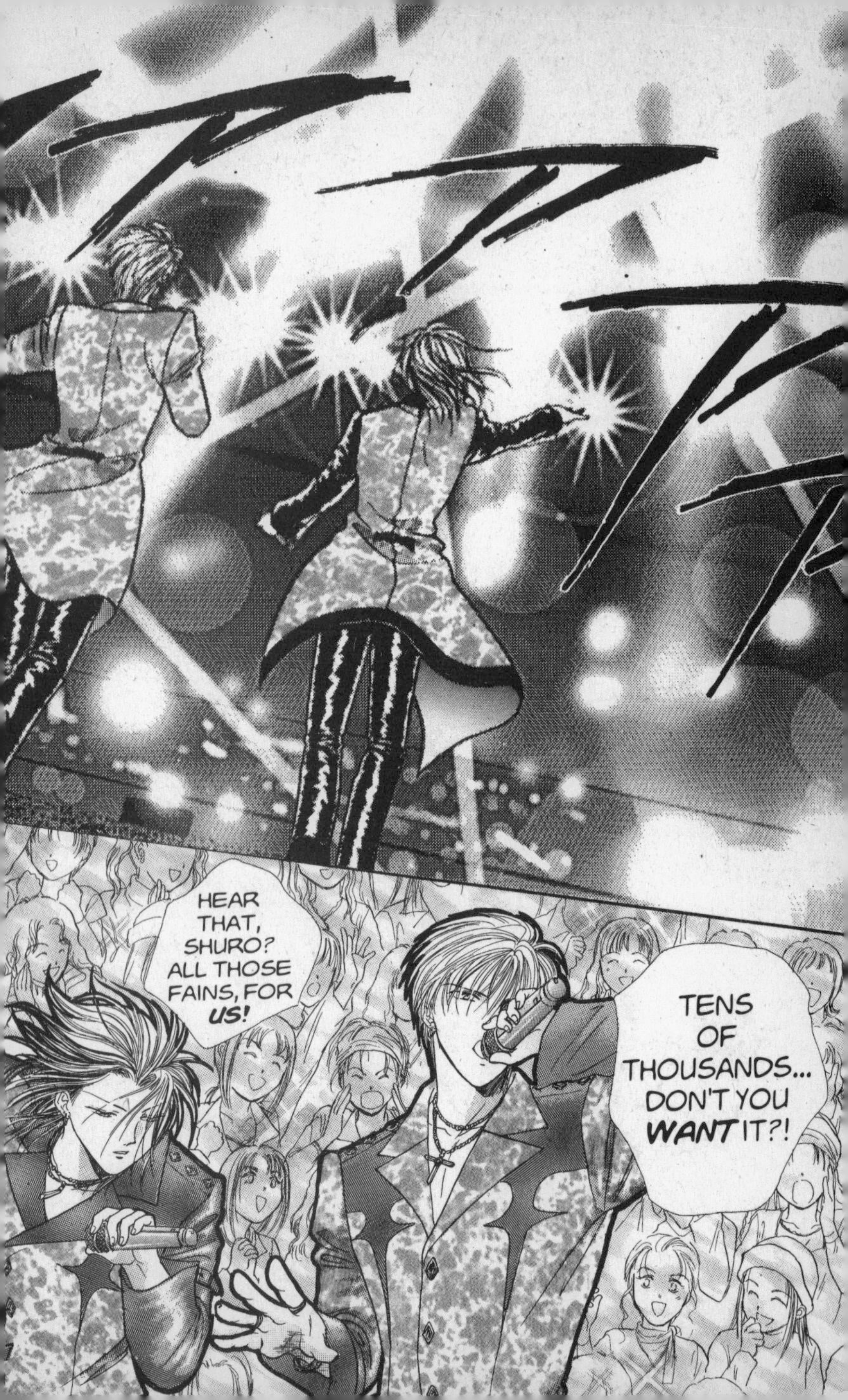

TENS OF THOUSANDS... DON'T YOU WANT IT?!
HEAR THAT, SHURO? ALL THOSE FAINS, FOR US!

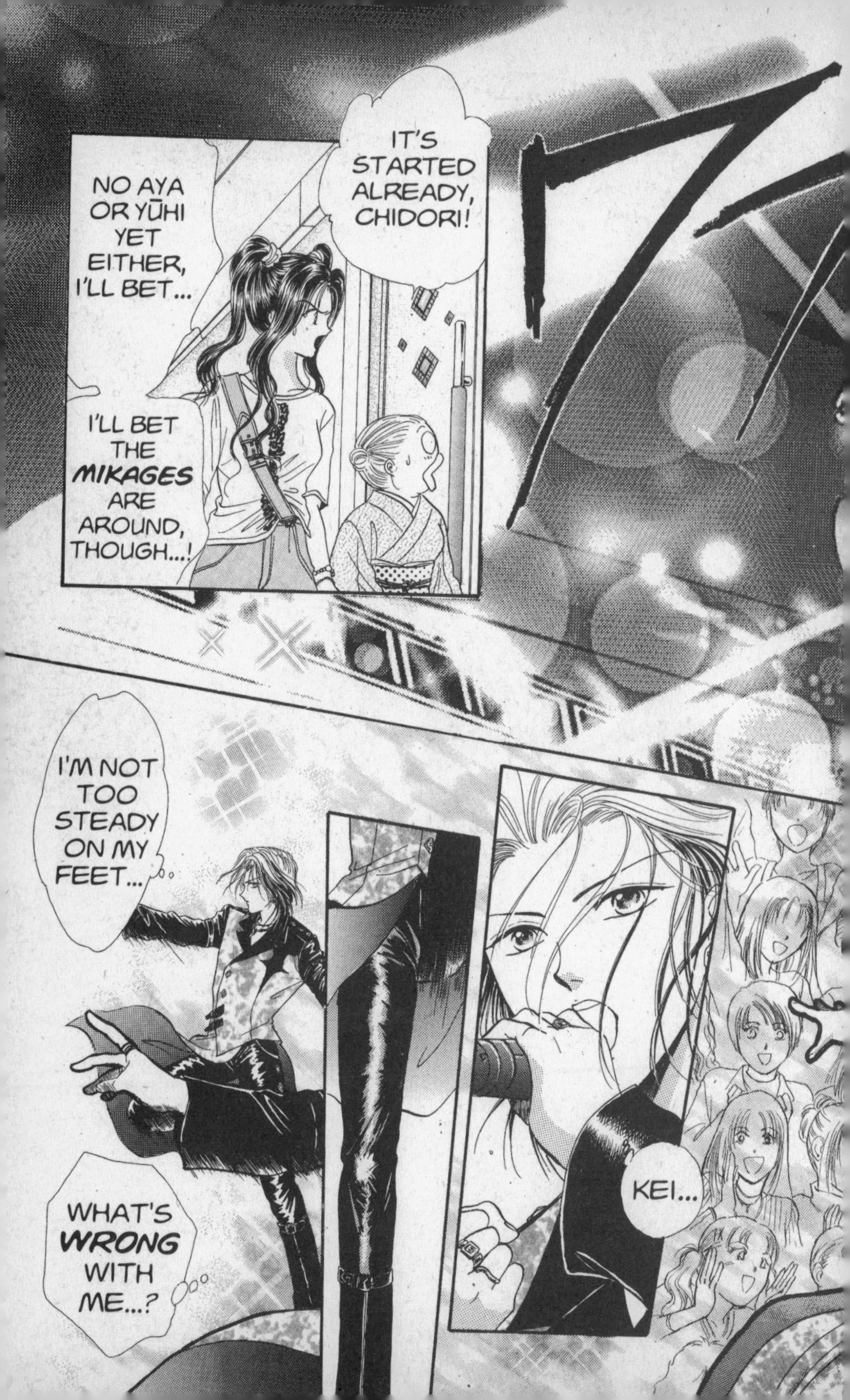
IT'S STARTED ALREADY, CHIDORI!
NO AYA OR YŪHI YET EITHER, I'LL BET...
I'LL BET THE ***MIKAGES*** ARE AROUND, THOUGH...!
KEI...
I'M NOT TOO STEADY ON MY FEET...
WHAT'S ***WRONG*** WITH ME...?

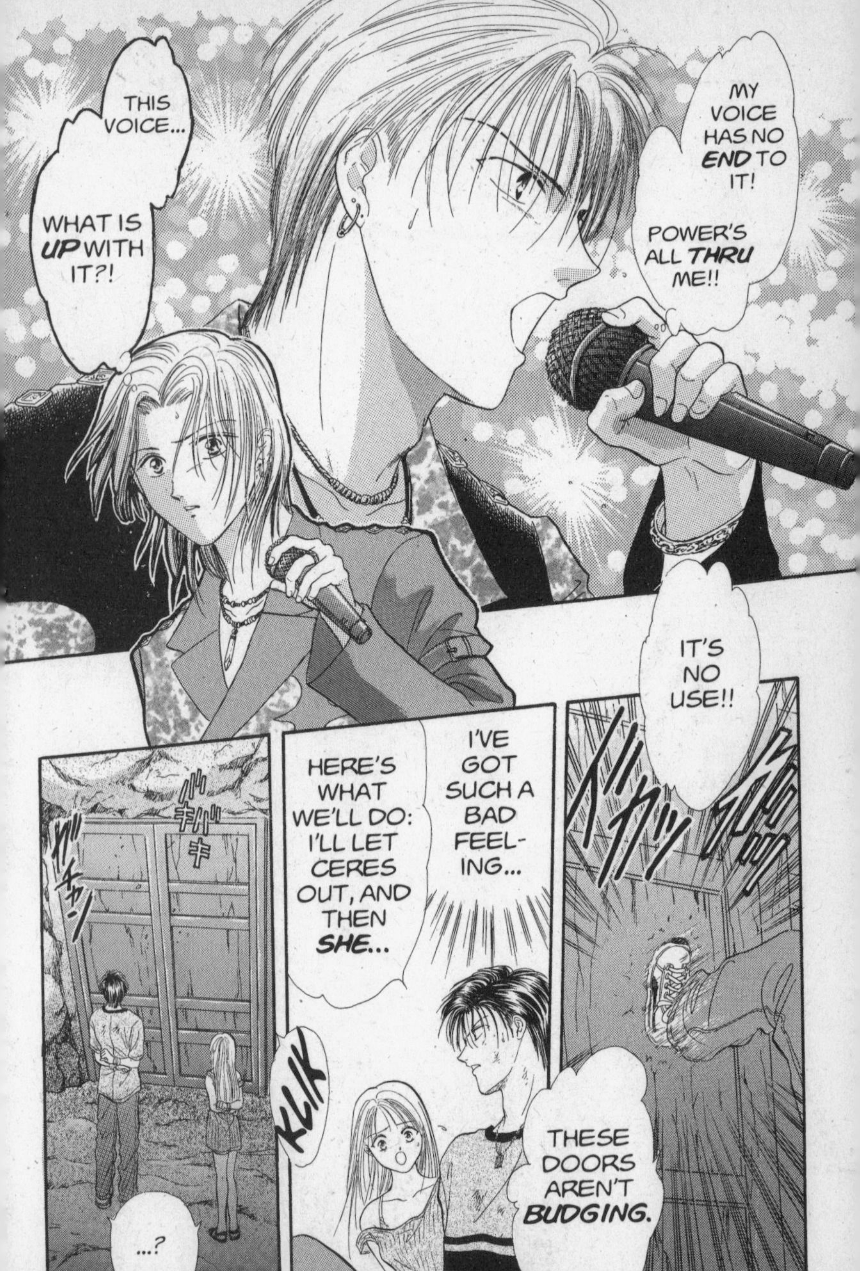
MY VOICE HAS NO END TO IT!
POWER'S ALL THRU ME!!
THIS VOICE...
WHAT IS UP WITH IT?!
IT'S NO USE!!
I'VE GOT SUCH A BAD FEEL- ING...
HERE'S WHAT WE'LL DO: I'LL LET CERES OUT, AND THEN SHE...
THESE DOORS AREN'T BUDGING.
KLIK
...?

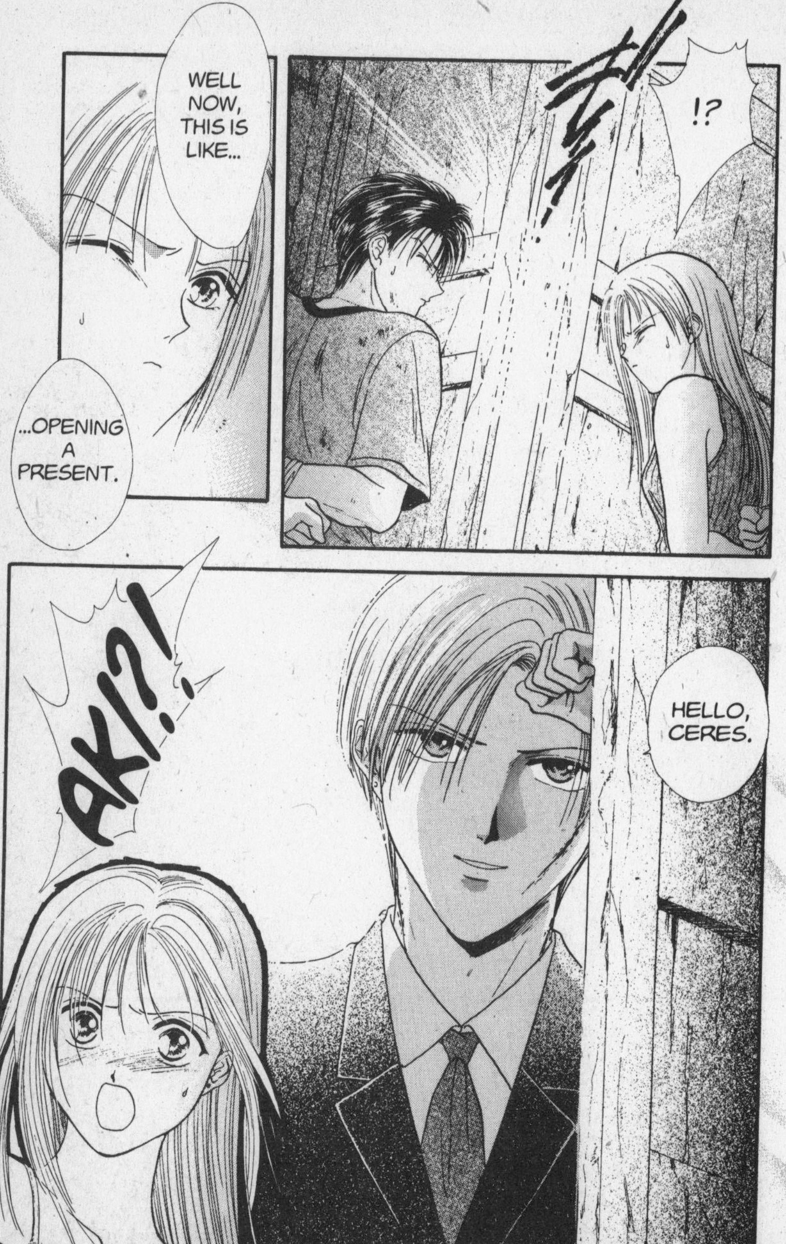
!?
WELL NOW, THIS IS LIKE...
...OPENING A PRESENT.
HELLO, CERES.
AKI?!

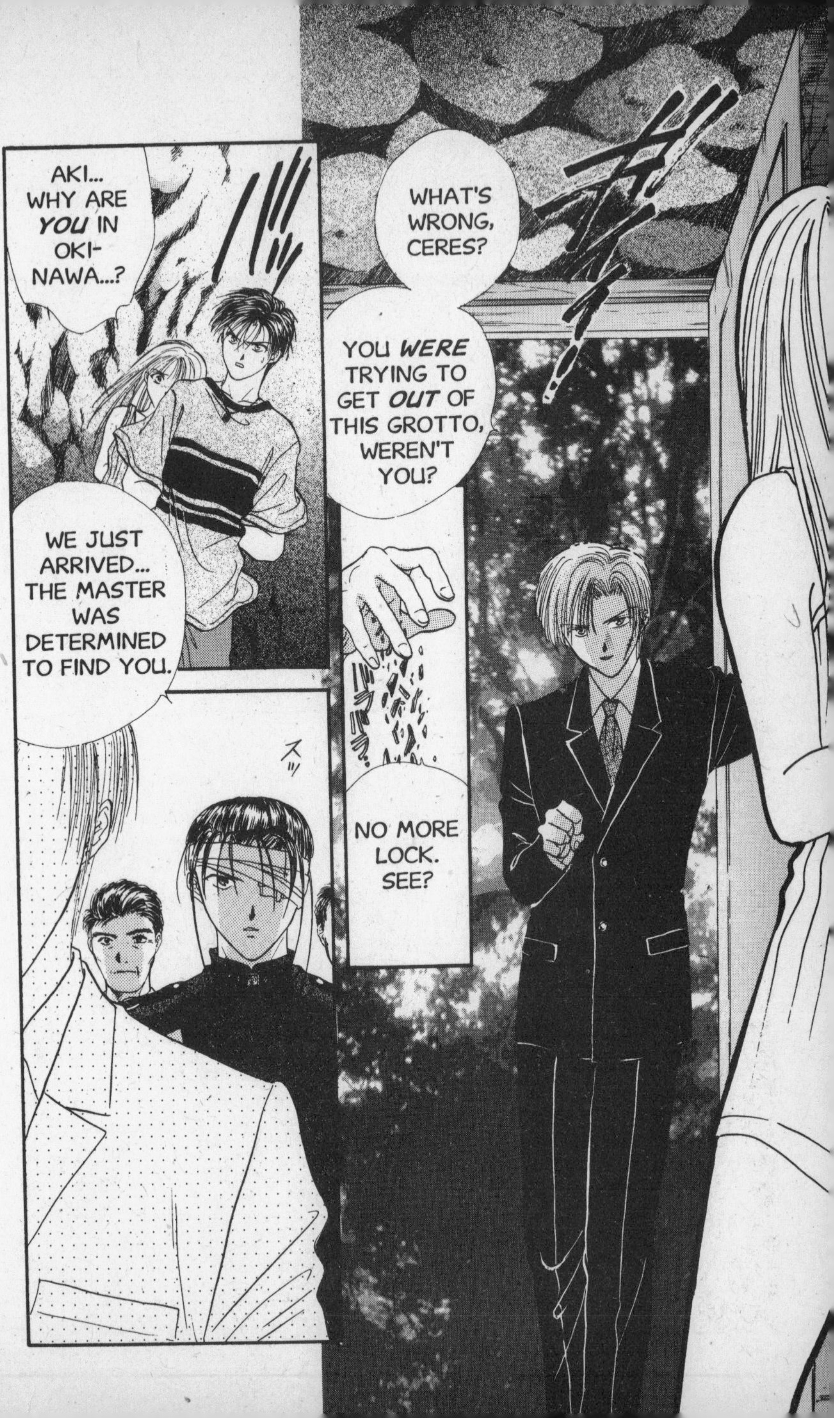
WHAT'S WRONG, CERES?
YOU WERE TRYING TO GET OUT OF THIS GROTTO, WEREN'T YOU?
NO MORE LOCK. SEE?
AKI... WHY ARE YOU IN OKI-NAWA...?
WE JUST ARRIVED... THE MASTER WAS DETERMINED TO FIND YOU.
スッ

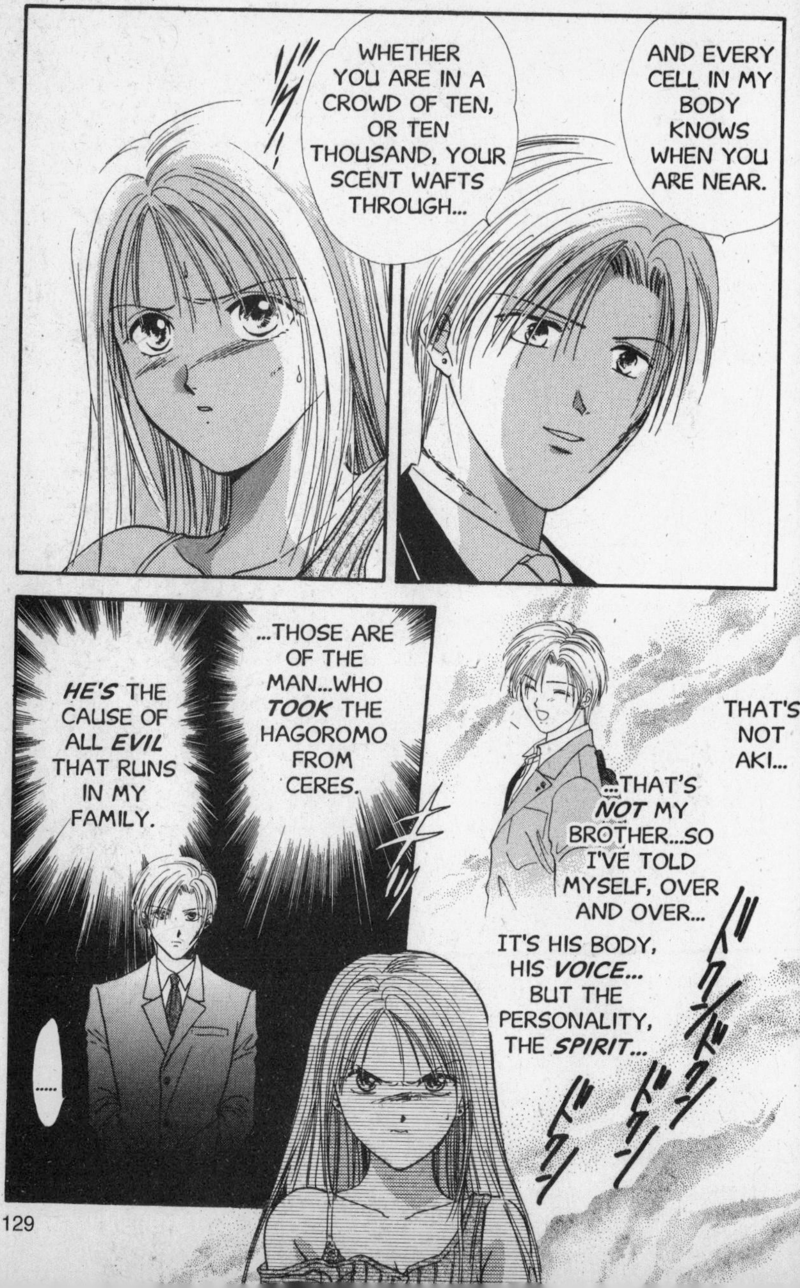
WHETHER YOU ARE IN A CROWD OF TEN, OR TEN THOUSAND, YOUR SCENT WAFTS THROUGH...
AND EVERY CELL IN MY BODY KNOWS WHEN YOU ARE NEAR.
THAT'S NOT AKI...
...THAT'S NOT MY BROTHER...SO I'VE TOLD MYSELF, OVER AND OVER...
IT'S HIS BODY, HIS VOICE... BUT THE PERSONALITY, THE SPIRIT...
...THOSE ARE OF THE MAN...WHO TOOK THE HAGOROMO FROM CERES.
HE'S THE CAUSE OF ALL EVIL THAT RUNS IN MY FAMILY.
.....

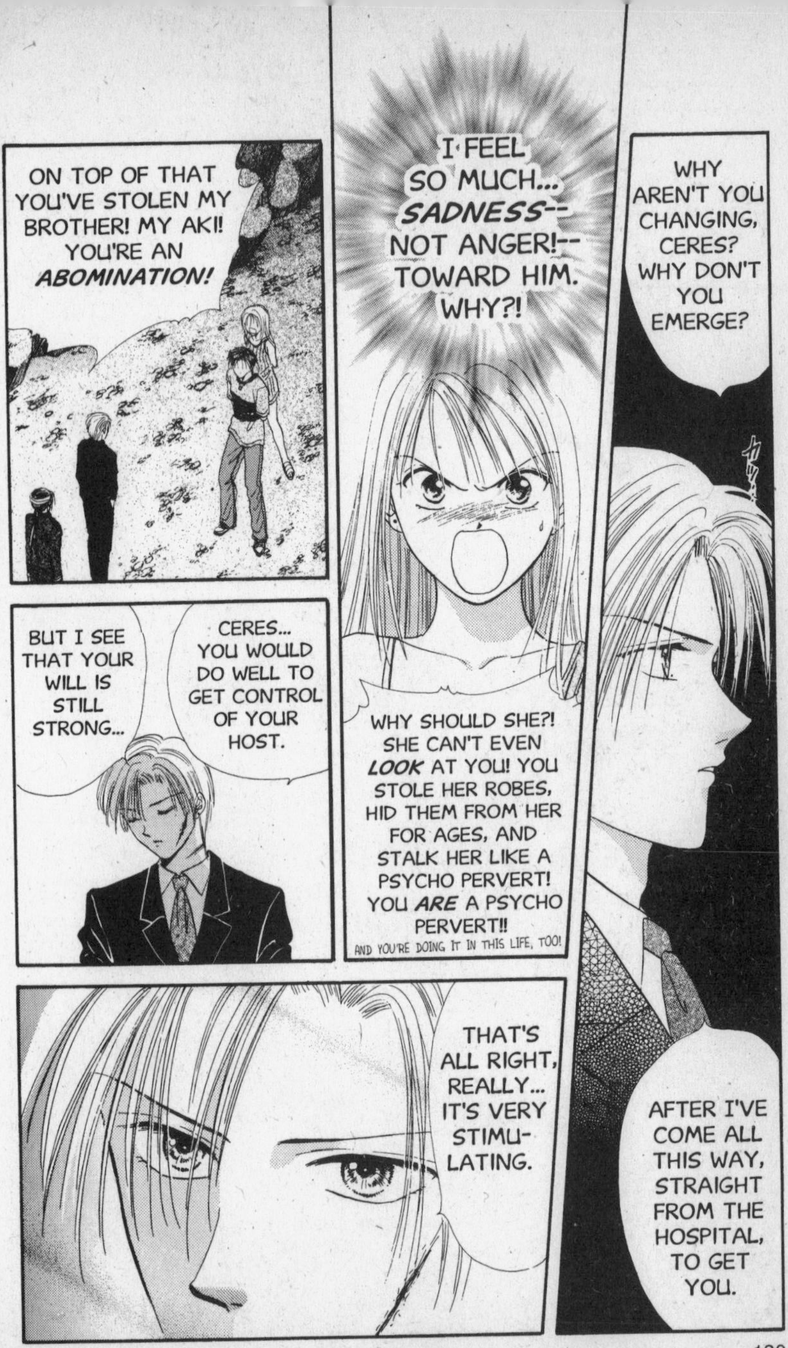
WHY AREN'T YOU CHANGING, CERES? WHY DON'T YOU EMERGE?
AFTER I'VE COME ALL THIS WAY, STRAIGHT FROM THE HOSPITAL, TO GET YOU.
I FEEL SO MUCH... SADNESS-- NOT ANGER!-- TOWARD HIM. WHY?!
WHY SHOULD SHE?! SHE CAN'T EVEN LOOK AT YOU! YOU STOLE HER ROBES, HID THEM FROM HER FOR AGES, AND STALK HER LIKE A PSYCHO PERVERT! YOU ARE A PSYCHO PERVERT!!
AND YOU'RE DOING IT IN THIS LIFE, TOO!
ON TOP OF THAT YOU'VE STOLEN MY BROTHER! MY AKI! YOU'RE AN ABOMINATION!
CERES... YOU WOULD DO WELL TO GET CONTROL OF YOUR HOST.
BUT I SEE THAT YOUR WILL IS STILL STRONG...
THAT'S ALL RIGHT, REALLY... IT'S VERY STIMULATING.

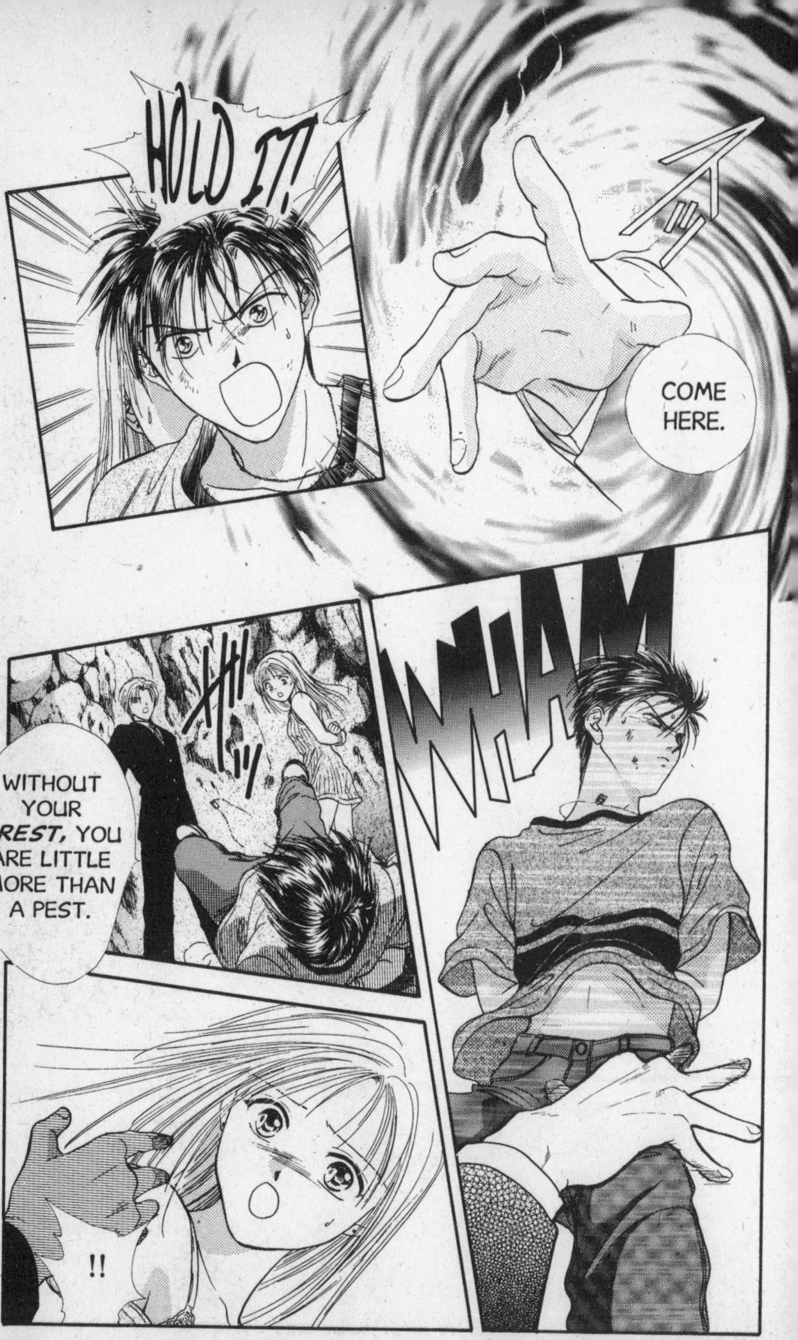
COME HERE.
HOLD IT!
WHAM
WITHOUT YOUR CREST, YOU ARE LITTLE MORE THAN A PEST.
!!

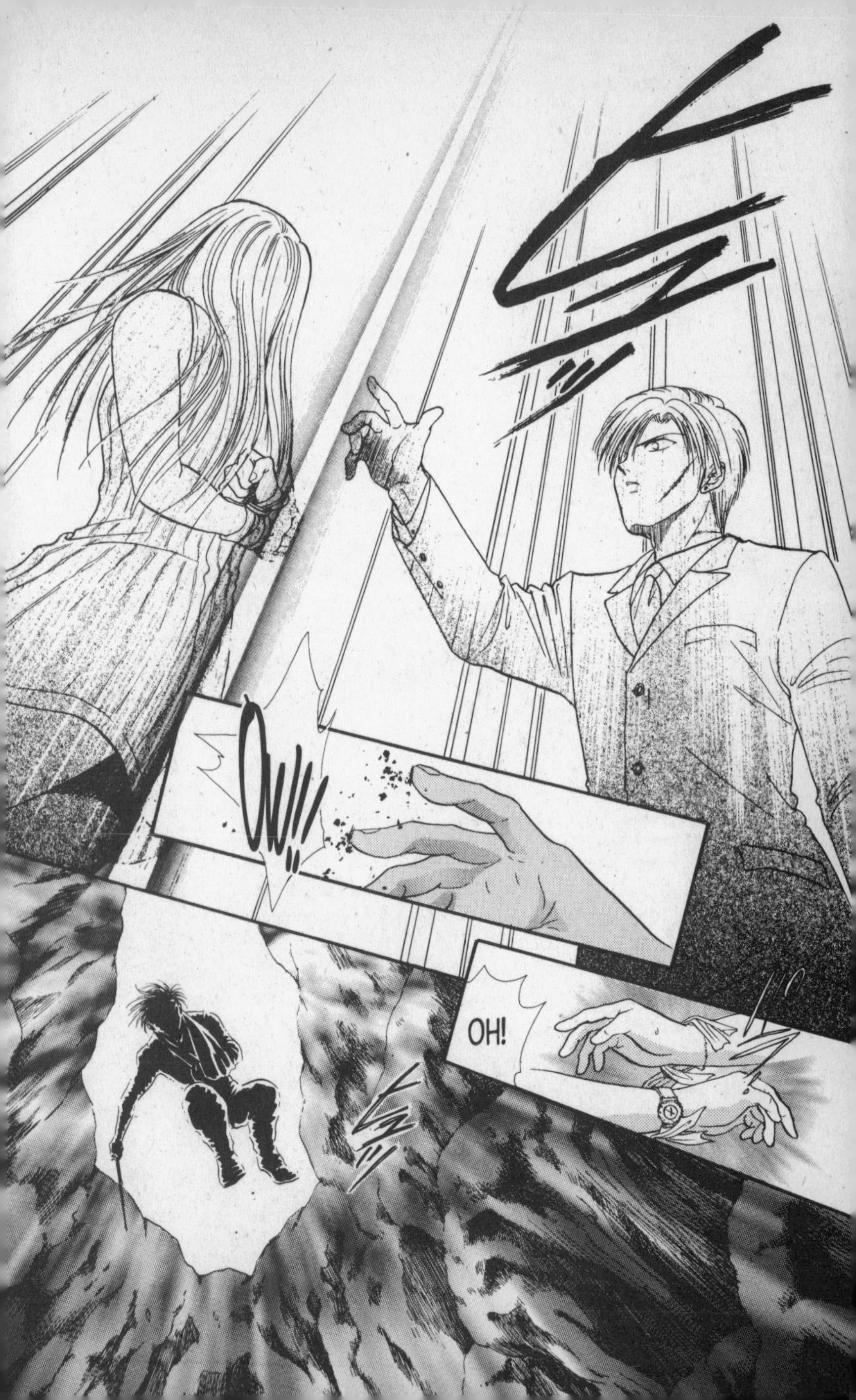
OW!!
OH!

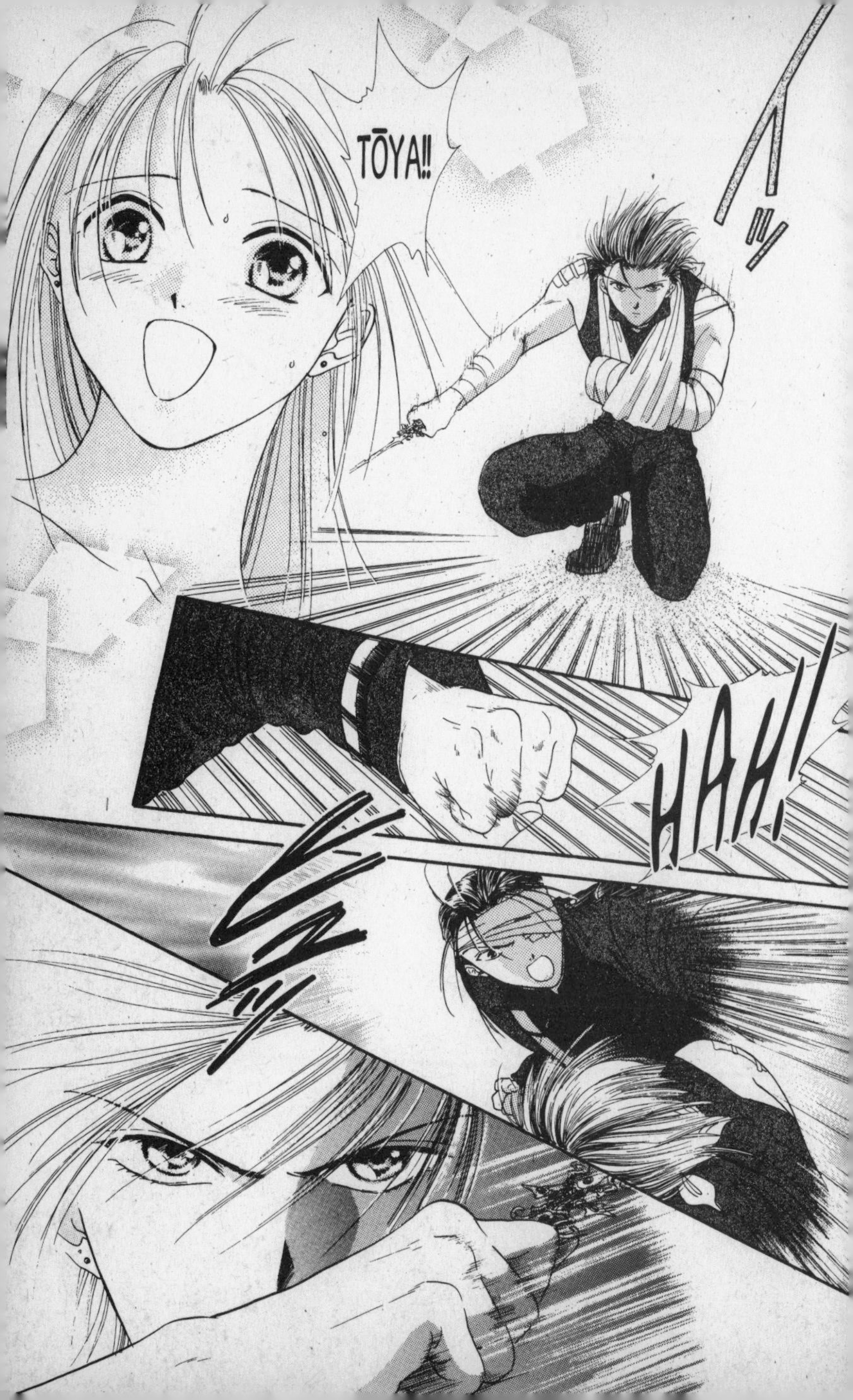
TŌYA!!
HAH!

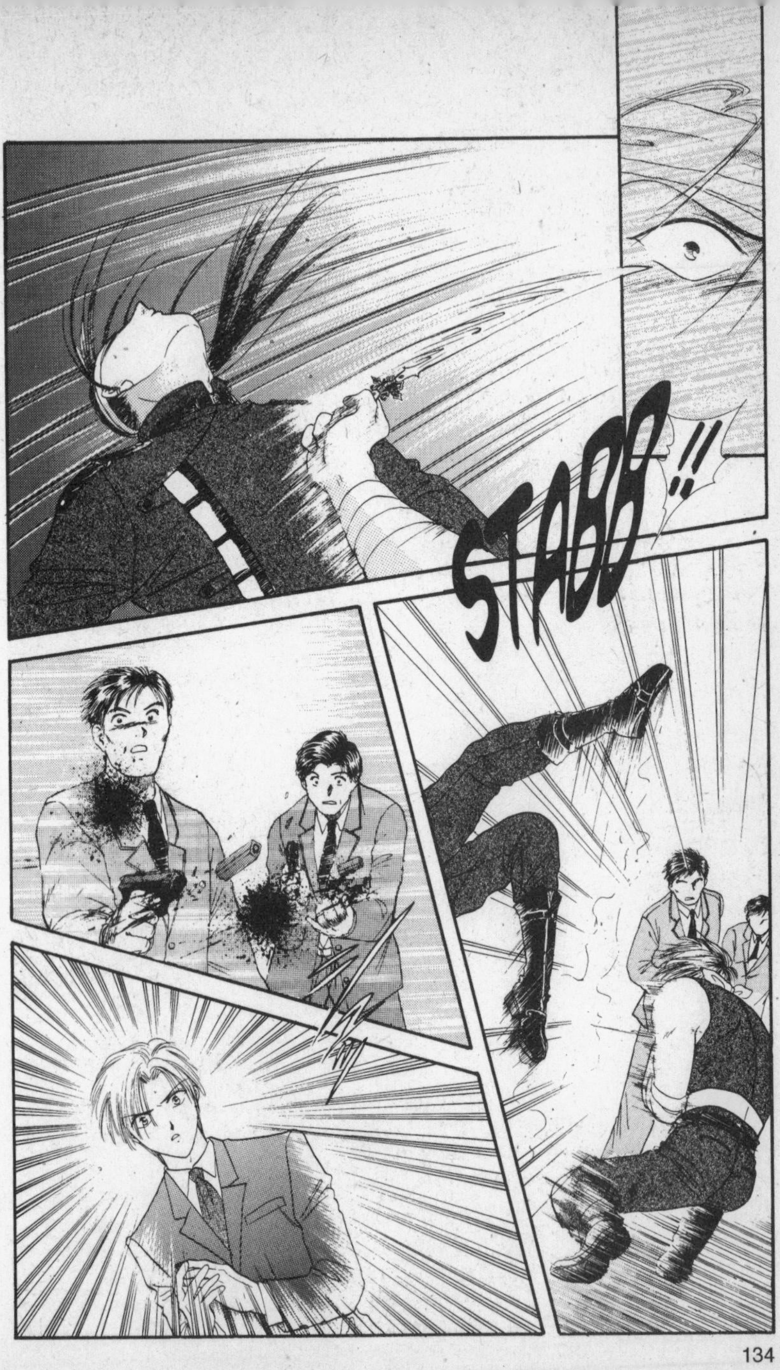
STABB!!

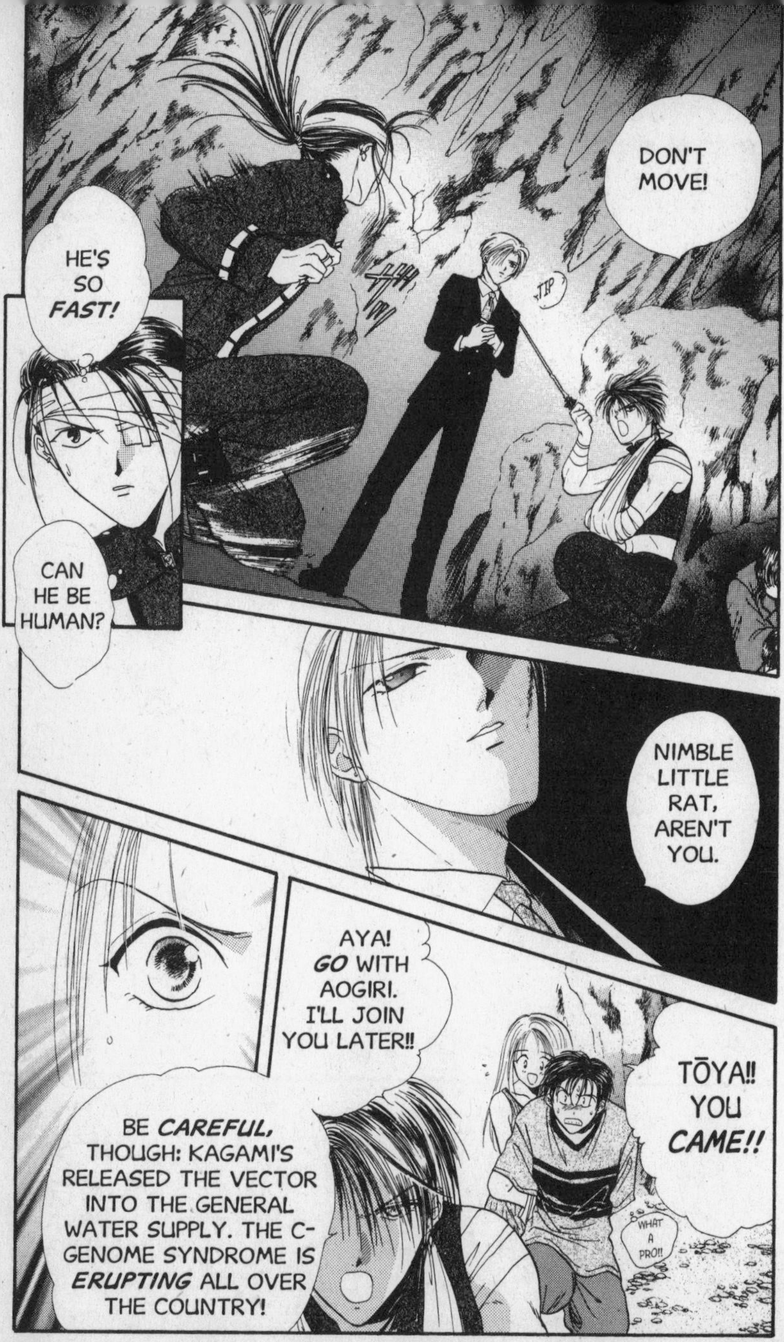
DON'T MOVE!
TIP
HE'S SO FAST!
CAN HE BE HUMAN?
NIMBLE LITTLE RAT, AREN'T YOU.
TŌYA!! YOU CAME!!
WHAT A PRO!!
AYA! GO WITH AOGIRI. I'LL JOIN YOU LATER!!
BE CAREFUL, THOUGH: KAGAMI'S RELEASED THE VECTOR INTO THE GENERAL WATER SUPPLY. THE C-GENOME SYNDROME IS ERUPTING ALL OVER THE COUNTRY!

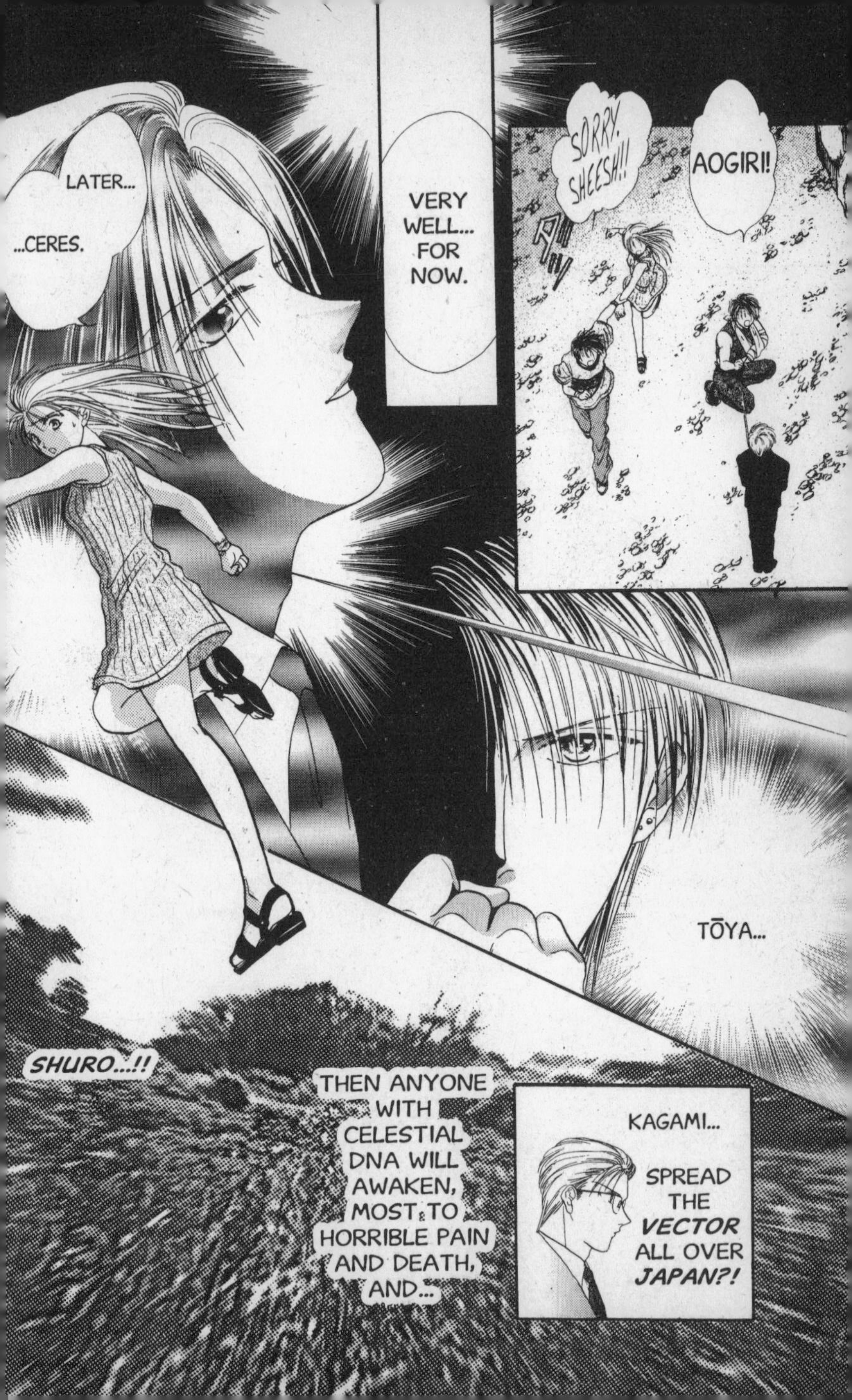
AOGIRI!
SORRY. SHEESH!!
VERY WELL... FOR NOW.
LATER...
...CERES.
TŌYA...
KAGAMI...
SPREAD THE VECTOR ALL OVER JAPAN?!
THEN ANYONE WITH CELESTIAL DNA WILL AWAKEN, MOST TO HORRIBLE PAIN AND DEATH, AND...
SHURO...!!

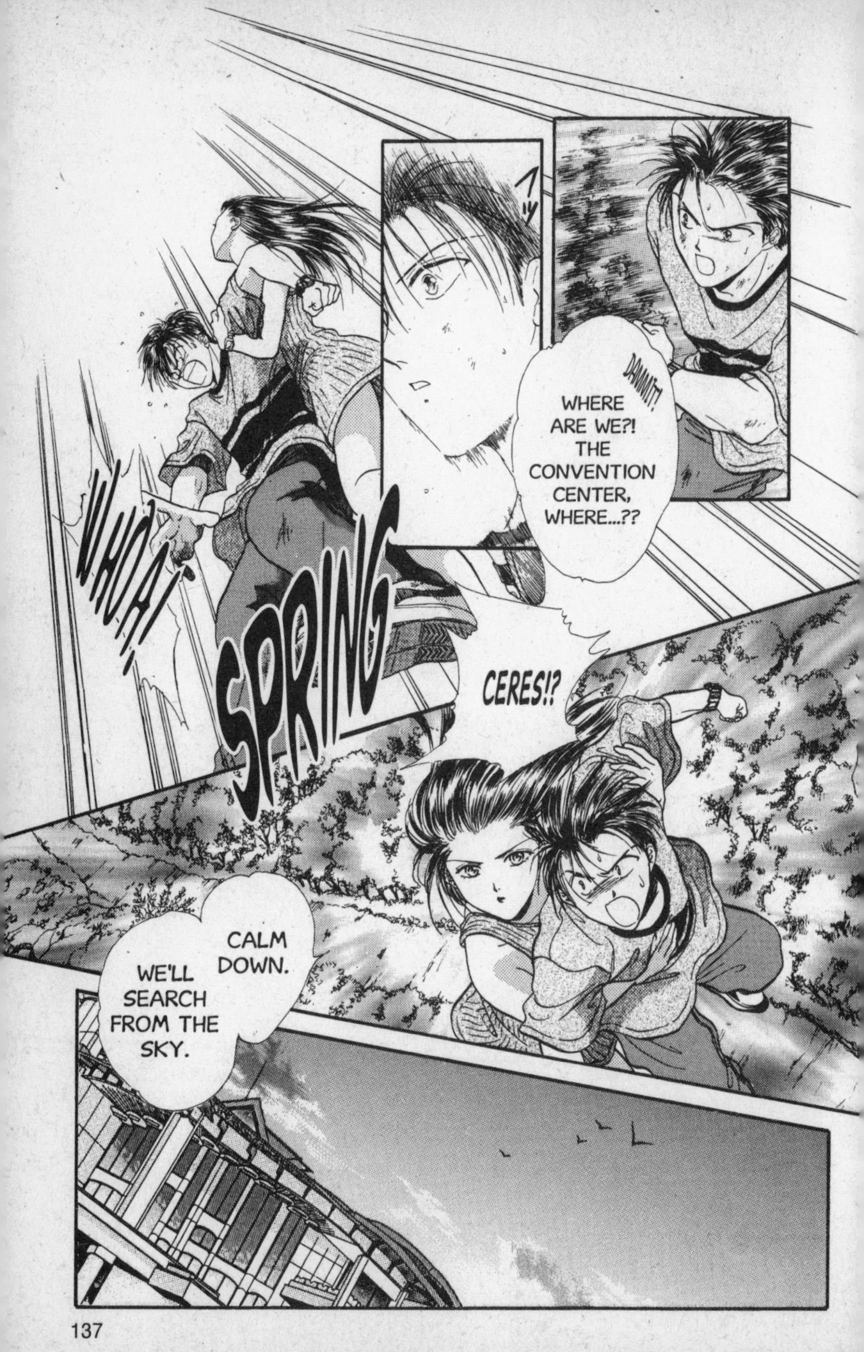
DAMMIT!
WHERE ARE WE?! THE CONVENTION CENTER, WHERE...??
WHOA!
SPRING
CERES!?
CALM DOWN.
WE'LL SEARCH FROM THE SKY.

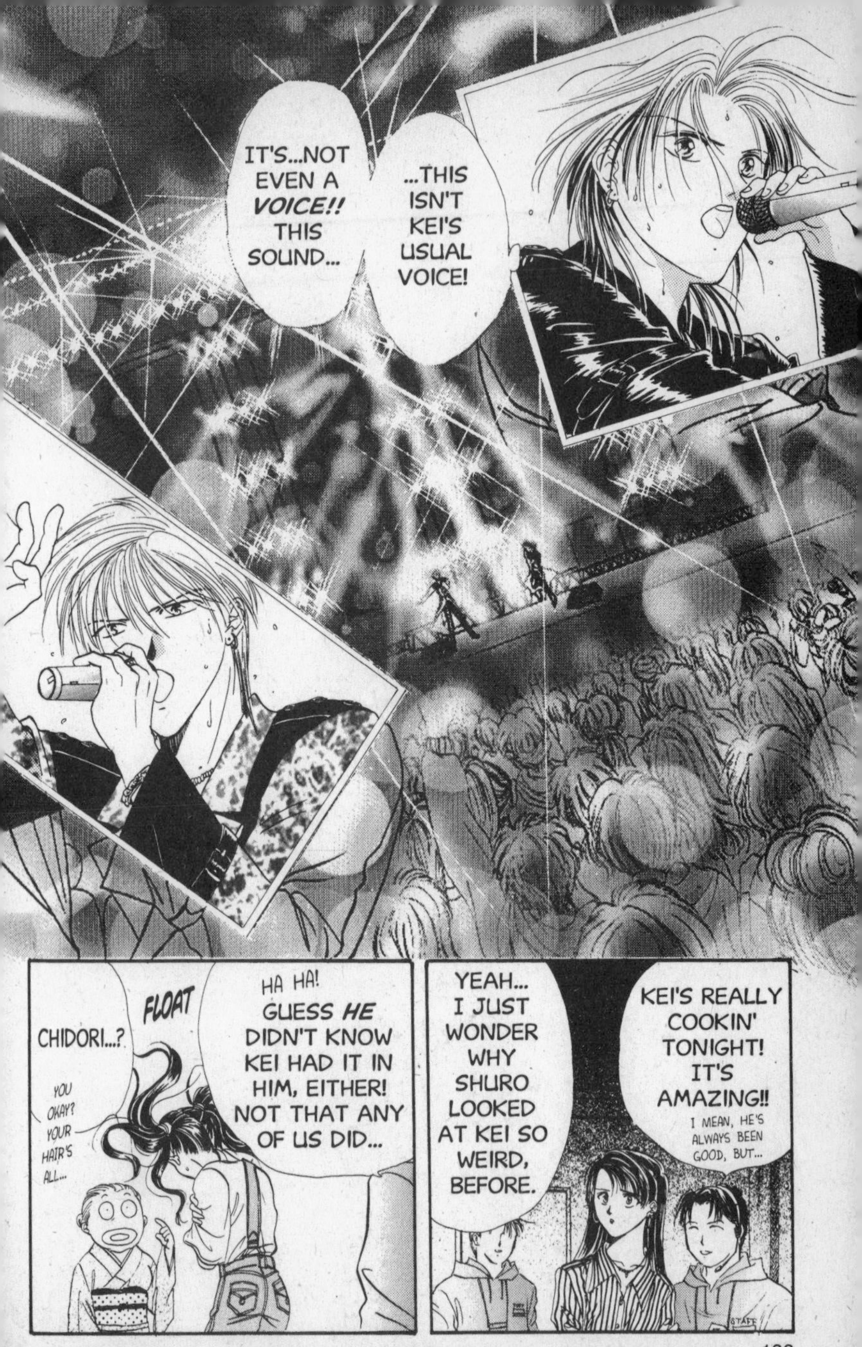
...THIS ISN'T KEI'S USUAL VOICE!
IT'S...NOT EVEN A *VOICE!!* THIS SOUND...
KEI'S REALLY COOKIN' TONIGHT! IT'S AMAZING!!
I MEAN, HE'S ALWAYS BEEN GOOD, BUT...
YEAH... I JUST WONDER WHY SHURO LOOKED AT KEI SO WEIRD, BEFORE.
HA HA! GUESS *HE* DIDN'T KNOW KEI HAD IT IN HIM, EITHER! NOT THAT ANY OF US DID...
FLOAT
CHIDORI...?
YOU OKAY? YOUR HAIR'S ALL...
STAFF

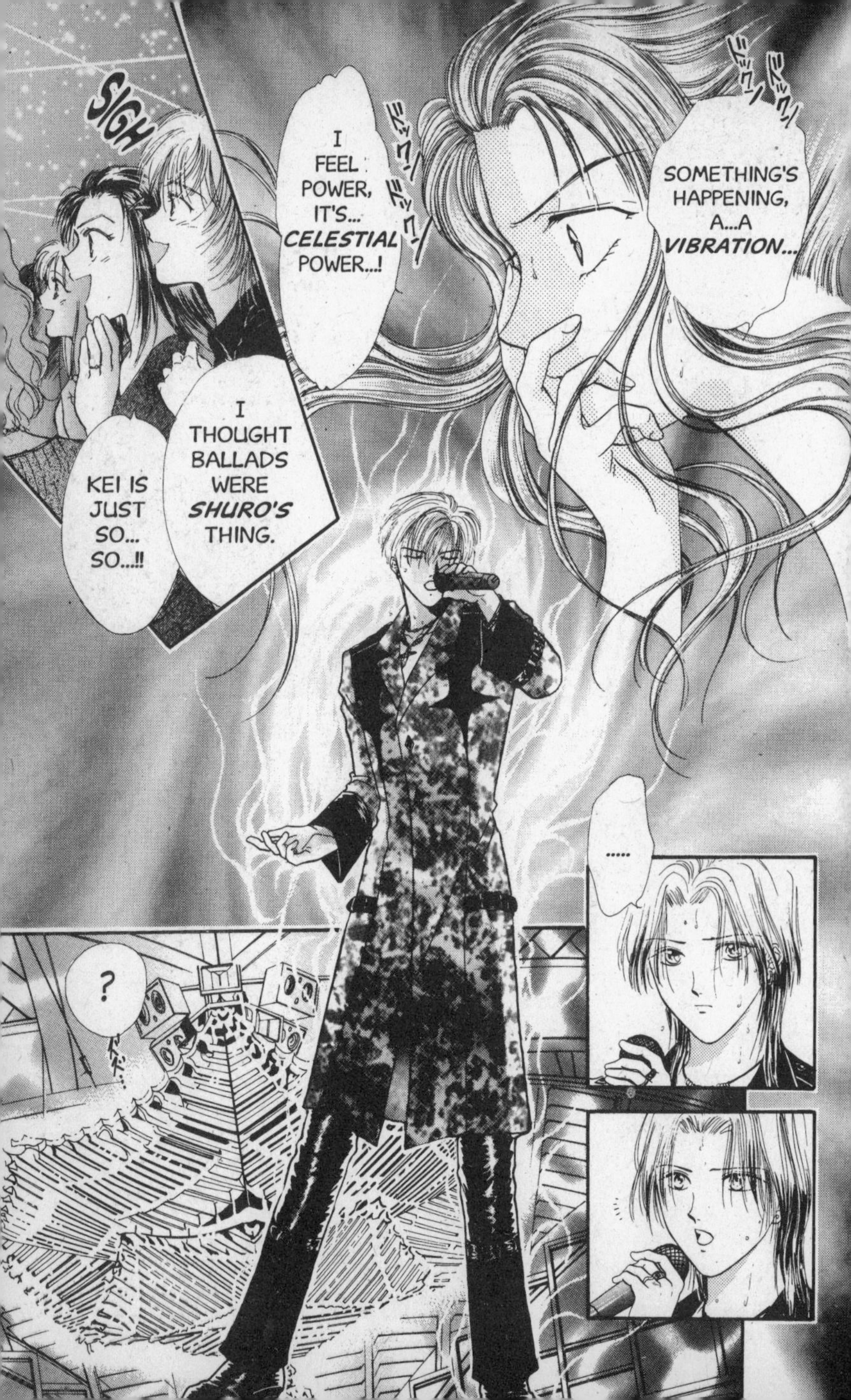
SOMETHING'S HAPPENING, A...A VIBRATION...
I FEEL POWER, IT'S... CELESTIAL POWER...!
SIGH
I THOUGHT BALLADS WERE SHURO'S THING.
KEI IS JUST SO... SO...!!
......
?

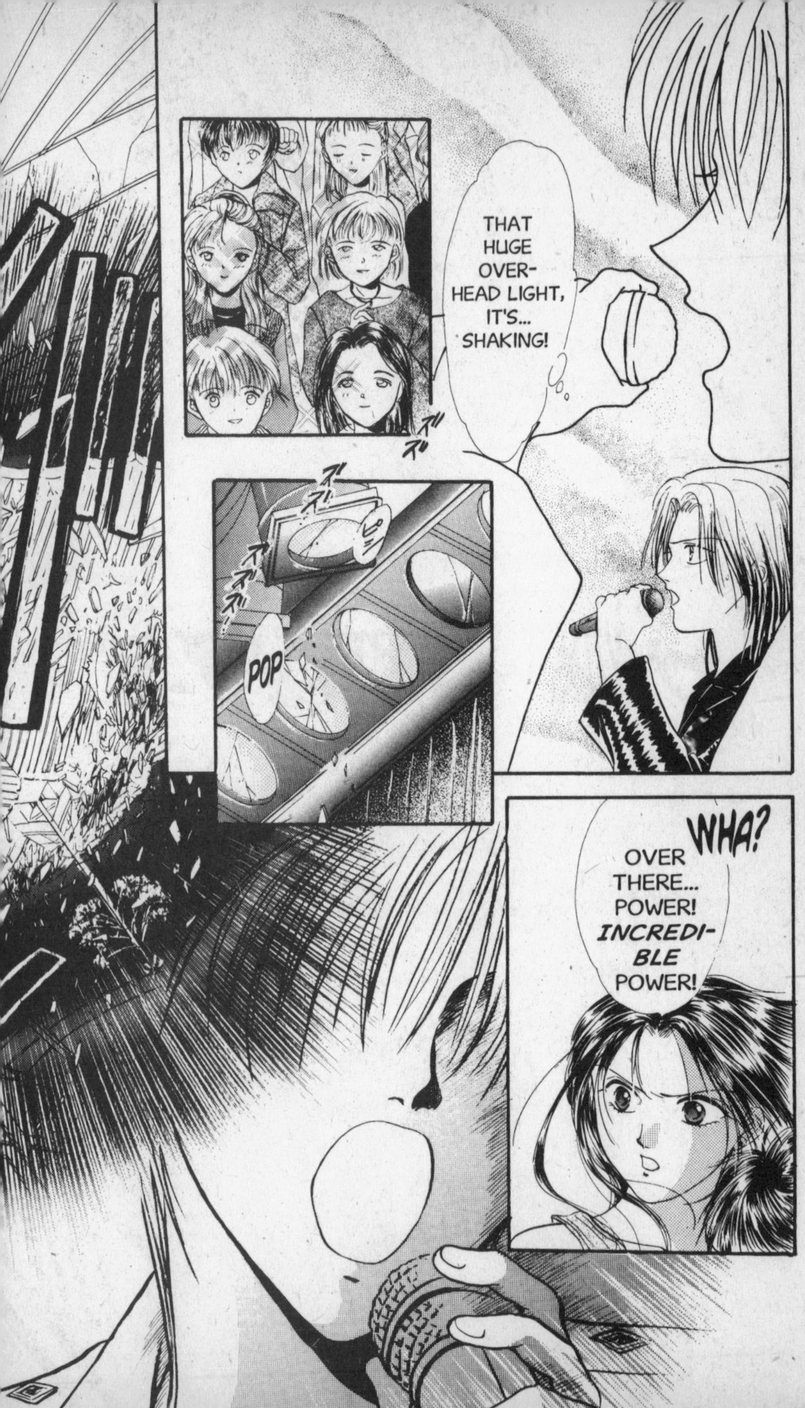
THAT HUGE OVER-HEAD LIGHT, IT'S... SHAKING!
POP
WHA?
OVER THERE... POWER! INCREDIBLE POWER!

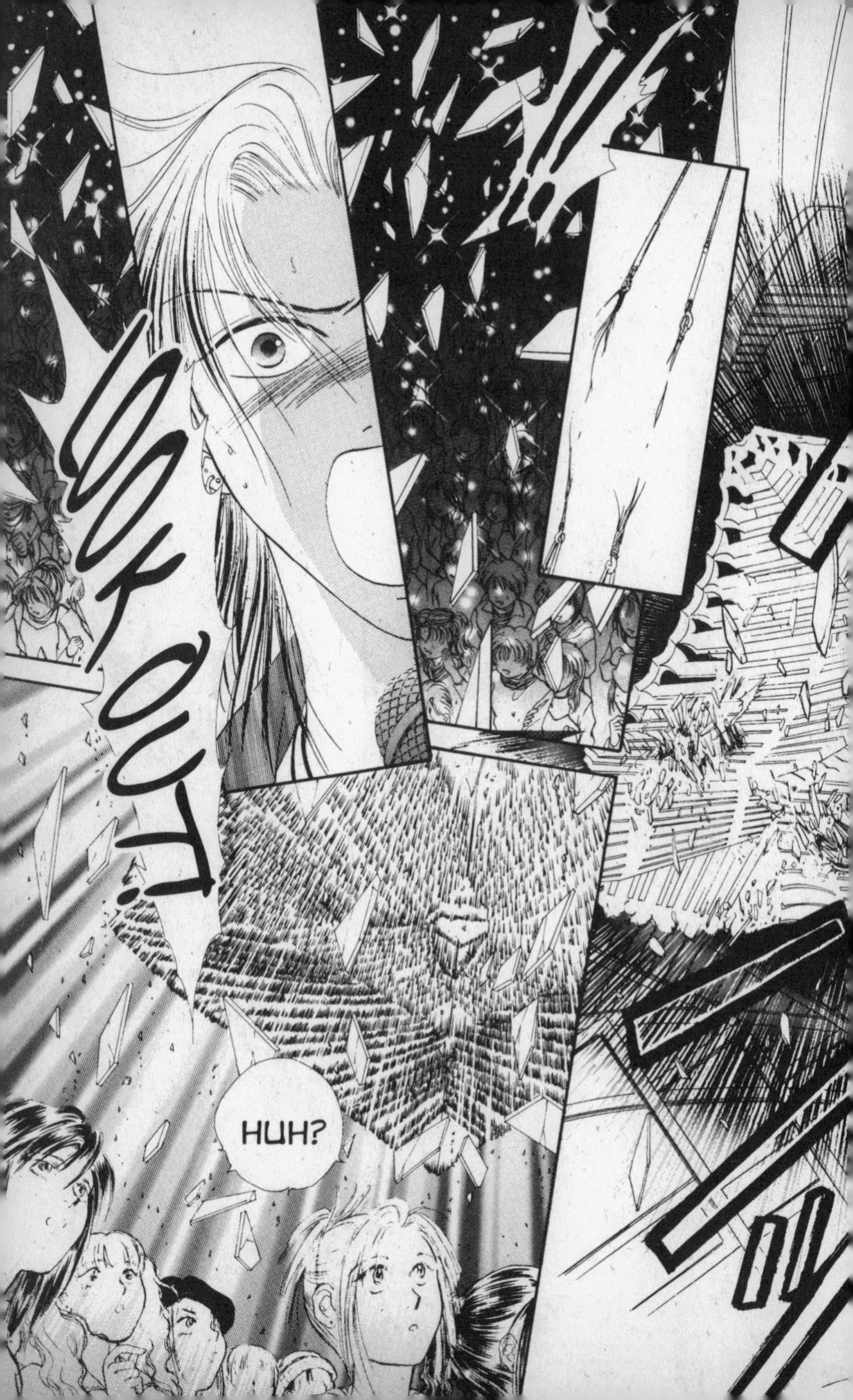
LOOK OUT!!
HUH?

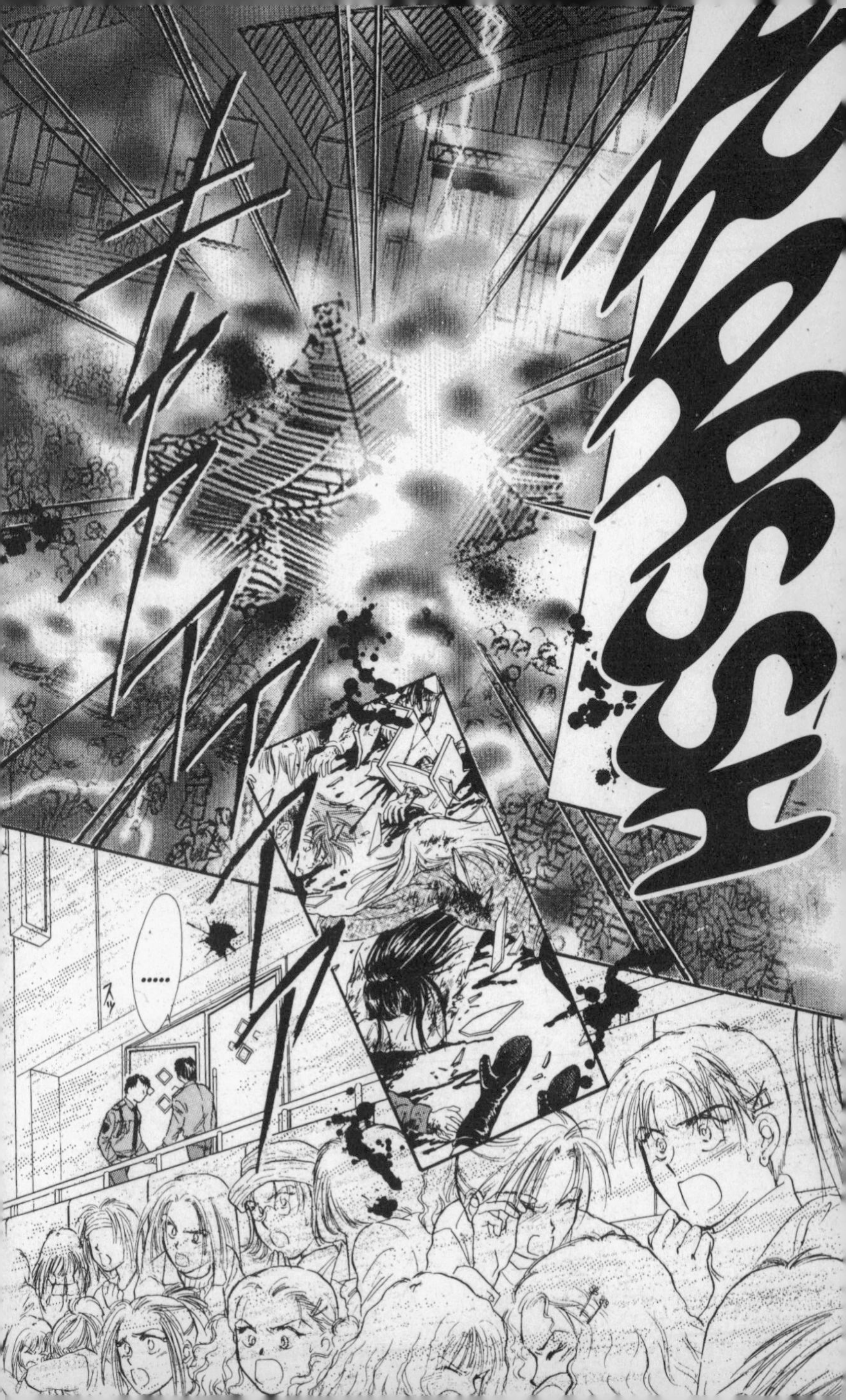
KRASSH
......

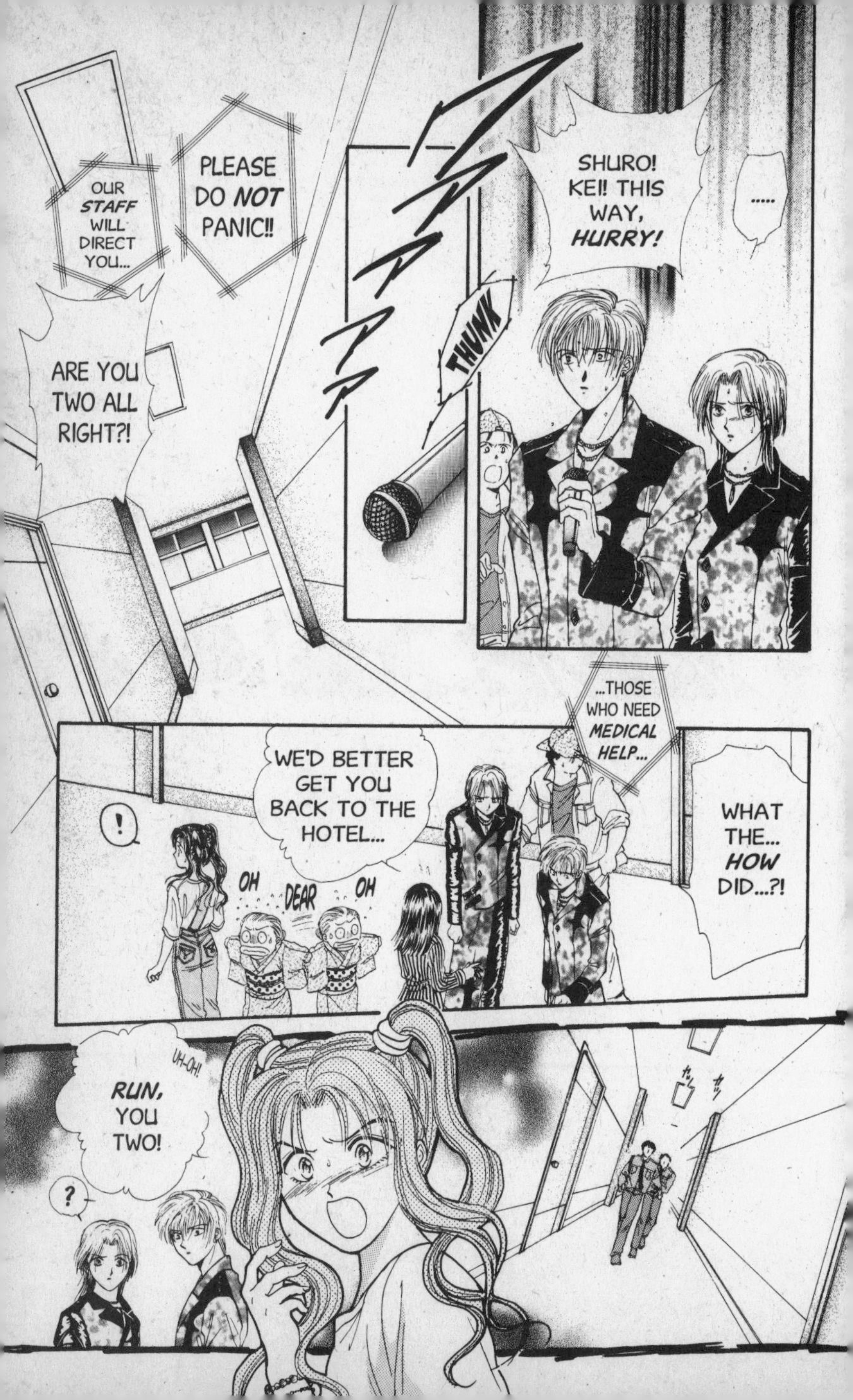
.....
SHURO! KEI! THIS WAY, HURRY!
THUNK
PLEASE DO NOT PANIC!!
OUR STAFF WILL DIRECT YOU...
ARE YOU TWO ALL RIGHT?!
...THOSE WHO NEED MEDICAL HELP...
WHAT THE... HOW DID...?!
WE'D BETTER GET YOU BACK TO THE HOTEL...
OH
DEAR
OH
!
UH-OH!
RUN, YOU TWO!
?

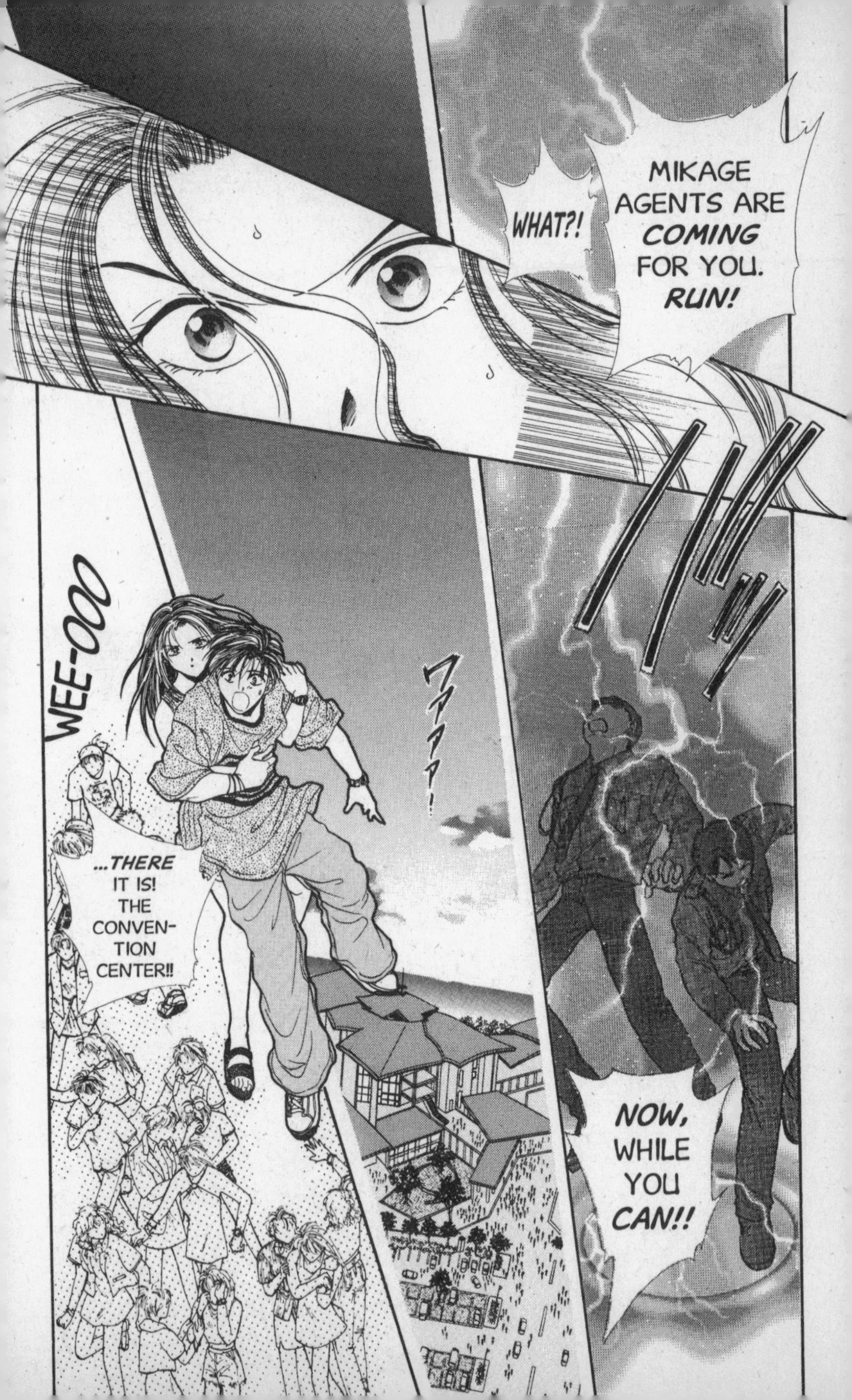
MIKAGE AGENTS ARE COMING FOR YOU. RUN!
WHAT?!
NOW, WHILE YOU CAN!!
WEE-OOO
ワァァァ!
...THERE IT IS! THE CONVEN-TION CENTER!!

Ceres: 6

"Being difficult" with Tōya is when Aya is most cute, I think. :-) It's like her to be upfront with her feelings, but that's also when she's being "girly"—acting like a child to get Tōya's attention. Not that I want it to be "all about the guy" with her—she holds it together when he's gone. When she **does** get to see him, though, she lets it all go. She wants that attention from him.

So! The love interests. Here's where all kinds of rules get broken. What I've done is split the role between Tōya and Yūhi. (Yūhi **does** seem more the typical love-interest, doesn't he?)

Let's talk about Tōya first. His attitude and background would make you **think** he's the love-interest, wouldn't they? I am so-o-o having fun with this. Has a love-interest **ever** been away so much from the main character...? Still, he manages to steal all the juicy scenes, and so has a devoted following. He's got it going on in the looks department, too. There are those who write to say, "I only read the series to see Tōya..." ...True, sometimes I **do** take upwards of an hour (!) just penciling one of his close-ups...I think maybe I'm trying to draw my most beautiful-est guy ever. What I like about Tōya is that, in the best sense, he's his own man. Guys shouldn't be tied to their girls. Tōya doesn't live **for** the heroine. When they say things like "Never leave me," girls are being selfish. I would never want a guy who just clings to a girl and doesn't even have his own life! And guys for their part, they shouldn't be all talk—especially not about the really important things. This is why I love how, in Volume 5, Tōya left the Aogiri house without a word. He knew what he had to do for Aki, and of course Aya was important to him too, but that was a whole separate thing. Just because he's the love-interest, I don't want Tōya to be the kind of guy who says cheesy lines and flirts all the time... (Wait, what am I saying here?)

Fans of Yūhi feel sorry for...

Oops! No more room.

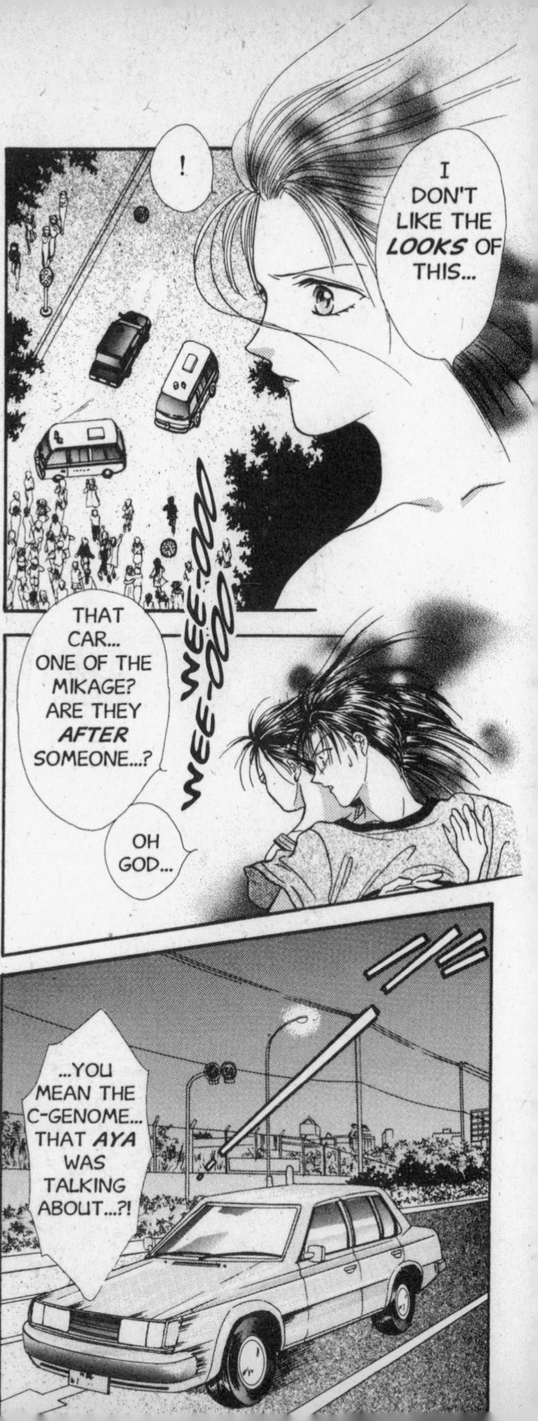

I DON'T LIKE THE *LOOKS* OF THIS...
!
WEE-OOO WEE-OOO
THAT CAR... ONE OF THE MIKAGE? ARE THEY *AFTER* SOMEONE...?
OH GOD...
...YOU MEAN THE C-GENOME... THAT *AYA* WAS TALKING ABOUT...?!

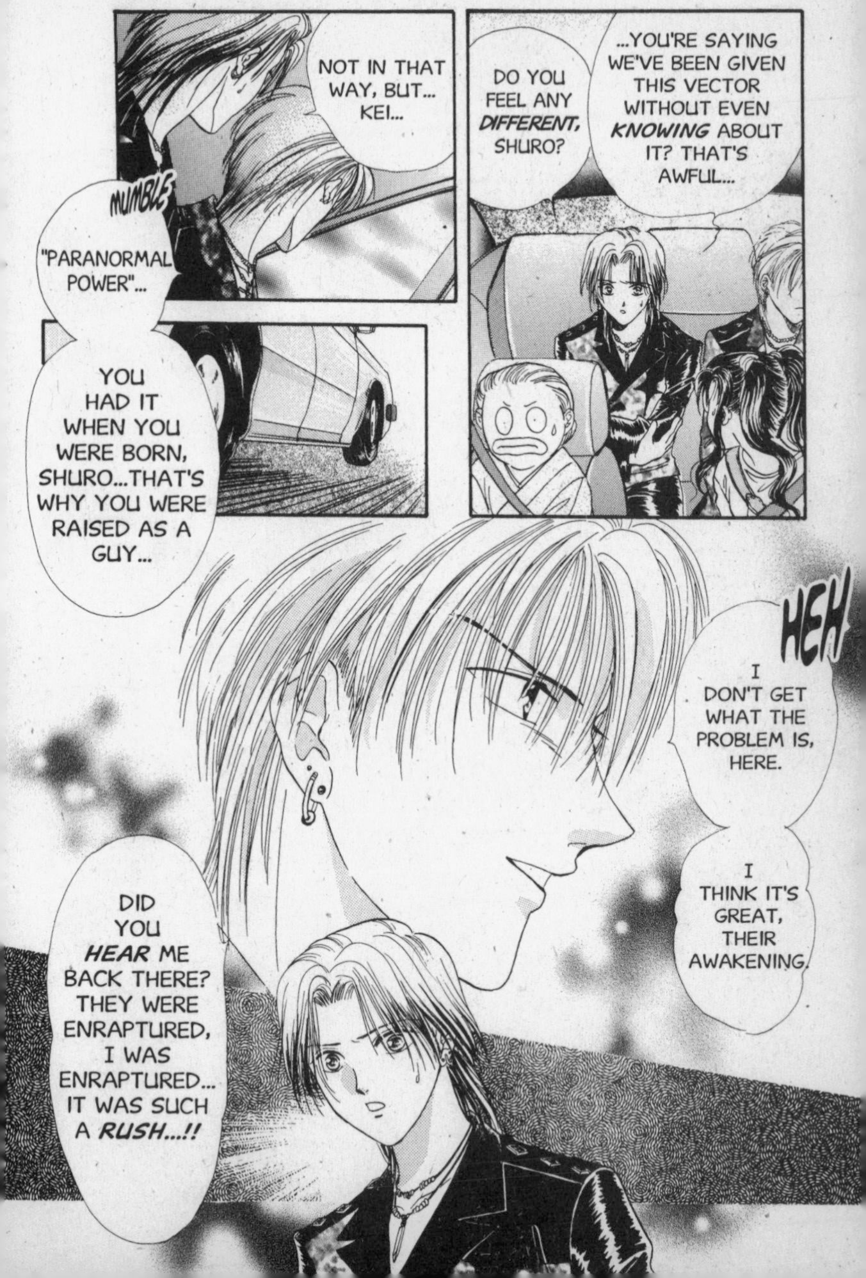

...YOU'RE SAYING WE'VE BEEN GIVEN THIS VECTOR WITHOUT EVEN *KNOWING* ABOUT IT? THAT'S AWFUL...
DO YOU FEEL ANY *DIFFERENT,* SHURO?
NOT IN THAT WAY, BUT... KEI...
MUMBLE
"PARANORMAL POWER"...
YOU HAD IT WHEN YOU WERE BORN, SHURO...THAT'S WHY YOU WERE RAISED AS A GUY...
HEH
I DON'T GET WHAT THE PROBLEM IS, HERE.
I THINK IT'S GREAT, THEIR AWAKENING.
DID YOU *HEAR* ME BACK THERE? THEY WERE ENRAPTURED, I WAS ENRAPTURED... IT WAS SUCH A *RUSH*...!!

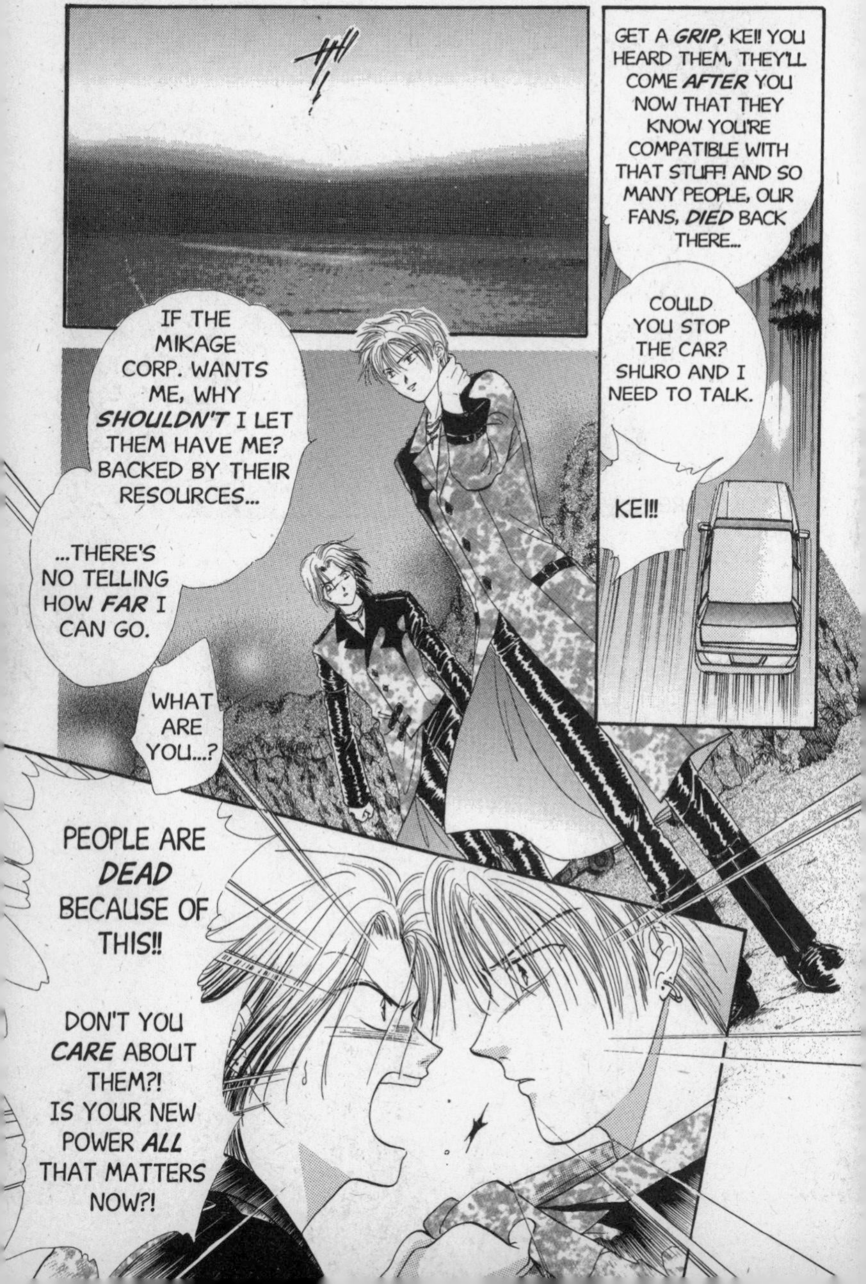
GET A *GRIP,* KEI! YOU HEARD THEM, THEY'LL COME *AFTER* YOU NOW THAT THEY KNOW YOU'RE COMPATIBLE WITH THAT STUFF! AND SO MANY PEOPLE, OUR FANS, *DIED* BACK THERE...
COULD YOU STOP THE CAR? SHURO AND I NEED TO TALK.
KEI!!
IF THE MIKAGE CORP. WANTS ME, WHY *SHOULDN'T* I LET THEM HAVE ME? BACKED BY THEIR RESOURCES...
...THERE'S NO TELLING HOW *FAR* I CAN GO.
WHAT ARE YOU...?
PEOPLE ARE *DEAD* BECAUSE OF THIS!!
DON'T YOU *CARE* ABOUT THEM?! IS YOUR NEW POWER *ALL* THAT MATTERS NOW?!

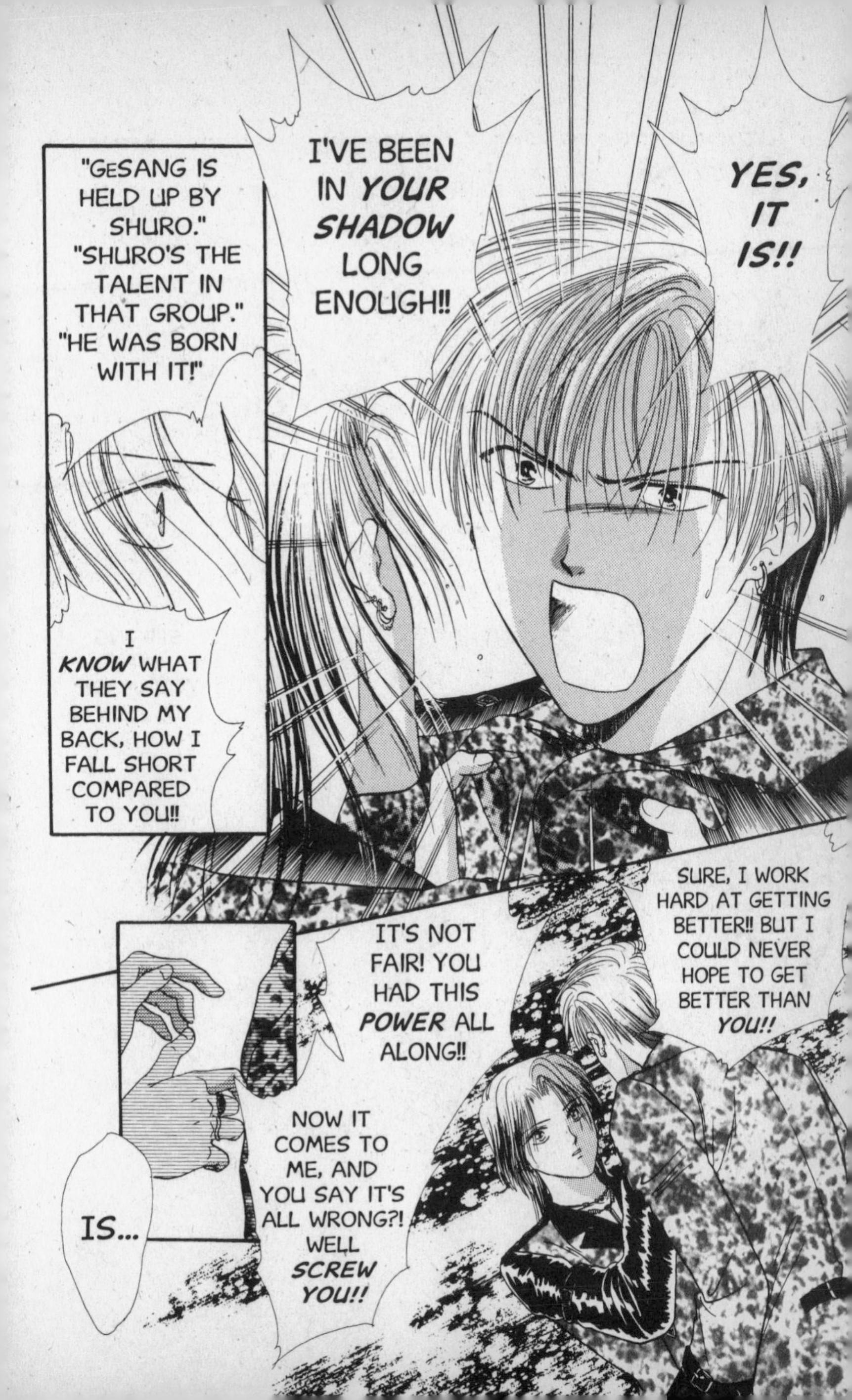
YES, IT IS!!
I'VE BEEN IN YOUR SHADOW LONG ENOUGH!!
"GESANG IS HELD UP BY SHURO." "SHURO'S THE TALENT IN THAT GROUP." "HE WAS BORN WITH IT!"
I KNOW WHAT THEY SAY BEHIND MY BACK, HOW I FALL SHORT COMPARED TO YOU!!
SURE, I WORK HARD AT GETTING BETTER!! BUT I COULD NEVER HOPE TO GET BETTER THAN YOU!!
IT'S NOT FAIR! YOU HAD THIS POWER ALL ALONG!!
NOW IT COMES TO ME, AND YOU SAY IT'S ALL WRONG?! WELL SCREW YOU!!
IS...

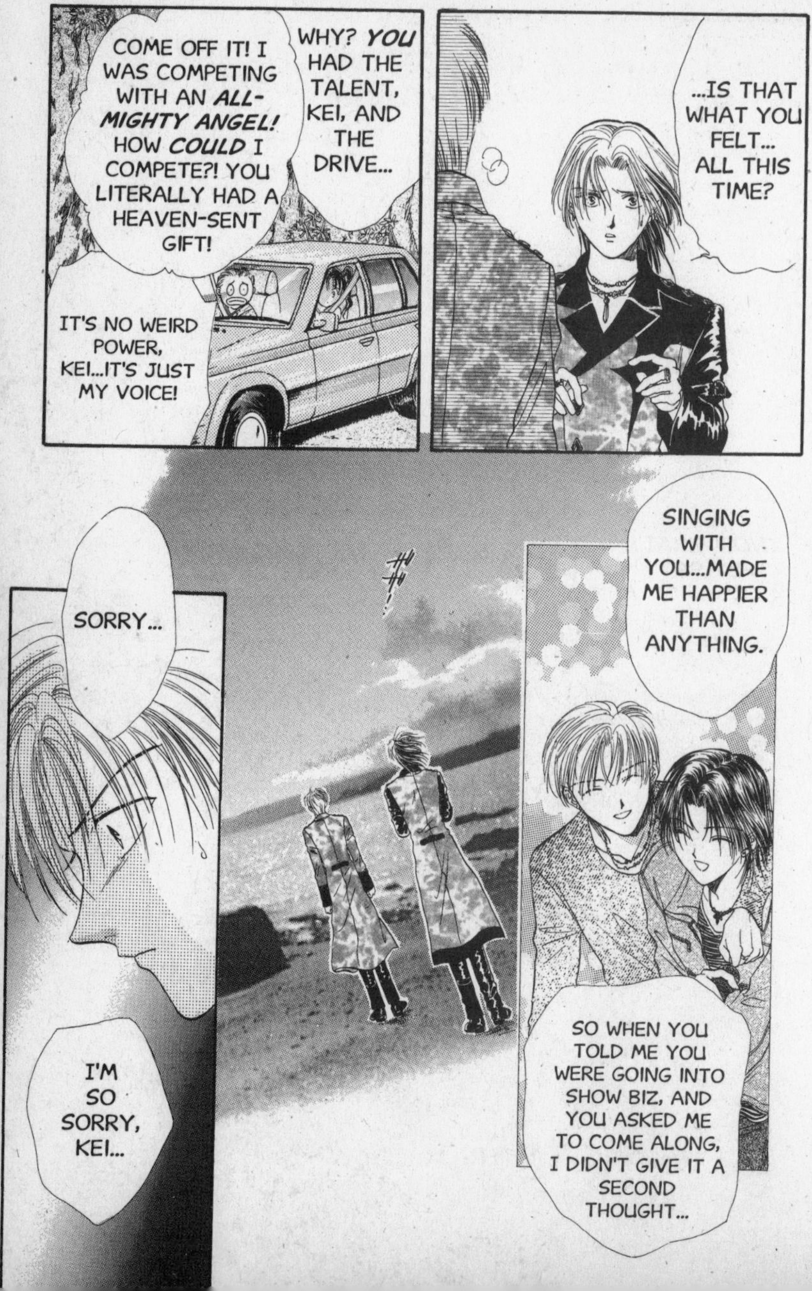
...IS THAT WHAT YOU FELT... ALL THIS TIME?
WHY? *YOU* HAD THE TALENT, KEI, AND THE DRIVE...
COME OFF IT! I WAS COMPETING WITH AN *ALL-MIGHTY ANGEL!* HOW *COULD* I COMPETE?! YOU LITERALLY HAD A HEAVEN-SENT GIFT!
IT'S NO WEIRD POWER, KEI...IT'S JUST MY VOICE!
SINGING WITH YOU...MADE ME HAPPIER THAN ANYTHING.
SO WHEN YOU TOLD ME YOU WERE GOING INTO SHOW BIZ, AND YOU ASKED ME TO COME ALONG, I DIDN'T GIVE IT A SECOND THOUGHT...
SORRY...
I'M SO SORRY, KEI...

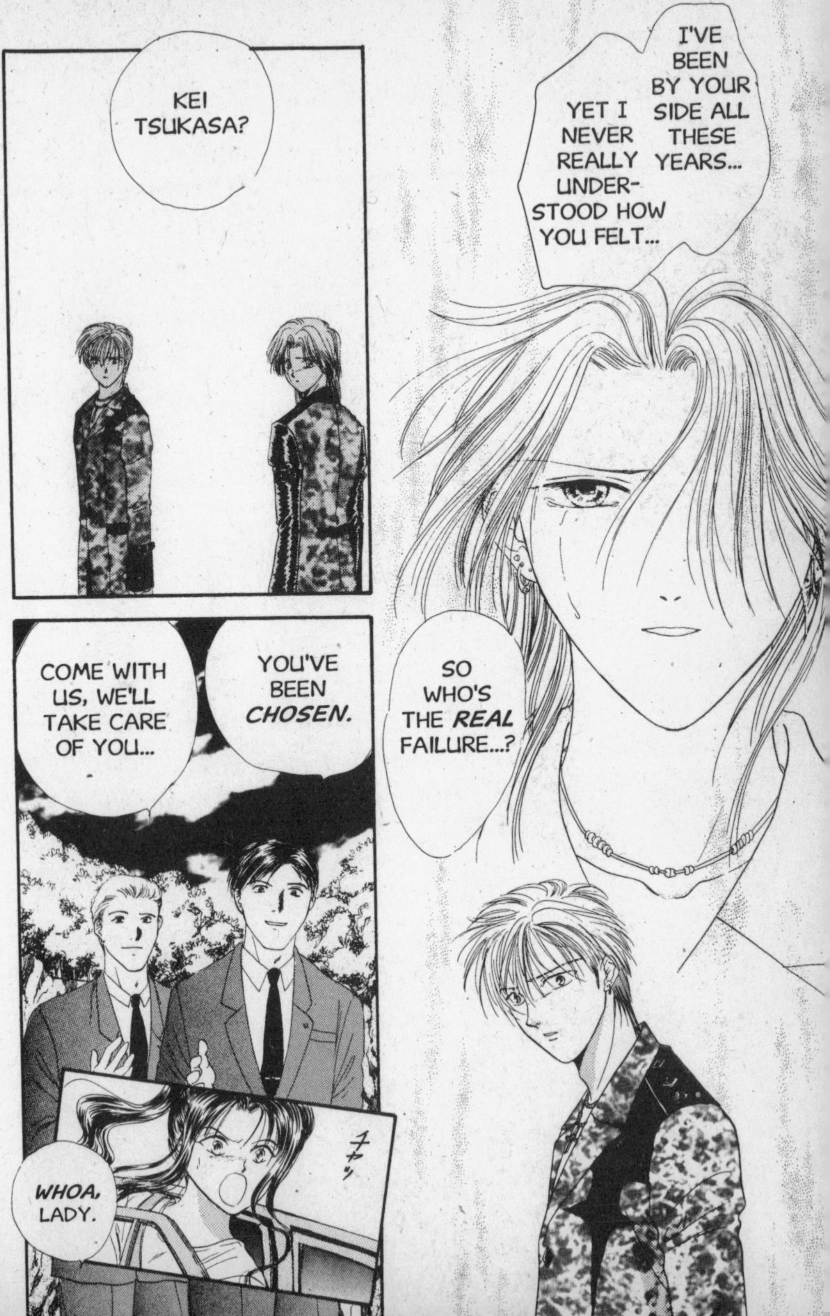
I'VE BEEN BY YOUR SIDE ALL THESE YEARS... YET I NEVER REALLY UNDER-STOOD HOW YOU FELT...
SO WHO'S THE *REAL* FAILURE...?
KEI TSUKASA?
YOU'VE BEEN *CHOSEN.*
COME WITH US, WE'LL TAKE CARE OF YOU...
チャッ
WHOA, LADY.

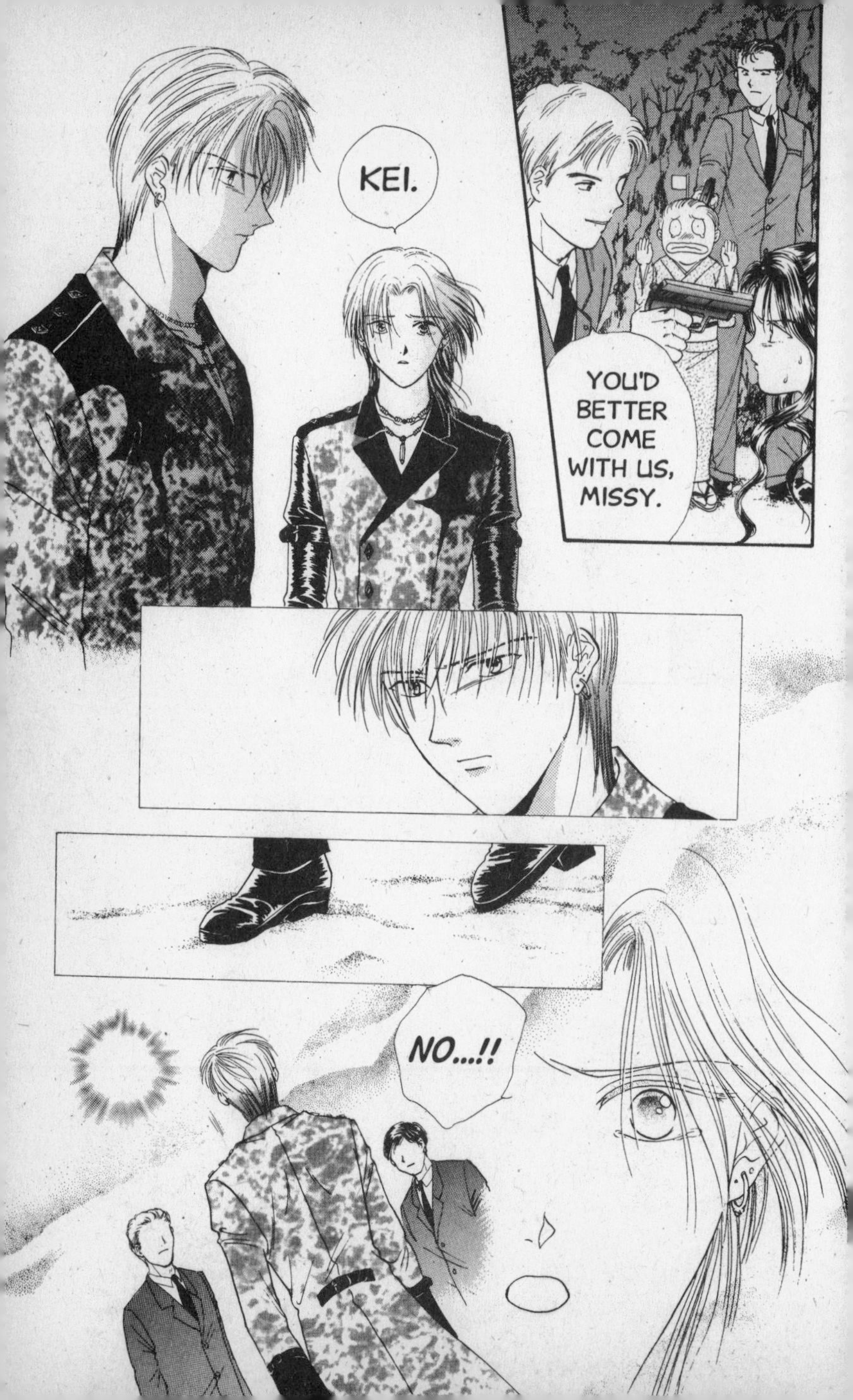
YOU'D BETTER COME WITH US, MISSY.
KEI.
NO...!!

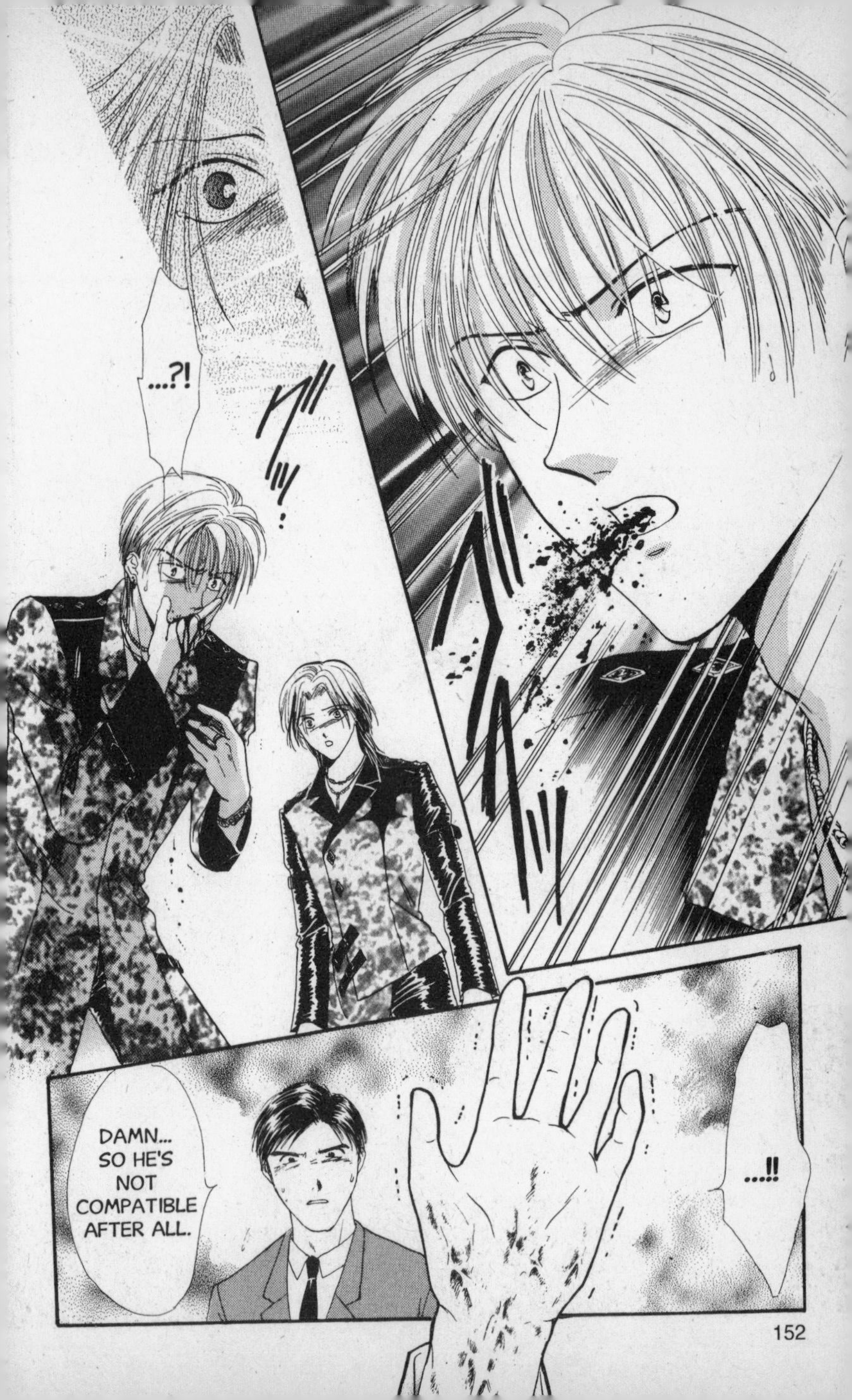
...?!
...!!
DAMN... SO HE'S NOT COMPATIBLE AFTER ALL.

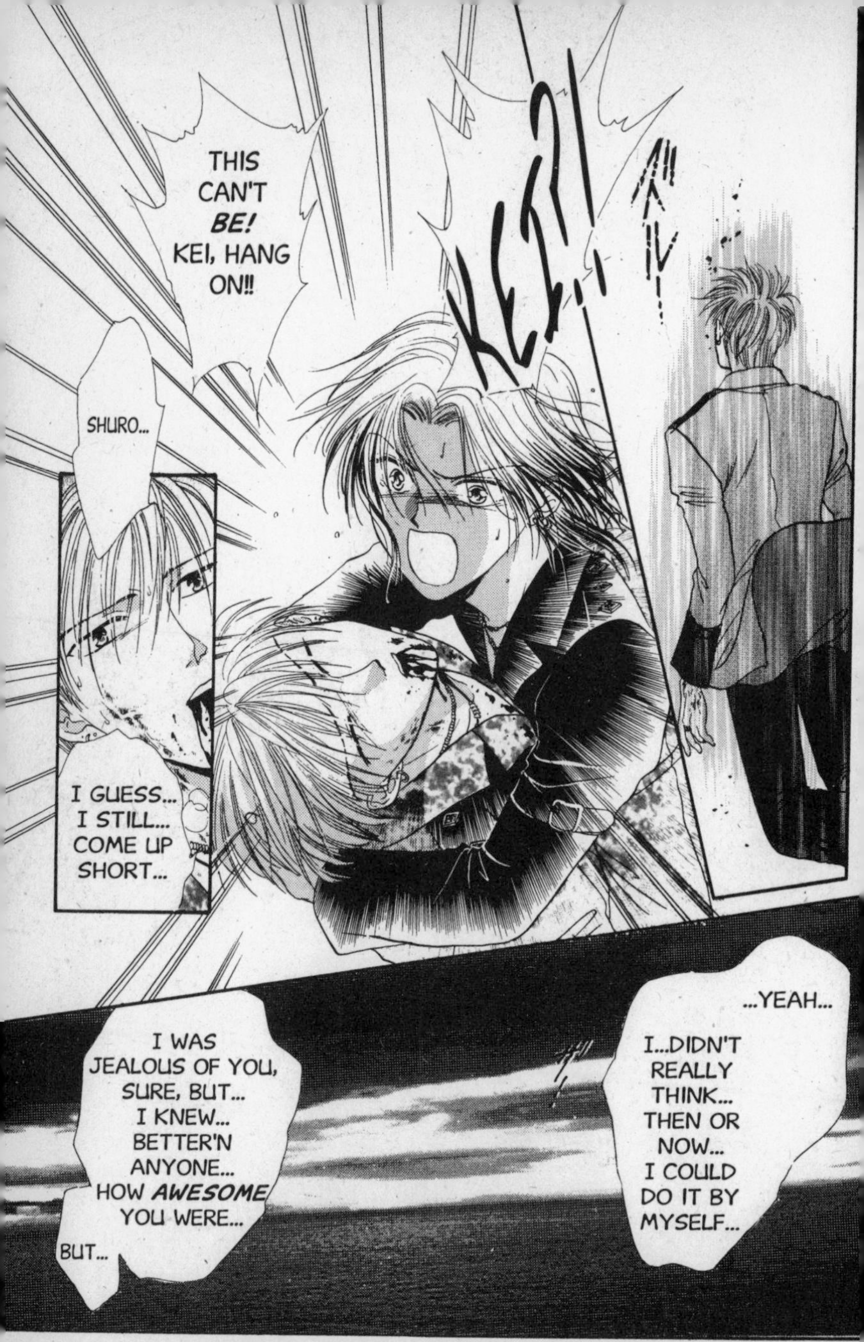
KEI?!
THIS CAN'T BE! KEI, HANG ON!!
SHURO...
I GUESS... I STILL... COME UP SHORT...
...YEAH...
I...DIDN'T REALLY THINK... THEN OR NOW... I COULD DO IT BY MYSELF...
I WAS JEALOUS OF YOU, SURE, BUT... I KNEW... BETTER'N ANYONE... HOW AWESOME YOU WERE...
BUT...

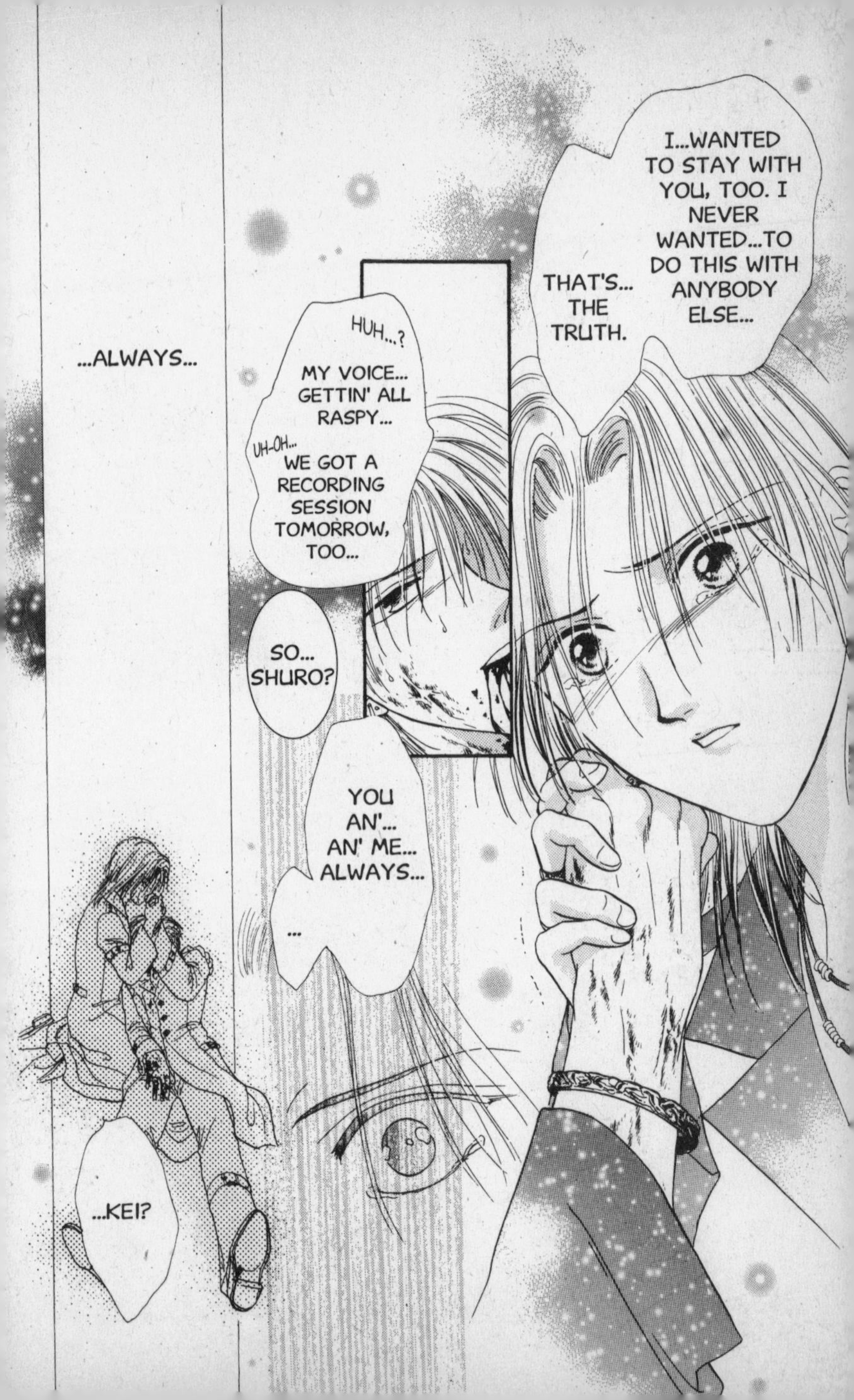
I...WANTED TO STAY WITH YOU, TOO. I NEVER WANTED...TO DO THIS WITH ANYBODY ELSE...
THAT'S... THE TRUTH.
HUH...?
MY VOICE... GETTIN' ALL RASPY...
UH-OH...
WE GOT A RECORDING SESSION TOMORROW, TOO...
SO... SHURO?
YOU AN'... AN' ME... ALWAYS...
...
...ALWAYS...
...KEI?

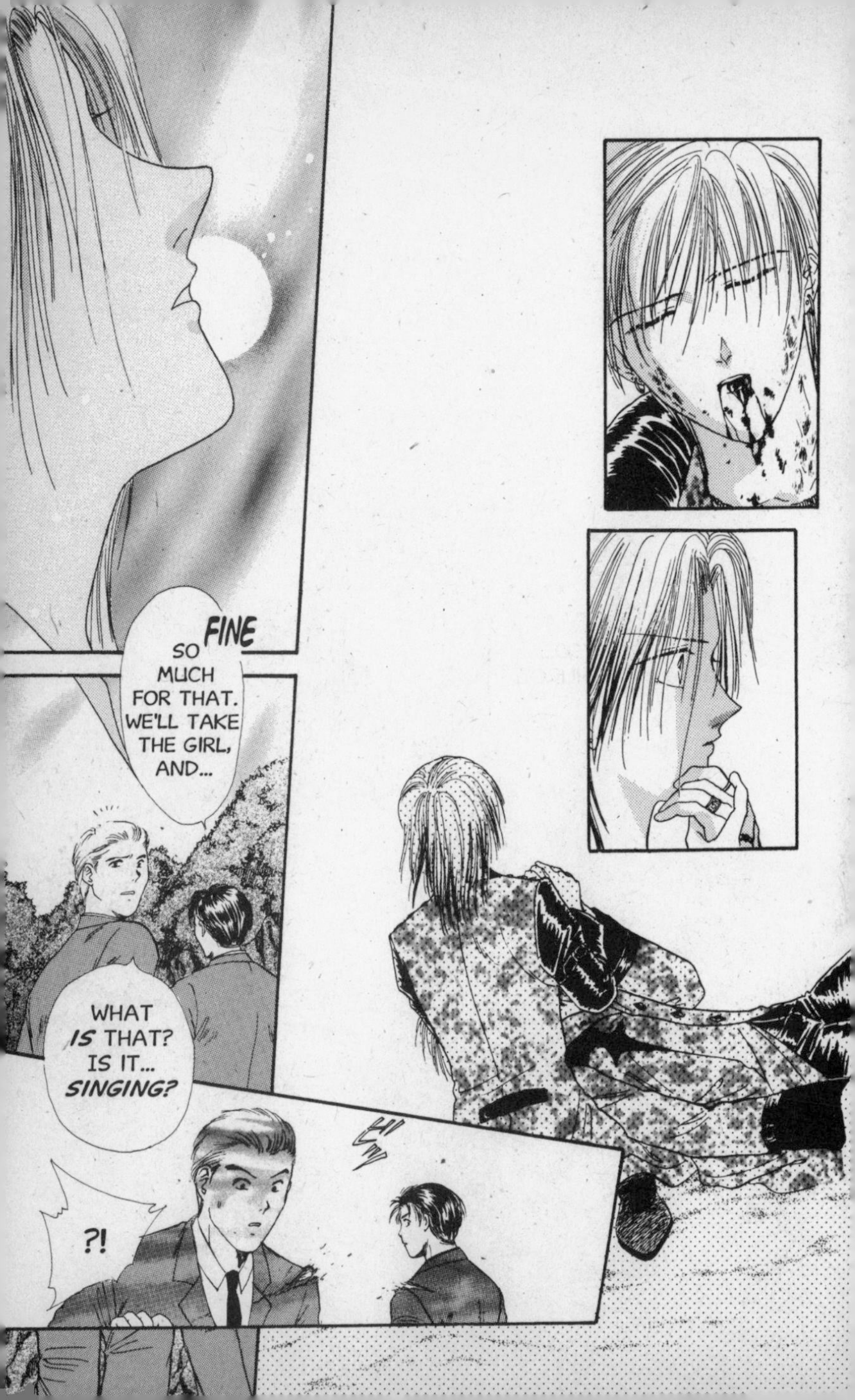
FINE
SO MUCH FOR THAT. WE'LL TAKE THE GIRL, AND...
WHAT *IS* THAT? IS IT... *SINGING?*
?!

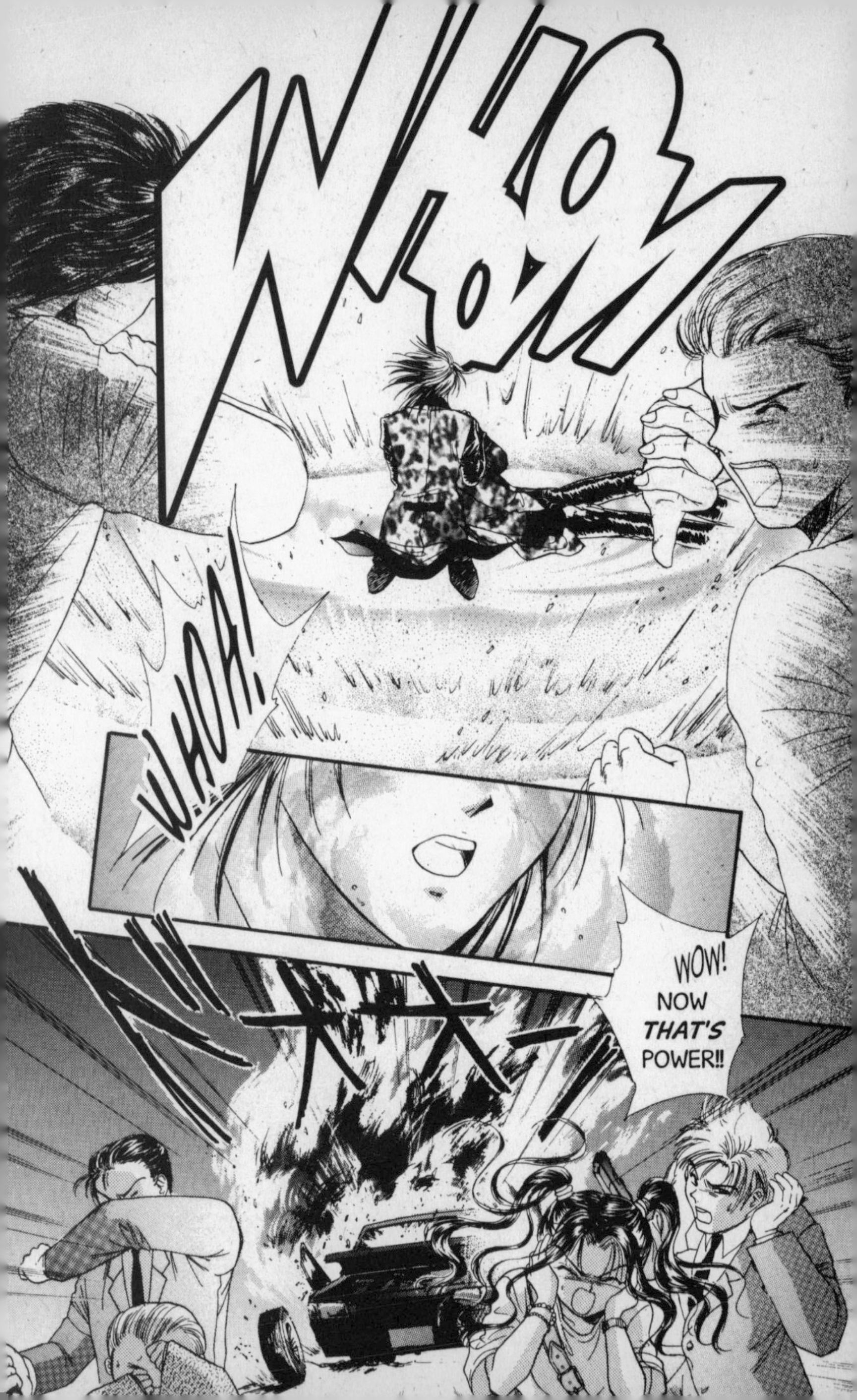
WHOOM
WHOA!
WOW! NOW THAT'S POWER!!

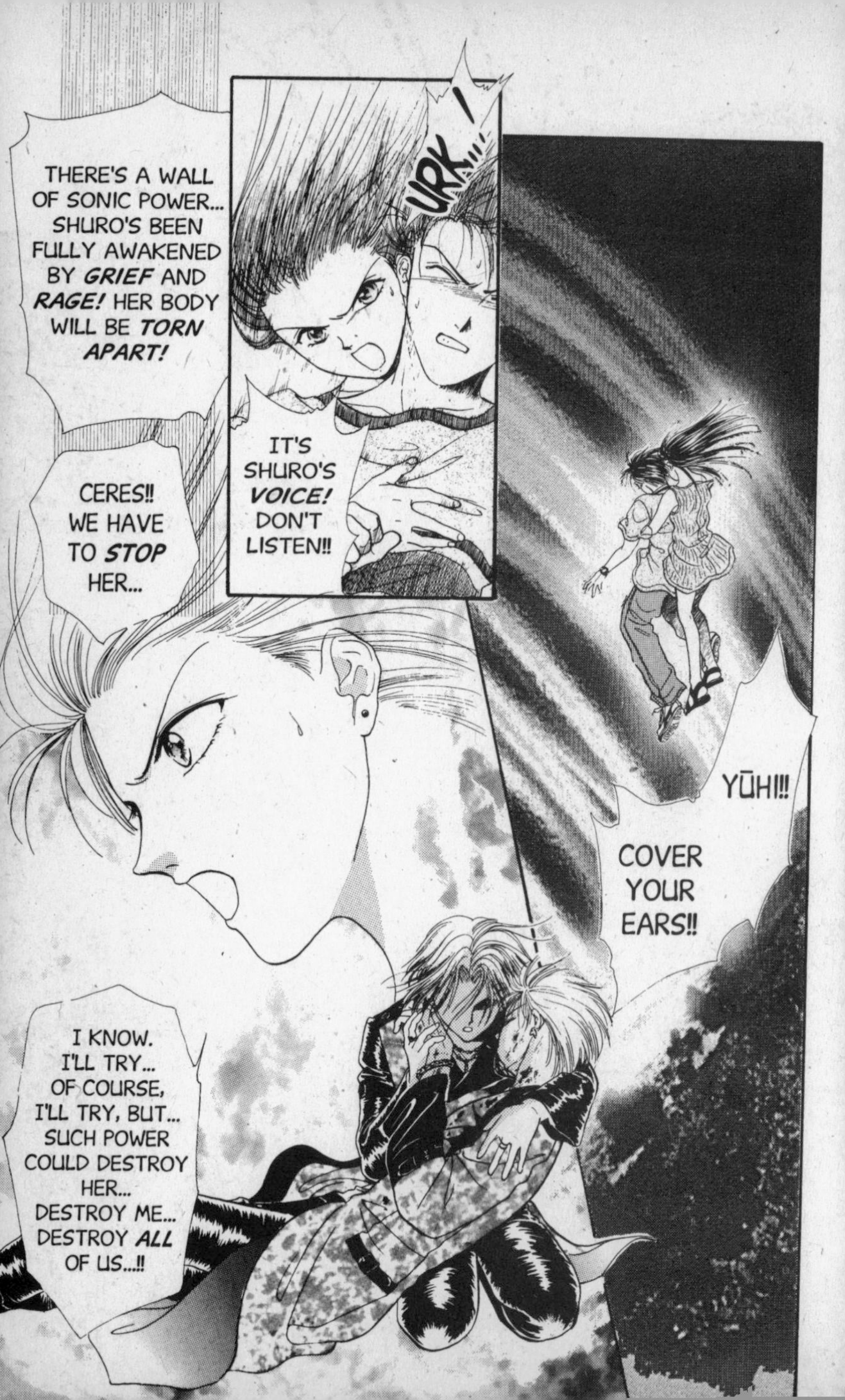
URK...!!
IT'S SHURO'S VOICE! DON'T LISTEN!!
YŪHI!!
COVER YOUR EARS!!
THERE'S A WALL OF SONIC POWER... SHURO'S BEEN FULLY AWAKENED BY GRIEF AND RAGE! HER BODY WILL BE TORN APART!
CERES!! WE HAVE TO STOP HER...
I KNOW. I'LL TRY... OF COURSE, I'LL TRY, BUT... SUCH POWER COULD DESTROY HER... DESTROY ME... DESTROY ALL OF US...!!

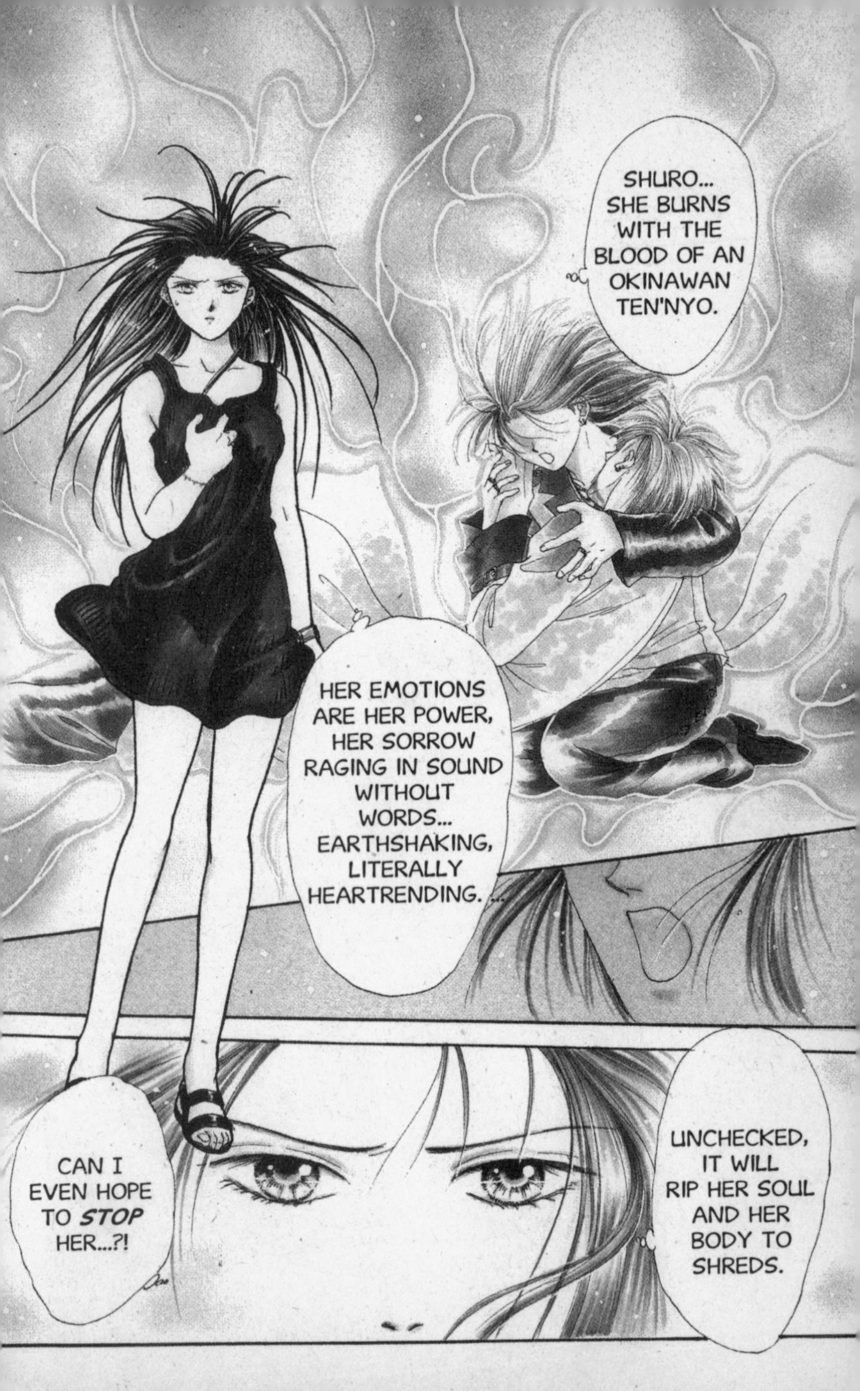
SHURO... SHE BURNS WITH THE BLOOD OF AN OKINAWAN TEN'NYO.
HER EMOTIONS ARE HER POWER, HER SORROW RAGING IN SOUND WITHOUT WORDS... EARTHSHAKING, LITERALLY HEARTRENDING.
UNCHECKED, IT WILL RIP HER SOUL AND HER BODY TO SHREDS.
CAN I EVEN HOPE TO *STOP* HER...?!

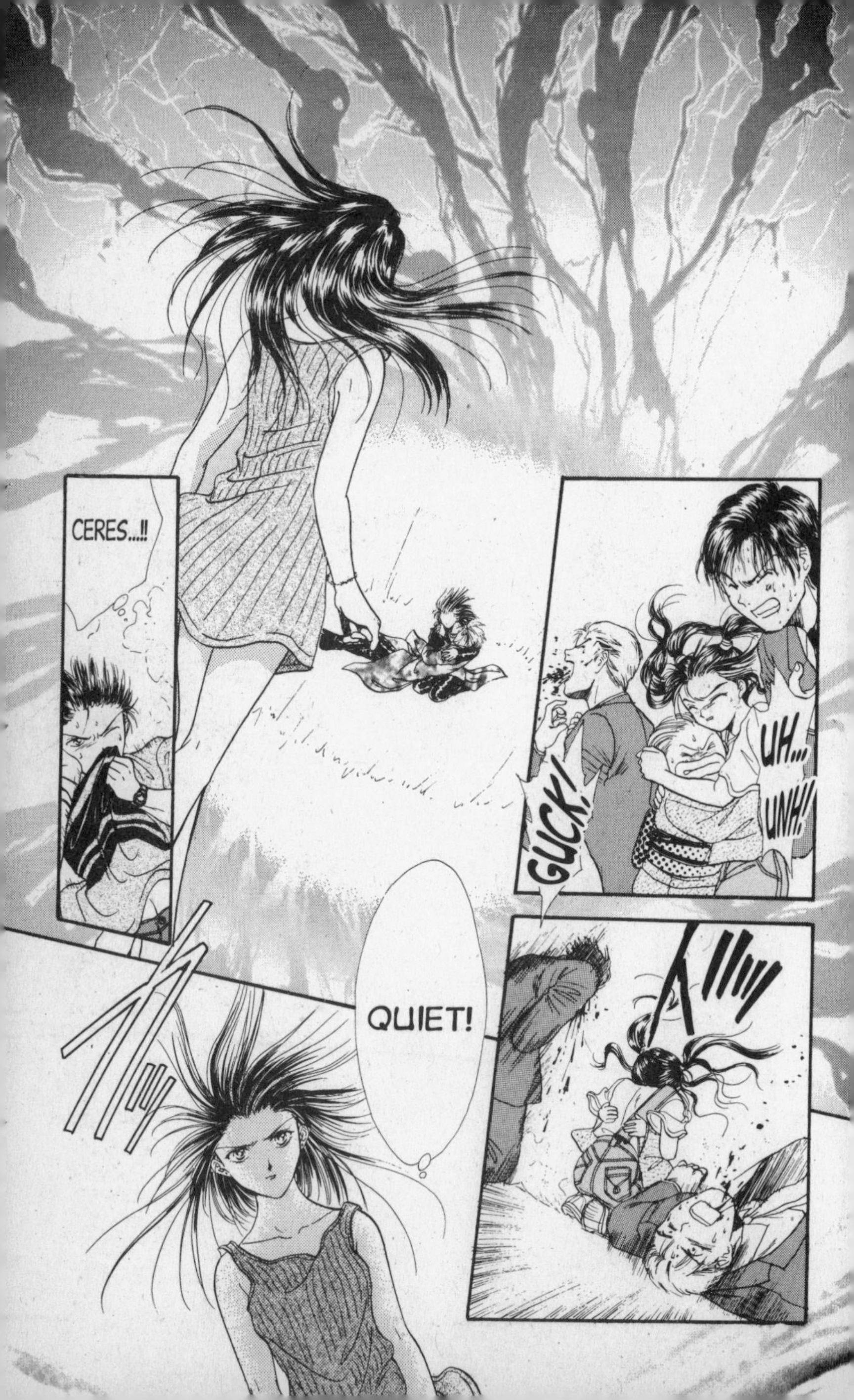
UH... UNH!!
GUCK!
CERES...!!
QUIET!

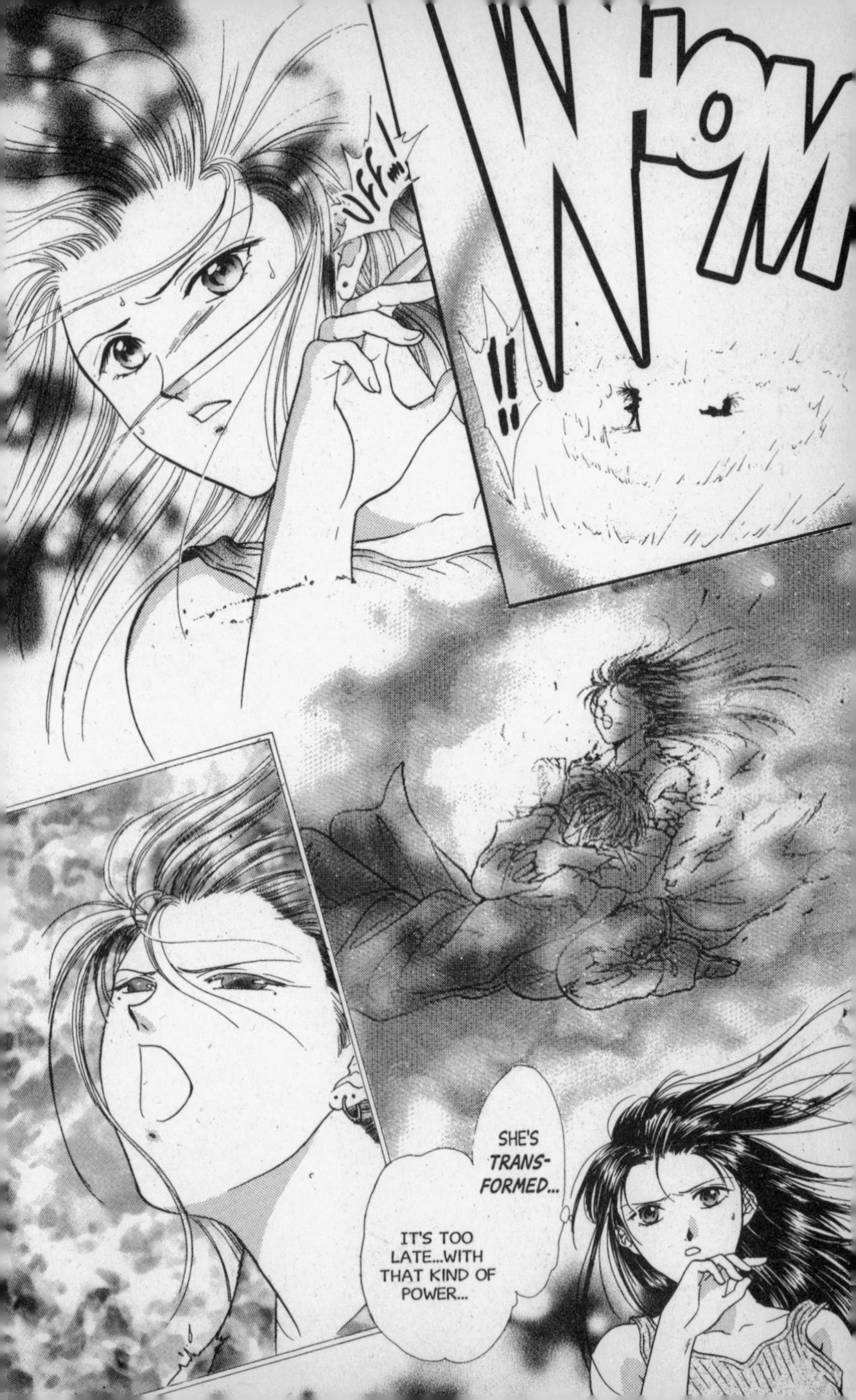

SHE'S TRANSFORMED...
IT'S TOO LATE...WITH THAT KIND OF POWER...

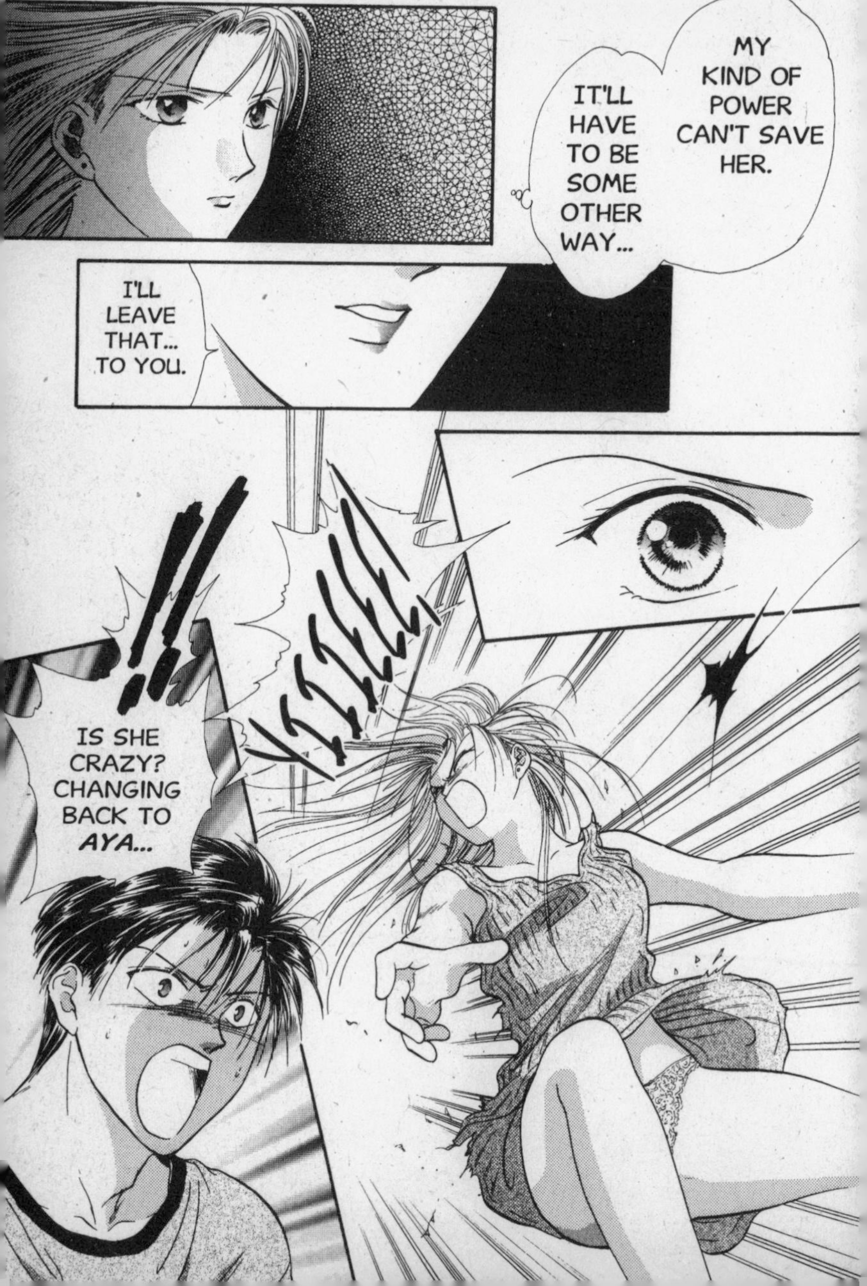
MY KIND OF POWER CAN'T SAVE HER.
IT'LL HAVE TO BE SOME OTHER WAY...
I'LL LEAVE THAT... TO YOU.
YIIEEE
!!
IS SHE CRAZY? CHANGING BACK TO *AYA*...

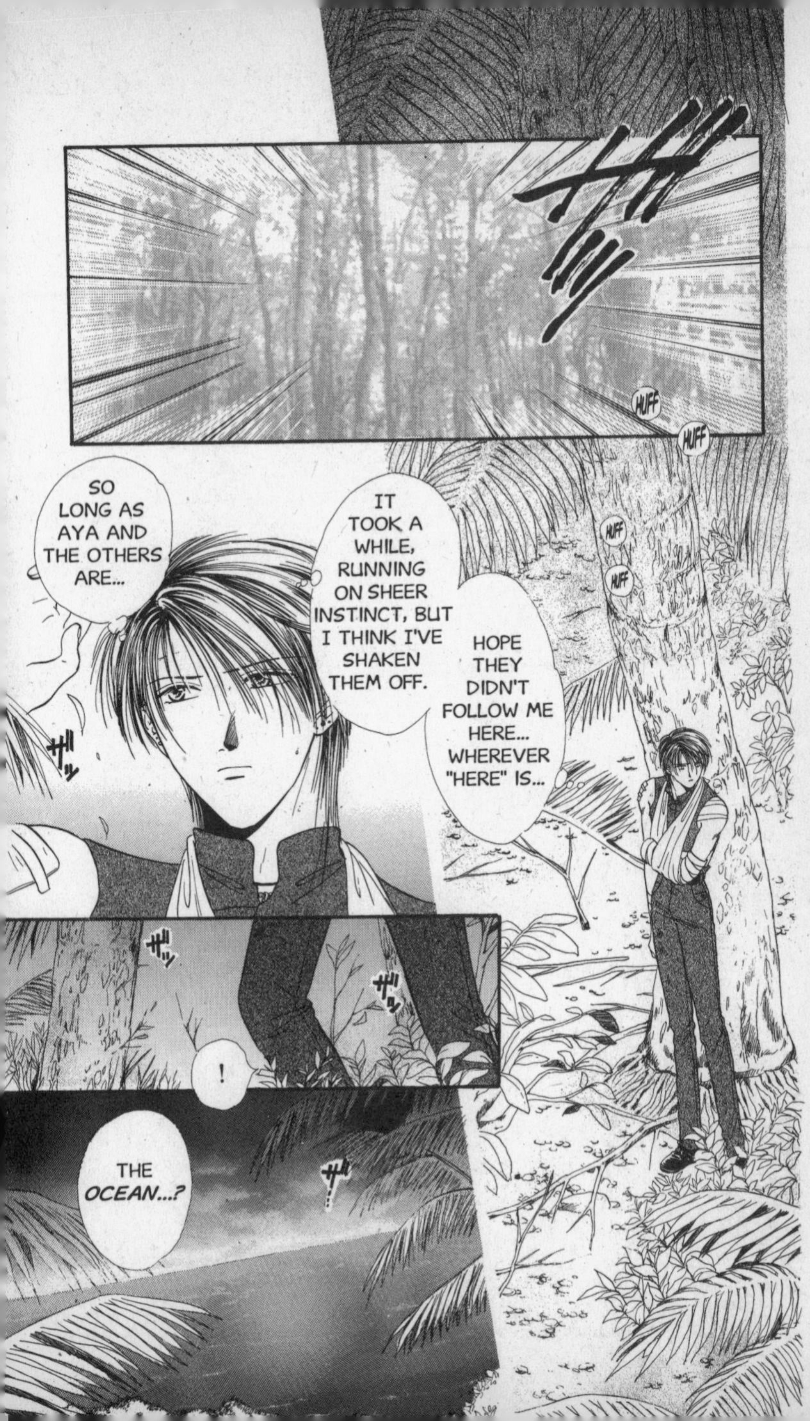
HUFF
HUFF
HUFF
HUFF
IT TOOK A WHILE, RUNNING ON SHEER INSTINCT, BUT I THINK I'VE SHAKEN THEM OFF.
HOPE THEY DIDN'T FOLLOW ME HERE... WHEREVER "HERE" IS...
SO LONG AS AYA AND THE OTHERS ARE...
!
THE *OCEAN*...?

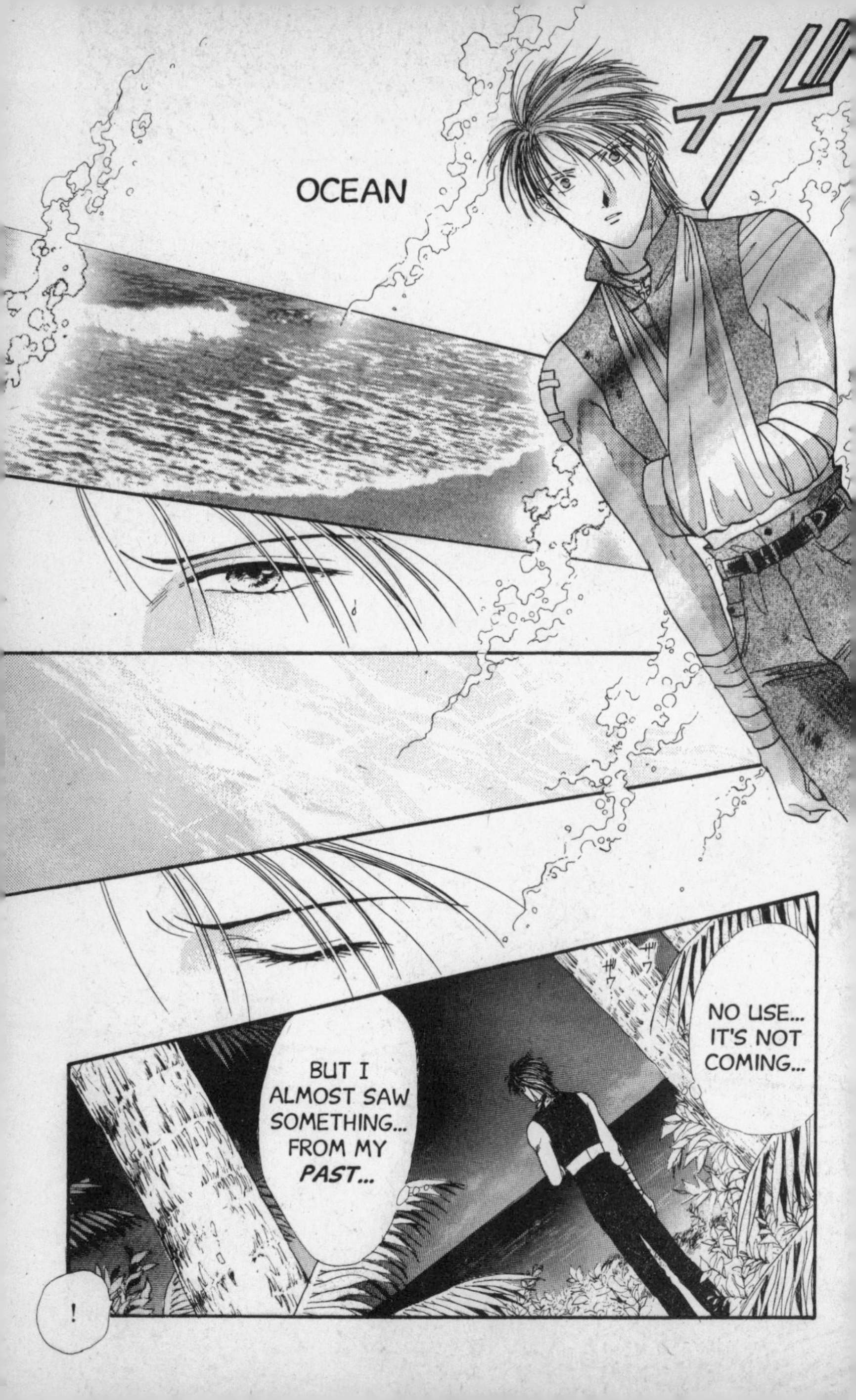
OCEAN
NO USE... IT'S NOT COMING...
BUT I ALMOST SAW SOMETHING... FROM MY *PAST*...
!

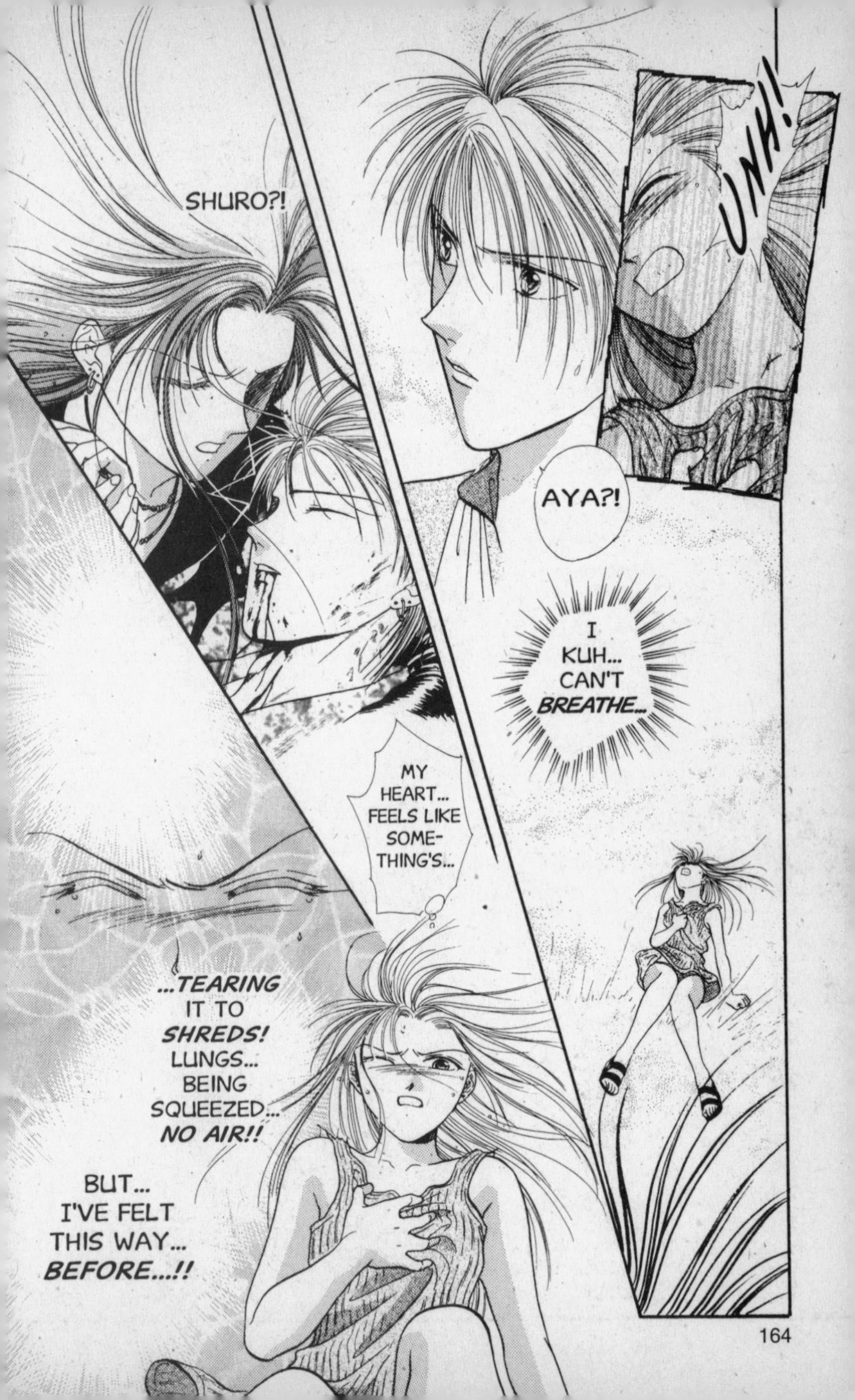
UNH!!
AYA?!
I KUH... CAN'T BREATHE...
SHURO?!
MY HEART... FEELS LIKE SOME-THING'S...
...TEARING IT TO SHREDS! LUNGS... BEING SQUEEZED... NO AIR!!
BUT... I'VE FELT THIS WAY... BEFORE...!!

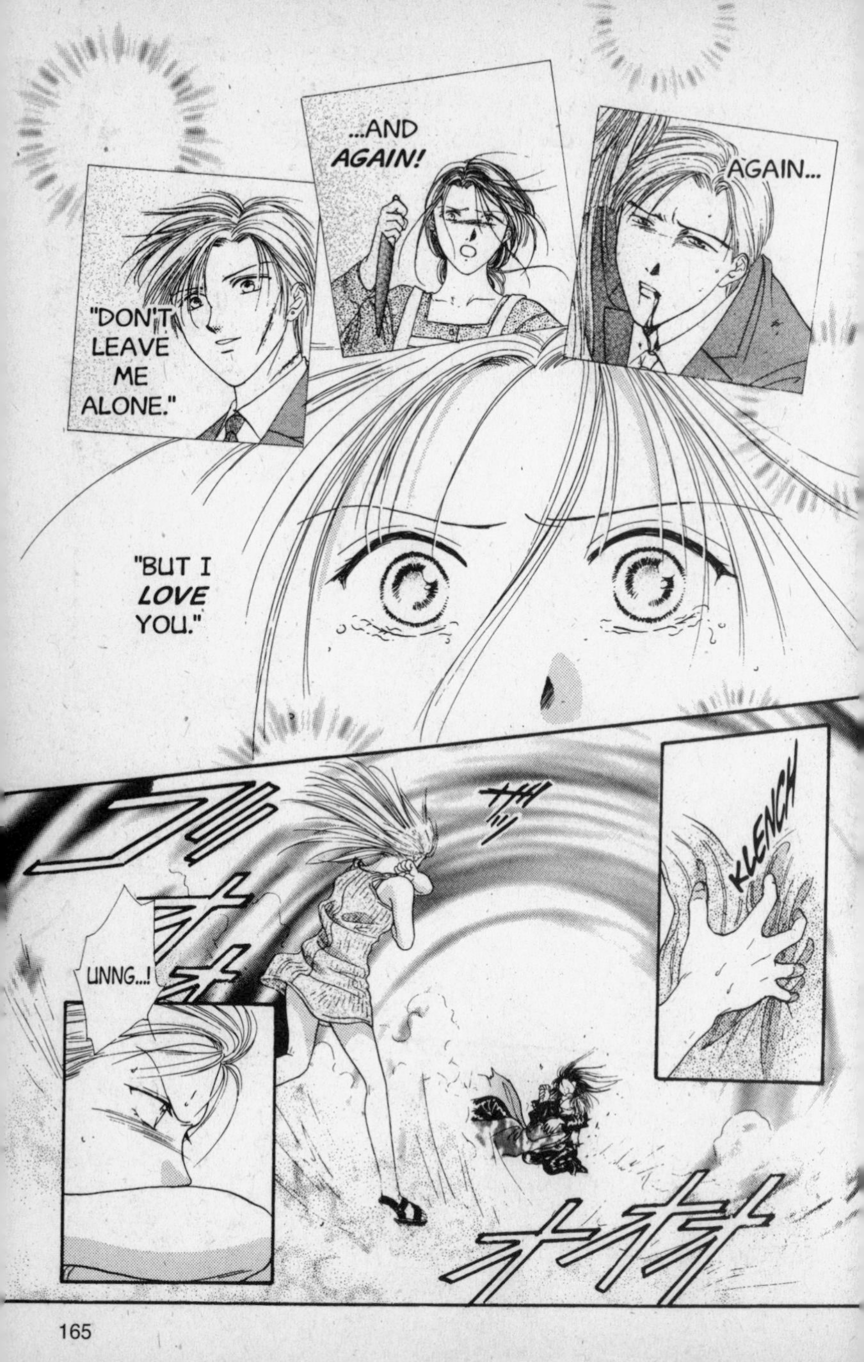
AGAIN...
...AND AGAIN!
"DON'T LEAVE ME ALONE."
"BUT I LOVE YOU."
KLENCH
UNNG...!

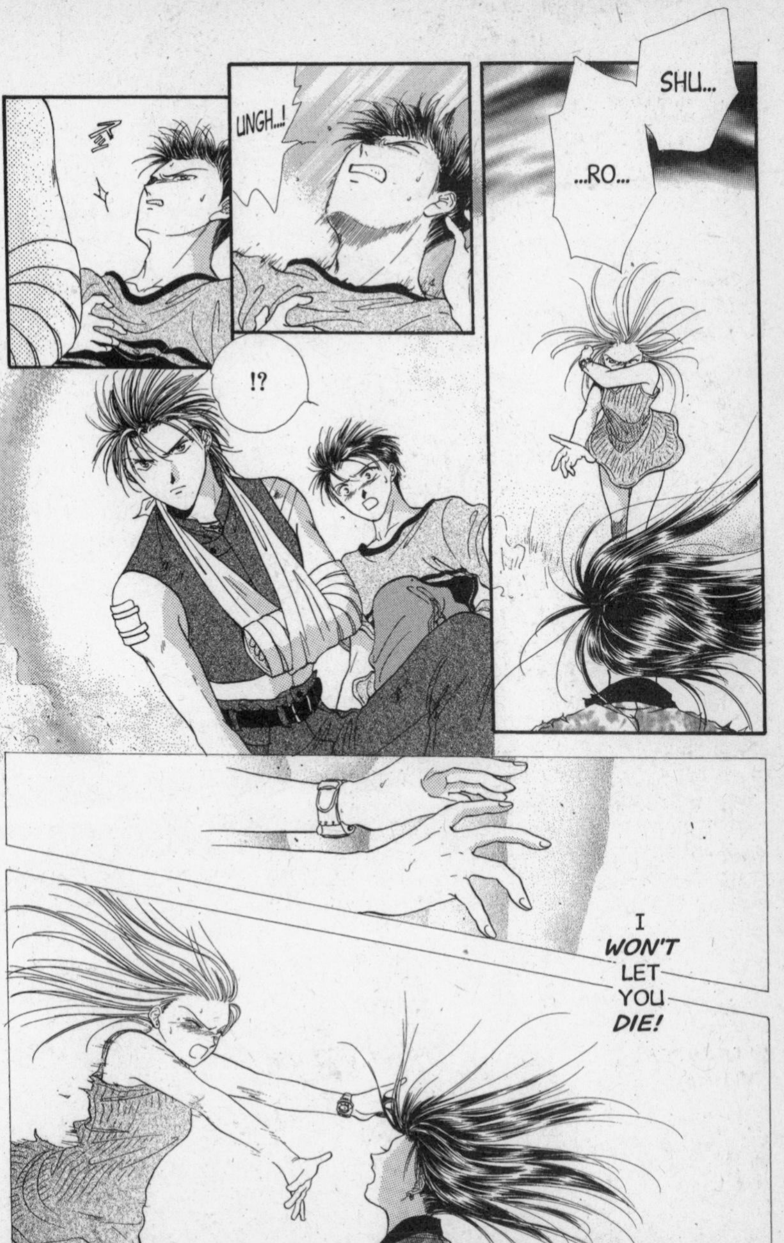
SHU...
...RO...
UNGH...!
!?
I *WON'T* LET YOU *DIE!*

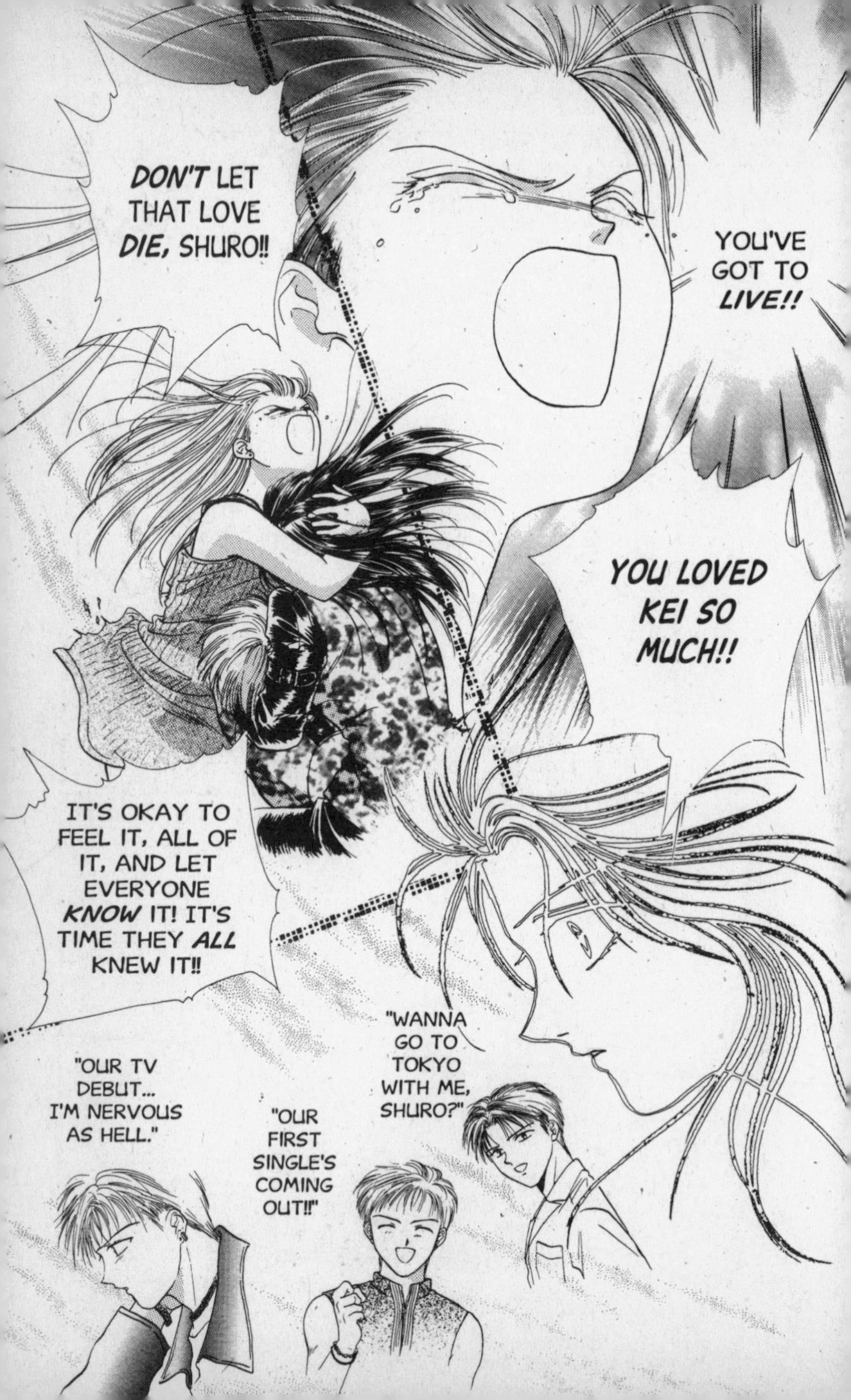
DON'T LET THAT LOVE *DIE,* SHURO!!
YOU'VE GOT TO *LIVE!!*
YOU LOVED KEI SO MUCH!!
IT'S OKAY TO FEEL IT, ALL OF IT, AND LET EVERYONE *KNOW* IT! IT'S TIME THEY *ALL* KNEW IT!!
"WANNA GO TO TOKYO WITH ME, SHURO?"
"OUR FIRST SINGLE'S COMING OUT!!"
"OUR TV DEBUT... I'M NERVOUS AS HELL."

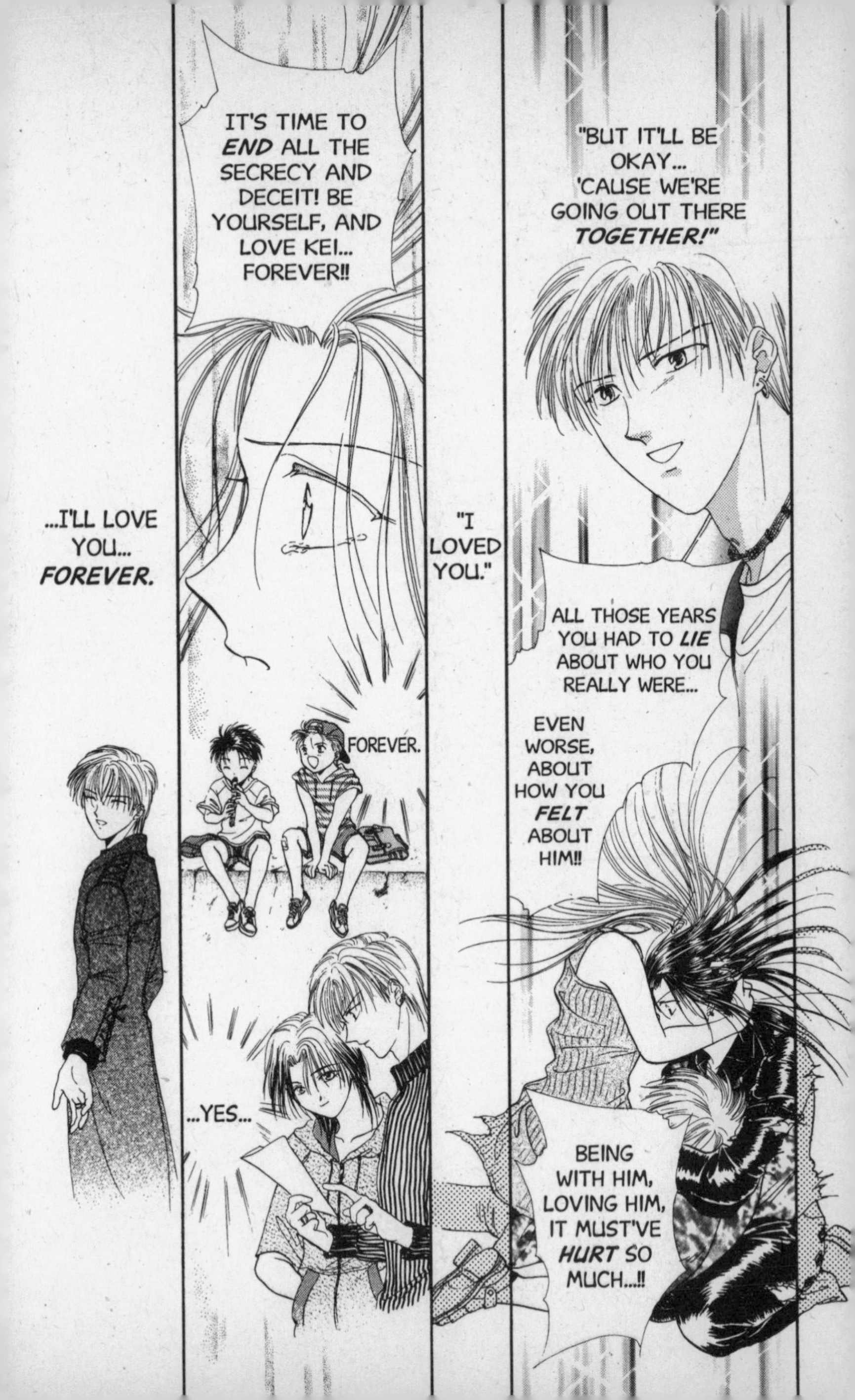
"BUT IT'LL BE OKAY... 'CAUSE WE'RE GOING OUT THERE TOGETHER!"
ALL THOSE YEARS YOU HAD TO LIE ABOUT WHO YOU REALLY WERE...
EVEN WORSE, ABOUT HOW YOU FELT ABOUT HIM!!
BEING WITH HIM, LOVING HIM, IT MUST'VE HURT SO MUCH...!!
"I LOVED YOU."
IT'S TIME TO END ALL THE SECRECY AND DECEIT! BE YOURSELF, AND LOVE KEI... FOREVER!!
FOREVER.
...YES...
...I'LL LOVE YOU... FOREVER.

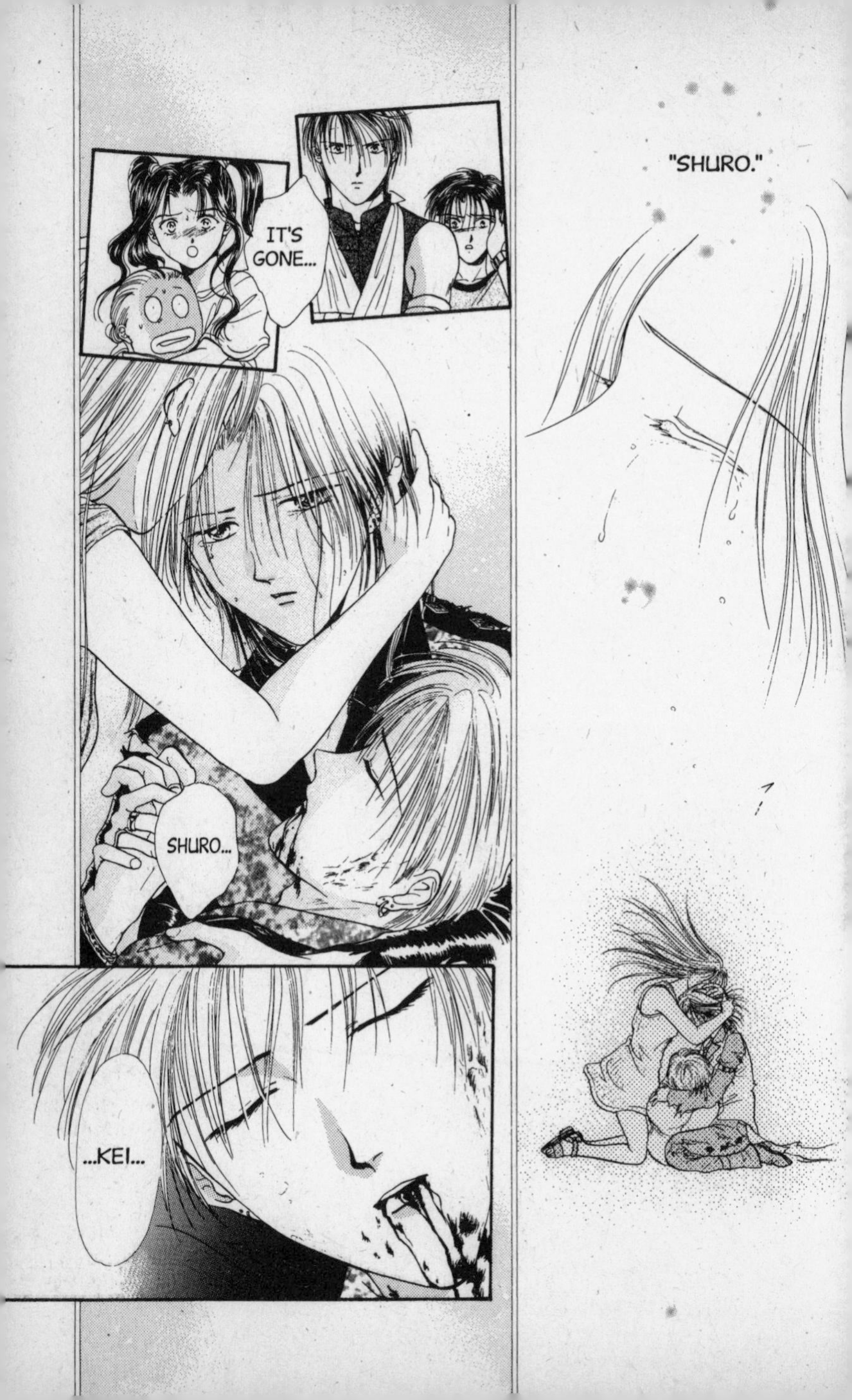
"SHURO."
IT'S GONE...
SHURO...
...KEI...

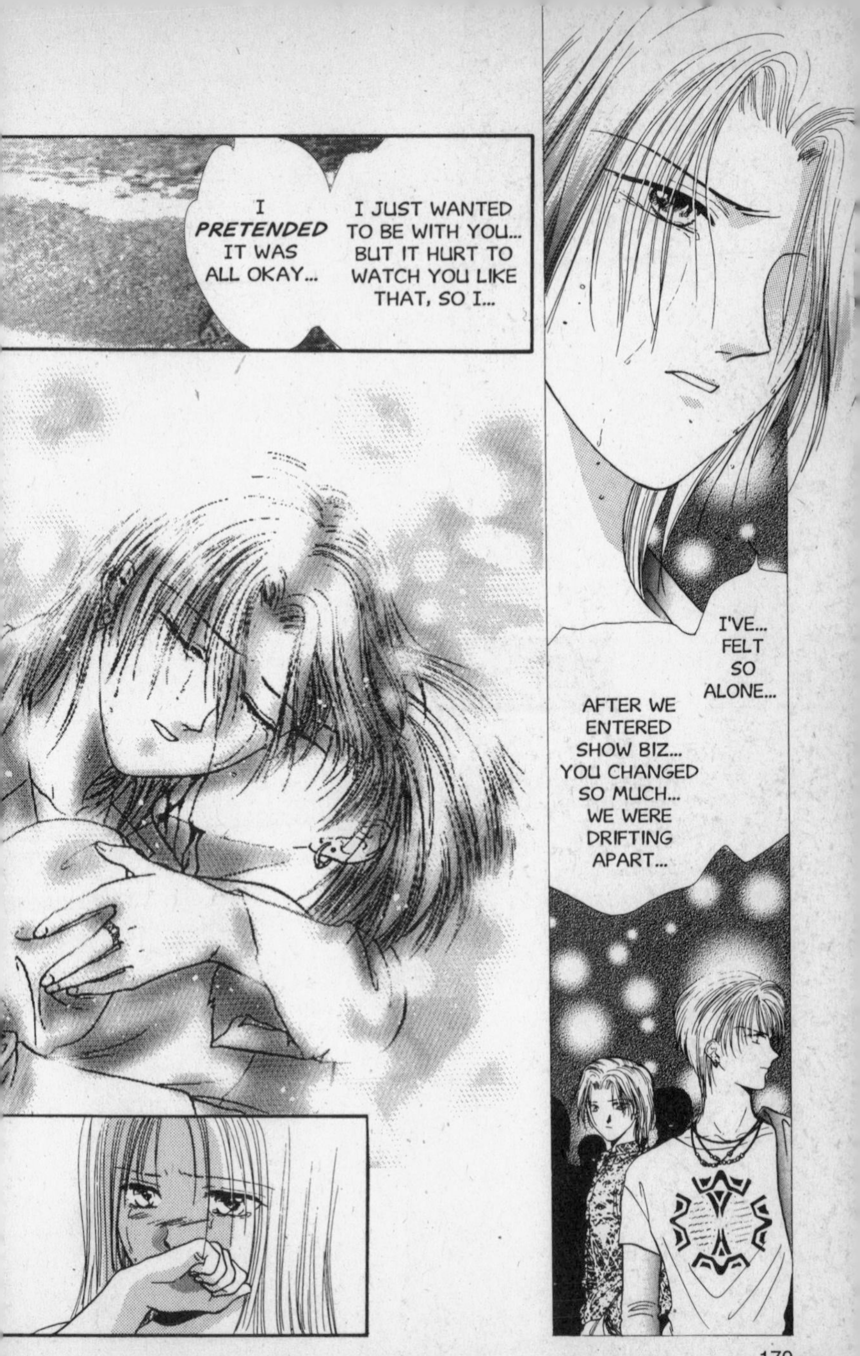
I'VE... FELT SO ALONE...
AFTER WE ENTERED SHOW BIZ... YOU CHANGED SO MUCH... WE WERE DRIFTING APART...
I JUST WANTED TO BE WITH YOU... BUT IT HURT TO WATCH YOU LIKE THAT, SO I...
I *PRETENDED* IT WAS ALL OKAY...

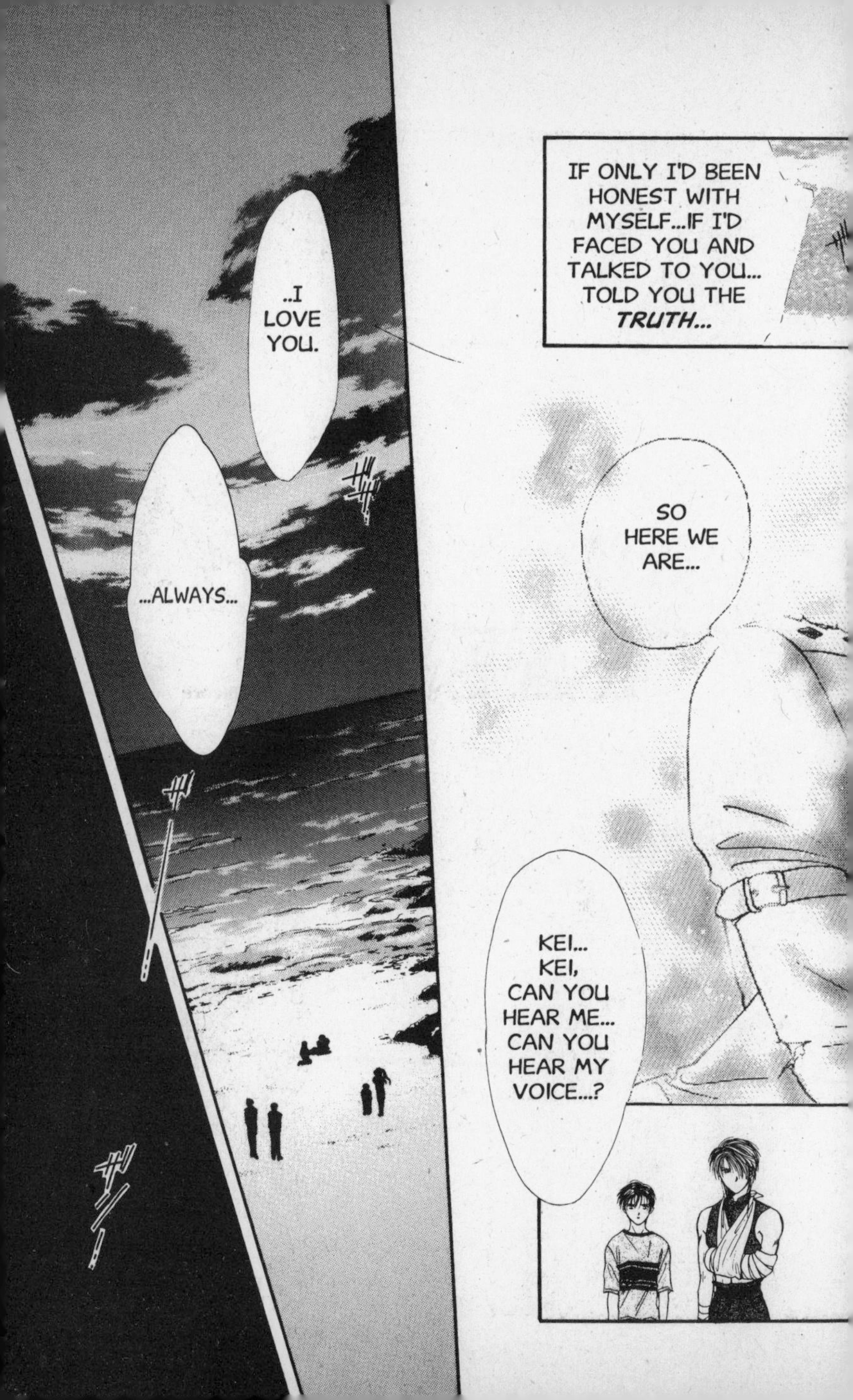
IF ONLY I'D BEEN HONEST WITH MYSELF...IF I'D FACED YOU AND TALKED TO YOU... TOLD YOU THE *TRUTH...*
SO HERE WE ARE...
KEI... KEI, CAN YOU HEAR ME... CAN YOU HEAR MY VOICE...?
..I LOVE YOU.
...ALWAYS...

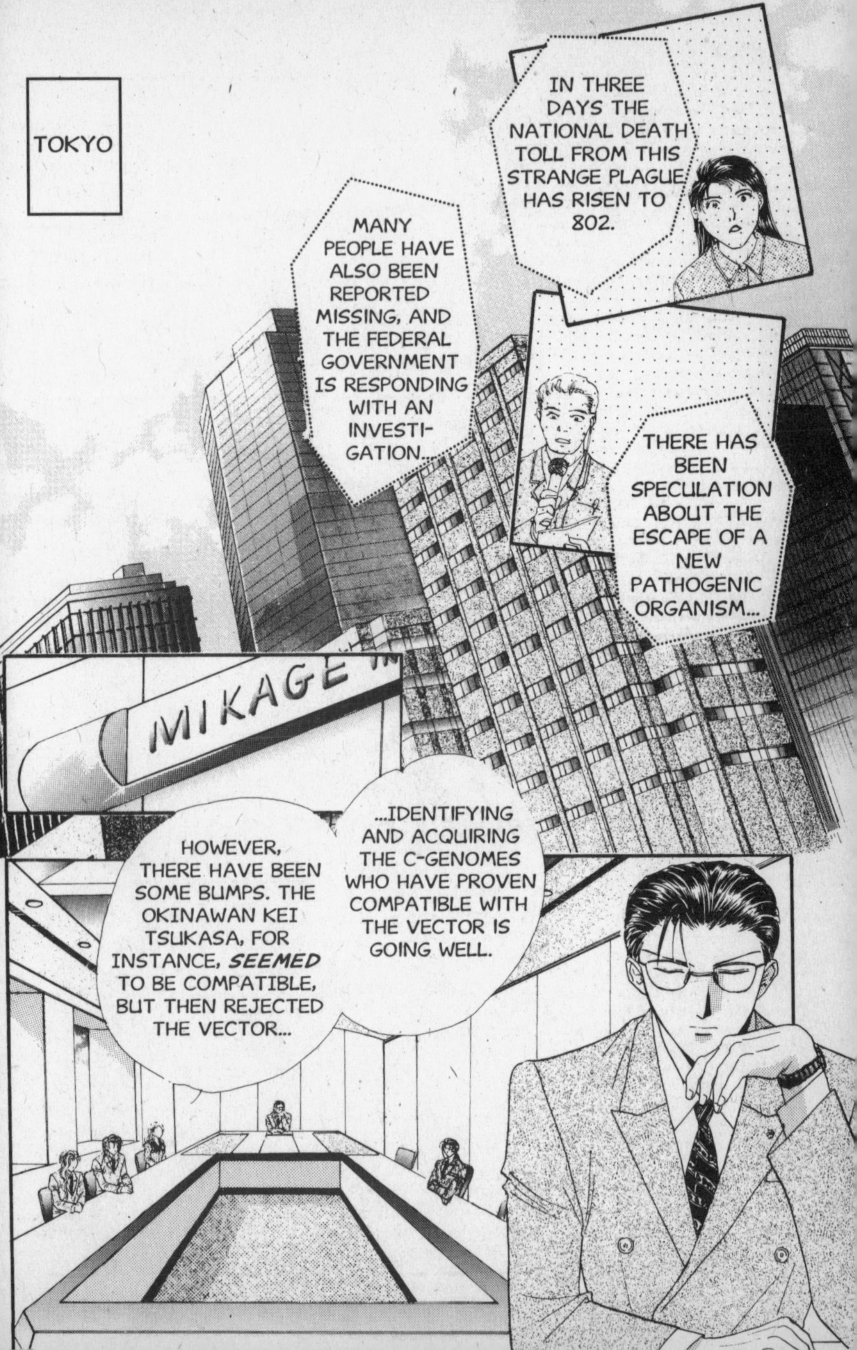

IN THREE DAYS THE NATIONAL DEATH TOLL FROM THIS STRANGE PLAGUE HAS RISEN TO 802.
TOKYO
MANY PEOPLE HAVE ALSO BEEN REPORTED MISSING, AND THE FEDERAL GOVERNMENT IS RESPONDING WITH AN INVESTI-GATION...
THERE HAS BEEN SPECULATION ABOUT THE ESCAPE OF A NEW PATHOGENIC ORGANISM...
MIKAGE
...IDENTIFYING AND ACQUIRING THE C-GENOMES WHO HAVE PROVEN COMPATIBLE WITH THE VECTOR IS GOING WELL.
HOWEVER, THERE HAVE BEEN SOME BUMPS. THE OKINAWAN KEI TSUKASA, FOR INSTANCE, *SEEMED* TO BE COMPATIBLE, BUT THEN REJECTED THE VECTOR...

Ceres: 6

Fans of Yūhi feel sorry for him, but I myself feel more sorry for Tōya. Some have questioned whether "having amnesia" is really such a big deal. Put yourself in his shoes. Not only does he not know anyone else, he doesn't even know himself. You can't be more alone than that. It **is** hard to imagine, I guess. But if you think about it another way, Toya can absorb lots of things—he's a blank slate. It's fun to read the different theories on who he "really" is (someone suggested "a former lover of Ceres," for example). Finally, though, as of this volume, we get another hint: The ocean. My assistants are still sticking with the "robot" theory...Tōya's supposed to be around 21, by the way. The interesting thing is, there's a sharp divide between "Tōya" fans and "Yūhi" fans. I guess that's only natural, as the two are such different types.
...Actually, though, Aki himself is getting more and more popular, especially since his personality change. (Why is that?) Do you like him more now because he's evil?
My assistant, "J" (who refers to herself, incidentally, as president of the "Aki Fan Club"), says Aki rocks when he's being nice, rocks when he's being evil, rocks even if he has a thing (oh, say it isn't so!) with Kagami or Toya. People rooting for an Aya-Aki connection...let's think about that for a moment, shall we? **They've** thought about what it means, haven't they?! Scarier still, maybe they **have...** :-)
There's a lot to look forward to in upcoming volumes, in more ways than one. But I'll cross that bridge when I come to it. (What bridge, you ask...?) Um...ah...uh....

Look, I'm running out of space again. I'll pick up this thread again next time. Since this volume takes place in Okinawa, I'd wanted to write about stuff like my research trip, but since I'll have had an autograph session in Okinawa by the time this volume is first published, I'll have to go into that more in the following volume. (I got a letter from a real celestial descendant—I really did!) I didn't use any local dialects, because it would've been too difficult to understand. I get dialects translated by actual locals.

Though there are times when it doesn't work. See you next time, in Volume 7.

The BGM soundtrack for "Ceres" now includes music from "The Ring," especially Tracks 6 and 7... [Feb '98]

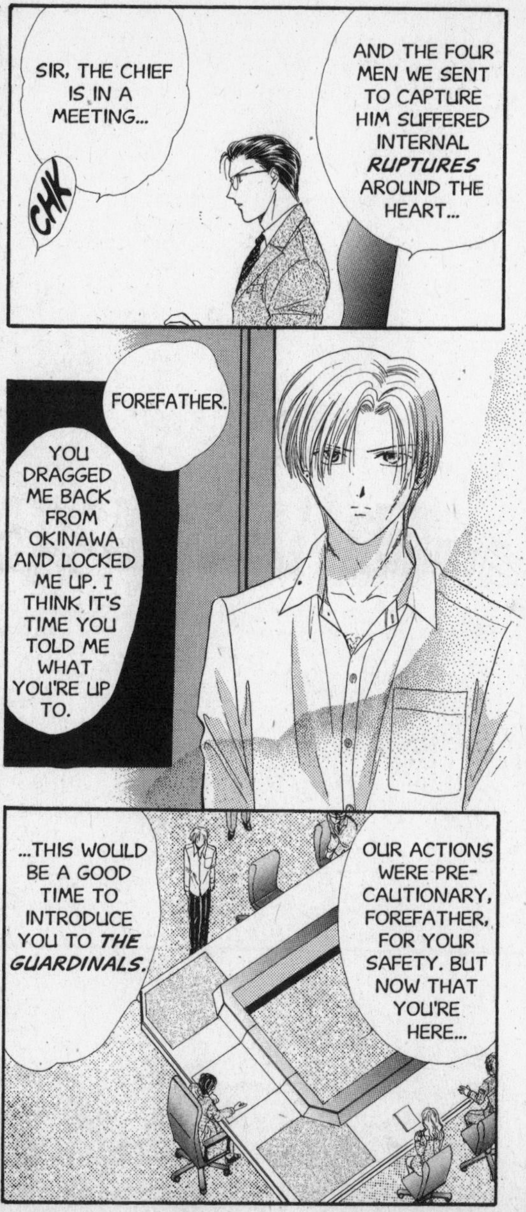

AND THE FOUR MEN WE SENT TO CAPTURE HIM SUFFERED INTERNAL *RUPTURES* AROUND THE HEART...
SIR, THE CHIEF IS IN A MEETING...
CHK
FOREFATHER.
YOU DRAGGED ME BACK FROM OKINAWA AND LOCKED ME UP. I THINK IT'S TIME YOU TOLD ME WHAT YOU'RE UP TO.
OUR ACTIONS WERE PRE-CAUTIONARY, FOREFATHER, FOR YOUR SAFETY. BUT NOW THAT YOU'RE HERE...
...THIS WOULD BE A GOOD TIME TO INTRODUCE YOU TO *THE GUARDINALS.*

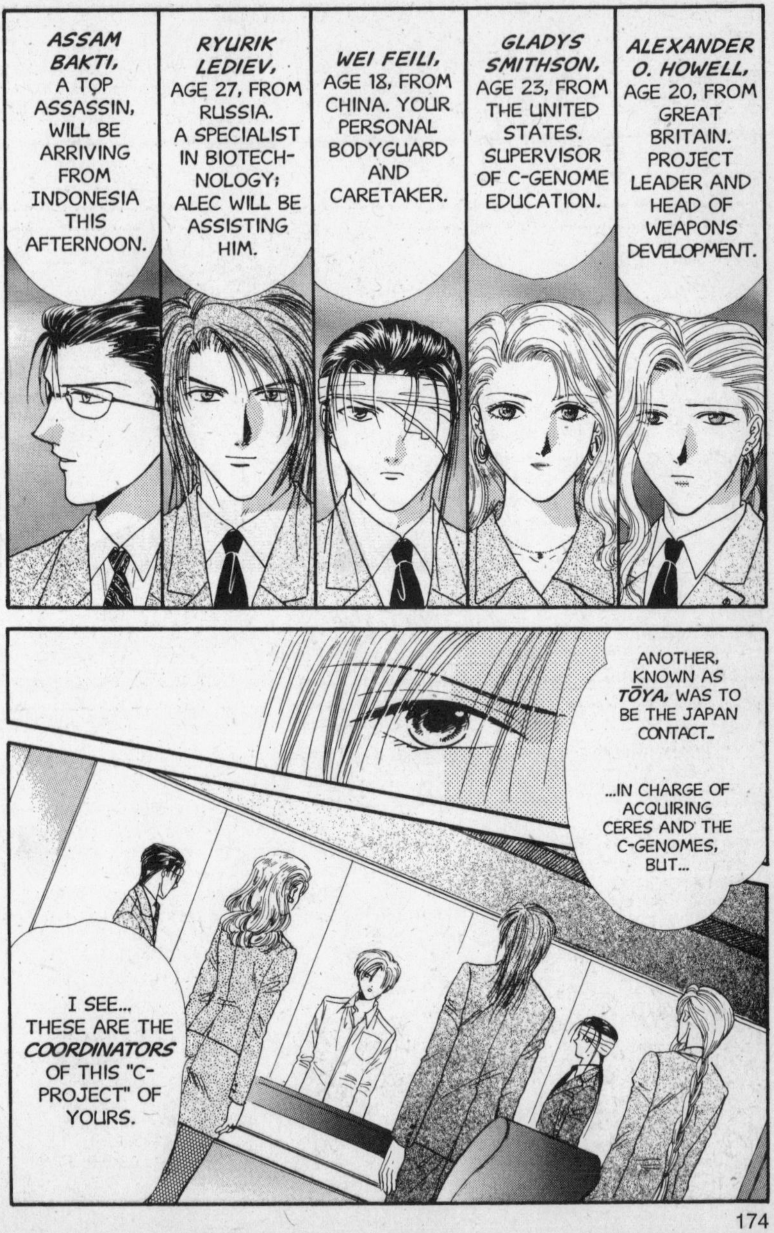

ALEXANDER O. HOWELL, AGE 20, FROM GREAT BRITAIN. PROJECT LEADER AND HEAD OF WEAPONS DEVELOPMENT.
GLADYS SMITHSON, AGE 23, FROM THE UNITED STATES. SUPERVISOR OF C-GENOME EDUCATION.
WEI FEILI, AGE 18, FROM CHINA. YOUR PERSONAL BODYGUARD AND CARETAKER.
RYURIK LEDIEV, AGE 27, FROM RUSSIA. A SPECIALIST IN BIOTECH-NOLOGY; ALEC WILL BE ASSISTING HIM.
ASSAM BAKTI, A TOP ASSASSIN, WILL BE ARRIVING FROM INDONESIA THIS AFTERNOON.
ANOTHER, KNOWN AS TŌYA, WAS TO BE THE JAPAN CONTACT...
...IN CHARGE OF ACQUIRING CERES AND THE C-GENOMES, BUT...
I SEE... THESE ARE THE COORDINATORS OF THIS "C-PROJECT" OF YOURS.

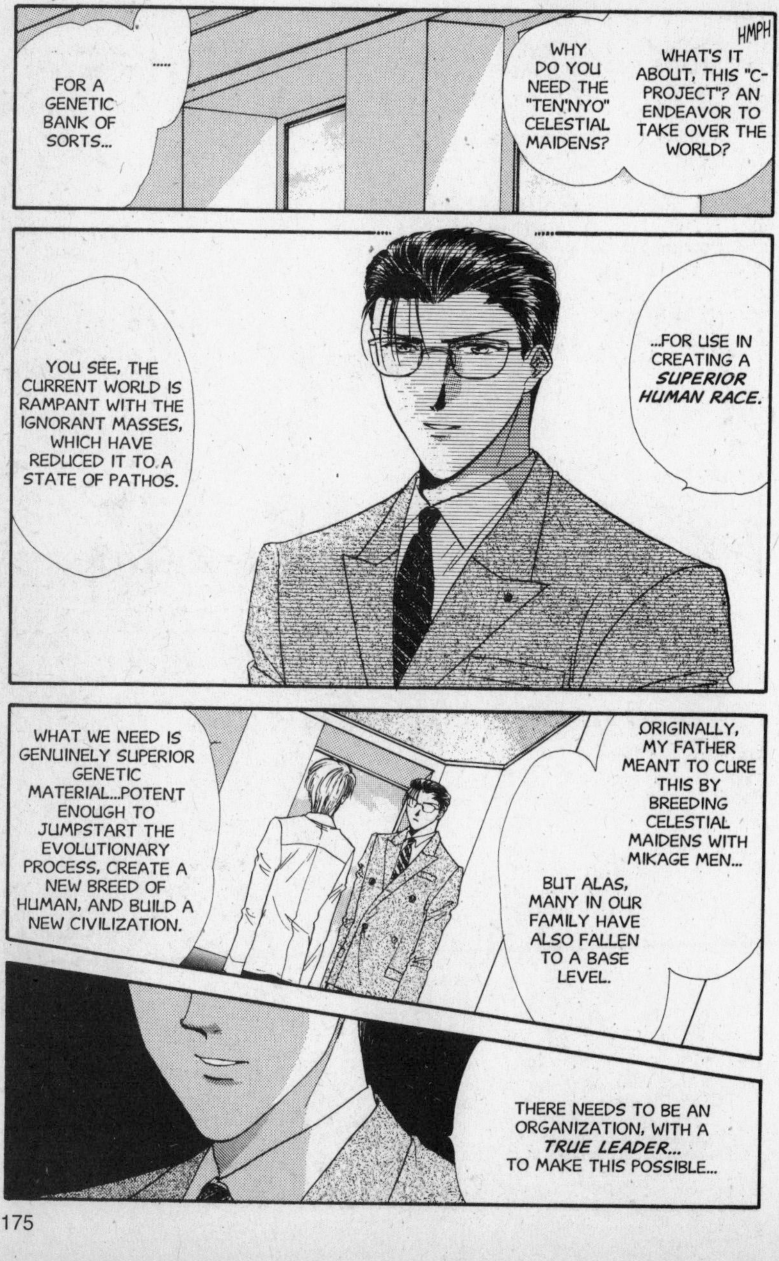
HMPH
WHAT'S IT ABOUT, THIS "C-PROJECT"? AN ENDEAVOR TO TAKE OVER THE WORLD?
WHY DO YOU NEED THE "TEN'NYO" CELESTIAL MAIDENS?
......
FOR A GENETIC BANK OF SORTS...
......
......
...FOR USE IN CREATING A *SUPERIOR HUMAN RACE.*
YOU SEE, THE CURRENT WORLD IS RAMPANT WITH THE IGNORANT MASSES, WHICH HAVE REDUCED IT TO A STATE OF PATHOS.
ORIGINALLY, MY FATHER MEANT TO CURE THIS BY BREEDING CELESTIAL MAIDENS WITH MIKAGE MEN...
BUT ALAS, MANY IN OUR FAMILY HAVE ALSO FALLEN TO A BASE LEVEL.
WHAT WE NEED IS GENUINELY SUPERIOR GENETIC MATERIAL...POTENT ENOUGH TO JUMPSTART THE EVOLUTIONARY PROCESS, CREATE A NEW BREED OF HUMAN, AND BUILD A NEW CIVILIZATION.
THERE NEEDS TO BE AN ORGANIZATION, WITH A *TRUE LEADER...* TO MAKE THIS POSSIBLE...

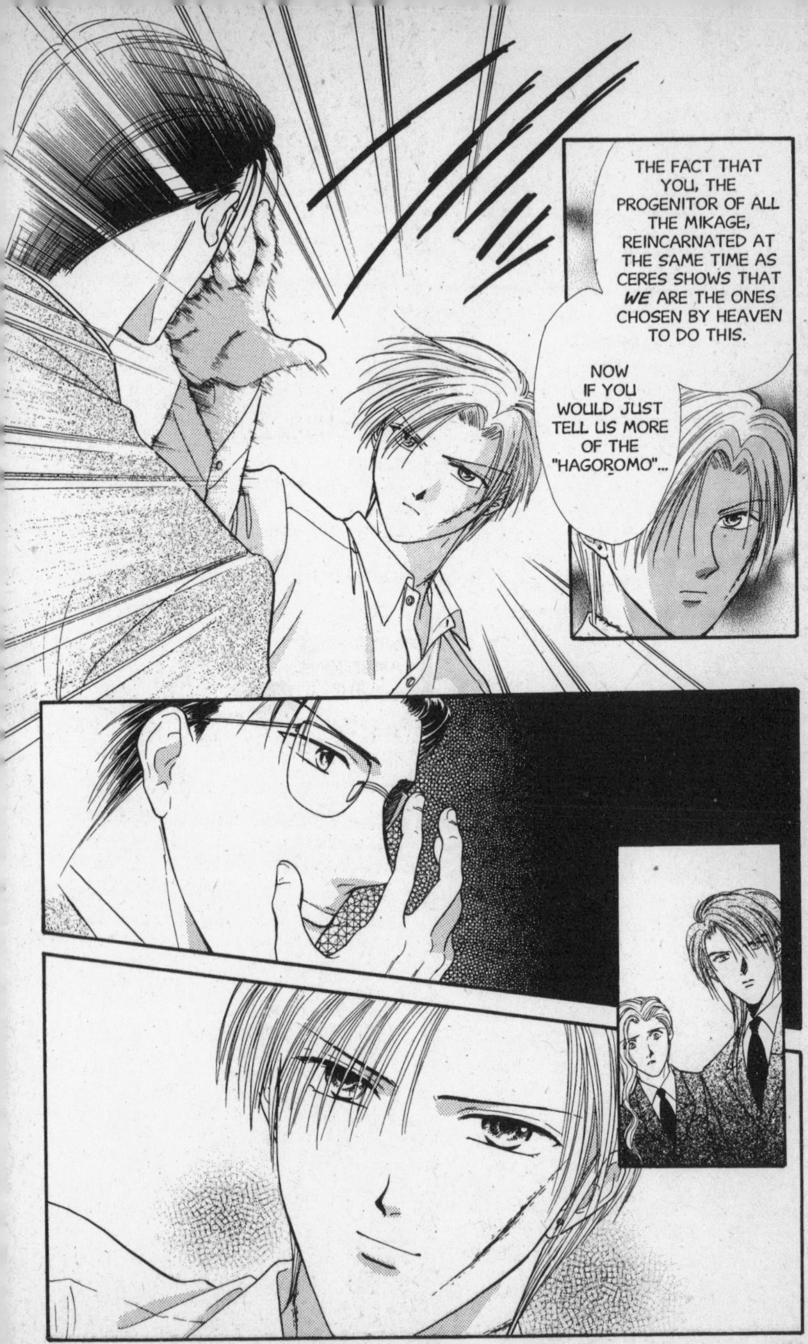
THE FACT THAT YOU, THE PROGENITOR OF ALL THE MIKAGE, REINCARNATED AT THE SAME TIME AS CERES SHOWS THAT *WE* ARE THE ONES CHOSEN BY HEAVEN TO DO THIS.
NOW IF YOU WOULD JUST TELL US MORE OF THE "HAGOROMO"...

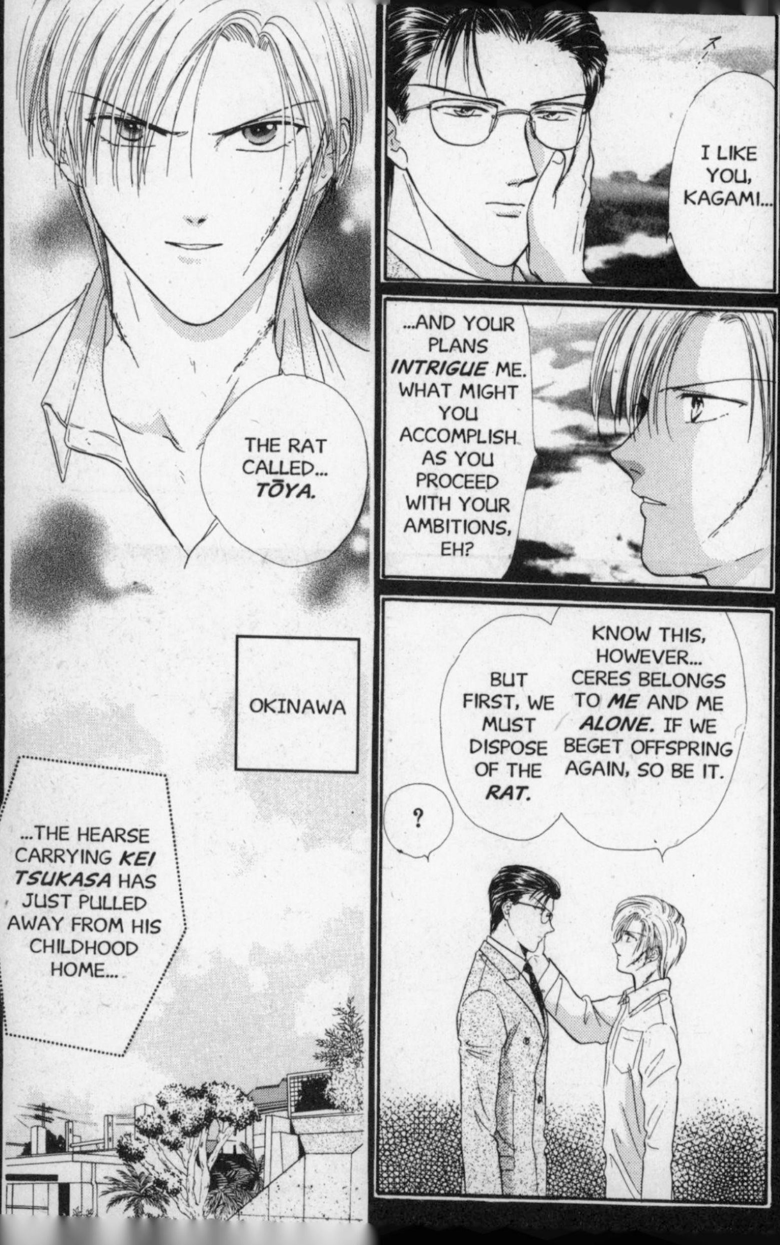
I LIKE YOU, KAGAMI...
...AND YOUR PLANS INTRIGUE ME. WHAT MIGHT YOU ACCOMPLISH AS YOU PROCEED WITH YOUR AMBITIONS, EH?
KNOW THIS, HOWEVER... CERES BELONGS TO ME AND ME ALONE. IF WE BEGET OFFSPRING AGAIN, SO BE IT.
BUT FIRST, WE MUST DISPOSE OF THE RAT.
?
THE RAT CALLED... TŌYA.
OKINAWA
...THE HEARSE CARRYING KEI TSUKASA HAS JUST PULLED AWAY FROM HIS CHILDHOOD HOME...

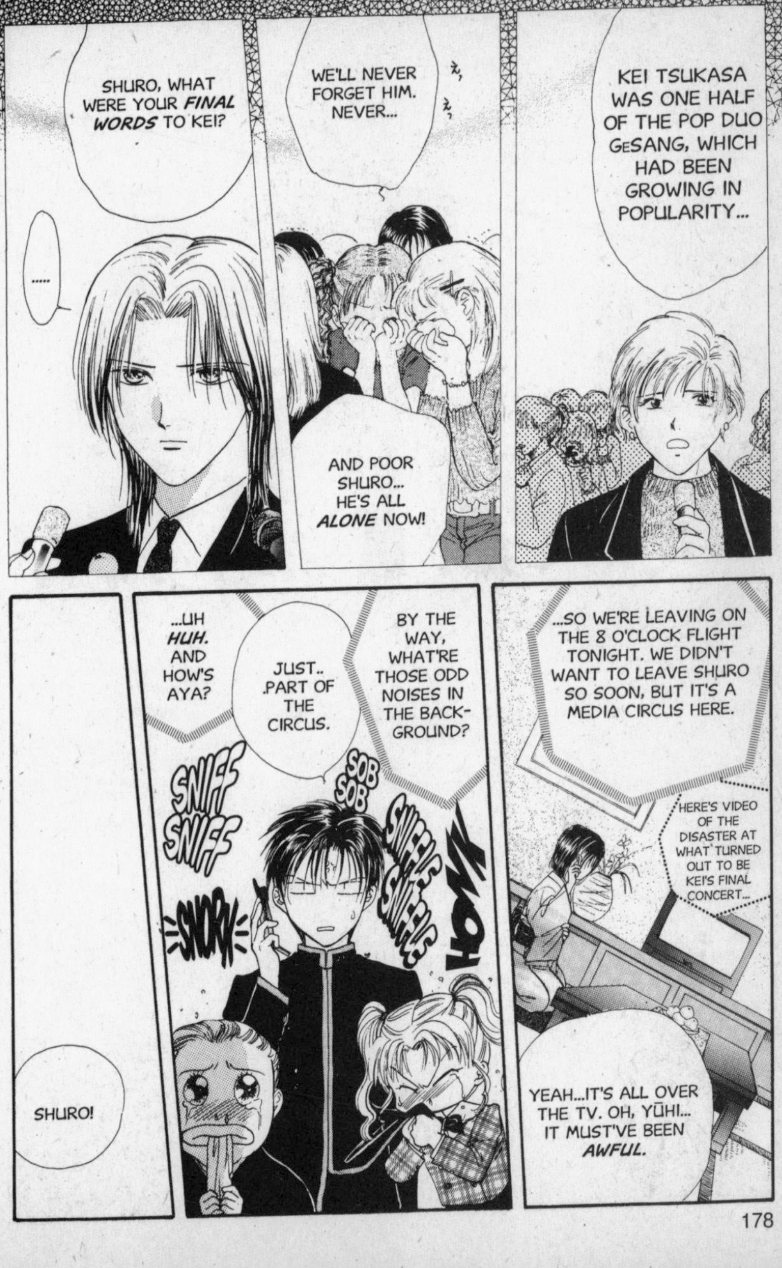
KEI TSUKASA WAS ONE HALF OF THE POP DUO GESANG, WHICH HAD BEEN GROWING IN POPULARITY...
WE'LL NEVER FORGET HIM. NEVER...
AND POOR SHURO... HE'S ALL *ALONE* NOW!
SHURO, WHAT WERE YOUR *FINAL WORDS* TO KEI?
......
...SO WE'RE LEAVING ON THE 8 O'CLOCK FLIGHT TONIGHT. WE DIDN'T WANT TO LEAVE SHURO SO SOON, BUT IT'S A MEDIA CIRCUS HERE.
HERE'S VIDEO OF THE DISASTER AT WHAT TURNED OUT TO BE KEI'S FINAL CONCERT...
YEAH...IT'S ALL OVER THE TV. OH, YŪHI... IT MUST'VE BEEN *AWFUL.*
BY THE WAY, WHAT'RE THOSE ODD NOISES IN THE BACK-GROUND?
JUST.. .PART OF THE CIRCUS.
...UH *HUH.* AND HOW'S AYA?
SOB SOB
HONK
SNIFF SNIFF
SNORK
SHURO!

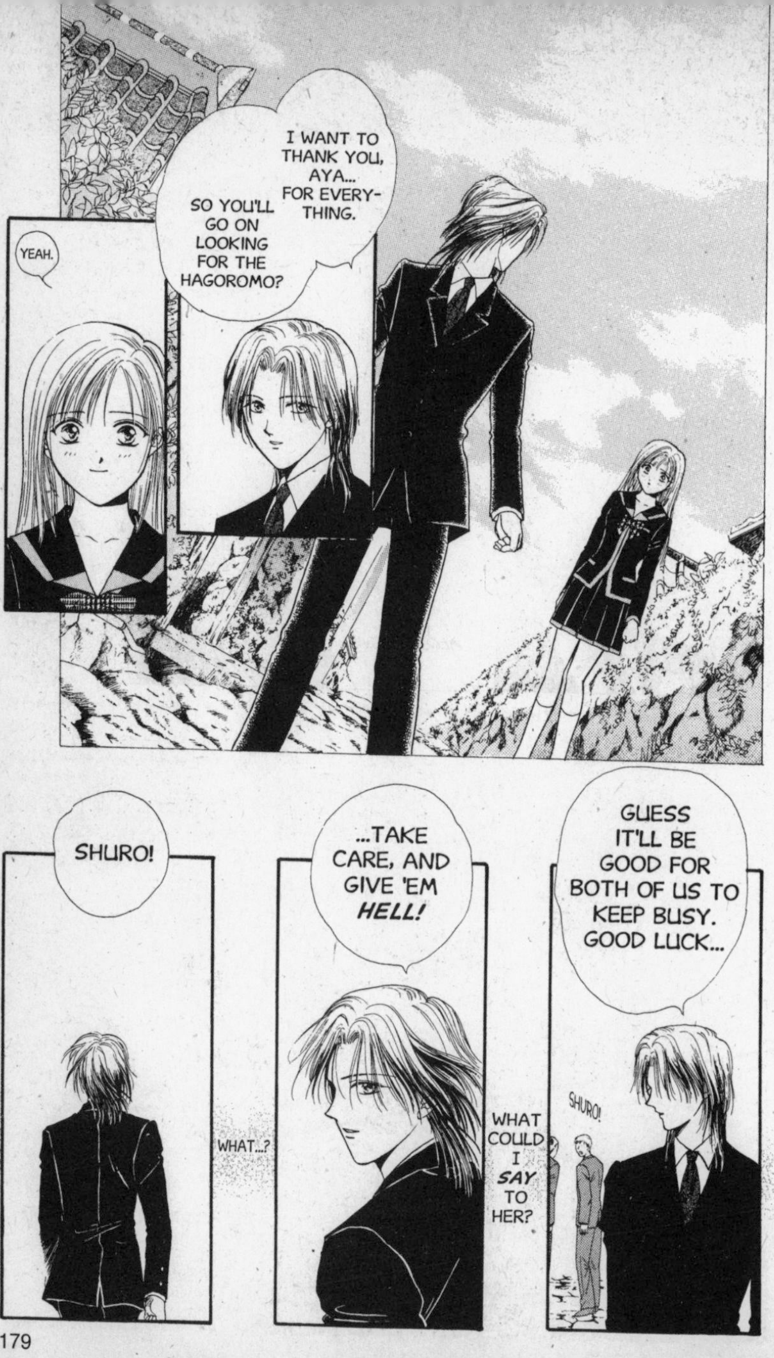
I WANT TO THANK YOU, AYA... FOR EVERYTHING.
SO YOU'LL GO ON LOOKING FOR THE HAGOROMO?
YEAH.
GUESS IT'LL BE GOOD FOR BOTH OF US TO KEEP BUSY. GOOD LUCK...
SHURO!
WHAT COULD I *SAY* TO HER?
...TAKE CARE, AND GIVE 'EM ***HELL!***
WHAT...?
SHURO!

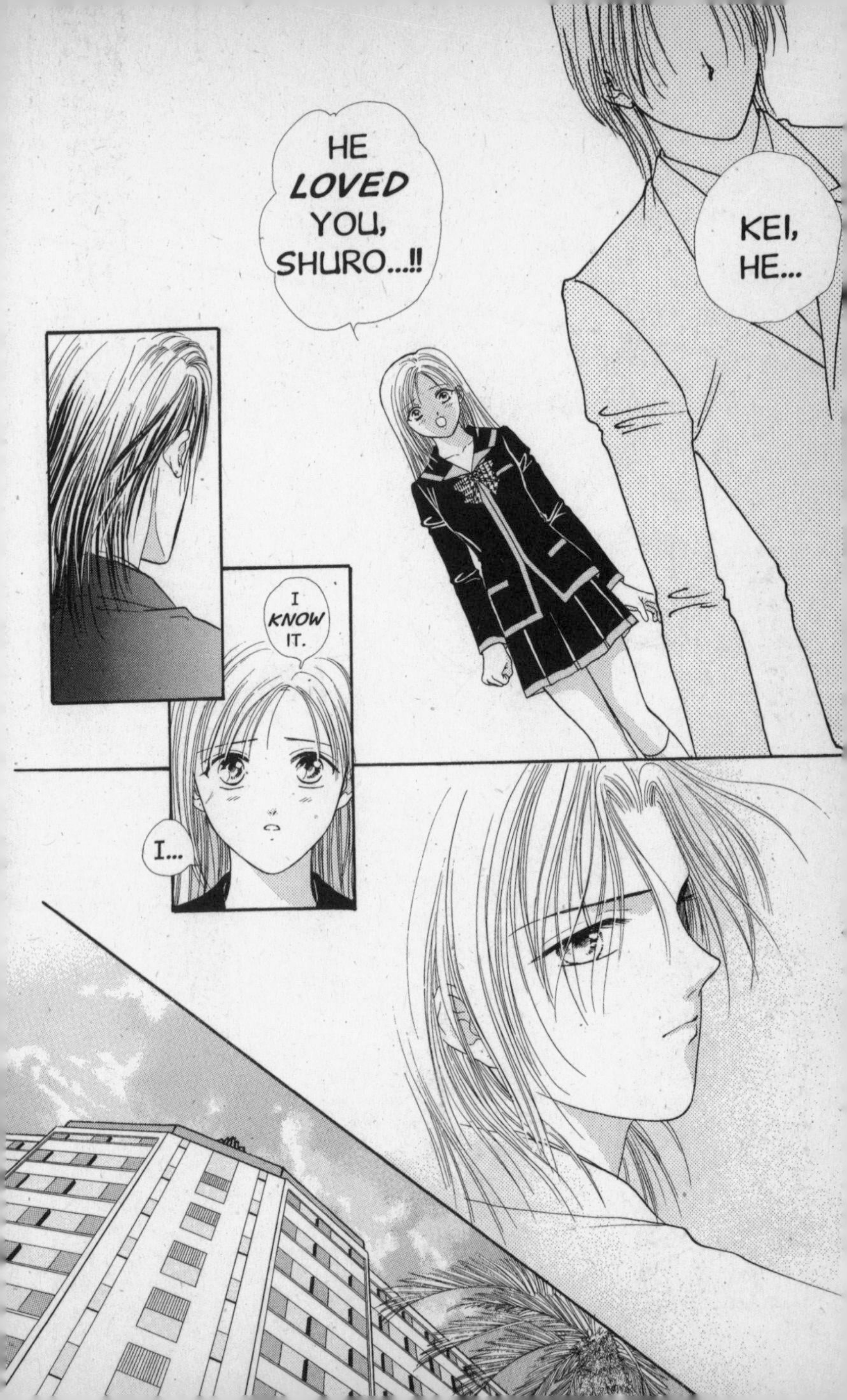
KEI, HE...
HE *LOVED* YOU, SHURO...!!
I *KNOW* IT.
I...

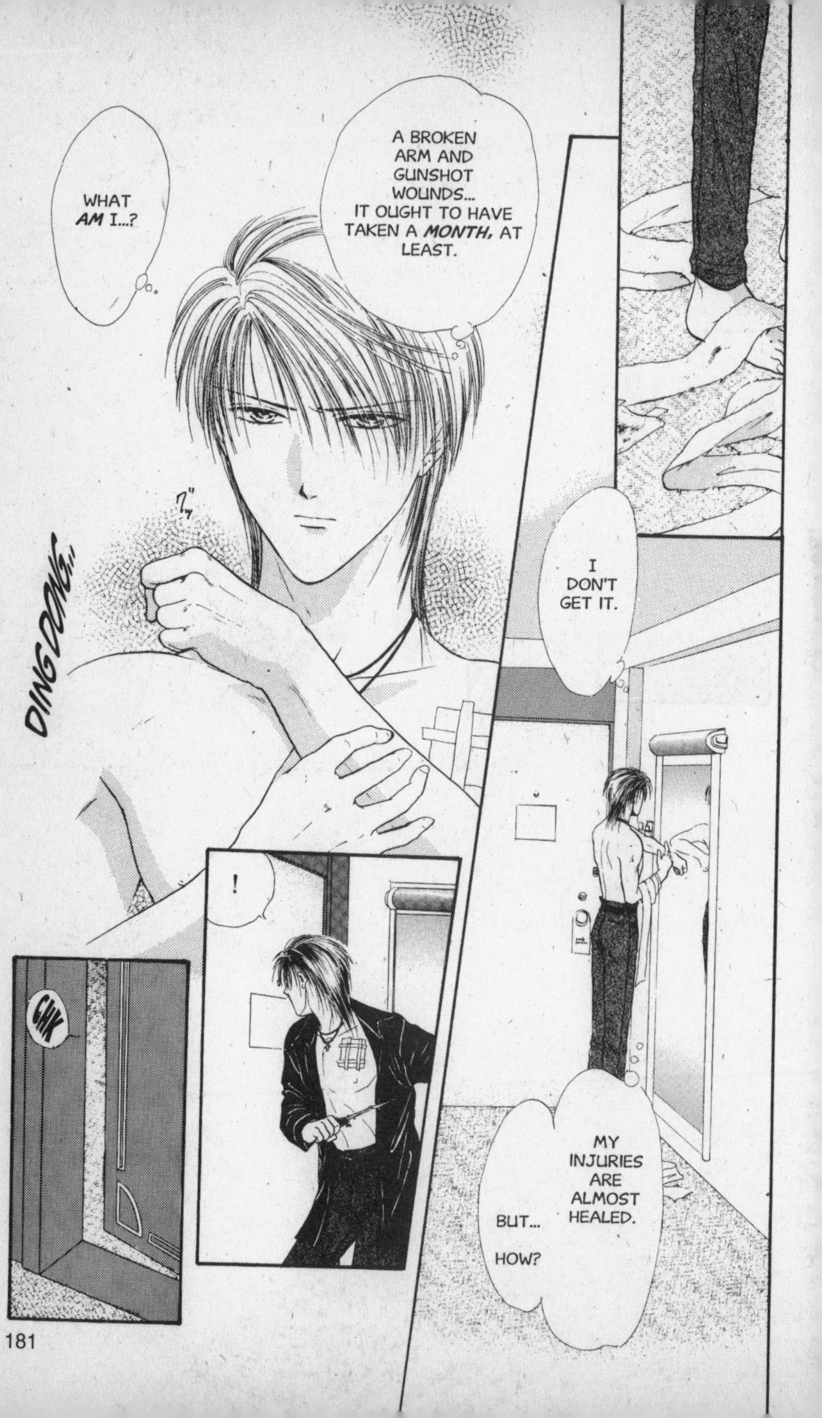
I DON'T GET IT.
MY INJURIES ARE ALMOST HEALED.
BUT... HOW?
A BROKEN ARM AND GUNSHOT WOUNDS... IT OUGHT TO HAVE TAKEN A *MONTH,* AT LEAST.
WHAT *AM* I...?
DING DONG...
!
CHK

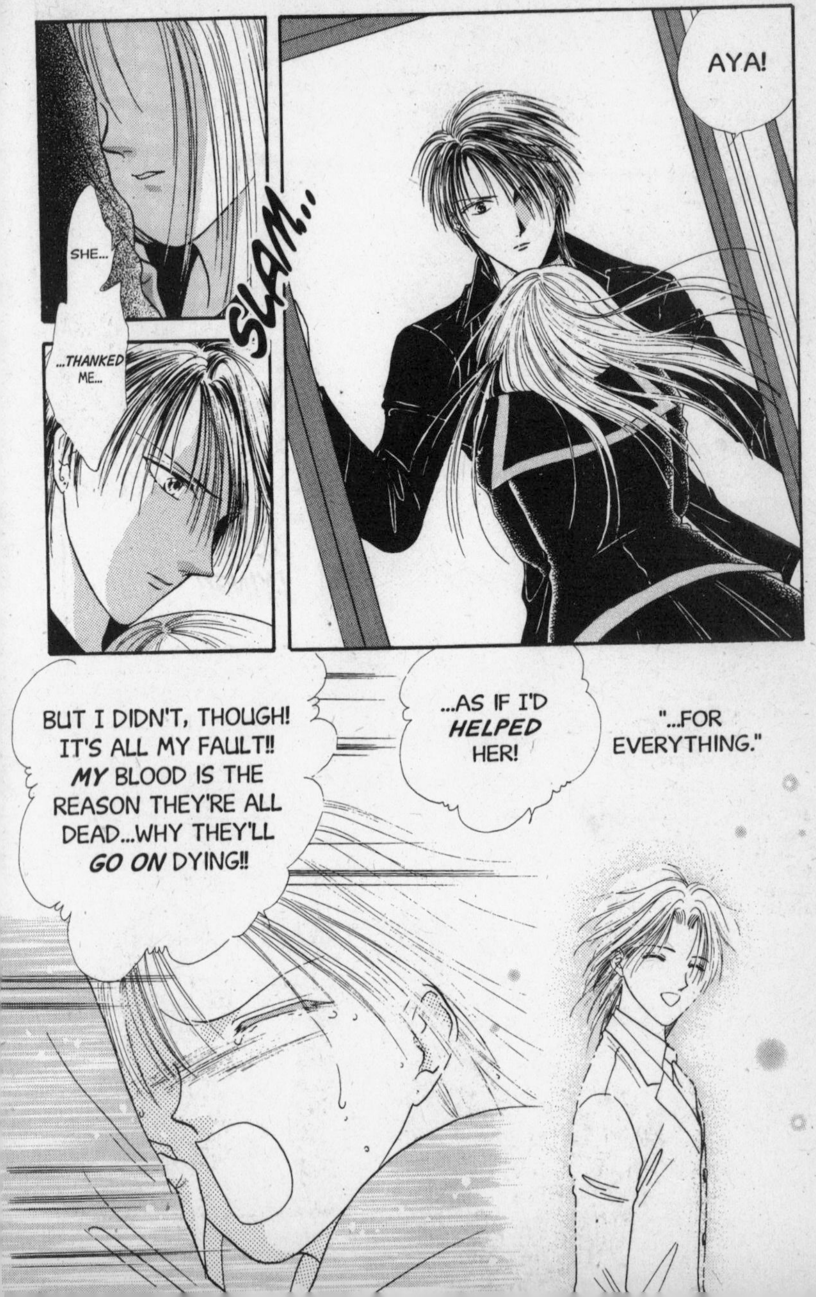
AYA!
SLAM...
SHE...
...THANKED ME...
"...FOR EVERYTHING."
...AS IF I'D HELPED HER!
BUT I DIDN'T, THOUGH! IT'S ALL MY FAULT!! MY BLOOD IS THE REASON THEY'RE ALL DEAD...WHY THEY'LL GO ON DYING!!

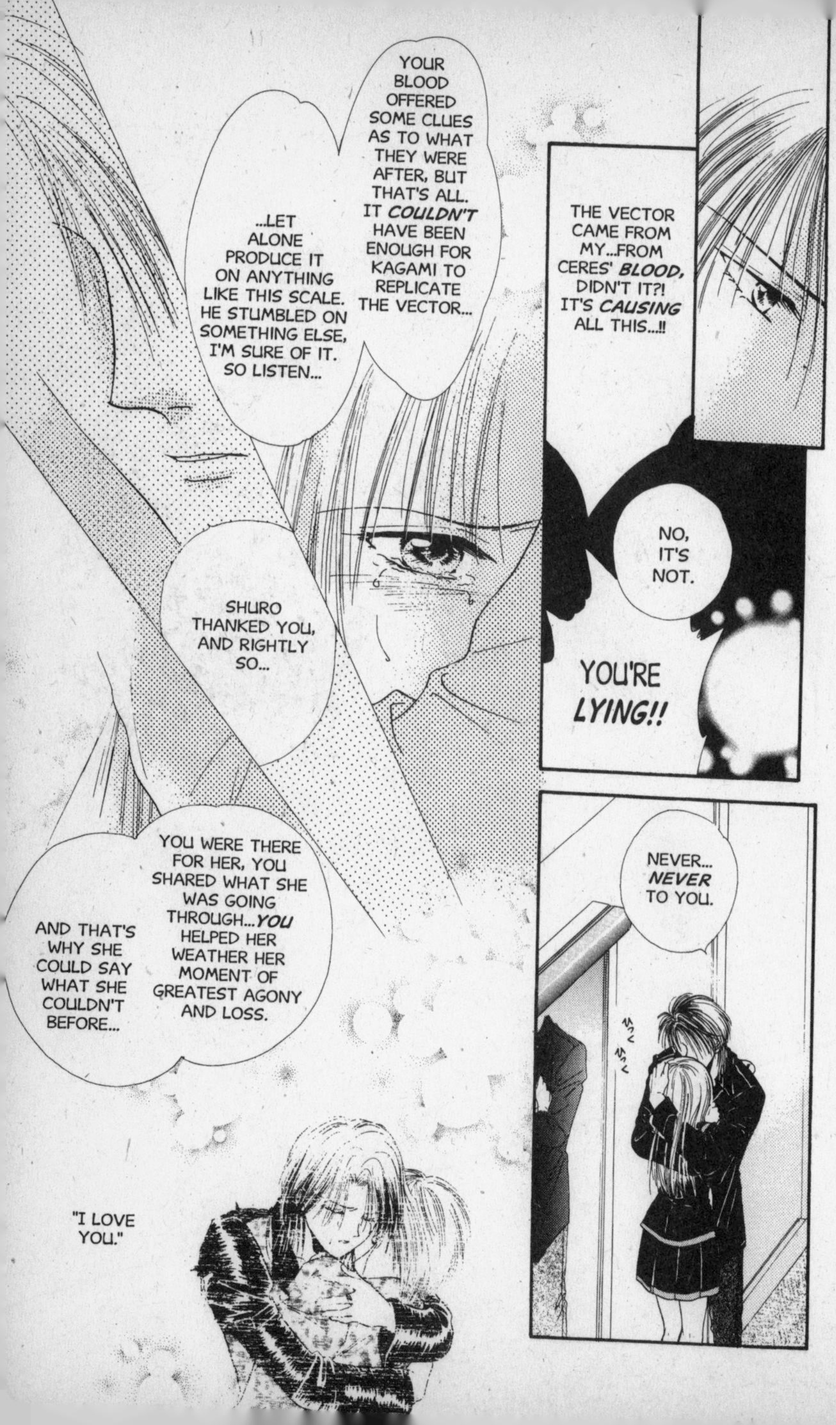
THE VECTOR CAME FROM MY...FROM CERES' *BLOOD,* DIDN'T IT?! IT'S *CAUSING* ALL THIS...!!
NO, IT'S NOT.
YOU'RE *LYING!!*
NEVER... ***NEVER*** TO YOU.
YOUR BLOOD OFFERED SOME CLUES AS TO WHAT THEY WERE AFTER, BUT THAT'S ALL. IT ***COULDN'T*** HAVE BEEN ENOUGH FOR KAGAMI TO REPLICATE THE VECTOR...
...LET ALONE PRODUCE IT ON ANYTHING LIKE THIS SCALE. HE STUMBLED ON SOMETHING ELSE, I'M SURE OF IT. SO LISTEN...
SHURO THANKED YOU, AND RIGHTLY SO...
YOU WERE THERE FOR HER, YOU SHARED WHAT SHE WAS GOING THROUGH...***YOU*** HELPED HER WEATHER HER MOMENT OF GREATEST AGONY AND LOSS.
AND THAT'S WHY SHE COULD SAY WHAT SHE COULDN'T BEFORE...
"I LOVE YOU."

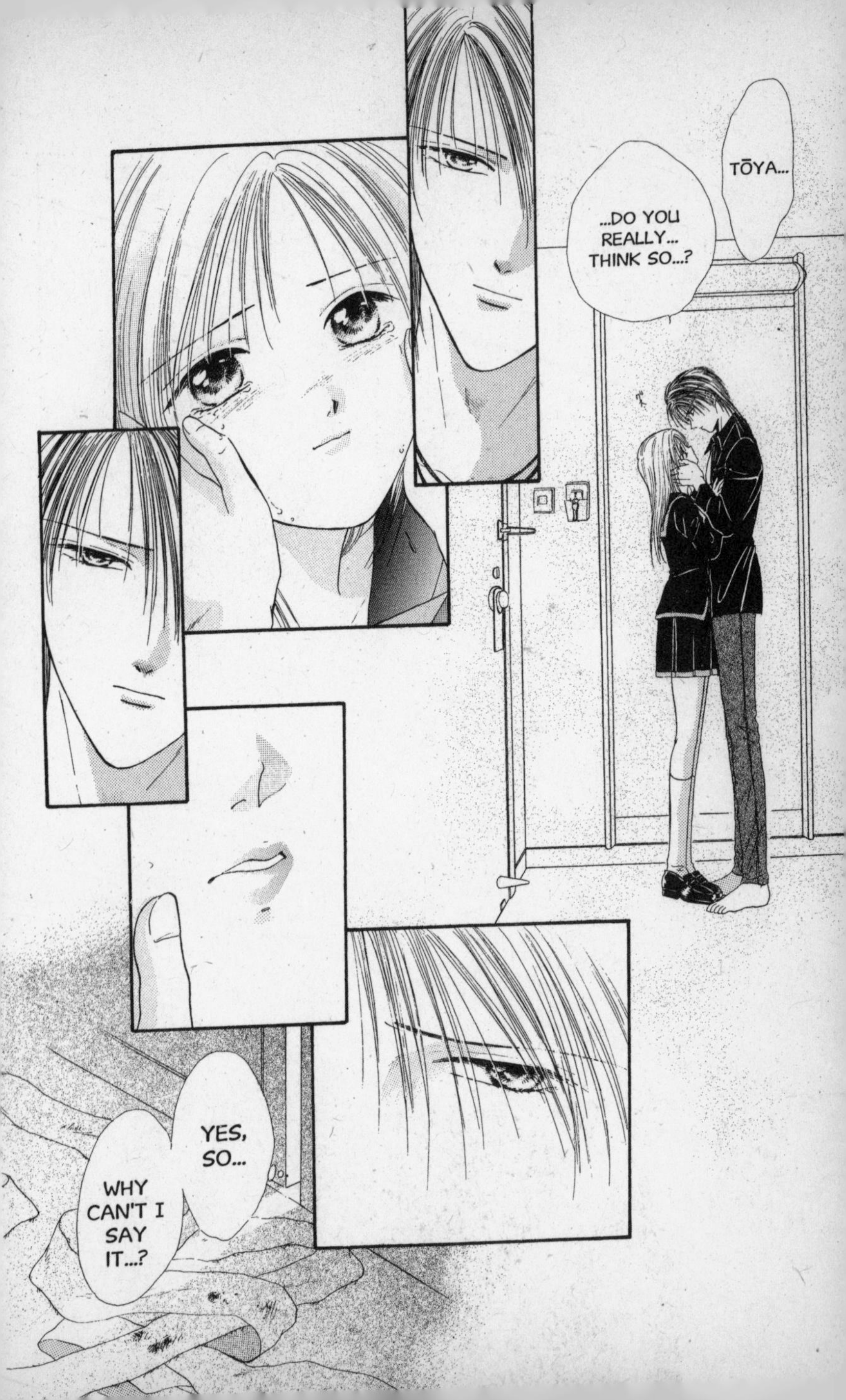
TŌYA...
...DO YOU REALLY... THINK SO...?
YES, SO...
WHY CAN'T I SAY IT...?

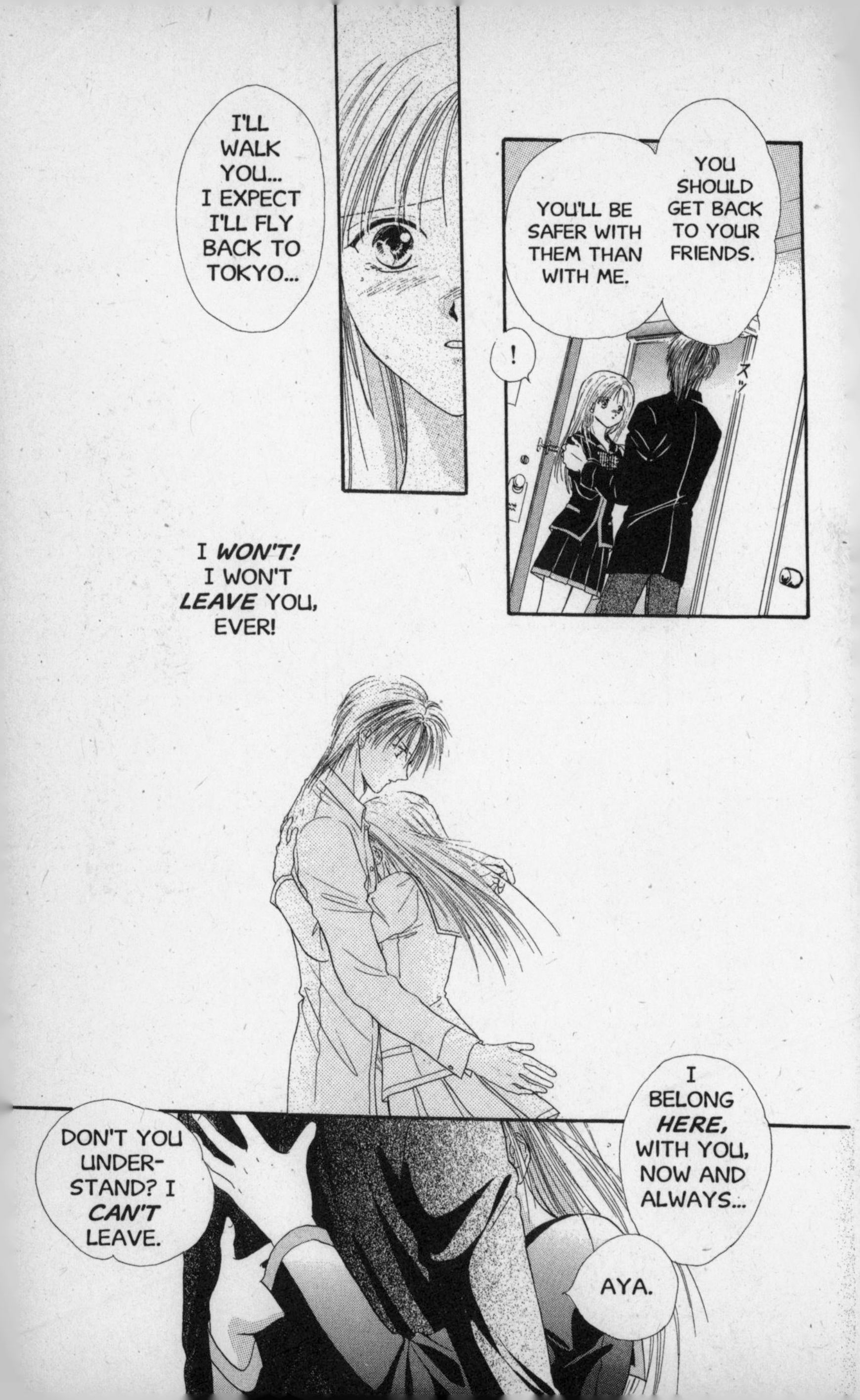
YOU SHOULD GET BACK TO YOUR FRIENDS.
YOU'LL BE SAFER WITH THEM THAN WITH ME.
ズッ
!
I'LL WALK YOU... I EXPECT I'LL FLY BACK TO TOKYO...
I *WON'T!* I WON'T *LEAVE* YOU, EVER!
I BELONG *HERE,* WITH YOU, NOW AND ALWAYS...
AYA.
DON'T YOU UNDER-STAND? I *CAN'T* LEAVE.

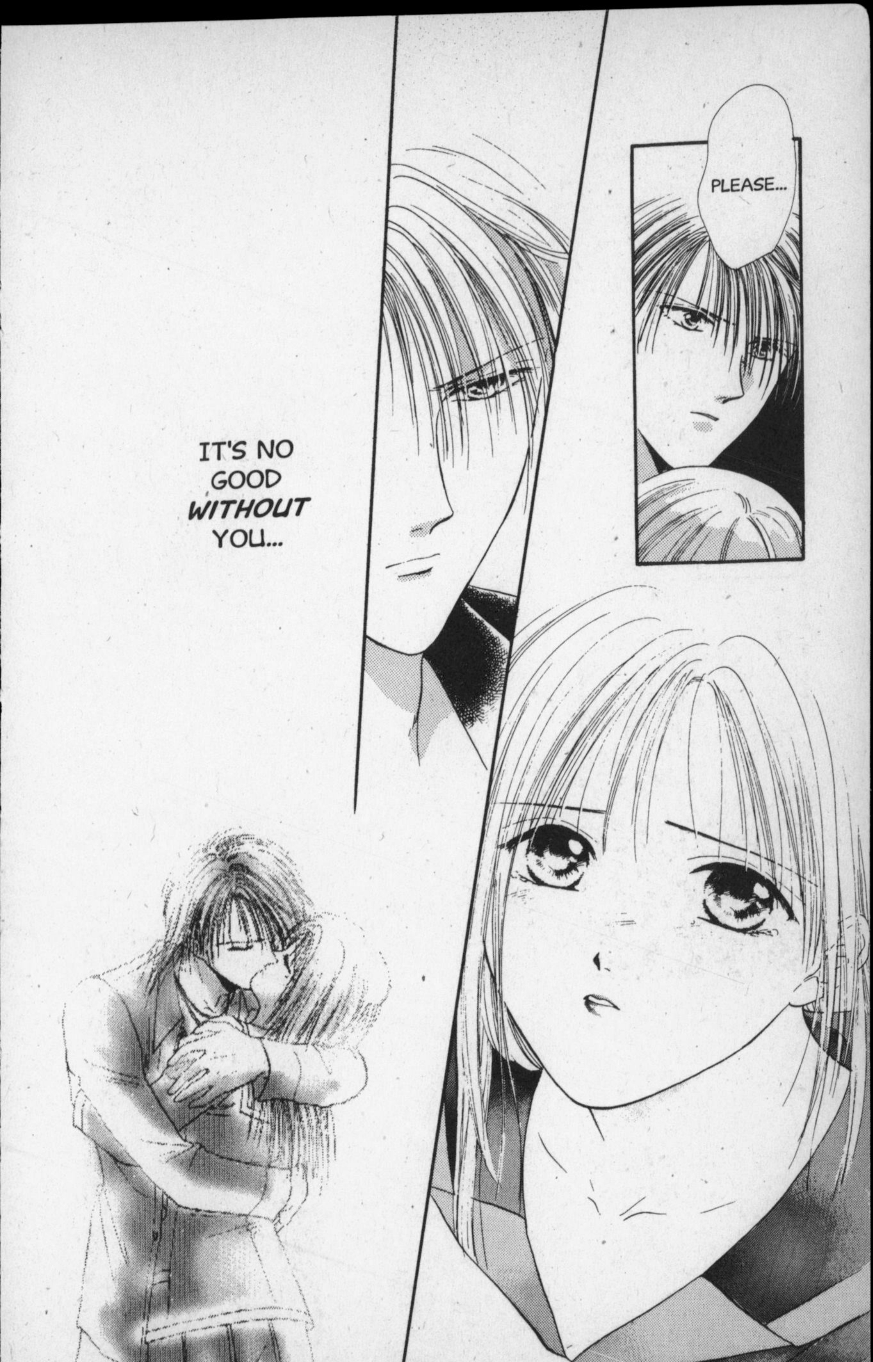
PLEASE...
IT'S NO GOOD *WITHOUT* YOU...

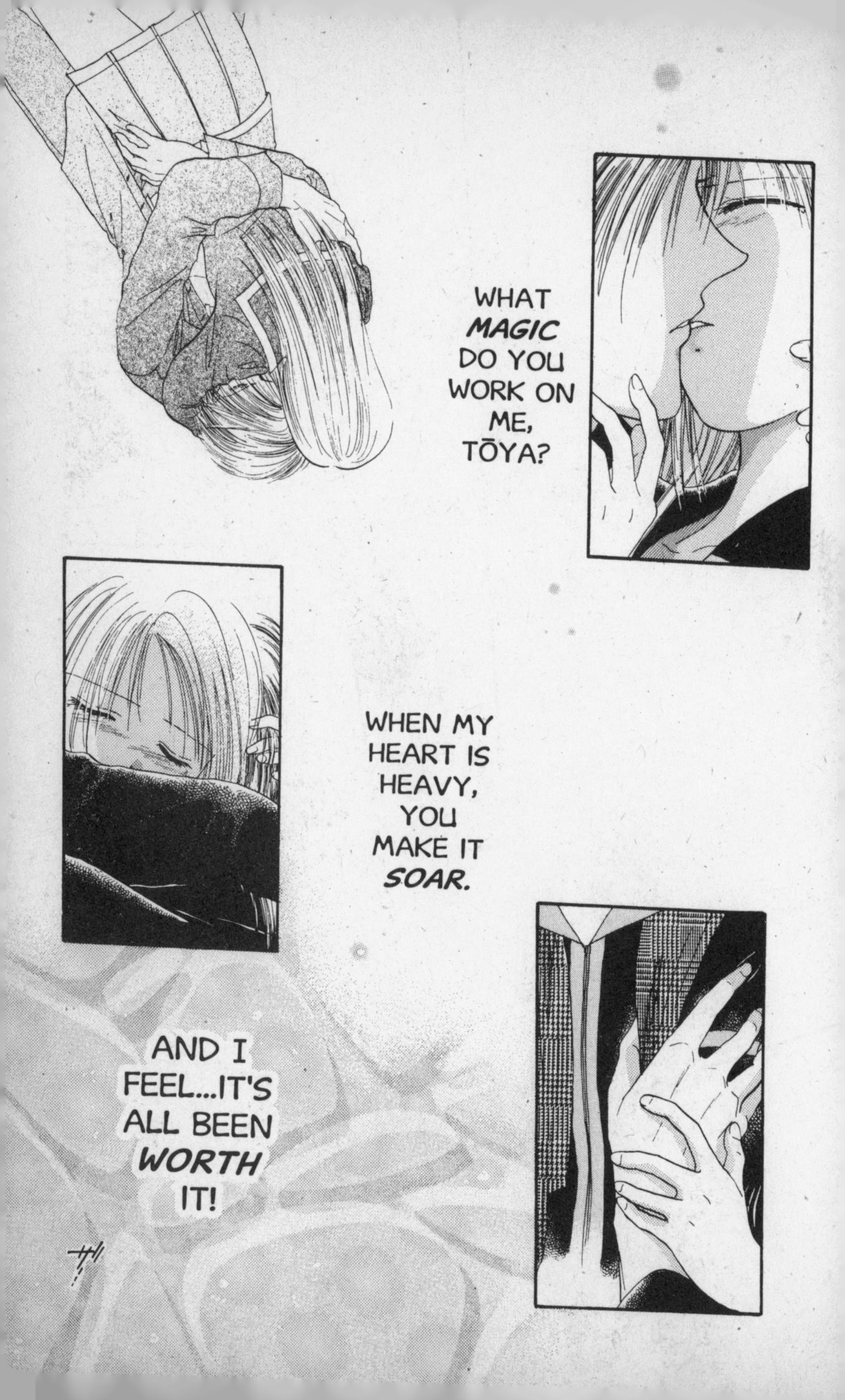
WHAT MAGIC DO YOU WORK ON ME, TŌYA?
WHEN MY HEART IS HEAVY, YOU MAKE IT SOAR.
AND I FEEL...IT'S ALL BEEN WORTH IT!

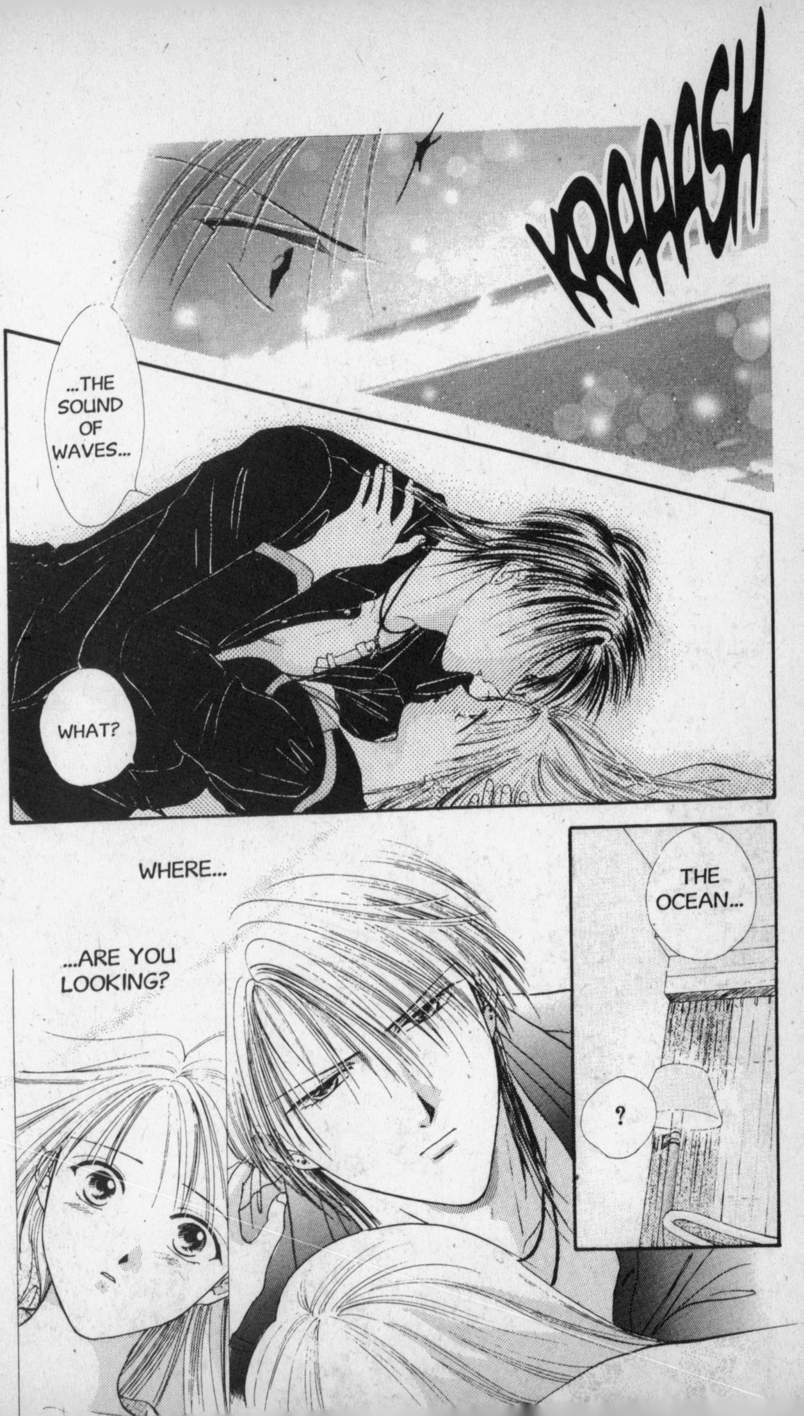
KRAAASH
...THE SOUND OF WAVES...
WHAT?
THE OCEAN...
?
WHERE...
...ARE YOU LOOKING?

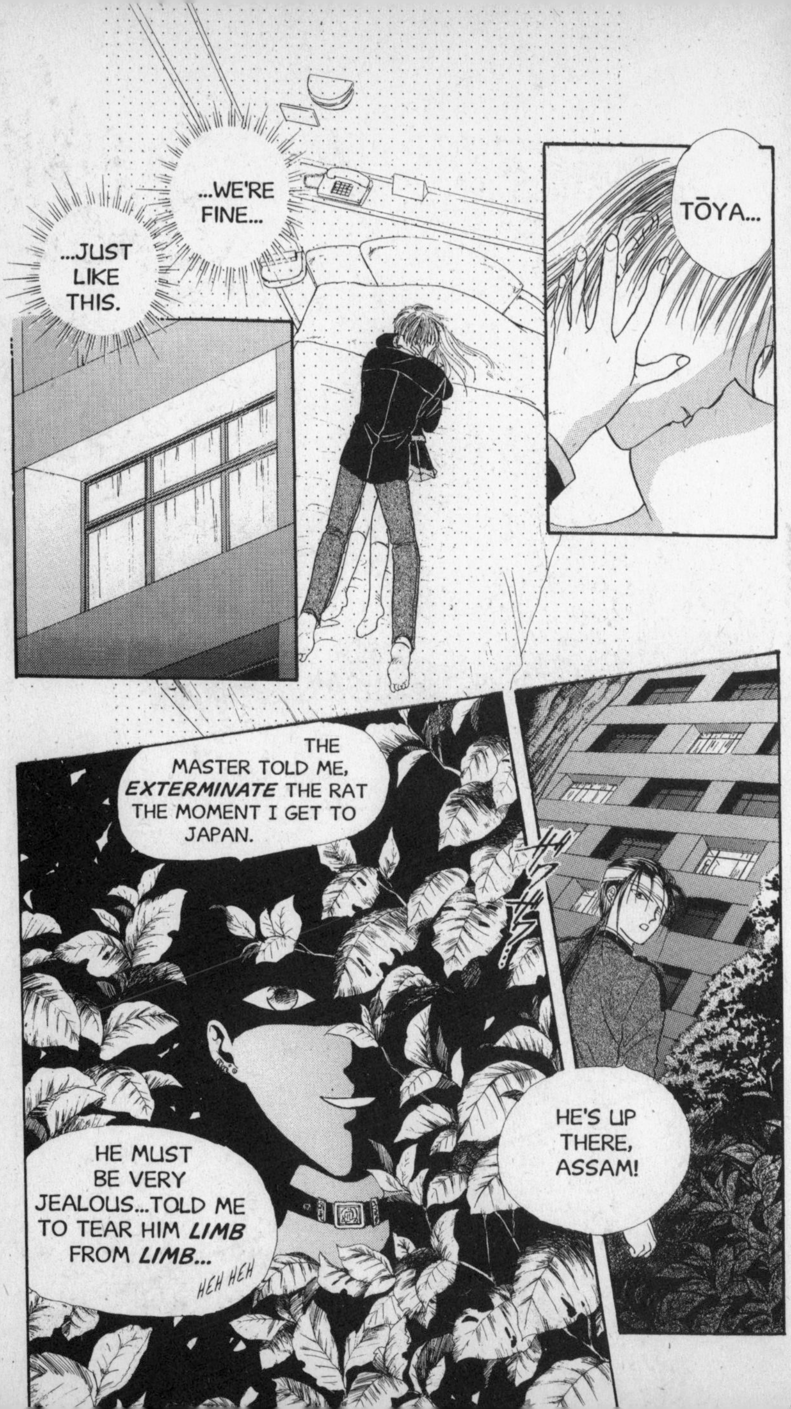
TŌYA...
...WE'RE FINE...
...JUST LIKE THIS.
HE'S UP THERE, ASSAM!
THE MASTER TOLD ME, EXTERMINATE THE RAT THE MOMENT I GET TO JAPAN.
HE MUST BE VERY JEALOUS...TOLD ME TO TEAR HIM LIMB FROM LIMB...
HEH HEH

The CERES Guide to Sound Effects

We've left most of the sound effects in CERES as Yuu Watase originally created them—in Japanese. VIZ has created this glossary to help you decipher, page-by-page and panel-by-panel, what all those foreign words and background noises mean. Use this guide to impress your friends with your new Japanese vocabulary. The glossary lists the page number then panel. For example, 3.1 indicates page 3, panel 1.

39.2 FX: Bun (smackdown!)
39.2 FX: Hyoi (quick movement, avoidance)
39.4 FX: Ha (quick gasp, sudden thought or epiphany, realization)
39.4 FX: Cha (opening door)
41.4 FX: Kya (girlish squeals— excitement or fear)
41.4 FX: Gi (Urk!)
42.2 FX: Shibu Shibu (dilly-dallying, prolonging the inevitable)
43.2 FX: Kotsu Kotsu (footsteps)
43.5 FX: Gashan (clang)
44.2 FX: Go'on Go'on (whirring of machinery)
46.3 FX: Shu (flung through air)
46.4 FX: Bishi (smarting impact)
46.5 FX: Shin (distinct absence of sound)
47.2 FX: Pi (electronic "beep")
50.1 FX: Cha (opening door)
50.2 FX: Gui (tug)
51.1 FX: Don (thud)
51.5 FX: Ba (quick or sudden movement, withdrawal or emergence)
52.2 FX: Kya Kya (girlish squeals— excitement or fear)
53.1 FX: Bu (sudden "splurt," spit-take)
53.2 FX: Gaku Gaku (violent shaking)
54.2 FX: Zui (eyes zooming in)
55.3 FX: Ji (fixed, unblinking stare)
55.4 FX: Paaaaan (suh-mack!)
56.3 FX: Dokun (heartbeat; variant [heavy] of "doki")
56.4 FX: Dokun Dokun Dokun Dokun Dokun Dokun Dokun (heartbeat; variant [heavy] of "doki)
57.3 FX: Doki (heartbeat)
58.1 FX: Za (sudden shift of sand)
58.5 FX: Doki (heartbeat)
59.2 FX: Dosa (heavy thudding)

8.2 FX: Kyaaaaa (girlish squeals— excitement or fear)
12.2 FX: Poro Poro Poro (plopping tears)
12.4 FX: Chichichi (tweeting bird[s])
13.1 FX: Pi Pi (bird sound)
13.1 FX: Basa Basa (fluttering wings)
13.3 FX: Doki (heartbeat)
13.5 FX: Gyu (squeeze, clench)
16.3 FX: Pera Pera (blah blah; ceaseless chatter)
17.4 FX: Boso (Mumble)
19.3 FX: Ba (quick or sudden movement, withdrawal or emergence)
19.4 FX: Kyaaaaaa (girlish squeals— excitement or fear)
20.5 FX: Gaba (quick "lift" exert)
21.4 FX: Ha? (What? Huh?)
23.1 FX: Gata Gatcha ("thunking" sounds)
23.2 FX: Ban (slam)
23.3 FX: Don (thud)
24.2 FX: Ka (purposeful step forward)
24.5 FX: Su (small passage of displaced air, as in movement)
29.4 FX: Fu (sigh-like laugh, contemplative sound)
30.4 FX: Ka (purposeful step forward)
32.5 FX: Ni (vocalized smile)
33.1 FX: Su (small passage of displaced air, as in movement)
33.2 FX: Gui (tug)
33.5 FX: Batan (slam)
34.1 FX: Ha Ha Ha (laughter)
34.2 FX: Ha (quick gasp, sudden thought or epiphany, realization)
35.3 FX: Pa (blink, widening eyes)
36.2 FX: Dokin Dokin Dokin Dokin (heart beat; variant [rapid] of "doki")
37.2 FX: Bashi (slap)
39.1 FX: Pofu (cushiony bosom)

85.5	FX:	Ba (sudden reveal, exposure, movement)
86.4	FX:	Jiro (inquisitive, gobsmacked stare)
87.3	FX:	Ton Ton Ton (feet on stairs)
87.3	FX:	Doki (heartbeat)
87.4	FX:	Wa Ha Ha Ha Ha Ha (uninhibited laughter)
89.1	FX:	Yoro (drunken stagger)
89.2	FX:	Yoro (drunken stagger)
89.3	FX:	Gu (landing of heavy hand)
89.4	FX:	Giku (startlement, twitch; variant [less pleasant] of "biku")
90.2	FX:	Mu (simmering anger)
91.3	FX:	Fu (sudden loss of gravity, sudden fade)
91.4	FX:	Heta (loss of posture, slump)
91.4	FX:	Pan ("brushing-off" exert/impact)
93.1	FX:	Ba (sudden reveal, exposure, movement)
94.2	FX:	Don (thud)
94.3	FX:	Ha'a Ha'a (labored breathing)
94.5	FX:	Ha'a Ha'a (labored breathing)
95.1	FX:	Dosu (thunk)
95.3	FX:	Zuru (quick slumping)
97.1	FX:	Donchan (par-tay!)
97.1	FX:	Wa Ha Ha Ha Ha (uninhibited laughter)
97.4	FX:	Su (small passage of displaced air, as in movement)
97.5	FX:	Doshi (sudden "smooshing" thrust)
98.2	FX:	Ja (running, rush of water)
98.2	FX:	Gobobobo (gurgling of water)
98.3	FX:	Gacha (unclicking of lock, latch)
98.3	FX:	Yotata (unsteady step)
99.2	FX:	Za (sudden shift of sand)
100.1	FX:	Za (sudden shift of sand)
100.4	FX:	Byu ("whoosh" of air, as in missed punch)
100.5	FX:	Yoro (drunken stagger)
101.1	FX:	Ba (sudden reveal, exposure, movement)
101.2	FX:	Pan (sweep of foot)
101.3	FX:	Dozaza ("skudding" into sand)
101.4	FX:	Su (small passage of displaced air, as in movement)
101.5	FX:	Doku Doku Doku (heartbeat; variant [strained] of "doki")
102.1	FX:	Pishi (smarting impact; variant [lighter] of "bishi")

59.5	FX:	Pasa (silky, shifting hair)
60.1	FX:	Dokun Dokun Dokun Dokun Dokun (heartbeat; variant [heavy] of "doki)
60.2	FX:	Biku (startlement, twitch)
61.3	FX:	Bi (ripping, rending of cloth)
62.4	FX:	Gan Gan Gan Gan Gan Gan (shock! stare! shock! stare!)
63.2	FX:	Ha (quick gasp, sudden thought or epiphany, realization)
65.3	FX:	Za—n (crashing of waves)
66.3	FX:	Zuzaza (heavy slide, drag)
66.3	FX:	Dosa (heavy thudding)
67.4	FX:	Kurun (double-take)
67.5	FX:	Ba (sudden reveal, exposure, movement)
68.1	FX:	Ha... (longish sigh)
68.4	FX:	Doki (heartbeat)
70.4	FX:	Ni (vocalized smile)
71.2	FX:	Bishi (smarting impact)
71.4	FX:	Peko (deferential bow)
72.1	FX:	Na— (first part of "Nan datte—?!," "What did you—?!")
72.3	FX:	Boka Boka Boka Boka (scolding blows)
72.4	FX:	Ki (piercing look)
73.2	FX:	Koso Koso (whispered speech)
73.5	FX:	Gon (unexpected upset, unpleasant surprise)
75.3	FX:	Fuwa (weightless float)
75.4	FX:	Beshi (inadvertent smack)
76.5	FX:	Jiro Jiro (inquisitive, gobsmacked stare)
77.2	FX:	Doki (heartbeat)
77.4	FX:	Shuru (loosening of constriction)
77.5	FX:	Doki Doki Doki Doki Doki (heartbeat)
78.1	FX:	Pasa (silky rustle of fabric)
80.3	FX:	Su (small passage of displaced air, as in movement)
80.4	FX:	Pachi (blink, widening eyes)
81.3	FX:	Gakkuri (doom, gloom)
82.1	FX:	Pon (hearty, encouraging pat)
82.2	FX:	Ton Ton Ton (feet on stairs)
82.2	FX:	Zawa Zawa (indistinct, unimportant speech)
82.5	FX:	Shuru (loosening of constriction)
83.2	FX:	Bi (ripping, rending of cloth)
83.3	FX:	Pi'i Bi (further rending of cloth; ripping, rending of cloth)
83.4	FX:	Bi Bi (ripping, rending of cloth)

120.3 FX: Dokun Dokun Dokun Dokun Dokun (heartbeat; variant [heavy] of "doki")

120.3 FX: Piku (startlement, twitch; variant [lighter] of "biku")

120.4 FX: Giku (startlement, twitch; variant [less pleasant] of "biku")

121.1 FX: Goron (roll-over)

121.1 FX: Ga ("connection" impact [as in "connecting knee"])

121.4 FX: Gyu Gyu (squeeze, clench)

121.4 FX: Giku (startlement, twitch; variant [less pleasant] of "biku")

122.1 FX: Ha (quick gasp, sudden thought or epiphany, realization)

122.3 FX: Zawa Zawa (indistinct, unimportant speech)

123.4 FX: Ka ("flash" of light)

124.1 FX: Waaaaaa (awestruck squeals—excitement or fear)

126.2 FX: Doka Ga (whack! krak! whack! smak-smak! bam!)

126.3 FX: Gacha (unclicking of lock, latch)

126.4 FX: Baki Baki ("cracking," as of wood)

126.4 FX: Gachan (unclicking of lock, latch; variant [definitive] of "gacha")

127.1 FX: Gi'i (slow, ominous creaking of door)

128.1 FX: Gi'i (slow, ominous creaking of door)

128.2 FX: Bara Bara (careless scattering)

128.3 FX: Ba (quick or sudden movement, withdrawal or emergence)

128.4 FX: Su (small passage of displaced air, as in movement)

129.2 FX: Zoku (shiver of fear)

129.3 FX: Dokun Dokun Dokun Dokun (heartbeat; variant [heavy] of "doki")

129.4 FX: Ki (piercing look)

130.1 FX: Katsu (footstep)

131.1 FX: Su (small passage of displaced air, as in movement)

131.3 FX: Do (krak! whack! smak-smak!; variant [less heavy] of "do")

131.4 FX: Za (skidding "thud")

132.1 FX: Hyu (sudden movement—up or down, side to side)

132.3 FX: Para (unraveling of bounds)

102.3 FX: Gaki Doka Bishi-Bishi Do'o (krak! whack! smak-smak! smarting impact; thud)

102.4 FX: Chichichi (tweeting bird[s])

103.2 FX: Buru Buru Buru (uncontrollable shaking, trembling)

103.3 FX: Buru Buru Buru (uncontrollable shaking, trembling)

103.5 FX: Ka (loud "crack" of violence)

104.1 FX: Kasha'aaan (shattering smash)

104.5 FX: Basa (fluttering wings)

105.2 FX: Gasha'aaan (shattering smash; variant [lighter] of "kasha'aaan")

105.3 FX: Pa Pa— (angry car horn)

105.3 FX: Pa— (angry car horn)

106.1 FX: Dokun Dokun Dokun Dokun Dokun (heartbeat; variant [heavy] of "doki")

106.3 FX: Pa (sudden "switching on")

107.5 FX: Guwan Guwan (head reeling)

108.3 FX: Zawa Zawa (indistinct, unimportant speech)

111.2 FX: Gatan (slam; sudden "thunk" of chair)

112.5 FX: Kotsu Kotsu Kotsu (footsteps)

114.1 FX: Pan (slap)

115.2 FX: Ha (quick gasp, sudden thought or epiphany, realization)

116.2 FX: Zukkun ("throb," especially of the groin area)

116.3 FX: Zuri Zuri (slow, dragging movement)

117.1 FX: Doki Doki Doki Doki Doki Doki Doki (heartbeat)

117.3 FX: Ha (quick gasp, sudden thought or epiphany, realization)

117.5 FX: Gura (topple)

117.6 FX: Dosa (heavy thudding)

118.1 FX: Gunya (squishy softness of Aya's pulchritude)

118.1 FX: U— (first part of "Uo-o-o-o," "Whoa-a-a-a!")

118.2 FX: Uo-o-o-o (first part of "Uo-o-o-o," "Whoa-a-a-a!")

119.1 FX: Do Do Do Do Do Do Do (heart-beat; variant [quick] of "doki")

120.1-2 FX: Tokun Tokun (heartbeat; variant [heavy] of "doki; variant [lighter] of "dokun")

153.4 FX: Za (crashing of waves; variant [less conclusive] of "za—n")
155.6 FX: Bi (ripping, rending of cloth)
156.1 FX: Go ("whomp")
156.3 FX: Do'oon (blasting eruption)
159.2 FX: Do (krak! whack! smak-smak!)
149.5 FX: Ka ("flash" of light)
160.1 FX: Don (thud)
162.1 FX: Za (slowish, unsubtle rustle)
162.2 FX: Ha'a Ha'a Ha'a (labored breathing)
162.3 FX: Za (slowish, unsubtle rustle)
162.4 FX: Za Za (slowish, unsubtle rustle)
162.5 FX: Za (crashing of waves; variant [less conclusive] of "za—n")
163.1 FX: Za (crashing of waves; variant [less conclusive] of "za—n")
163.6 FX: Zawa Zawa (gentle rustling, as of palm fronds)
165.5 FX: Giri (desperate clench)
165.6 FX: Za (sudden shift of sand)
165.6 FX: Go'ooooo (rumbling roar)
166.3 FX: Su (small passage of displaced air, as in movement)
169.1 FX: Fu (sudden loss of gravity, sudden fade)
171.4 FX: Zaza Za— (crashing of waves; variant [less conclusive] of "za—n")
171.5 FX: Zan (crashing of waves; variant [less conclusive] of "za—n")
173.1 FX: Cha (opening door)
176.2 FX: Ba (quick or sudden movement, withdrawal or emergence)
177.1 FX: Su (small passage of displaced air, as in movement)
178.2 FX: E, E (small, inarticulate cries)
181.3 FX: Gu (clench)
181.5 FX: Cha (opening door)
182.2 FX: Batan (slam)
183.3 FX: Hikku Hikku (hitching of sobs)
184.1 FX: Gusu (sniffling sob)
185.1 FX: Su (small passage of displaced air, as in movement)
187.3 FX: Za (crashing of waves; variant [less conclusive] of "za—n")
188.1 FX: Zan (crashing of waves; variant [less conclusive] of "za—n")
189.5 FX: Zawa Zawa (gentle rustling, as of palm fronds)

132.4 FX: Hyu (sudden movement—up or down, side to side)
133.1 FX: To (krak! whack! smak-smak!; variant [even lighter, easier] of "do")
133.3 FX: Hyu (sudden movement—up or down, side to side)
134.2 FX: Ba (quick or sudden movement, withdrawal or emergence)
134.4 FX: Shu (flung through air)
135.1 FX: Za (skidding "thud")
136.1 FX: Da (dash of movement)
137.2 FX: Fu (sudden loss of gravity, sudden fade)
137.3 FX: Ba (quick or sudden movement, withdrawal or emergence)
138.3 FX: Zawa (effortless float)
139.1 FX: Dokkun Dokkun Dokkun Dokkun (heartbeat; variant [more pronounced] of "dokun")
139.2 FX: Ho'o (breathless sigh)
139.5 FX: Zuzu (rattling vibration)
140.3 FX: Zuzu Zuzu Zuzuzu (rattling vibration; building vibrations)
140.3 FX: Pishi (small "cracking")
140.5 FX: Ban (heavy separation)
142.1 FX: Dosha'aaan (shattering smash; variant [heavier] of "kasha'aaan")
142.2 FX: Kyaaaaaa (girlish squeals—excitement or fear)
142.4 FX: Su (small passage of displaced air, as in movement)
143.2 FX: Goton (hollow "thunk")
143.2 FX: Waaaaa (awestruck squeals—excitement or fear)
143.5 FX; Ka Ka (purposeful step forward)
144.1 FX: Ba (quick or sudden movement, withdrawal or emergence)
144.3 FX: Waaaa (awestruck squeals—excitement or fear)
144.4 FX: U— (incoming siren)
145.3 FX: Ba— ("vroom")
147.2 FX; Za (crashing of waves; variant [less conclusive] of "za—n")
149.4 FX: Zaza (crashing of waves; variant [less conclusive] of "za—n")
150.4 FX: Cha (opening door)
152.1 FX: Gofu (gurgly, liquid coughing-up)
152.3 FX; Gu ("urk"-like cough)
153.1 FX: Zuru (quick slumping)

Yuu Watase was born on March 5 in a town near Osaka, and she was raised there before moving to Tokyo to follow her dream of creating manga. In the decade since her debut short story, *PAJAMA DE OJAMA* ("An Intrusion in Pajamas"), she has produced more than 50 compiled volumes of short stories and continuing series. Perhaps most well known for her smash-hit fantasy/romance stories *FUSHIGI YÛGI: THE MYSTERIOUS PLAY* and *CERES CELESTIAL LEGEND*, her latest work, *APPARE JIPANGU*, is set in the Edo Period and is about a girl who cures people of their sadness. It is currently being serialized in *SHÔJO COMIC*.

Hello, and welcome to *CERES*, Volume 6! It certainly has been an adjustment, getting to know not only the characters and the story, but becoming more familiar with *CERES* creator Watase herself, via the charming, informal sidebars she's scattered throughout the series. Isn't it interesting how many manga creators seem to be into video games? I suppose that, when you live the kinds of lives that they do—secluded away, scribbling frantically, always having your editor's deadlines hanging over your head like the Sword of Damocles—maybe video games are the perfect distraction. You don't have to leave the apartment, you can play them at any hour of the day or night, you get to enjoy the creative efforts of others, in a medium that's not so far off from your own. (Hm, any of this sound familiar? I think there's a new Sims expansion pack out this month with my name on it....) Till next time,

Avery Gotoh, Editor

If you enjoyed *CERES: CELESTIAL LEGEND*, here are some other titles VIZ recommends you read:

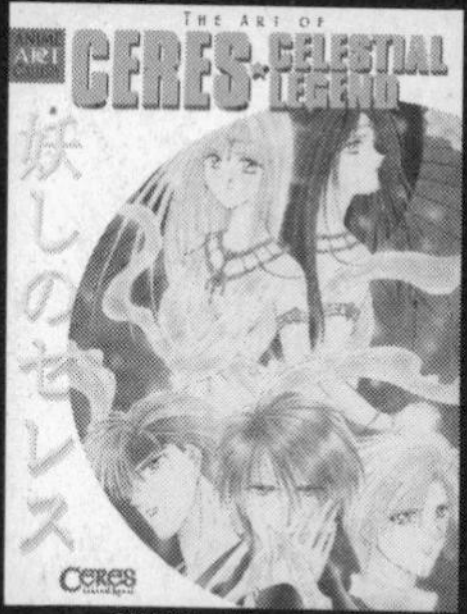
THE ART OF
CERES
CELESTIAL LEGEND

THE ART OF CERES: CELESTIAL LEGEND gives Yuu Watase fans another chance to drool over her artwork. The book contains full-color and black-and-white images from the series, plus character summaries, story background information and an interview with Ms. Watase.

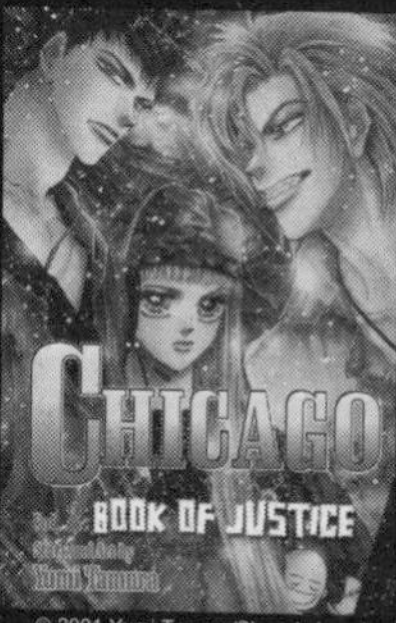
CHICAGO
BOOK OF JUSTICE

CHICAGO is an untraditional shôjo adventure by acclaimed artist Yumi Tamura. When their entire rescue team is wiped out, Rei, a tomboy heroine with brains and brawn, and her cool, handsome partner, Uozumi, begin uncovering the mystery that killed their squad. Their first clue is in the south-Shinjuku bar called Chicago.

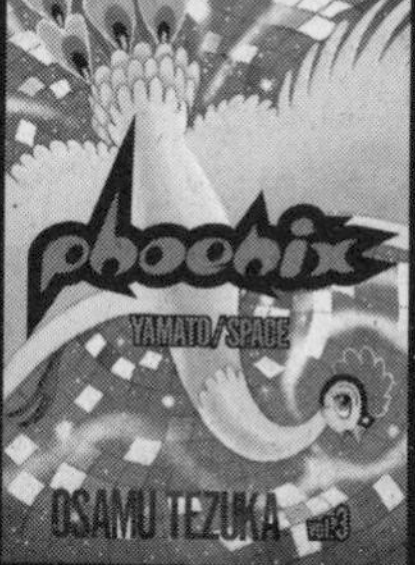
phoenix
YAMATO/SPACE
OSAMU TEZUKA

PHOENIX: A TALE OF THE FUTURE is a seminal work in the history of manga, the epic *PHOENIX* series by "God of Manga" Osamu Tezuka is one of the classics and is a must read for all manga fans regardless of genre. *A TALE OF THE FUTURE* is a sci-fi apocalyptic tale of the future that starts off being part *BLADE RUNNER* and part *LOGAN'S RUN*, but ends up being much much more.

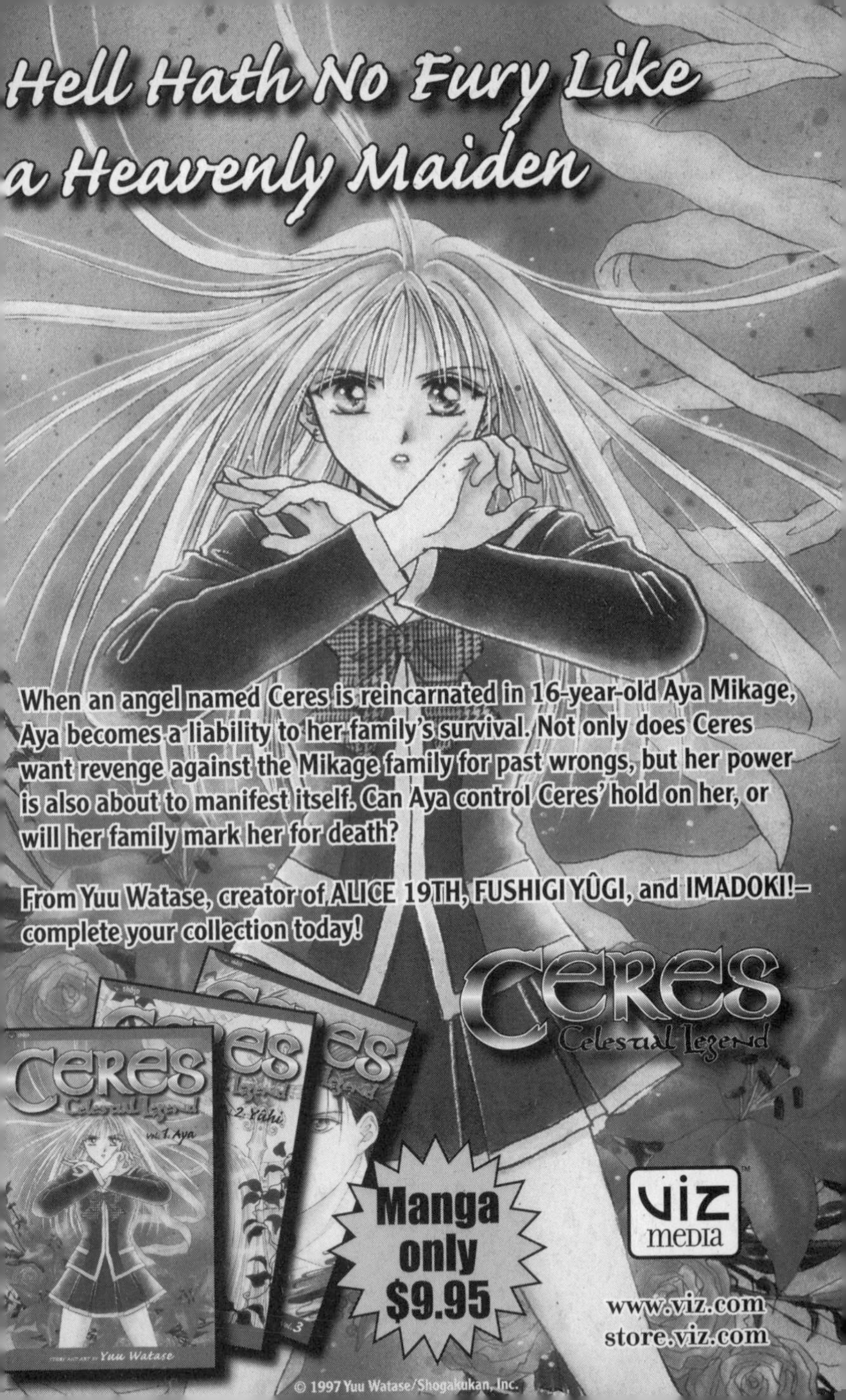
Hell Hath No Fury Like a Heavenly Maiden
When an angel named Ceres is reincarnated in 16-year-old Aya Mikage, Aya becomes a liability to her family's survival. Not only does Ceres want revenge against the Mikage family for past wrongs, but her power is also about to manifest itself. Can Aya control Ceres' hold on her, or will her family mark her for death?
From Yuu Watase, creator of ALICE 19TH, FUSHIGI YÛGI, and IMADOKI!–complete your collection today!
Ceres Celestial Legend
Ceres Celestial Legend vol. 1: Aya
Yuu Watase
vol. 2: Yûhi
vol. 3
Manga only $9.95
viz media
www.viz.com
store.viz.com
© 1997 Yuu Watase/Shogakukan, Inc.

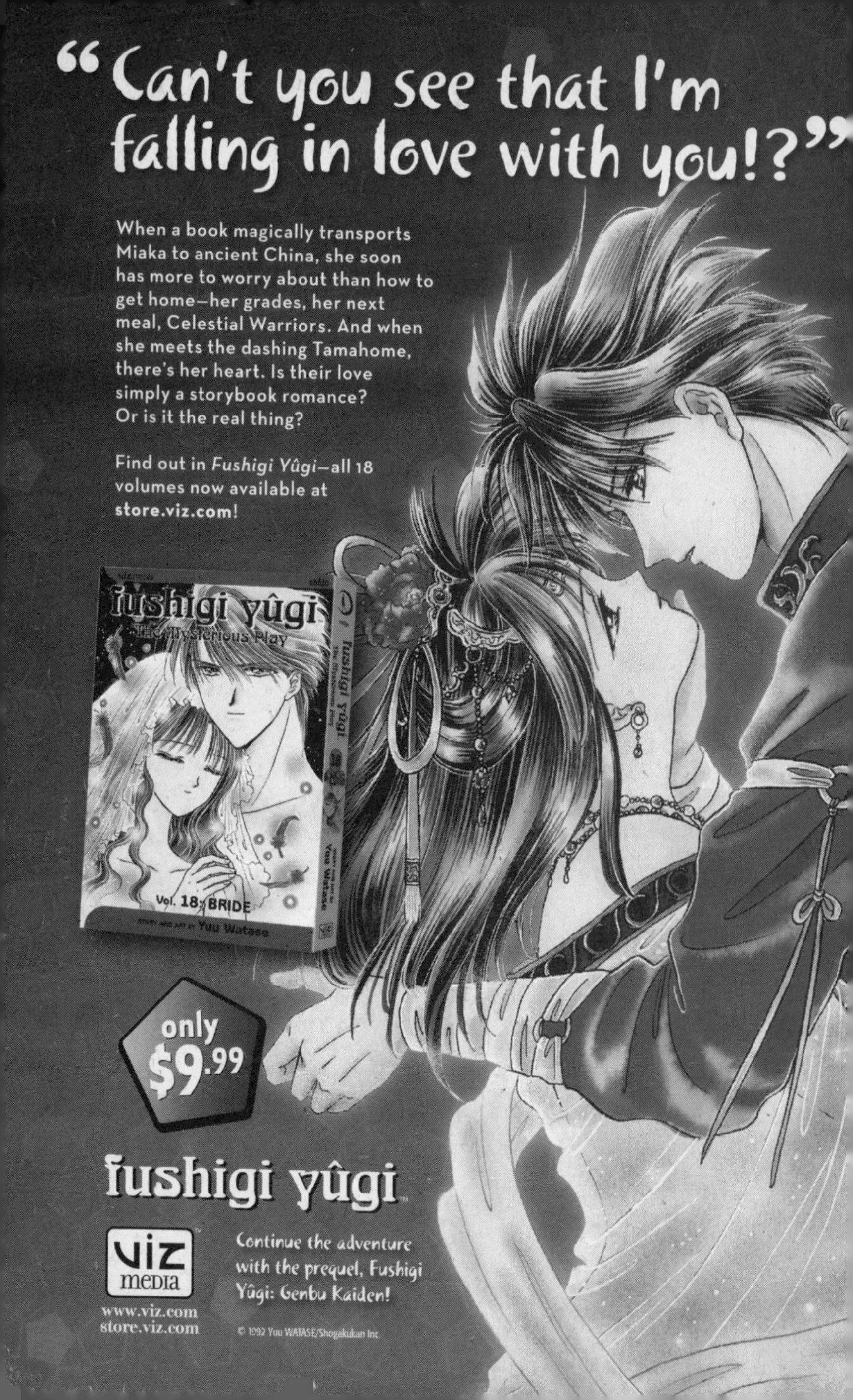
"Can't you see that I'm falling in love with you!?"
When a book magically transports Miaka to ancient China, she soon has more to worry about than how to get home—her grades, her next meal, Celestial Warriors. And when she meets the dashing Tamahome, there's her heart. Is their love simply a storybook romance? Or is it the real thing?
Find out in Fushigi Yûgi—all 18 volumes now available at store.viz.com!
fushigi yûgi
The Mysterious Play
Vol. 18: BRIDE
Yuu Watase
only $9.99
fushigi yûgi™
viz media
www.viz.com
store.viz.com
Continue the adventure with the prequel, Fushigi Yûgi: Genbu Kaiden!
© 1992 Yuu WATASE/Shogakukan Inc.

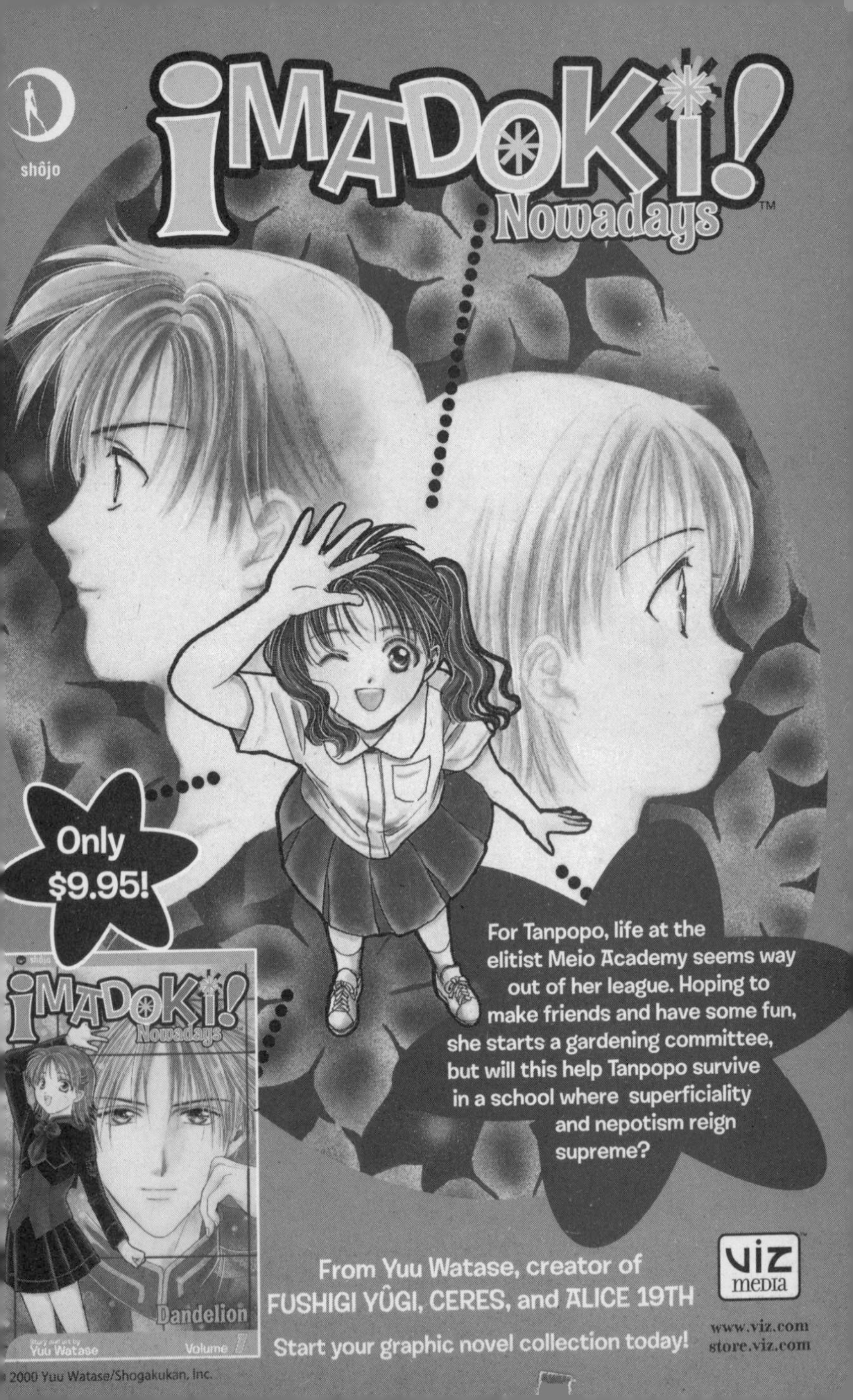
shôjo
IMADOKI!
Nowadays™
Only $9.95!
For Tanpopo, life at the elitist Meio Academy seems way out of her league. Hoping to make friends and have some fun, she starts a gardening committee, but will this help Tanpopo survive in a school where superficiality and nepotism reign supreme?
IMADOKI! Nowadays
Dandelion
Yuu Watase
Volume 1
From Yuu Watase, creator of FUSHIGI YÛGI, CERES, and ALICE 19TH
Start your graphic novel collection today!
VIZ media
www.viz.com
store.viz.com
© 2000 Yuu Watase/Shogakukan, Inc.

LOVE SHOJO? LET US KNOW!

☐ Please do NOT send me information about VIZ Media products, news and events, special offers, or other information.

☐ Please do NOT send me information from VIZ' trusted business partners.

Name: _____

Address: _____

City: _____ **State:** _____ **Zip:** _____

E-mail: _____

☐ Male ☐ Female **Date of Birth** (mm/dd/yyyy): ___ / ___ / ___ (Under 13? Parental consent required)

What race/ethnicity do you consider yourself? (check all that apply)

☐ White/Caucasian ☐ Black/African American ☐ Hispanic/Latino

☐ Asian/Pacific Islander ☐ Native American/Alaskan Native ☐ Other: _____

What VIZ shojo title(s) did you purchase? (indicate title(s) purchased)

_____

What other shojo titles from other publishers do you own? _____

_____

Reason for purchase: (check all that apply)

☐ Special offer ☐ Favorite title / author / artist / genre

☐ Gift ☐ Recommendation ☐ Collection

☐ Read excerpt in VIZ manga sampler ☐ Other _____

Where did you make your purchase? (please check one)

☐ Comic store ☐ Bookstore ☐ Mass/Grocery Store

☐ Newsstand ☐ Video/Video Game Store

☐ Online (site:_____) ☐ Other _____

How many shojo titles have you purchased in the last year? How many were VIZ shojo titles?
(please check one from each column)

SHOJO MANGA
- ☐ None
- ☐ 1 – 4
- ☐ 5 – 10
- ☐ 11+

VIZ SHOJO MANGA
- ☐ None
- ☐ 1 – 4
- ☐ 5 – 10
- ☐ 11+

What do you like most about shojo graphic novels? (check all that apply)

- ☐ Romance
- ☐ Drama / conflict
- ☐ Fantasy
- ☐ Comedy
- ☐ Real-life storylines
- ☐ Relatable characters
- ☐ Other ______________________________

Do you purchase every volume of your favorite shojo series?

- ☐ Yes! Gotta have 'em as my own
- ☐ No. Please explain: ______________________________

Who are your favorite shojo authors / artists? ______________________________

____

What shojo titles would like you translated and sold in English? ______________________________

____

THANK YOU! Please send the completed form to:

NJW Research
ATTN: VIZ Media Shojo Survey
42 Catharine Street
Poughkeepsie, NY 12601

Your privacy is very important to us. All information provided will be used for internal purposes only and will not be sold or otherwise divulged.